Charles Lamb, Alfred Ainger

Poems, Plays and Miscellaneous Essays

Charles Lamb, Alfred Ainger

Poems, Plays and Miscellaneous Essays

ISBN/EAN: 9783744712910

Printed in Europe, USA, Canada, Australia, Japan

Cover: Foto ©Thomas Meinert / pixelio.de

More available books at **www.hansebooks.com**

POEMS PLAYS

AND

MISCELLANEOUS ESSAYS

OF

CHARLES LAMB

WITH INTRODUCTION AND NOTES BY

ALFRED AINGER

London
MACMILLAN AND CO.
AND NEW YORK
1888

INTRODUCTION.

The present volume, with its predecessor the *Essays of Elia*, contains all of Lamb's miscellaneous writings that he had himself selected for preservation in a permanent shape. Twice during his lifetime were issued collections of his prose and verse,—the *Works of Charles Lamb*, published by the Olliers in 1818, and the *Album Verses* issued by Edward Moxon in 1830. The volume now presented is made up of the contents of these two works.

Nothing has been omitted, but a few additions have been made, on a principle which I will explain. When Lamb collected his poems in 1818, he omitted from them certain pathetic verses which had been wrung from him by the first and deepest sorrow of his life—his mother's death. These he had printed when the calamity was still recent, most of them in a slender volume of blank verse written jointly by Charles Lloyd and himself in 1802. But in later years he naturally and rightly shrank from recalling to his beloved sister events in which she had taken so terrible a part. Such a reason for their omission has long ceased to exist, and accordingly they are here restored, as nearly as possible in the order of their composition. Again, after Lamb's death his literary executors—who had better reason than we can have for knowing which of the fugitive verses written between 1830 and his death in 1834 Lamb most valued—added in the subsequent editions of his writings some half a dozen pieces that had appeared in newspapers and journals. These have been accordingly retained in the present edition. But other occasional verses—a few translations, epilogues and prologues, epigrams and political squibs, which have been of late years carefully gleaned by editors of Lamb, are not here included, and the volume makes no claim, in their sense of the word, to possess the merit of completeness. Without suggesting or believing that even the lightest trifles of a humorist like Lamb are not worthy of preservation, I yet cherish a strong opinion that when a writer has himself chosen for the people "of his best," that *best* should be at least kept separate from matter of less worth. Acting on the same principle, I have left for a concluding volume (should it be called for) those slighter prose essays and *jeux d'esprit* which have been collected of late years, and entitled not, I think, very felicitously, *Eliana*.

I have arranged the poems as far as possible in chronological order. Lamb put so much of his personal history into his verse that when so presented it forms a delightful running commentary upon his life and education. In his early sonnets we read of his happy holiday seasons with his grandmother, Mrs. Field, at Blakesware, and the first and only love romance of his life. Then we are reminded of such alleviations of his sad and monotonous family story as were afforded by a rare excursion to the seaside or the more frequent visit to the theatre, or best of all by his correspondence or occasional meetings with Coleridge and Lloyd. Then, for a while, the verse becomes darkened by domestic calamity, and the sonnet measure of Bowles gives place to the blank verse of Cowper, whose pious example seems to have given courage to Lamb's own deep sense of need to express itself in verse. But as we read on, we trace mind and spirit recovering from their great shock, and braced by new friendships and fresh literary interests and sympathies. A fleeting passion for Hester Savory inspires his sweetest lyric, and his struggle with the seductions of his "sweet enemy," Tobacco, produces the first and most remarkable of those poems in which he shewed himself the disciple of Wither and Jonson and the later Elizabethans, and "sealed himself," as was said in that elder time, "of the tribe of Ben." And lastly, when poverty and domestic anxiety no longer press, and his unique genius is gradually revealed to himself as well as to others—as life becomes gladdened and enriched by the sympathy of admiring friends, Wordsworth and Hunt, Barton and Hood, Talfourd and Crabb Robinson, his verse still flows, reflecting with the same genial transparency the changed condition of things. And when towards the end, "genius declines with him," to use his own expression, but he "grows clever"—when, moreover, his fame is fixed and secure and there is no need to write, save for his friends' gratification, since "cash at Leadenhall" means "corn in Egypt"—he is always ready to make happy by an acrostic or some other poetical conceit all the young ladies among his friends and neighbours who come round him with their albums.

As I have just intimated, the chronological order enables us to trace the succession of literary influences under which his verse was produced. Beginning, as his friend Coleridge also began, from an emotional impulse given by the sonnets of Bowles, he passes for a while under the dominion of Cowper, but his studies in a widely different poetic school begin very shortly to assert themselves, and to retain control over him for the rest of his life. In 1805, when he wrote his *Farewell to Tobacco*, he confided to Wordsworth that it was George Wither who had supplied him with the metre and in part with the manner of his verse. And from this time onward the seven-syllabled trochaic couplet of the *Shepherd's Hunting* becomes his "darling measure," as it had been Wither's. It was in fact one of the commonest lyric measures of the great Elizabethans. Lamb knew it well from Shakspere's "On a day (alack the day)," and Beaumont's *Lines on the Tombs*, and many a song and epigram of Fletcher and Jonson. But it was exceptionally characteristic of Wither, and from the day that Lamb came under its spell, it is clear that no other metre came so naturally to him or seemed to fit so well his peculiar gift. His most distinctive verse—such as his lines to Thornton Hunt, or on the death of Thomas Hood's infant child—is henceforth composed in it. And it denotes, I think, a confident assurance in Lamb of a certain kinship with the Elizabethans, that he felt no misgivings that the same verdict might be passed upon him as upon a despised singer of Queen Anne's day, and that *his* Muse might also be labelled *Namby-Pamby*. He knew, as he has so finely said of Ambrose Philips, that it is the poet who makes the metre, not "the metre the poet;" and he felt that in his degree (however modestly he might estimate that degree) he possessed a faculty that would make itself felt, as in Wither and Fletcher, through the jingle of the short line and the rapidly recurring rhyme. In his verse, therefore, as in the best of his serious prose, I still think that Lamb may be reckoned as among the last of the Elizabethans.

A kind and generous reviewer of my Edition of *Elia* has taken exception to my use of this phrase, and given reasons for thinking that Lamb was as much indebted to the literary influences of the eighteenth century as to those of the sixteenth and seventeenth. In this opinion I am quite at one with my critic, but I cannot agree with him that Lamb, while having much in common with the last century humorists, ever shewed himself a despiser or disparager of their excellences. The careless depreciation of the eighteenth century, now so common, had hardly begun in Lamb's day, and if it had, he would have been the last to countenance it. Although Lamb had his perversenesses and prejudices as a critic, it was always against individuals and never against classes or schools of writers, still less against the centuries which produced them. He was intimately acquainted with the poets, essayists, and novelists of the last century. Pope's couplets he seems to have had by heart, and was never weary of quoting and applying them; Defoe and Swift, Addison and Steele, were to him dear and familiar friends.

When he declares that "the pen of Yorick and none since his could have drawn entire" the character of his brother, James Elia, or dwells with such loving emphasis on the well-worn "Circulating Library *Tom Jones* or *Vicar of Wakefield*, speaking of the thousand thumbs that have turned over their pages with delight," it is impossible to mistake the writer's own devout affection for these masterpieces of the imagination. In his earliest prose essays he adopts quite naturally the form and manner of the *Tatler*, when he sits down to address his views of men and things to "Mr. Reflector." But when he is most decidedly the literary successor of the great masters who built the Essay upon Steele's happy venture, he bears upon him no less decidedly the traits of a very different ancestry. And he remains, and seems likely to remain, the last of the moderns whose affinity with the genius of the Elizabethan age enabled him to write, at one moment, in the "soluta oratio"—the "linked sweetness long drawn out" of Jeremy Taylor; and at another with the closely-blended wit and tenderness of the later Euphuists; and in both so to write as one who was "to the manner born." "Hang the age!" exclaimed Lamb one day, when some Editor objected to his style as out of harmony with the taste of the day—"Hang the age! I will write for Antiquity!" And in a sense this remained always his habit. Even in the lightest and hastiest of his effusions some flavour of the antique, in metre or in manner, always clung to him. The attraction he felt for the *Acrostic* was clearly due to the circumstance that it was a favourite amusement of the Elizabethans, and it was really with a fond reminiscence of the metrical conceits

"That so did take Eliza and our James,"

that he was always ready to enshrine in this manner the names of his young lady friends. I may be allowed to quote in this place a hitherto unprinted copy of album verses, kindly given me by Mrs. Augustus de Morgan, the daughter of Lamb's old acquaintance, the Rev. William Frend. Mrs. de Morgan—then Miss Sophia Frend—had set up an album, after the pleasant fashion of those days, and had applied to Lamb to write the introductory verses. The following was his response to the invitation, and I copy the verses from the original manuscript :—

TO THE BOOK.

Little Casket ! Storehouse rare
Of rich conceits to please the Fair !
Happiest he of mortal men—
(I crown him monarch of the pen)—
To whom Sophia deigns to give
The flattering prerogative
To inscribe his name in chief,
On thy first and maiden Leaf.
When thy pages shall be full
With what brighter wits can cull
Of the Tender or Romantic—
Creeping Prose, or Verse Gigantic—
Which thy spaces so shall cram
That the Bee-like Epigram
(Which a two-fold tribute brings,
Honey gives at once, and *stings*)
Hath not room left wherewithal
To infix its tiny scrawl ;
Haply some more youthful swain,
Striving to describe his pain
And the Damsel's ear to seize
With more expressive lays than these,
When he finds his own excluded
And these counterfeits intruded,
While, loitering in the Muses' bower
He overstaid the eleventh hour
Till the Tables filled—shall fret,
Die, or sicken with regret
Or into a shadow pine :
While this triumphant verse of mine
Like to some favoured stranger-guest
Bidden to a good man's Feast
Shall sit—by merit less than Fate—
In the upper Seat in State !

A trifle, evidently thrown off in haste, and more lax in the metre than is usual with him, but yet in cadence, in the use of the parenthesis, in a certain charming effect of never-endingness, impregnate with the rhythm of him who wrote :—

> Though sometime my song I raise
> To unusèd heights of praise
> (And brake forth as I shall please
> Into strange *Hyperboles*)
> 'Tis to shew conceit has found
> Worth beyond expression's bound.
> Though her breath I do compare
> To the sweet'st perfumes that are ;
> Or, her eies that are so bright
> To the morning's cheerefull light,
> Yet I doe it not so much
> To inferre that she is such ;
> As to shew that being blest
> With what merrits name of best,
> She appeares more faire to me
> Than all creatures else that be.

Of the Prose included in this volume I have said all that seems necessary in the notes. All the Essays here given were written before 1818—that is to say, before any of the finest of the *Elia* Series. As I have elsewhere pointed out, Lamb's critical faculty ripened early, and the criticisms on the Elizabethan dramatists, and the two Papers on Hogarth and on Shakspere's Tragedies, are specimens of his faculty at its very highest. The comments on Shakspere's dramatic contemporaries have now been before the world since 1808, but there is much for the critic to learn from them still. In these days when *ghastliness* is the commonest resource of novelist and dramatist, and is accepted by so many readers as an evidence of *power*, it may be not unprofitable to read and digest Lamb's remark upon the secret of Webster, and the feebleness of would-be Websters—"Inferior geniuses may 'upon horror's head horrors accumulate,' but they cannot do this. They mistake quantity for quality; they 'terrify babes with painted devils,' but they know not how a soul is to be moved. Their terrors want dignity—their affrightments are without decorum."

Nothing again can be finer and better worth saying than his comment on Fuller's vision of Wickliffe's ashes, dispersed from the Avon to the Severn, and then into the narrow seas and into the main ocean, and so "all the world over":—"I have seen this passage smiled at and set down as a quaint conceit of old Fuller. But what is not a conceit to those who read it in a temper different from that in which the writer composed it? The most pathetic parts of poetry to cold tempers seem and are nonsense, as divinity was to the Greeks foolishness. When Richard II., meditating on his own utter annihilation as to royalty, cries out,

> 'O that I were a mockery king of snow
> To melt before the sun of Bolingbroke.'

"If we have been going on pace for pace with the passion before, this sudden conversion of a strong-felt metaphor into something to be actually realised in nature, like that of Jeremiah, 'Oh! that my head were waters, and mine eye a fountain of tears,' is strictly and strikingly natural; but come unprepared upon it, and it is a conceit; and so is a 'head' turned into 'waters.'" And Lamb might have foreseen certain æsthetic developments of seventy years later when he warned men, in his Essay on Hogarth, against "that disgust at common life, that *tædium quotidianarum formarum*, which an unrestricted passion for ideal forms and beauties is in danger of producing." Lastly, that sudden illuminating faculty, which belongs to Lamb above all other critics, is shewn in such a passage as that on Wither's Fourth Eclogue of the *Shepherd's Hunting*—"The praises of Poetry have been often sung in ancient and in modern times; strange powers have been ascribed to it of influence over animate and inanimate auditors; its force over fascinated crowds has been acknowledged; but, before Wither, no one ever celebrated its power *at home*, the wealth and the strength which this divine gift confers upon its possessor. Fame, and that too after death, was all which hitherto the poets had promised themselves from their art. It seems to have been left to Wither to discover that poetry was a present possession, as well as a rich reversion; and that the Muse had promise of both lives—of this, and of that which is to come."

It is as a critic that Lamb will be found at his best in this volume. The lighter humorous papers were written while yet the essay in his hands was only in process of moulding. He starts, as I have said, from the models freshest in his memory, the papers in the *Tatler* and *Spectator*, and in seeking to preserve their forms and turns of expression he is clearly hampered, though it does not prevent his striking out humorous fancies of rare quality. But, as yet, the humour is more that of Sterne and Swift than of the genuine Elian flavour. Swift might have imagined the man of enormous appetite, of whom it is explained that the disease was not in his family, but that his father "had a tedious custom of sitting long at his meals," and his mother "swallowed her victuals very fast," and that perhaps "he took after both." And Yorick himself would have been delighted to describe the sensations of the gentleman who had been hanged and then resuscitated, on meeting some years afterwards the public executioner wearing "a waistcoat that had been his."

I have, as on former occasions, to thank many friends for information and assistance of varied kind. To Mr. A. C. Swinburne my acknowledgments are specially due for having allowed me to examine Lamb's manuscript annotations written in the interleaved copy of Wither, now in Mr. Swinburne's possession. I have also to thank Mr. W. S. Ayrton, of Saltburn-by-the-Sea, the son of Lamb's old friend, Mr. William Ayrton, the eminent musical critic, and (as before) the family of the late Mr. Arthur Loveday, for permission to quote from unpublished letters of Lamb's.

June 1884.

Dedication

TO

SAMUEL TAYLOR COLERIDGE.

(Prefixed to Lamb's Collected Works in 1818.)

MY DEAR COLERIDGE—
    You will smile to see the slender labours of your friend designated by the title of *Works:* but such was the wish of the gentlemen who have kindly undertaken the trouble of collecting them, and from their judgment could be no appeal.

It would be a kind of disloyalty to offer to any one but yourself a volume containing the *early pieces*, which were first published among your poems, and were fairly derivatives from you and them. My friend Lloyd and myself came into our first battle (authorship is a sort of warfare) under cover of the greater Ajax. How this association, which shall always be a dear and proud recollection to me, came to be broken,—who snapped the threefold cord,—whether yourself (but I know that was not the case) grew ashamed of your former companions,—or whether (which is by much the more probable) some ungracious bookseller was author of the separation,—I cannot tell;—but wanting the support of your friendly elm (I speak for myself), my vine has, since that time, put forth few or no fruits; the sap (if ever it had any) has become, in a manner, dried up and extinct: and you will find your old associate, in his second volume, dwindled into prose and *criticism*.

Am I right in assuming this as the cause? or is it that, as years come upon us (except with some more healthy-happy spirits), life itself loses much of its poetry for us? we transcribe but what we read in the great volume of Nature; and, as the characters grow dim, we turn off, and look another way. You yourself write no *Christabels*, nor *Ancient Mariners*, now.

Some of the Sonnets, which shall be carelessly turned over by the general reader, may happily awaken in you remembrances, which I should be sorry should be ever totally extinct—the memory

> Of summer days and of delightful years—

even so far back as to those old suppers at our old * * *[1] Inn,—when life was fresh, and topics exhaustless,—and you first kindled in me, if not the power, yet the love of poetry, and beauty, and kindliness—

> What words have I heard
> Spoke at the Mermaid!

The world has given you many a shrewd nip and gird since that time, but either my eyes are grown dimmer, or my old friend is the *same*, who stood before me three-and-twenty years ago—his hair a little confessing the hand of time, but still shrouding the same capacious brain,—his heart not altered, scarcely where it "alteration finds."

One piece, Coleridge, I have ventured to publish in its original form, though I have heard you complain of a certain over-imitation of the antique in the style. If I could see any way of getting rid of the objection, without rewriting it entirely, I would make some sacrifices. But when I wrote *John Woodvil*, I never proposed to myself any distinct deviation from common English. I had been newly initiated in the writings of our elder dramatists; Beaumont and Fletcher, and Massinger, were then a *first*

---

[1] The *Salutation and Cat*, a tavern near Smithfield, where Lamb and Coleridge were fond of meeting in early days.

love; and from what I was so freshly conversant in, what wonder if my language imperceptibly took a tinge? The very *time*, which I had chosen for my story, that which immediately followed the Restoration, seemed to require, in an English play, that the English should be of rather an older cast, than that of the precise year in which it happened to be written. I wish it had not some faults, which I can less vindicate than the language.—

   I remain,
    My dear Coleridge,
     Yours,
      With unabated esteem,
         C. LAMB.

CONTENTS.

POEMS.

PAGE

SONNETS—
'Was it some sweet device' 1
'When last I roved' 1
'The Lord of Light shakes off' . . . 2
'A timid grace sits trembling' . . . 2
'We were two pretty babes' . . . 3
'Methinks how dainty sweet it were' . . 3
'If from my lips' 4
'Friend of my earliest years' . . . 4
'O, I could laugh to hear the midnight wind' . 5
'As when a child' 5

TO SARA AND HER SAMUEL 6
TO THE POET COWPER 7
CHILDHOOD 7
THE GRANDAME 8
THE SABBATH BELLS. 9
FANCY EMPLOYED ON DIVINE SUBJECTS . . 9
THE TOMB OF DOUGLAS 10
TO CHARLES LLOYD, AN UNEXPECTED VISITOR . 11
A VISION OF REPENTANCE 13

CONTENTS.

	PAGE
To Charles Lloyd	15
Written on the Day of my Aunt's Funeral	16
Written a Year after the Events	17
Written soon after the Preceding Poem	19
Written on Christmas Day 1797	20
The Old Familiar Faces	21
Composed at Midnight	22
Living without God in the World	23
John Woodvil (A Tragedy in Five Acts)	25
The Witch (A Dramatic Sketch of the Seventeenth Century)	66
A Ballad (Noting the difference of rich and poor)	68
Ballad (From the German)	69
Hester	69
A Farewell to Tobacco	70
Lines on the Celebrated Picture (By Leonardo da Vinci)	75
The Three Friends	75
To a River in which a Child was drowned	81
Queen Oriana's Dream	82
To T. L. H.—A Child	83
To Miss Kelly	84
On the Sight of Swans in Kensington Gardens	85
The Family Name	85
To John Lamb, Esq., of the South-Sea House	86
To Martin Charles Burney	86
Written at Cambridge on the 15th August, 1819	87
To the Author of Poems, published under the Name of Barry Cornwall	87
Sonnet: Work	88

CONTENTS.

	PAGE
SONNET: LEISURE	88
To J. S. KNOWLES, ESQ. (On his Tragedy of Virginius)	89
IN THE ALBUM OF LUCY BARTON	89
TO THE EDITOR OF THE 'EVERY-DAY BOOK'	90
THE YOUNG CATECHIST	91
ANGEL HELP	92
ON AN INFANT DYING AS SOON AS BORN	93
THE CHRISTENING	95
IN THE ALBUM OF MISS ——	96
THE GIPSY'S MALISON	96
IN THE ALBUM OF A CLERGYMAN'S LADY	97
IN THE AUTOGRAPH BOOK OF MRS. SERJEANT W——	97
IN THE ALBUM OF A VERY YOUNG LADY	98
IN THE ALBUM OF A FRENCH TEACHER	98
IN THE ALBUM OF MISS DAUBENY	99
IN THE ALBUM OF MRS. JANE TOWERS	100
IN THE ALBUM OF CATHERINE ORKNEY	100
IN MY OWN ALBUM	101
TO BERNARD BARTON	102
SHE IS GOING	103
TO A YOUNG FRIEND (On her twenty-first Birthday)	103
TO THE SAME	104
HARMONY IN UNLIKENESS	105
TO A CELEBRATED FEMALE PERFORMER IN 'THE BLIND BOY'	105
TO SAMUEL ROGERS, ESQ.	106
TO CAROLINE MARIA APPLEBEE	106
TO CECILIA CATHERINE LAWTON	107
TO A LADY WHO DESIRED ME TO WRITE HER EPITAPH	108
ANOTHER (To her youngest Daughter)	108

CONTENTS.

	PAGE
TRANSLATIONS. From the Latin of Vincent Bourne—	
On a Sepulchral Statue of an Infant Sleeping	109
The Rival Bells	109
Epitaph on a Dog	109
The Ballad Singers	110
To David Cook, of the Parish of St. Margaret's, Westminster, Watchman	112
On a Deaf and Dumb Artist	114
Newton's Principia	114
The Housekeeper	115
The Female Orators	115
PINDARIC ODE TO THE TREAD-MILL	116
EPICEDIUM (Going or Gone)	119
THE WIFE'S TRIAL; OR, THE INTRUDING WIDOW (A Dramatic Poem)	122
'O LIFT WITH REVERENT HAND'.	150
IN THE ALBUM OF ROTHA QUILLINAN	150
TO DORA WORDSWORTH	151
IN THE ALBUM OF EDITH SOUTHEY	151
THE SELF-ENCHANTED	152
TO A FRIEND, ON HIS MARRIAGE	152
TO LOUISA M——	153
FREE THOUGHTS ON SEVERAL EMINENT COMPOSERS	154
TO MARGARET W——	155

PROSE.

ROSAMUND GRAY	157
CURIOUS FRAGMENTS (Extracted from a Common-place Book	197
HYPOCHONDRIACUS	204

CONTENTS.

	PAGE
Recollections of Christ's Hospital	206
On the Tragedies of Shakspere	220
Characters of Dramatic Writers, Contemporary with Shakspere	241
Specimens from the Writings of Fuller	262
On the Genius and Character of Hogarth	272
On the Poetical Works of George Wither	295
The Londoner	301
On Burial Societies; and the Character of an Undertaker	304
On the Danger of confounding Moral with Personal Deformity	311
On the Inconveniences resulting from being Hanged	319
On the Melancholy of Tailors	330
Hospita on the Immoderate Indulgence of the Pleasures of the Palate	335
Edax on Appetite	339
Mr. H——: A Farce	348
Notes	377

POEMS.

1

WAS it some sweet device of Faëry
That mock'd my steps with many a lonely glade,
And fancied wanderings with a fair-hair'd maid?
Have these things been? or what rare witchery,
Impregning with delights the charmed air,
Enlighted up the semblance of a smile
In those fine eyes? methought they spake the while
Soft soothing things, which might enforce despair
To drop the murdering knife, and let go by
His foul resolve. And does the lonely glade
Still court the footsteps of the fair-hair'd maid?
Still in her locks the gales of summer sigh?
While I forlorn do wander, reckless where,
And 'mid my wanderings meet no Anna there.
                                        1795.

2.

WHEN last I roved these winding wood-walks green,
Green winding walks, and shady pathways sweet,
Ofttimes would Anna seek the silent scene,
Shrouding her beauties in the lone retreat.

No more I hear her footsteps in the shade:
Her image only in these pleasant ways
Meets me self-wandering, where in happier days
I held free converse with the fair-hair'd maid.
I pass'd the little cottage which she loved,
The cottage which did once my all contain;
It spake of days which ne'er must come again,
Spake to my heart, and much my heart was moved.
"Now fair befall thee, gentle maid!" said I,
And from the cottage turn'd me with a sigh.

1795.

3.

The Lord of Light shakes off his drowsyhed;
Fresh from his couch up springs the lusty sun,
And girds himself his mighty race to run.
Meantime, by truant love of rambling led
I turn my back on thy detested walls,
Proud city, and thy sons I leave behind,
A selfish, sordid, money-getting kind
Who shut their ears when holy Freedom calls.
I pass not thee so lightly, humble spire,
That mindest me of many a pleasure gone,
Of merriest days of love and Islington,
Kindling anew the flames of past desire;
And I shall muse on thee, slow journeying on,
To the green plains of pleasant Hertfordshire.

1795.

4.

A timid grace sits trembling in her eye,
As loth to meet the rudeness of men's sight,
Yet shedding a delicious lunar light,
That steeps in kind oblivious ecstasy
The care-crazed mind, like some still melody:
Speaking most plain the thoughts which do possess

Her gentle sprite : peace, and meek quietness,
And innocent loves, and maiden purity :
A look whereof might heal the cruel smart
Of changed friends, or fortune's wrongs unkind ;
Might to sweet deeds of mercy move the heart
Of him who hates his brethren of mankind.
Turn'd are those lights from me, who fondly yet
Past joys, vain loves, and buried hopes regret.
1795.

5.

WE were two pretty babes, the youngest she,
The youngest, and the loveliest far, I ween,
And INNOCENCE her name. The time has been,
We two did love each other's company ;
Time was, we two had wept to have been apart.
But when by show of seeming good beguiled,
I left the garb and manners of a child,
And my first love for man's society,
Defiling with the world my virgin heart—
My loved companion dropped a tear, and fled,
And hid in deepest shades her awful head.
Beloved, who shall tell me where thou art—
In what delicious Eden to be found—
That I may seek thee the wide world around ?
1795.

6.

METHINKS how dainty sweet it were, reclined
Beneath the vast out-stretching branches high
Of some old wood, in careless sort to lie,
Nor of the busier scenes we left behind
Aught envying. And, O Anna ! mild-eyed maid !
Beloved ! I were well content to play
With thy free tresses all a summer's day,
Losing the time beneath the greenwood shade.

Or we might sit and tell some tender tale
Of faithful vows repaid by cruel scorn,
A tale of true love, or of friend forgot;
And I would teach thee, lady, how to rail
In gentle sort, on those who practise not
Or love or pity, though of woman born.

1795.

7.

IF from my lips some angry accents fell,
Peevish complaint, or harsh reproof unkind,
'Twas but the error of a sickly mind
And troubled thoughts, clouding the purer well,
And waters clear of Reason; and for me
Let this my verse the poor atonement be—
My verse, which thou to praise wert ever inclined
Too highly, and with a partial eye to see
No blemish. Thou to me didst ever show
Kindest affection; and would ofttimes lend
An ear to the desponding love-sick lay,
Weeping my sorrows with me, who repay
But ill the mighty debt of love I owe,
Mary, to thee, my sister and my friend.

1795.

8.

FRIEND of my earliest years and childish days,
My joys, my sorrows, thou with me hast shared,
Companion dear; and we alike have fared,
Poor pilgrims we, through life's unequal ways.
It were unwisely done, should we refuse
To cheer our path, as featly as we may,—
Our lonely path to cheer, as travellers use,
With merry song, quaint tale, or roundelay.
And we will sometimes talk past troubles o'er,
Of mercies shown, and all our sickness healed,

And in His judgments God remembering love:
And we will learn to praise God evermore,
For these "glad tidings of great joy," revealed
By that sooth messenger, sent from above.
                                        1797.

9.

WRITTEN AT MIDNIGHT, BY THE SEA-SIDE AFTER A VOYAGE.

O, I could laugh to hear the midnight wind,
That, rushing on its way with careless sweep,
Scatters the ocean waves. And I could weep
Like to a child. For now to my raised mind
On wings of winds comes wild-eyed Phantasy,
And her rude visions give severe delight.
O winged bark! how swift along the night
Pass'd thy proud keel; nor shall I let go by
Lightly of that drear hour the memory,
When wet and chilly on thy deck I stood,
Unbonneted, and gazed upon the flood,
Even till it seem'd a pleasant thing to die,—
To be resolved into th' elemental wave,
Or take my portion with the winds that rave.
                                        1795.

10.

As when a child on some long winter's night
Affrighted clinging to its grandame's knees
With eager wondering and perturb'd delight
Listens strange tales of fearful dark decrees
Mutter'd to wretch by necromantic spell;
Or of those hags, who at the witching time
Of murky midnight ride the air sublime,
And mingle foul embrace with fiends of hell:
Cold Horror drinks its blood! Anon the tear

More gentle starts, to hear the beldame tell
Of pretty babes, that loved each other dear,
Murder'd by cruel Uncle's mandate fell:
Even such the shivering joys thy tones impart,
Even so thou, SIDDONS! meltest my sad heart!

1794.

TO SARA AND HER SAMUEL.

WAS it so hard a thing?—I did but ask
A fleeting holiday. One little week,
Or haply two, had bounded my request.
What if the jaded steer, who all day long
Had borne the heat and labour of the plough,
When evening came, and her sweet cooling hour,
Should seek to trespass on a neighbour copse,
Where greener herbage waved, or clearer streams
Invited him to slake his burning thirst?
That man were crabbed, who should say him nay:
That man were churlish who should drive him thence.

A blessing light upon your heads, ye good,
Ye hospitable pair! I may not come,
To catch on Clifden's heights the summer gale;
I may not come, a pilgrim, to the banks
Of Avon, lucid stream, to taste the wave
Which Shakspeare drank, our British Helicon!
Or with mine eye intent on Redcliffe towers,
To muse in tears on that mysterious youth,
Cruelly slighted, who to London walls,
In evil hour, shaped his disastrous course.

Complaint begone: begone, unkind reproof:
Take up, my song, take up a merrier strain,
Forget again, and lo! from Avon's vales
Another "minstrel" cometh! Youth endeared,
God and good angels guide thee on thy way,
And gentler fortunes wait the friends I love.

July 5, 1796.

TO THE POET COWPER.

Cowper, I thank my God that thou art healed!
Thine was the sorest malady of all;
And I am sad to think that it should light
Upon the worthy head! But thou art healed,
And thou art yet, we trust, the destined man
Born to reanimate the lyre, whose chords
Have slumbered, and have idle lain so long;
To the immortal sounding of whose strings
Did Milton frame the stately pacèd verse;
Among whose wires with light finger playing,
Our elder bard, Spenser, a gentle name,
The lady Muses' dearest darling child,
Elicited the deftest tunes yet heard
In hall or bower, taking the delicate ear
Of Sidney and his peerless maiden Queen.

Thou, then, take up the mighty epic strain,
Cowper, of England's Bards the wisest and the best.
                                           1796.

CHILDHOOD.

In my poor mind it is most sweet to muse
Upon the days gone by; to act in thought
Past seasons o'er, and be again a child;
To sit in fancy on the turf-clad slope
Down which the child would roll; to pluck gay flowers,
Make posies in the sun, which the child's hand
(Childhood offended soon, soon reconciled,)
Would throw away, and straight take up again,
Then fling them to the winds, and o'er the lawn
Bound with so playful and so light a foot,
That the pressed daisy scarce declined her head.

THE GRANDAME.

On the green hill-top,
Hard by the house of prayer, a modest roof,
And not distinguish'd from its neighbour barn,
Save by a slender-tapering length of spire,
The Grandame sleeps. A plain stone barely tells
The name and date to the chance passenger.
For lowly-born was she, and long had eat,
Well-earn'd, the bread of service:—hers was else
A mounting spirit, one that entertain'd
Scorn of base action, deed dishonourable,
Or aught unseemly. I remember well
Her reverend image: I remember, too,
With what a zeal she served her master's house;
And how the prattling tongue of garrulous age
Delighted to recount the oft-told tale
Or anecdote domestic. Wise she was,
And wondrous skill'd in genealogies,
And could in apt and voluble terms discourse
Of births, of titles, and alliances;
Of marriages, and intermarriages;
Relationship remote, or near of kin;
Of friends offended, family disgraced,
Maiden high-born, but wayward, disobeying
Parental strict injunctions, and regardless
Of unmix'd blood, and ancestry remote,
Stooping to wed with one of low degree.
But these are not thy praises; and I wrong
Thy honour'd memory, recording chiefly
Things light or trivial. Better 'twere to tell,
How with a nobler zeal, and warmer love,
She served her *heavenly Master*. I have seen
That reverend form bent down with age and pain,
And rankling malady. Yet not for this
Ceased she to praise her Maker, or withdraw
Her trust in Him, her faith, and humble hope;

So meekly had she learn'd to bear her cross—
For she had studied patience in the school
Of Christ; much comfort she had thence derived,
And was a *follower* of the NAZARENE.

THE SABBATH BELLS.

THE cheerful Sabbath bells, wherever heard,
Strike pleasant on the sense, most like the voice
Of one, who from the far-off hills proclaims
Tidings of good to Zion: chiefly when
Their piercing tones fall *sudden* on the ear
Of the contemplant, solitary man,
Whom thoughts abstruse or high have chanced to lure
Forth from the walks of men, revolving oft,
And oft again, hard matter, which eludes
And baffles his pursuit, thought-sick and tired
Of controversy, where no end appears,
No clue to his research, the lonely man
Half wishes for society again.
Him, thus engaged, the Sabbath bells salute
Sudden! his heart awakes: his ears drink in
The cheering music; his relenting soul
Yearns after all the joys of social life
And softens with the love of human kind.

FANCY EMPLOYED ON DIVINE SUBJECTS.

THE truant fancy was a wanderer ever,
A lone enthusiast maid.   She loves to walk
In the bright visions of empyreal light,
By the green pastures, and the fragrant meads,
Where the perpetual flowers of Eden blow:
By crystal streams, and by the living waters,
Along whose margin grows the wondrous tree

Whose leaves shall heal the nations; underneath
Whose holy shade a refuge shall be found
From pain and want, and all the ills that wait
On mortal life, from sin and death for ever.

THE TOMB OF DOUGLAS.

(See the Tragedy of that name.)

WHEN her son, her Douglas, died,
To the steep rock's fearful side
Fast the frantic mother hied—

  O'er her blooming warrior dead
Many a tear did Scotland shed,
And shrieks of long and loud lament
From her Grampian hills she sent.

  Like one awakening from a trance
She met the shock of Lochlin's[1] lance;
On her rude invader foe
Return'd an hundredfold the blow,
Drove the taunting spoiler home;
  Mournful thence she took her way
To do observance at the tomb
  Where the son of Douglas lay

  Round about the tomb did go
In solemn state and order slow,
Silent pace, and black attire,
Earl or Knight, or good Esquire;
Whoe'er by deeds of valour done
In battle had high honours won;
Whoe'er in their pure veins could trace
The blood of Douglas' noble race.

[1] Denmark.

With them the flower of minstrels came,
And to their cunning harps did frame
In doleful numbers piercing rhymes,
Such strains as in the older times
Had soothed the spirit of Fingal,
Echoing thro' his father's hall.

"Scottish maidens, drop a tear
O'er the beauteous Hero's bier!
Brave youth, and comely 'bove compare,
All golden shone his burnish'd hair;
Valour and smiling courtesy
Play'd in the sunbeams of his eye.
Closed are those eyes that shone so fair,
And stain'd with blood his yellow hair.
Scottish maidens, drop a tear
O'er the beauteous Hero's bier!

"Not a tear, I charge you, shed
For the false Glenalvon dead;
Unpitied let Glenalvon lie,
Foul stain to arms and chivalry!

"Behind his back the traitor came,
And Douglas died without his fame.
Young light of Scotland early spent,
Thy country thee shall long lament,
And oft to after-times shall tell,
In Hope's sweet prime my Hero fell."

TO CHARLES LLOYD, AN UNEXPECTED VISITOR.

ALONE, obscure, without a friend,
A cheerless, solitary thing,
Why seeks my Lloyd the stranger out?
What offering can the stranger bring

Of social scenes, home-bred delights,
　　That him in aught compensate may
For Stowey's pleasant winter nights,
　　For loves and friendships far away?

In brief oblivion to forego
　　Friends such as thine, so justly dear,
And be awhile with me content
　　To stay, a kindly loiterer, here.

For this a gleam of random joy
　　Hath flush'd my unaccustom'd cheek;
And with an o'ercharged bursting heart,
　　I feel the thanks I cannot speak.

O! sweet are all the Muses' lays,
　　And sweet the charm of matin bird—
'Twas long since these estrangèd ears
　　The sweeter voice of friend had heard.

The voice hath spoke: the pleasant sounds
　　In memory's ear in after-time
Shall live, to sometimes rouse a tear,
　　And sometimes prompt an honest rhyme.

For when the transient charm is fled,
　　And when the little week is o'er,
To cheerless, friendless solitude
　　When I return, as heretofore,

Long, long, within my aching heart,
　　The grateful sense shall cherish'd be;
I'll think less meanly of myself,
　　That Lloyd will sometimes think on me.

　　　　　　　　　　　　　Jan. 1797.

A VISION OF REPENTANCE.

I saw a famous fountain in my dream,
  Where shady pathways to a valley led;
A weeping willow lay upon that stream,
  And all around the fountain brink were spread
Wide branching trees, with dark green leaf rich clad,
  Forming a doubtful twilight—desolate and sad.

The place was such, that whoso enter'd in,
  Disrobèd was of every earthly thought,
And straight became as one that knew not sin,
  Or to the world's first innocence was brought;
Enseem'd it now, he stood on holy ground,
In sweet and tender melancholy wrapt around.

A most strange calm stole o'er my soothèd sprite:
  Long time I stood, and longer had I staid,
When lo! I saw, saw by the sweet moonlight,
  Which came in silence o'er that silent shade,
Where near the fountain SOMETHING like DESPAIR
Made of that weeping willow garlands for her hair.

And eke with painful fingers she inwove
  Many an uncouth stem of savage thorn—
"The willow garland, *that* was for her love,
  And *these* her bleeding temples would adorn."
With sighs her heart nigh burst, salt tears fast fell,
As mournfully she bended o'er that sacred well.

To whom when I address'd myself to speak,
  She lifted up her eyes, and nothing said;
The delicate red came mantling o'er her cheek,
  And, gathering up her loose attire, she fled
To the dark covert of that woody shade,
And in her goings seem'd a timid gentle maid.

Revolving in my mind what this should mean,
　　And why that lovely lady plainèd so;
Perplex'd in thought at that mysterious scene,
　　And doubting if 'twere best to stay or go,—
I cast mine eyes in wistful gaze around,
When from the shades came slow a small and plaintive sound:

　"Pysche[1] am I, who love to dwell
　　In these brown shades, this woody dell,
　　Where never busy mortal came,
　　Till now, to pry upon my shame.

　"At thy feet what thou dost see
　　The waters of repentance be,
　　Which, night and day, I must augment
　　With tears, like a true penitent,

　"If haply so my day of grace
　　Be not yet past; and this lone place,
　　O'er-shadowy, dark, excludeth hence
　　All thoughts but grief and penitence."

　"*Why dost thou weep, thou gentle maid!*
　　And wherefore in this barren shade
　　Thy hidden thoughts with sorrow feed?
　　Can thing so fair repentance need?"

　"O! I have done a deed of shame,
　　And tainted is my virgin fame,
　　And stain'd the beauteous maiden white,
　　In which my bridal robes were dight."

　"*And who the promised spouse, declare:*
　　And what those bridal garments were."

　"Severe and saintly righteousness
　　Composed the clear white bridal dress;

[1] The Soul.

JESUS, the son of Heaven's high King,
Bought with His blood the marriage-ring.

"A wretched sinful creature, I
Deem'd lightly of that sacred tie,
Gave to a treacherous WORLD my heart,
And play'd the foolish wanton's part.

"Soon to these murky shades I came,
To hide from the sun's light my shame.
And still I haunt this woody dell,
And bathe me in that healing well,
Whose waters clear have influence
From sin's foul stains the soul to cleanse;

"And night and day I them augment
With tears, like a true penitent,
Until, due expiation made,
And fit atonement fully paid,
The Lord and Bridegroom me present,
Where in sweet strains of high consent,
God's throne before, the Seraphim
Shall chaunt the ecstatic marriage hymn."

"*Now Christ restore thee soon*"—I said,
And thenceforth all my dream was fled.

1797.

TO CHARLES LLOYD.

A STRANGER, and alone, I past those scenes
We past so late together; and my heart
Felt something like desertion, when I look'd
Around me, and the well-known voice of friend
Was absent, and the cordial look was there
No more to smile on me. I thought on Lloyd;

All he had been to me. And now I go
Again to mingle with a world impure,
With men who make a mock of holy things
Mistaken, and of man's best hope think scorn.
The world does much to warp the heart of man,
And I may sometimes join its idiot laugh.
Of this I now complain not. Deal with me
Omniscient Father! as thou judgest best,
And in Thy season *tender* Thou my heart.
I pray not for myself; I pray for him,
Whose soul is sore perplex'd: shine Thou on him,
Father of Lights! and in the difficult paths
Make plain his way before him. His own thoughts
May he not think, his own ends not pursue;
So shall he best perform Thy will on earth,
Greatest and Best, Thy will be ever ours!

August 1797.

WRITTEN ON THE DAY OF MY AUNT'S FUNERAL.

Thou too art dead . . . . ! very kind
Hast thou been to me in my childish days,
Thou best good creature. I have not forgot
How thou didst love thy Charles, when he was yet
A prating schoolboy: I have not forgot
The busy joy on that important day,
When, childlike, the poor wanderer was content
To leave the bosom of parental love,
His childhood's play-place, and his early home,
For the rude fosterings of a stranger's hand,
Hard uncouth tasks, and schoolboy's scanty fare.
How did thine eye peruse him round and round,
And hardly know him in his yellow coats,[1]
Red leathern belt, and gown of russet blue!

[1] The dress of Christ's Hospital.

Farewell, good aunt!
Go thou and occupy the same grave-bed
Where the dead mother lies.
Oh my dear mother, oh thou dear dead saint!
Where's now that placid face, where oft hath sat
A mother's smile, to think her son should thrive
In this bad world when she was dead and gone;
And where a tear hath sat (take shame, O son!)
When that same child has proved himself unkind.
One parent yet is left—a wretched thing,
A sad survivor of his buried wife,
A palsy-smitten, childish, old, old man,
A semblance most forlorn of what he was,
A merry cheerful man. A merrier man,
A man more apt to frame matter for mirth,
Mad jokes, and antics for a Christmas eve;
Making life social, and the laggard time
To move on nimbly, never yet did cheer
The little circle of domestic friends.
February 1797.

WRITTEN A YEAR AFTER THE EVENTS.

ALAS! how am I changed! Where be the tears,
The sobs, and forced suspensions of the breath,
And all the dull desertions of the heart,
With which I hung o'er my dead mother's corse?
Where be the blest subsidings of the storm
Within, the sweet resignedness of hope
Drawn heavenward, and strength of filial love,
In which I bow'd me to my Father's will?
My God, and my Redeemer! keep not Thou
My soul in brute and sensual thanklessness
Seal'd up; oblivious ever of that dear grace
And health restored to my long-loved friend,
Long-loved, and worthy known. Thou didst not leave
Her soul in death! O leave not now, my Lord,

Thy servants in far worse, in spiritual death!
And darkness blacker than those fearèd shadows
Of the valley all must tread.   Lend us Thy balms,
Thou dear Physician of the sin-sick soul,
And heal our cleansèd bosoms of the wounds
With which the world has pierced us thro' and thro'.
Give us new flesh, new birth.   Elect of heaven
May we become; in Thine election sure
Contain'd, and to one purpose steadfast drawn,
Our soul's salvation!
     Thou, and I, dear friend,
With filial recognition sweet, shall know
One day the face of our dear mother in heaven;
And her remember'd looks of love shall greet
With looks of answering love; her placid smiles
Meet with a smile as placid, and her hand
With drops of fondness wet, nor fear repulse.
Be witness for me, Lord, I do not ask
Those days of vanity to return again
(Nor fitting me to ask, nor Thee to give).
Vain loves and wanderings with a fair-hair'd maid,
Child of the dust as I am, who so long
My captive heart steep'd in idolatry
And creature-loves.   Forgive me, O my Maker!
If in a mood of grief I sin almost
In sometimes brooding on the days long past,
And from the grave of time wishing them back,
Days of a mother's fondness to her child,
Her little one.
     O where be now those sports,
And infant play-games? where the joyous troops
Of children, and the haunts I did so love?
O my companions, O ye lovèd names
Of friend or playmate dear; gone are ye now;
Gone diverse ways; to honour and credit some,
And some, I fear, to ignominy and shame!
I only am left, with unavailing grief,
To mourn one parent dead, and see one live

Of all life's joys bereft and desolate:
Am left with a few friends, and one, above
The rest, found faithful in a length of years,
Contented as I may, to bear me on
To the not unpeaceful evening of a day
Made black by morning storms!

September 1797.

WRITTEN SOON AFTER THE PRECEDING POEM.

Thou should'st have longer lived, and to the grave
Have peacefully gone down in full old age!
Thy children would have tended thy gray hairs.
We might have sat, as we have often done,
By our fireside, and talk'd whole nights away,
Old times, old friends, and old events recalling;
With many a circumstance, of trivial note,
To memory dear, and of importance grown.
How shall we tell them in a stranger's ear?
A wayward son ofttimes was I to thee;
And yet, in all our little bickerings,
Domestic jars, there was, I know not what,
Of tender feeling, that were ill exchanged
For this world's chilling friendships, and their smiles
Familiar, whom the heart calls strangers still.
A heavy lot hath he, most wretched man!
Who lives the last of all his family;
He looks around him, and his eye discerns
The face of the stranger, and his heart is sick.
Man of the world, what canst thou do for him?
Wealth is a burden, which he could not bear;
Mirth a strange crime, the which he dares not act;
And wine no cordial, but a bitter cup.
For wounds like his Christ is the only cure,
And gospel promises are his by right,

For these were given to the poor in heart.
Go, preach thou to him of a world to come,
Where friends shall meet and know each other's face.
Say less than this, and say it to the winds.

October 1797.

WRITTEN ON CHRISTMAS DAY, 1797.

I AM a widow'd thing, now thou art gone!
Now thou art gone, my own familiar friend,
Companion, sister, helpmate, counsellor!
Alas! that honoured mind, whose sweet reproof
And meekest wisdom in times past have smooth'd
The unfilial harshness of my foolish speech,
And made me loving to my parents old,
(Why is this so, ah, God! why is this so?)
That honour'd mind become a fearful blank,
Her senses lock'd up, and herself kept out
From human sight or converse, while so many
Of the foolish sort are left to roam at large,
Doing all acts of folly, and sin, and shame?
Thy paths are mystery!
                Yet I will not think,
Sweet friend, but we shall one day meet, and live
In quietness, and die so, fearing God.
Or if *not*, and these false suggestions be
A fit of the weak nature, loth to part
With what it loved so long, and held so dear;
If thou art to be taken, and I left
(More sinning, yet unpunish'd, save in thee),
It is the will of God, and we are clay
In the potter's hands; and, at the worst, are made
From absolute nothing, vessels of disgrace,
Till, His most righteous purpose wrought in us,
Our purified spirits find their perfect rest.

THE OLD FAMILIAR FACES.

WHERE are they gone, the old familiar faces?

I had a mother, but she died, and left me,
Died prematurely in a day of horrors—
All, all are gone, the old familiar faces.

I have had playmates, I have had companions,
In my days of childhood, in my joyful school-days—
All, all are gone, the old familiar faces.

I have been laughing, I have been carousing,
Drinking late, sitting late, with my bosom cronies—
All, all are gone, the old familiar faces.

I loved a love once, fairest among women.
Closed are her doors on me, I must not see her—
All, all are gone, the old familiar faces.

I have a friend, a kinder friend has no man.
Like an ingrate, I left my friend abruptly;
Left him, to muse on the old familiar faces.

Ghost-like, I paced round the haunts of my childhood.
Earth seem'd a desert I was bound to traverse,
Seeking to find the old familiar faces.

Friend of my bosom, thou more than a brother!
Why wert not thou born in my father's dwelling?
So might we talk of the old familiar faces.

For some they have died, and some they have left me,
And some are taken from me; all are departed;
All, all are gone, the old familiar faces.

January 1798.

COMPOSED AT MIDNIGHT.

From broken visions of perturbèd rest
I wake, and start, and fear to sleep again.
How total a privation of all sounds,
Sights, and familiar objects, man, bird, beast,
Herb, tree, or flower, and prodigal light of heaven!
'Twere some relief to catch the drowsy cry
Of the mechanic watchman, or the noise
Of revel, reeling home from midnight cups.
Those are the moanings of the dying man,
Who lies in the upper chamber; restless moans,
And interrupted only by a cough
Consumptive, torturing the wasted lungs.
So in the bitterness of death he lies,
And waits in anguish for the morning's light.
What can that do for him, or what restore?
Short taste, faint sense, affecting notices,
And little images of pleasures past,
Of health, and active life—(health not yet slain,
Nor the other grace of life, a good name, sold
For sin's black wages). On his tedious bed
He writhes, and turns him from th' accusing light,
And finds no comfort in the sun, but says
"When night comes I shall get a little rest."
Some few groans more, death comes, and there an end.
'Tis darkness and conjecture all beyond;
Weak nature fears, though charity must hope,
And fancy, most licentious on such themes,
Where decent reverence well had kept her mute,
Hath o'er-stock'd hell with devils, and brought down
By her enormous fablings, and mad lies,
Discredit on the gospel's serious truths
And salutary fears. The man of parts,
Poet, or prose declaimer, on his couch
Lolling, like one indifferent, fabricates
A heaven of gold, where he, and such as he,

Their heads encompassèd with crowns, their heels
With fine wings garlanded, shall tread the stars,
Beneath their feet, heaven's pavement, far removed
From damnèd spirits, and the torturing cries
Of men, his brethren, fashion'd of the earth,
As he was, nourish'd with the self-same breath,
Belike his kindred or companions once,
Through everlasting ages now divorced,
In chains and savage torments, to repent
Short years of folly on earth. Their groans unheard
In heaven, the saint nor pity feels, nor care,
For those thus sentenced—pity might disturb,
The delicate sense and most divine repose
Of spirits angelical. Blessed be God,
The measures of His judgments are not fix'd
By man's erroneous standard. He discerns
No such inordinate difference and vast
Betwixt the sinner and the saint, to doom
So disproportion'd fates. Compared with Him,
No man on earth is holy call'd: they best
Stand in His sight approved, who at His feet
Their little crowns of virtue cast, and yield
To Him of His own works the praise, His due.

LIVING WITHOUT GOD IN THE WORLD.

Mystery of God! thou brave and beauteous world,
Made fair with light and shade and stars and flowers,
Made fearful and august with woods and rocks;
Jagg'd precipice, black mountain, sea in storms,
Sun, over all, that no co-rival owns,
But thro' Heaven's pavement rides as in despite
Or mockery of the littleness of man!
I see a mighty arm, by man unseen,
Resistless, not to be controll'd, that guides,
In solitude of unshared energies,
All these thy ceaseless miracles, O world!
Arm of the world, I view thee, and I muse

On Man, who, trusting in his mortal strength,
Leans on a shadowy staff, a staff of dreams.
We consecrate our total hopes and fears
To idols, flesh and blood, our love (heaven's due),
Our praise and admiration; praise bestow'd
By man on man, and acts of worship done
To a kindred nature, certes do reflect
Some portion of the glory and rays oblique
Upon the politic worshipper,—so man
Extracts a pride from his humility.
Some braver spirits of the modern stamp
Affect a Godhead nearer: these talk loud
Of mind, and independent intellect,
Of energies omnipotent in man;
And man of his own fate artificer;
Yea, of his own life lord, and of the days
Of his abode on earth, when time shall be,
That life immortal shall become an art,
Or Death, by chymic practices deceived,
Forego the scent, which for six thousand years
Like a good hound he has follow'd, or at length
More manners learning, and a decent sense
And reverence of a philosophic world,
Relent, and leave to prey on carcasses.
But these are fancies of a few: the rest,
Atheists, or Deists only in the name,
By word or deed deny a God. They eat
Their daily bread, and draw the breath of heaven
Without or thought or thanks; heaven's roof to them
Is but a painted ceiling hung with lamps,
No more, that lights them to their purposes.
They wander "loose about," they nothing see,
Themselves except, and creatures like themselves,
Short-lived, short-sighted, impotent to save.
So on their dissolute spirits, soon or late,
Destruction cometh "like an armèd man,"
Or like a dream of murder in the night,
Withering their mortal faculties, and breaking
The bones of all their pride.   1798.

JOHN WOODVIL:

A TRAGEDY IN FIVE ACTS

CHARACTERS.

SIR WALTER WOODVIL.
JOHN, } his sons.
SIMON,
LOVEL, } pretended friends of John.
GRAY,
SANDFORD, Sir Walter's old Steward.
MARGARET, Orphan Ward of Sir Walter.
FOUR GENTLEMEN, John's riotous companions.
SERVANTS.

SCENE.—*For the most part at Sir Walter's mansion in Devonshire; at other times in the forest of Sherwood.*
TIME.—*Soon after the Restoration.*

ACT THE FIRST.

SCENE.—*A Servants' Apartment in Woodvil Hall. Servants drinking.—Time, the Morning.*

A Song by DANIEL.

"When the King enjoys his own again."

Peter. A delicate song. Where didst learn it, fellow?

Daniel. Even there, where thou learnest thy oaths and thy politics—at our master's table. Where else should a serving-man pick up his poor accomplishments?

Martin. Well spoken, Daniel. O rare Daniel!—his oaths and his politics! excellent!

Francis. And where didst pick up thy knavery, Daniel?

Pet. That came to him by inheritance. His family have supplied the shire of Devon, time out of mind, with good thieves and bad serving-men. All of his race have come into the world without their conscience.

Mar. Good thieves, and bad serving-men? Better and better. I marvel what Daniel hath got to say in reply.

Dan. I marvel more when thou wilt say anything to the purpose, thou shallow serving-man, whose swiftest conceit carries thee no higher than to apprehend with difficulty the stale jests of us thy compeers. When wast ever known to club thy own particular jest among us?

Mar. Most unkind Daniel, to speak such biting things of me!

Fran. See—if he hath not brought tears into the poor fellow's eyes with the saltness of his rebuke.

Dan. No offence, brother Martin—I meant none. 'Tis true, Heaven gives gifts and withholds them. It has been pleased to bestow upon me a nimble invention to the manufacture of a jest; and upon thee, Martin, an indifferent bad capacity to understand my meaning.

Mar. Is that all? I am content. Here's my hand.

Fran. Well, I like a little innocent mirth myself, but never could endure bawdry.

Dan. Quot homines tot sententiæ.

Mar. And what is that?

Dan. 'Tis Greek, and argues difference of opinion.

Mar. I hope there is none between us.

Dan. Here's to thee, brother Martin (*drinks*).

Mar. And to thee, Daniel (*drinks*).

Fran. And to thee, Peter (*drinks*).

Pet. Thank you, Francis. And here's to thee (*drinks*).

Mar. I shall be fuddled anon.

Dan. And drunkenness I hold to be a very despicable vice.

All. Oh! a shocking vice. [*They drink round.*

Pet. Inasmuch as it taketh away the understanding.

Dan. And makes the eyes red.

Pet. And the tongue to stammer.

Dan. And to blab out secrets.

(*During this conversation they continue drinking.*)

Pet. Some men do not know an enemy from a friend when they are drunk.

Dan. Certainly sobriety is the health of the soul.

Mar. Now I know I am going to be drunk.

Dan. How canst tell, dry-bones?

Mar. Because I begin to be melancholy. That's always a sign.

Fran. Take care of Martin, he'll topple off his seat else.   [MARTIN *drops asleep.*

Pet. Times are greatly altered since young master took upon himself the government of this household.

All. Greatly altered.

Fran. I think everything be altered for the better since his Majesty's blessed restoration.

Pet. In Sir Walter's days there was no encouragement given to good housekeeping.

All. None.

Dan. For instance, no possibility of getting drunk before two in the afternoon.

Pet. Every man his allowance of ale at breakfast—his quart!

All. A quart!! (*in derision*).

Dan. Nothing left to our own sweet discretions.

Pet. Whereby it may appear, we were treated more like beasts than what we were—discreet and reasonable serving-men.

All. Like beasts.

Mar. (*opening his eyes*). Like beasts!

Dan. To sleep, wag-tail!

Fran. I marvel all this while where the old gentleman has found means to secrete himself. It seems no man has heard of him since the day of the King's return. Can any tell, why our young master, being favoured by the court, should not have interest to procure his father's pardon.

Dan. Marry, I think 'tis the obstinacy of the old Knight, that will not be beholden to the court for his safety.

Mar. Now that is wilful.

Fran. But can any tell me the place of his concealment?

Pet. That cannot I; but I have my conjectures.

Dan. Two hundred pounds, as I hear, to the man that shall apprehend him.

Fran. Well, I have my suspicions.

Pet. And so have I.

Mar. And I can keep a secret.

Fran. (*to* PETER). Warwickshire you mean (*aside*).

Pet. Perhaps not.

Fran. Nearer, perhaps.

Pet. I say nothing.

Dan. I hope there is none in this company would be mean enough to betray him.

All. O Lord, surely not.

[*They drink to* SIR WALTER'S *safety.*

Fran. I have often wondered how our master came to be excepted by name in the late Act of Oblivion.

Dan. Shall I tell the reason?

All. Ay, do.

Dan. 'Tis thought he is no great friend to the present happy establishment.

All. Oh! monstrous!

Pet. Fellow-servants, a thought strikes me. Do we, or do we not, come under the penalties of the Treason Act, by reason of our being privy to this man's concealment!

All. Truly, a sad consideration.

To them enters SANDFORD *suddenly.*

Sandford. You well-fed and unprofitable grooms,
Maintain'd for state, not use;
You lazy feasters at another's cost,
That eat like maggots into an estate,
And do as little work,
Being indeed but foul excrescences,
And no just parts in a well-order'd family;
You base and rascal imitators,
Who act up to the height your master's vices,

But cannot read his virtues in your bond :
Which of you, as I enter'd, spake of betraying?
Was it you, or you, or, thin-face, was it you?
    Mar. Whom does he call thin-face?
    Sand. No prating, loon, but tell me who he was,
That I may brain the villain with my staff,
That seeks Sir Walter's life!
You miserable men,
With minds more slavish than your slave's estate,
Have you that noble bounty so forgot,
Which took you from the looms, and from the ploughs,
Which better had ye follow'd, fed ye, clothed ye,
And entertain'd ye in a worthy service,
Where your best wages was the world's repute,
That thus ye seek his life, by whom ye live?
Have you forgot, too,
How often in old times
Your drunken mirths have stunn'd day's sober ears,
Carousing full cups to Sir Walter's health?
Whom now ye would betray, but that he lies
Out of the reach of your poor treacheries.
This learn from me,
Our master's secret sleeps with trustier tongues,
Than will unlock themselves to carles like you.
Go, get you gone, you knaves. Who stirs? this staff
Shall teach you manners else.
    All. Well, we are going.
    Sand. And quickly, too, ye had better, for I see
Young mistress Margaret coming this way.
                [*Exeunt all but* SANDFORD.

Enter MARGARET, *as in a fright, pursued by a Gentleman, who, seeing* SANDFORD, *retires muttering a curse.*

        SANDFORD.   MARGARET.

    Sand. Good-morrow to my fair mistress. 'Twas a chance
I saw you, lady, so intent was I
On chiding hence these graceless serving-men,
Who cannot break their fast at morning meals

Without debauch and mis-timed riotings.
This house hath been a scene of nothing else,
But atheist riot and profane excess,
Since my old master quitted all his rights here.

 Marg. Each day I endure fresh insult from the scorn
Of Woodvil's friends, the uncivil jests
And free discourses of the dissolute men
That haunt this mansion, making me their mirth.

 Sand. Does my young master know of these affronts?

 Marg. I cannot tell. Perhaps he has not been told.
Perhaps he might have seen them if he would.
I have known him more quick-sighted. Let that pass.
All things seem changed, I think. I had a friend
(I can't but weep to think him alter'd too)—
These things are best forgotten: but I knew
A man, a young man, young, and full of honour,
That would have pick'd a quarrel for a straw,
And fought it out to the extremity,
E'en with the dearest friend he had alive,
On but a bare surmise, a possibility,
That Margaret had suffer'd an affront.
Some are too tame that were too splenetic once.

 Sand. 'Twere best he should be *told* of these affronts.

 Marg. I am the daughter of his father's friend,
Sir Walter's orphan ward.
I am not his servant-maid, that I should wait
The opportunity of a gracious hearing,
Inquire the times and seasons when to put
My peevish prayer up at young Woodvil's feet,
And sue to him for slow redress, who was
Himself a suitor late to Margaret.
I am somewhat proud: and Woodvil taught me pride.
I was his favourite once, his playfellow in infancy,
And joyful mistress of his youth.
None once so pleasant in his eyes as Margaret.
His conscience, his religion Margaret was,
His dear heart's confessor, a heart within that heart,
And all dear things summ'd up in her alone.

As Margaret smiled or frown'd John lived or died:
His dress, speech, gesture, studies, friendships, all
Being fashioned to her liking.
His flatteries taught me first this self-esteem,
His flatteries and caresses, while he loved.
The world esteem'd her happy, who had won
His heart, who won all hearts;
And ladies envied me the love of Woodvil.

   Sand. He doth affect the courtier's life too much,
Whose art is to forget,
And that has wrought this seeming change in him,
That was by nature noble.
'Tis these court plagues, that swarm about our house,
Have done the mischief, making his fancy giddy
With images of state preferment, place,
Tainting his generous spirits with ambition.

   Marg. I know not how it is;
A cold protector is John grown to me.
The mistress and presumptive wife of Woodvil
Can never stoop so low to supplicate
A man, her equal, to redress those wrongs,
Which he was bound first to prevent:
But which his own neglects have sanction'd rather,
Both sanction'd and provoked: a mark'd neglect,
And strangeness fastening bitter on his love,
His love which long has been upon the wane.
For me, I am determined what to do:
To leave this house this night, and lukewarm John,
And trust for food to the Earth and Providence.

   Sand. O lady, have a care
Of these indefinite and spleen-bred resolves.
You know not half the dangers that attend
Upon a life of wandering, which your thoughts now
Feeling the swellings of a lofty anger,
To your abusèd fancy, as 'tis likely,
Portray without its terrors, painting *lies*
And representments of fallacious liberty—
You know not what it is to leave the roof that shelters you.

Marg. I have thought on every possible event,
The dangers and discouragements you speak of,
Even till my woman's heart hath ceased to fear them,
And cowardice grows enamour'd of rare accidents,
Nor am I so unfurnish'd as you think,
Of practicable schemes.
    Sand. Now God forbid ; think twice of this, dear lady.
    Marg. I pray you spare me, Mr. Sandford,
And once for all believe, nothing can shake my purpose.
    Sand. But what course have you thought on ?
    Marg. To seek Sir Walter in the forest of Sherwood.
I have letters from young Simon,
Acquainting me with all the circumstances
Of their concealment, place, and manner of life,
And the merry hours they spend in the green haunts
Of Sherwood, nigh which place they have ta'en a house
In the town of Nottingham, and pass for foreigners,
Wearing the dress of Frenchmen.—
All which I have perused with so attent
And childlike longings, that to my doting ears
Two sounds now seem like one,
One meaning in two words, Sherwood and Liberty.—
And, gentle Mr. Sandford,—
'Tis you that must provide now
The means of my departure, which for safety
Must be in boy's apparel.
    Sand. Since you will have it so
(My careful age trembles at all may happen)
I will engage to furnish you.
I have the keys of the wardrobe, and can fit you
With garments to your size.
I know a suit
Of lively Lincoln Green, that shall much grace you
In the wear, being glossy fresh, and worn but seldom.
Young Stephen Woodvil wore them while he lived.
I have the keys of all this house and passages,
And ere day break will rise and let you forth.
What things soe'er you have need of I can furnish you ;

And will provide a horse and trusty guide
To bear you on your way to Nottingham.—
  Marg. That once this day and night were fairly past!
For then I'll bid this house and love farewell;
Farewell, sweet Devon; farewell, lukewarm John:
For with the morning's light will Margaret be gone.
Thanks, courteous Mr. Sandford.— [*Exeunt divers ways.*

ACT THE SECOND.

Scene.—*An Apartment in Woodvil Hall.*

John Woodvil—*alone.*

(*Reading parts of a letter.*)

The Letter.

"When Love grows cold, and indifference has usurped upon old esteem, it is no marvel if the world begin to account *that* dependence, which hitherto has been esteemed honourable shelter. The course I have taken (in leaving this house, not easily wrought thereunto) seemed to me best for the once-for-all releasing of yourself (who in times past have deserved well of me) from the now daily and not to be endured tribute of forced love, and ill-dissembled reluctance of affection.   "Margaret."

Gone! gone! my girl? so hasty, Margaret!
And never a kiss at parting? shallow loves,
And likings of a ten days' growth, use courtesies,
And show red eyes at parting. Who bids "farewell"
In the same tone he cries "God speed you, sir?"
Or tells of joyful victories at sea,
Where he hath ventures? does not rather muffle
His organs to emit a leaden sound,
To suit the melancholy dull "farewell,"
Which They in Heaven not use?—
So peevish, Margaret?

D

But 'tis the common error of your sex,
When our idolatry slackens, or grows less,
(As who of woman born can keep his faculty,
Of Admiration, being a decaying faculty,
For ever strain'd to the pitch? or can at pleasure
Make it renewable, as some appetites are,
As namely, Hunger, Thirst?)—this being the case,
They tax us with neglect, and love grown cold,
Coin plainings of the perfidy of men,
Which into maxims pass, and apothegms
To be retail'd in ballads.—
     I know them all.
They are jealous, when our larger hearts receive
More guests than one. (Love in a woman's heart
Being all in one.) For me, I am sure I have room here
For more disturbers of my sleep than one.
Love shall have part, but Love shall not have all.
Ambition, Pleasure, Vanity, all by turns,
Shall lie in my bed, and keep me fresh and waking;
Yet Love not be excluded.—Foolish wench,
I could have loved her twenty years to come,
And still have kept my liking. But since 'tis so,
Why, fare thee well, old play-fellow! I'll try
To squeeze a tear for old acquaintance' sake.
I shall not grudge so much.——

To him enters LOVEL.

Lov. Bless us, Woodvil! what is the matter? I protest, man, I thought you had been weeping.

Wood. Nothing is the matter, only the wench has forced some water into my eyes, which will quickly disband.

Lov. I cannot conceive you.

Wood. Margaret is flown.

Lov. Upon what pretence?

Wood. Neglect on my part: which it seems she has had the wit to discover, maugre all my pains to conceal it.

Lov. Then you confess the charge?

Wood. To say the truth, my love for her has of late stopped short on this side idolatry.

Lov. As all good Christians should, I think.

Wood. I am sure, I could have loved her still within the limits of warrantable love.

Lov. A kind of brotherly affection, I take it.

Wood. We should have made excellent man and wife in time.

Lov. A good old couple, when the snows fell, to crowd about a sea-coal fire, and talk over old matters.

Wood. While each should feel, what neither cared to acknowledge, that stories oft repeated may at last come to lose some of their grace by the repetition.

Lov. Which both of you may yet live long enough to discover. For, take my word for it, Margaret is a bird, that will come back to you without a lure.

Wood. Never, never, Lovel. Spite of my levity, with tears I confess it, she was a lady of most confirmed honour, of an unmatchable spirit, and determinate in all virtuous resolutions; not hasty to anticipate an affront, nor slow to feel, where just provocation was given.

Lov. What made you neglect her, then?

Wood. Mere levity and youthfulness of blood, a malady incident to young men, physicians call it caprice. Nothing else. He that slighted her knew her value: and 'tis odds, but for thy sake, Margaret, John will yet go to his grave a bachelor. [*A noise heard as of one drunk and singing.*

Lov. Here comes one that will quickly dissipate these humours.

Enter one drunk.

Drunken Man. Good-morrow to you, gentlemen. Mr. Lovel, I am your humble servant. Honest Jack Woodvil, I will get drunk with you to-morrow.

Wood. And why to-morrow, honest Mr. Freeman?

Drunk. M. I scent a traitor in that question. A beastly question. Is it not his Majesty's birthday? the day of all days in the year, on which King Charles the Second was graciously pleased to be born. (*Sings*)

"Great pity 'tis such days as those should come but once a year."

Lov. Drunk in a morning! foh! how he stinks.

Drunk. M. And why not drunk in a morning? canst tell, bully?

Wood. Because being the sweet and tender infancy of the day, methinks it should ill-endure such early blightings.

Drunk. M. I grant you, 'tis in some sort the youth and tender nonage of the day. Youth is bashful, and I give it a cup to encourage it. (*Sings*) "Ale that will make Grimalkin prate."—At noon I drink for thirst, at night for fellowship, but above all I love to usher in the bashful morning under the auspices of a freshening stoup of liquor. (*Sings*) "Ale in a Saxon rumkin then Makes valour burgeon in tall men."—But I crave pardon. I fear I keep that gentleman from serious thoughts. There be those that wait for me in the cellar.

Wood. Who are they?

Drunk. M. Gentlemen, my good friends, Cleveland, Delaval, and Truby. I know by this time they are all clamorous for me. [*Exit singing.*

Wood. This keeping of open house acquaints a man with strange companions.

Enter at another door, Three calling for HARRY FREEMAN.

Harry Freeman, Harry Freeman.
He is not here. Let us go look for him.
Where is Freeman?
Where is Harry?

[*Exeunt the Three, calling for* FREEMAN.

Wood. Did you ever see such gentry? (*laughing*). These are they, that fatten on ale and tobacco in a morning, drink burnt brandy at noon to promote digestion, and piously conclude with quart bumpers after supper to prove their loyalty.

Lov. Come, shall we adjourn to the Tennis Court?

Wood. No, you shall go with me into the gallery,

where I will show you the *Vandyke* I have purchased:
"The late king taking leave of his children."

Lov. I will but adjust my dress, and attend you.
[*Exit* LOVEL.

Wood. (alone). Now universal England getteth drunk
For joy that Charles, her monarch, is restored:
And she, that sometime wore a saintly mask,
The stale-grown vizor from her face doth pluck,
And weareth now a suit of morris bells,
With which she jingling goes through all her towns and
    villages.
The baffled factions in their houses skulk:
The commonwealthsman, and state machinist,
The cropp'd fanatic, and fifth-monarchy-man,
Who heareth of these visionaries now?
They and their dreams have ended. Fools do sing,
Where good men yield God thanks; but politic spirits,
Who live by observation, note these changes
Of the popular mind, and thereby serve their ends.
Then why not I? What's Charles to me, or Oliver,
But as my own advancement hangs on one of them?
I to myself am chief.——I know,
Some shallow mouths cry out, that I am smit
With the gauds and show of state, the point of place,
And trick of precedence, the ducks, and nods,
Which weak minds pay to rank. 'Tis not to sit
In place of worship at the royal masques,
Their pastimes, plays, and Whitehall banquetings,
For none of these,
Nor yet to be seen whispering with some great one,
Do I affect the favours of the court.
I would be great, for greatness hath great *power*,
And that's the fruit I reach at.—
Great spirits ask great play-room. Who could sit,
With these prophetic swellings in my breast,
That prick and goad me on, and never cease,
To the fortunes something tells me I was born to?
Who, with such monitors within to stir him,

Would sit him down with lazy arms across,
An unit, a thing without a name in the state,
A something to be govern'd, not to govern,
A fishing, hawking, hunting country gentleman? [*Exit.*

Scene.—*Sherwood Forest.*

SIR WALTER WOODVIL, SIMON WOODVIL
(*disguised as Frenchmen*).

Sir Wal. How fares my boy, Simon, my youngest born,
My hope, my pride, young Woodvil, speak to me?
Some grief untold weighs heavy at thy heart:
I know it by thy alter'd cheer of late.
Thinkest thy brother plays thy father false?
It is a mad and thriftless prodigal,
Grown proud upon the favours of the court;
Court manners, and court fashions, he affects,
And in the heat and uncheck'd blood of youth,
Harbours a company of riotous men,
All hot, and young, court-seekers like himself,
Most skilful to devour a patrimony;
And these have eat into my old estates,
And these have drain'd thy father's cellars dry;
But these so common faults of youth not named,
(Things which themselves outgrow, left to themselves)
I know no quality that stains his honour.
My life upon his faith and noble mind,
Son John could never play thy father false.

Sim. I never thought but nobly of my brother,
Touching his honour and fidelity,
Still I could wish him charier of his person,
And of his time more frugal, than to spend
In riotous living, graceless society,
And mirth unpalatable, hours better employ'd
(With those persuasive graces nature lent him)
In fervent pleadings for a father's life.

Sir Wal. I would not owe my life to a jealous court,

Whose shallow policy I know it is,
On some reluctant acts of prudent mercy,
(Not voluntary, but extorted by the times,
In the first tremblings of new-fixed power,
And recollection smarting from old wounds,)
On these to build a spurious popularity.
Unknowing what free grace or mercy mean,
They fear to punish, therefore do they pardon.
For this cause have I oft forbid my son,
By letters, overtures, open solicitings,
Or closet-tamperings, by gold or fee,
To beg or bargain with the court for my life.

 Sim. And John has ta'en you, father, at your word,
True to the letter of his paternal charge.

 Sir Wal. Well, my good cause, and my good conscience, boy,
Shall be for sons to me, if John prove false.
Men die but once, and the opportunity
Of a noble death is not an every-day fortune :
It is a gift which noble spirits pray for.

 Sim. I would not wrong my brother by surmise ;
I know him generous, full of gentle qualities,
Incapable of base compliances,
No prodigal in his nature, but affecting
This show of bravery for ambitious ends.
He drinks, for 'tis the humour of the court,
And drink may one day wrest the secret from him,
And pluck you from your hiding-place in the sequel.

 Sir Wal. Fair death shall be my doom, and foul life is.
Till when, we'll live as free in this green forest,
As yonder deer, who roam unfearing treason ;
Who seem the Aborigines of this place,
Of Sherwood theirs by tenure.—

 Sim. 'Tis said, that Robert Earl of Huntingdon,
Men call'd him Robin Hood, an outlaw bold,
With a merry crew of hunters here did haunt,
Not sparing the king's venison. May one believe
The antique tale ?

    Sir Wal. There is much likelihood,
Such bandits did in England erst abound,
When polity was young. I have read of the pranks
Of that mad archer, and of the tax he levied
On travellers, whatever their degree,
Baron, or knight, whoever pass'd these woods,
Layman, or priest, not sparing the bishop's mitre
For spiritual regards; nay once, 'tis said,
He robb'd the king himself.
    Sim. A perilous man (*smiling*).
    Sir Wal. How quietly we live here,
Unread in the world's business,
And take no note of all its slippery changes.
'Twere best we make a world among ourselves,
A little world,
Without the ills and falsehoods of the greater;
We two being all the inhabitants of ours,
And kings and subjects both in one.—
    Sim. Only the dangerous errors, fond conceits,
Which make the business of that greater world,
Must have no place in ours:
As namely, riches, honours, birth, place, courtesy,
Good fame and bad, rumours and popular noises,
Books, creeds, opinions, prejudices national,
Humours particular,
Soul-killing lies, and truths that work small good,
Feuds, factions, enmities, relationships,
Loves, hatreds, sympathies, antipathies,
And all the intricate stuff quarrels are made of.

    MARGARET *enters in boy's apparel.*

    Sir Wal. What pretty boy have we here?
    Marg. Bonjour, messieurs. Ye have handsome English
        faces,
I should have ta'en you else for other two,
I came to seek in the forest.
    Sir Wal. Who are they?
    Marg. A gallant brace of Frenchmen, curl'd monsieurs,

That, men say, haunt these woods, affecting privacy,
More than the manner of their countrymen.
   Sim. We have here a wonder.
The face is Margaret's face.
   Sir Wal. The face is Margaret's, but the dress the same
My Stephen sometime wore.
(*To* MARG.) Suppose us them; whom do men say we are?
Or know you what you seek?
   Marg. A worthy pair of exiles,
Two whom the politics of state revenge,
In final issue of long civil broils,
Have houseless driven from your native France
To wander idle in these English woods,
Where now ye live; most part
Thinking on home, and all the joys of France,
Where grows the purple vine.
   Sir Wal. These woods, young stranger,
And grassy pastures, which the slim deer loves,
Are they less beauteous than the land of France,
Where grows the purple vine?
   Marg. I cannot tell.
To an indifferent eye both show alike
'Tis not the scene,
But all familiar objects in the scene,
Which now ye miss, that constitute a difference.
Ye had a country, exiles, ye have none now;
Friends had ye, and much wealth, ye now have nothing;
Our manners, laws, our customs all are foreign to you,
I know ye loathe them, cannot learn them readily:
And there is reason, exiles, ye should love
Our English earth less than your land of France,
Where grows the purple vine; where all delights grow
Old custom has made pleasant.
   Sir Wal. You, that are read
So deeply in our story, what are you?
   Marg. A bare adventurer; in brief a woman,
That put strange garments on, and came thus far
To seek an ancient friend:

And having spent her stock of idle words,
And feeling some tears coming,
Hastes now to clasp Sir Walter Woodvil's knees,
And beg a boon for Margaret, his poor ward (*kneeling*).
    Sir Wal. Not at my feet, Margaret, not at my feet.
    Marg. Yes, till her suit is answer'd.
    Sir Wal. Name it.
    Marg. A little boon, and yet so great a grace,
She fears to ask it.
    Sir Wal. Some riddle, Margaret?
    Marg. No riddle, but a plain request.—
    Sir Wal. Name it.
    Marg. Free liberty of Sherwood.
And leave to take her lot with you in the forest.
    Sir Wal. A scant petition, Margaret, but take it,
Seal'd with an old man's tears.—
Rise, daughter of Sir Rowland.
(*Addresses them both*) O you most worthy,
You constant followers of a man proscribed,
Following poor misery in the throat of danger;
Fast servitors to crazed and penniless poverty,
Serving poor poverty without hope of gain;
Kind children of a sire unfortunate;
Green clinging tendrils round a trunk decay'd,
Which needs must bring on you timeless decay;
Fair living forms to a dead carcase join'd;—
What shall I say?
Better the dead were gather'd to the dead,
Than death and life in disproportion meet.—
Go, seek your fortunes, children.—
    Sim. Why, whither should we go?
    Sir Wal. You to the court, where now your brother
        John
Commits a rape on Fortune:—
    Sim. Luck to John!
A light-heel'd strumpet, when the sport is done.
    Sir Wal. You to the sweet society of your equals,
Where the world's fashion smiles on youth and beauty:

Marg. Where young men's flatteries cozen young maids' beauty,
There pride oft gets the vantage hand of duty,
There sweet humility withers.

Sim. Mistress Margaret,
How fared my brother John, when you left Devon?

Marg. John was well, sir.

Sim. 'Tis now nine months almost,
Since I saw home. What new friends has John made?
Or keeps he his first love?—I did suspect
Some foul disloyalty. Now do I know,
John has proved false to her, for Margaret weeps.
It is a scurvy brother.

Sir Wal. Fie upon it!
All men are false, I think. The date of love
Is out, expired, its stories all grown stale,
O'erpast, forgotten, like an antique tale
Of Hero and Leander.

Sim. I have known some men that are too general-contemplative for the narrow passion. I am in some sort a *general* lover.

Marg. In the name of the boy-god, who plays at hoodman-blind with the Muses, and cares not whom he catches: what is it *you* love?

Sim. Simply, all things that live,
From the crook'd worm to man's imperial form,
And God-resembling likeness. The poor fly,
That makes short holyday in the sunbeam,
And dies by some child's hand. The feeble bird
With little wings, yet greatly venturous
In the upper sky. The fish in th' other element,
That knows no touch of eloquence. What else?
Yon tall and elegant stag,
Who paints a dancing shadow of his horns
In the water, where he drinks.

Marg. I myself love all these things, yet so as with a difference:—for example, some animals better than others, some men rather than other men; the nightingale before

the cuckoo, the swift and graceful palfrey before the slow
and asinine mule. Your humour goes to confound all
qualities.
What sports do you use in the forest?

   Sim. Not many; some few, as thus:—
To see the sun to bed, and to arise,
Like some hot amorist with glowing eyes,
Bursting the lazy bands of sleep that bound him,
With all his fires and travelling glories round him:
Sometimes the moon on soft night clouds to rest,
Like beauty nestling in a young man's breast,
And all the winking stars, her handmaids, keep
Admiring silence, while those lovers sleep:
Sometimes outstretch'd, in very idleness,
Nought doing, saying little, thinking less,
To view the leaves, thin dancers upon air,
Go eddying round; and small birds, how they fare,
When mother Autumn fills their beaks with corn,
Filch'd from the careless Amalthea's horn;
And how the woods berries and worms provide
Without their pains, when earth has nought beside
To answer their small wants:
To view the graceful deer come tripping by,
Then stop, and gaze, then turn, they know not why,
Like bashful younkers in society:
To mark the structure of a plant or tree;
And all fair things of earth, how fair they be.

   Marg. (*smiling*). And afterwards them paint in
     simile.—

   Sir Wal. Mistress Margaret will have need of some
     refreshment.
Please you, we have some poor viands within—

   Marg. Indeed I stand in need of them.

   Sir Wal. Under the shade of a thick-spreading tree,
Upon the grass, no better carpeting,
We'll eat our noon-tide meal; and, dinner done,
One of us shall repair to Nottingham,
To seek some safe night-lodging in the town,

Where you may sleep, while here with us you dwell,
By day, in the forest, expecting better times
And gentler habitations, noble Margaret.—
  Sim. Allons, young Frenchman—
  Marg. Allons, Sir Englishman. The time has been,
I've studied love-lays in an English tongue,
And been enamour'd of rare poesy:
Which now I must unlearn. Henceforth,
Sweet mother-tongue, old English speech, adieu;
For Margaret has got new name and language new.
[Exeunt.

ACT THE THIRD.

Scene.—*An Apartment of State in Woodvil Hall.— Cavaliers drinking.*

JOHN WOODVIL, LOVEL, GRAY, *and four more.*

  John. More mirth, I beseech you, gentlemen—
Mr. Gray, you are not merry.—
  Gray. More wine, say I, and mirth shall ensue in course. What! we have not yet above three half-pints a man to answer for. Brevity is the soul of drinking, as of wit. Despatch, I say. More wine. (*Fills.*)
  1st Gent. I entreat you, let there be some order, some method, in our drinkings. I love to lose my reason with my eyes open, to commit the deed of drunkenness with forethought and deliberation. I love to feel the fumes of the liquor gathering here, like clouds.
  2d Gent. And I am for plunging into madness at once. Damn order, and method, and steps, and degrees, that he speaks of. Let confusion have her legitimate work.
  Lov. I marvel why the poets, who of all men, methinks, should possess the hottest livers, and most empyreal fancies, should affect to see such virtues in cold water.
  Gray. Virtue in cold water! ha! ha! ha!—
  John. Because your poet born hath an internal wine,

richer than Lippara or Canaries, yet uncrushed from any grapes of earth, unpressed in mortal wine-presses.

3d Gent. What may be the name of this wine?

John. It hath as many names as qualities. It is denominated indifferently, wit, conceit, invention, inspiration; but its most royal and comprehensive name is *fancy*.

3d Gent. And where keeps he this sovereign liquor?

John. Its cellars are in the brain, whence your true poet deriveth intoxication at will; while his animal spirits, catching a pride from the quality and neighbourhood of their noble relative, the brain, refuse to be sustained by wines and stimuli of earth.

3d Gent. But is your poet-born always tipsy with this liquor?

John. He hath his stoopings and reposes; but his proper element is the sky, and in the suburbs of the empyrean.

3d Gent. Is your wine-intellectual so exquisite? henceforth I, a man of plain conceit, will in all humility content my mind with canaries.

4th Gent. I am for a song or a catch. When will the catches come on, the sweet wicked catches?

John. They cannot be introduced with propriety before midnight. Every man must commit his twenty bumpers first. We are not yet well roused. Frank Lovel, the toast stands with you.

Lov. Gentlemen, the Duke. (*Fills.*)

All. The Duke. (*They drink.*)

Gray. Can any tell, why his Grace, being a Papist——

John. Pshaw! we will have no questions of state now. Is not this his Majesty's birthday?

Gray. What follows?

John. That every man should sing, and be joyful, and ask no questions.

2d Gent. Damn politics, they spoil drinking.

3d Gent. For certain, 'tis a blessed monarchy.

2d Gent. The cursed fanatic days we have seen! The times have been when swearing was out of fashion.

3d Gent. And drinking.

1st Gent. And wenching.

Gray. The cursed yeas and forsooths, which we have heard uttered, when a man could not rap out an innocent oath, but straight the air was thought to be infected.

Lov. 'Twas a pleasant trick of the saint, which that trim puritan, *Swear-not-at-all Smooth-speech* used, when his spouse chid him with an oath for committing with his servant-maid, to cause his house to be fumigated with burnt brandy, and ends of scripture, to disperse the devil's breath, as he termed it.

All. Ha! ha! ha!

Gray. But 'twas pleasanter, when the other saint, *Resist-the-devil-and-he-will-flee-from-thee Pureman* was overtaken in the act, to plead an *illusio visûs*, and maintain his sanctity upon a supposed power in the adversary to counterfeit the shapes of things.

All. Ha! ha! ha!

John. Another round, and then let every man devise what trick he can in his fancy, for the better manifesting our loyalty this day.

Gray. Shall we hang a puritan?

John. No, that has been done already in Coleman Street.

2d Gent. Or fire a conventicle?

John. That is stale too.

3d Gent. Or burn the Assembly's Catechism?

4th Gent. Or toast the king's health, every man standing upon his head naked?

John (to LOVEL*).* We have here some pleasant madness.

3d Gent. (dashing his glass down). Pshaw, damn these acorn cups, they would not drench a fairy. Who shall pledge me in a pint bumper, while we drink the king's health upon our knees?

Lov. Why on our knees, cavalier?

John (smiling). For more devotion, to be sure. (*To a servant*) Sirrah, fetch the gilt goblets.

(*The goblets are brought. They drink the king's health kneeling. A shout of general approbation following the first appearance of the goblets.*)

John. We have here the unchecked virtues of the grape. How the vapours curl upwards! It were a life of gods to dwell in such an element: to see, and hear, and talk brave things. Now fie upon these casual potations. That a man's most exalted reason should depend upon the ignoble fermentation of a fruit, which sparrows pluck at as well as we!

Gray (*aside to* LOVEL). Observe how he is ravished.

Lov. Vanity and gay thoughts of wine do meet in him and engender madness.

(*While the rest are engaged in a wild kind of talk,* JOHN *advances to the front of the stage and soliloquises.*)

John. My spirits turn to fire, they mount so fast.
My joys are turbulent, my hopes show like fruition.
These high and gusty relishes of life, sure,
Have no allayings of mortality in them.
I am too hot now and o'ercapable,
For the tedious processes, and creeping wisdom,
Of human acts, and enterprises of a man.
I want some seasonings of adversity,
Some strokes of the old mortifier, Calamity,
To take these swellings down, divines call vanity.

1st Gent. Mr. Woodvil, Mr. Woodvil.

2d Gent. Where is Woodvil?

Gray. Let him alone. I have seen him in these lunes before. His abstractions must not taint the good mirth.

John (*continuing to soliloquise*). O for some friend now,
To conceal nothing from, to have no secrets.
How fine and noble a thing is confidence,
How reasonable too, and almost godlike!
Fast cement of fast friends, band of society,
Old natural go-between in the world's business,
Where civil life and order, wanting this cement,
Would presently rush back

Into the pristine state of singularity,
And each man stand alone.

A Servant enters.

Serv. Gentlemen, the fireworks are ready.

1st Gent. What be they ?

Lov. The work of London artists, which our host has provided in honour of this day.

2d Gent. 'Sdeath, who would part with his wine for a rocket ?

Lov. Why truly, gentlemen, as our kind host has been at the pains to provide this spectacle, we can do no less than be present at it. It will not take up much time. Every man may return fresh and thirsting to his liquor.

3d Gent. There is reason in what he says.

2d Gent. Charge on then, bottle in hand. There's husbandry in that.

[*They go out, singing. Only* LOVEL *remains, who observes* WOODVIL.

John (still talking to himself). This Lovel here's of a
    tough honesty,
Would put the rack to the proof. He is not of that sort.
Which haunt my house, snorting the liquors,
And, when their wisdoms are afloat with wine,
Spend vows as fast as vapours, which go off,
Even with the fumes, their fathers. He is one,
Whose sober morning actions
Shame not his o'ernight's promises ;
Talks little, flatters less, and makes no promises ;
Why this is he, whom the dark-wisdom'd fate
Might trust her counsels of predestination with,
And the world be no loser.
Why should I fear this man ?
(*Seeing* LOVEL.) Where is the company gone ?

Lov. To see the fireworks, where you will be expected
    to follow.
But I perceive you are better engaged.

John. I have been meditating this half-hour

E

On all the properties of a brave friendship,
The mysteries that are in it, the noble uses,
Its limits withal, and its nice boundaries.
Exempli gratia, how far a man
May lawfully forswear himself for his friend;
What quantity of lies, some of them brave ones,
He may lawfully incur in a friend's behalf;
What oaths, blood-crimes, hereditary quarrels,
Night-brawls, fierce words, and duels in the morning,
He need not stick at, to maintain his friend's honour, or
    his cause.
  Lov. I think many men would die for their friends.
  John. Death! why 'tis nothing. We go to it for sport,
To gain a name, or purse, or please a sullen humour,
When one has worn his fortune's livery threadbare,
Or his spleen'd mistress frowns. Husbands will venture
    on it,
To cure the hot fits and cold shakings of jealousy.
A friend, sir, must do more.
  Lov. Can he do more than die?
  John. To serve a friend this he may do. Pray mark
    me.
Having a law within (great spirits feel one)
He cannot, ought not to be bound by any
Positive laws or ordinances extern,
But may reject all these: by the law of friendship
He may do so much, be they, indifferently,
Penn'd statutes, or the land's unwritten usages,
As public fame, civil compliances,
Misnamed honour, trust in matter of secrets,
All vows and promises, the feeble mind's religion,
(Binding our morning knowledge to approve
What last night's ignorance spake);
The ties of blood withal, and prejudice of kin.
Sir, these weak terrors
Must never shake me. I know what belongs
To a worthy friendship. Come, you shall have my con-
    fidence.

Lov. I hope you think me worthy.

John. You will smile to hear now—
Sir Walter never has been out of the island.

Lov. You amaze me.

John. That same report of his escape to France
Was a fine tale, forged by myself—
Ha! ha!
I knew it would stagger him.—

Lov. Pray, give me leave.
Where has he dwelt, how lived, how lain conceal'd?
Sure I may ask so much.

John. From place to place, dwelling in no place long,
My brother Simon still hath borne him company,
('Tis a brave youth, I envy him all his virtues.)
Disguised in foreign garb, they pass for Frenchmen,
Two Protestant exiles from the Limosin
Newly arrived. Their dwelling's now at Nottingham,
Where no soul knows them.

Lov. Can you assign any reason why a gentleman of Sir Walter's known prudence should expose his person so lightly?

John. I believe, a certain fondness,
A child-like cleaving to the land that gave him birth
Chains him like fate.

Lov. I have known some exiles thus
To linger out the term of the law's indulgence,
To the hazard of being known.—

John. You may suppose sometimes,
They use the neighbouring Sherwood for their sport,
Their exercise and freer recreation.—
I see you smile. Pray now, be careful.

Lov. I am no babbler, sir; you need not fear me.

John. But some men have been known to talk in their sleep,
And tell fine tales that way.—

Lov. I have heard so much. But, to say truth, I mostly sleep alone.

John. Or drink, sir? do you never drink too freely?
Some men will drink, and tell you all their secrets.

 Lov. Why do you question me, who know my habits?
 John. I think you are no sot,
No tavern-troubler, worshipper of the grape;
But all men drink sometimes,
And veriest saints at festivals relax,
The marriage of a friend, or a wife's birthday.
 Lov. How much, sir, may a man with safety drink?
  (*smiling*).
 John. Sir, three half-pints a day is reasonable;
I care not if you never exceed that quantity.
 Lov. I shall observe it;
On holidays two quarts.—
 John. Or stay; you keep no wench?
 Lov. Ha!
 John. No painted mistress for your private hours?
You keep no whore, sir?
 Lov. What does he mean?
 John. Who for a close embrace, a toy of sin,
And amorous praising of your worship's breath,
In rosy junction of four melting lips,
Can kiss out secrets from you?
 Lov. How strange this passionate behaviour shows in
  you!
Sure you think me some weak one.
 John. Pray pardon me some fears.
You have now the pledge of a dear father's life.
I am a son—would fain be thought a loving one;
You may allow me some fears: do not despise me,
If, in a posture foreign to my spirit,
And by our well-knit friendship I conjure you,
Touch not Sir Walter's life.— (*Kneels.*)
You see these tears. My father's an old man.
Pray let him live.
 Lov. I must be bold to tell you, these new freedoms
Show most unhandsome in you.
 John (*rising*). Ha! do you say so?
Sure, you are not grown proud upon my secret!
Ah! now I see it plain. He would be babbling.

No doubt a garrulous and hard-faced traitor—
But I'll not give you leave.   (*Draws.*)
    Lov. What does this madman mean?
    John. Come, sir; here is no subterfuge.
You must kill me, or I kill you.
    Lov. (*drawing*). Then self-defence plead my excuse.
Have at you, sir.   (*They fight.*)
    John. Stay, sir.
I hope you have made your will.
If not, 'tis no great matter.
A broken Cavalier has seldom much
He can bequeath: an old worn peruke,
A snuff-box with a picture of Prince Rupert,
A rusty sword he'll swear was used at Naseby,
Though it ne'er came within ten miles of the place;
And, if he's very rich,
A cheap edition of the *Icon Basilike*,
Is mostly all the wealth he dies possess'd of.
You say few prayers, I fancy;—
So to it again.
        (*They fight again.* Lovel *is disarmed.*)
    Lov. You had best now take my life. I guess you
        mean it.
    John (*musing*). No:—men will say I fear'd him, if I
        kill'd him.
Live still, and be a traitor in thy wish,
But never act thy thought, being a coward.
That vengeance, which thy soul shall nightly thirst for,
And this disgrace I've done you cry aloud for,
Still have the will without the power to execute.
So now I leave you.
Feeling a sweet security. No doubt
My secret shall remain a virgin for you!—
        (*Goes out, smiling in scorn.*)
    Lov. (*rising*). For once you are mistaken in your man.
The deed you wot of shall forthwith be done.
A bird let loose, a secret out of hand,
Returns not back. Why, then, 'tis baby policy

To menace him who hath it in his keeping.
I will go look for Gray;
Then Northward ho! such tricks as we shall play
Have not been seen, I think, in merry Sherwood,
Since the days of Robin Hood, that archer good.

ACT THE FOURTH.

SCENE.—*An Apartment in Woodvil Hall.*

John Woodvil (alone). A weight of wine lies heavy on my head,
The unconcocted follies of last night.
Now all those jovial fancies, and bright hopes,
Children of wine, go off like dreams.
This sick vertigo here
Preacheth of temperance, no sermon better.
These black thoughts, and dull melancholy,
That stick like burrs to the brain, will they ne'er leave me?
Some men are full of choler, when they are drunk;
Some brawl of matter foreign to themselves;
And some, the most resolvèd fools of all,
Have told their dearest secrets in their cups.

SCENE.—*The Forest.*

SIR WALTER. SIMON. LOVEL. GRAY.

Lov. Sir, we are sorry we cannot return your *French* salutation.

Gray. Nor otherwise consider this garb you trust to, than as a poor disguise.

Lov. Nor use much ceremony with a traitor.

Gray. Therefore, without much induction of superfluous words, I attach you, Sir Walter Woodvil, of high treason in the king's name.

Lov. And of taking part in the great Rebellion against our late lawful sovereign, Charles the First.

Sim. John has betrayed us, father.

Lov. Come, sir, you had best surrender fairly. We know you, sir.

Sim. Hang ye, villains, ye are two better known than trusted. I have seen those faces before. Are ye not two beggarly retainers, trencher-parasites, to John? I think ye rank above his footmen. A sort of bed and board-worms—locusts that invest our house; a leprosy that long has hung upon its walls and princely apartments, reaching to fill all the corners of my brother's once noble heart.

Gray. We are his friends.

Sim. Fie, sir, do not weep. How these rogues will triumph! Shall I whip off their heads, father?

(*Draws.*)

Lov. Come, sir, though this show handsome in you, being his son, yet the law must have its course.

Sim. And if I tell you, the law shall not have its course, cannot ye be content? Courage, father; shall such things as these apprehend a man? Which of ye will venture upon me?—Will you, Mr. Constable self-elect? or you, sir, with a pimple on your nose, got at Oxford by hard drinking, your only badge of loyalty?

Gray. 'Tis a brave youth—I cannot strike at him.

Sim. Father, why do you cover your face with your hands? Why do you fetch your breath so hard? See, villains, his heart is burst! O, villains, he cannot speak. One of you run for some water: quickly, ye knaves; will ye have your throats cut? [*They both slink off.* How is it with you, Sir Walter? Look up, sir; the villains are gone. He hears me not, and this deep disgrace of treachery in his son hath touched him even to the death. O most distuned and distempered world, where sons talk their aged fathers into their graves! Garrulous and diseased world, and still empty, rotten, and hollow *talking* world, where good men decay, states

turn round in an endless mutability, and still for the
worse, nothing is at a stay, nothing abides, but vanity,
chaotic vanity.—Brother, adieu!
There lies the parent stock which gave us life,
Which I will see consign'd with tears to earth.
Leave thou the solemn funeral rites to me,
Grief and a true remorse abide with thee.
[Bears in the body.

SCENE.—*Another part of the Forest.*

Marg. (alone). It was an error merely, and no crime,
An unsuspecting openness in youth,
That from his lips the fatal secret drew,
Which should have slept like one of nature's mysteries,
Unveil'd by any man.—
Well, he is dead!
And what should Margaret do in the forest?
O ill-starr'd John!
O Woodvil, man enfeoffed to despair!
Take thy farewell of peace.
O never look again to see good days,
Or close thy lids in comfortable nights,
Or ever think a happy thought again,
If what I have heard be true.—
Forsaken of the world must Woodvil live,
If he did tell these men.
No tongue must speak to him, no tongue of man
Salute him, when he wakes up in a morning;
Or bid "good-night" to John. Who seeks to live
In amity with thee, must for thy sake
Abide the world's reproach. What then?
Shall Margaret join the clamours of the world
Against her friend? O undiscerning world,
That cannot from misfortune separate guilt,
No, not in thought! O never, never, John.
Prepared to share the fortunes of her friend
For better or for worse thy Margaret comes,

To pour into thy wounds a healing love,
And wake the memory of an ancient friendship.
And pardon me, thou spirit of Sir Walter,
Who, in compassion to the wretched living,
Have but few tears to waste upon the dead.

Scene.—*Woodvil Hall.*

Sandford *and* Margaret (*as from a journey*).

Sand. The violence of the sudden mischance hath so wrought in him, who by nature is allied to nothing *less* than a self-debasing humour of dejection, that I have never seen anything more changed and spirit-broken. He hath, with a peremptory resolution, dismissed the partners of his riots and late hours, denied his house and person to their most earnest solicitings, and will be seen by none. He keeps ever alone, and his grief (which is solitary) does not so much seem to possess and govern in him, as it is by him, with a wilfulness of most manifest affection, entertained and cherished.

Marg. How bears he up against the common rumour?

Sand. With a strange indifference, which whosoever dives not into the niceness of his sorrow, might mistake for obdurate and insensate. Yet are the wings of his pride for ever clipt; and yet a virtuous predominance of filial grief is so ever uppermost, that you may discover his thoughts, less troubled with conjecturing what living opinions will say and judge of his deeds, than absorbed and buried with the dead, whom his indiscretion made so.

Marg. I knew a greatness ever to be resident in him, to which the admiring eyes of men should look up even in the declining and bankrupt state of his pride. Fain would I see him, fain talk with him; but that a sense of respect, which is violated, when without deliberation we press into the society of the unhappy, checks and holds me back. How, think you, he would bear my presence?

Sand. As of an assured friend, whom in the forgetfulness of his fortunes he passed by. See him you must; but not to-night. The newness of the sight shall move the bitterest compunction and the truest remorse; but afterwards, trust me, dear lady, the happiest effects of a returning peace, and a gracious comfort, to him, to you, and all of us.

Marg. I think he would not deny me. He hath ere this received farewell letters from his brother, who hath taken a resolution to estrange himself, for a time, from country, friends, and kindred, and to seek occupation for his sad thoughts in travelling in foreign places, where sights remote and extern to himself may draw from him kindly and not painful ruminations.

Sand. I was present at the receipt of the letter. The contents seemed to affect him, for a moment, with a more lively passion of grief than he has at any time outwardly shown. He wept with many tears (which I had not before noted in him) and appeared to be touched with a sense as of some unkindness; but the cause of their sad separation and divorce quickly recurring, he presently returned to his former inwardness of suffering.

Marg. The reproach of his brother's presence at this hour should have been a weight more than could be sustained by his already oppressed and sinking spirit. Meditating upon these intricate and wide-spread sorrows hath brought a heaviness upon me, as of sleep. How goes the night?

Sand. An hour past sunset. You shall first refresh your limbs (tired with travel) with meats and some cordial wine, and then betake your no less wearied mind to repose.

Marg. A good rest to us all.

Sand. Thanks, lady.

ACT THE FIFTH.

JOHN WOODVIL (*dressing*).

John. How beautiful (*handling his mourning*)
And comely do these mourning garments show!
Sure Grief hath set his sacred impress here,
To claim the world's respect! they note so feelingly
By outward types the serious man within.
Alas! what part or portion can I claim
In all the decencies of virtuous sorrow,
Which other mourners use?
This black attire, abstraction from society,
Good thoughts, and frequent sighs, and seldom smiles,
A cleaving sadness native to the brow.
All sweet condolements of like-grievèd friends,
(That steal away the sense of loss almost)
Men's pity and good offices
Which enemies themselves do for us then,
Putting their hostile disposition off,
As we put off our high thoughts and proud looks.
                            [*Pauses and observes the pictures.*
These pictures must be taken down:
The portraitures of our most ancient family
For nigh three hundred years! How have I listen'd,
To hear Sir Walter, with an old man's pride,
Holding me in his arms a prating boy,
And pointing to the pictures where they hung,
Repeat by course their worthy histories,
(As Hugh de Widville, Walter, first of the name,
And Anne the handsome, Stephen, and famous John:
Telling me, I must be his famous John)
But that was in old times,
Now, no more
Must I grow proud upon our house's pride.
I rather, I, by most unheard-of crimes,
Have backward tainted all their noble blood,
Rased out the memory of an ancient family,

And quite reversed the honours of our house—
Who now shall sit and tell us anecdotes?
The secret history of his own times,
And fashions of the world when he was young:
How England slept out three and twenty years,
While Carr and Villiers ruled the baby King:
The costly fancies of the pedant's reign,
Balls, feastings, huntings, shows in allegory,
And Beauties of the court of James the First.

MARGARET enters.

John. Comes Margaret here to witness my disgrace?
O lady, I have suffer'd loss,
And diminution of my honour's brightness.
You bring some images of old times, Margaret,
That should be now forgotten.

Marg. Old times should never be forgotten, John.
I came to talk about them with my friend.

John. I did refuse you, Margaret, in my pride.

Marg. If John rejected Margaret in his pride,
(As who does not, being splenetic, refuse
Sometimes old play-fellows) the spleen being gone,
The offence no longer lives.
O Woodvil, those were happy days,
When we two first began to love. When first,
Under pretence of visiting my father,
(Being then a stripling nigh upon my age)
You came a-wooing to his daughter, John,
Do you remember,
With what a coy reserve and seldom speech,
(Young maidens must be chary of their speech)
I kept the honours of my maiden pride?
I was your favourite then.

John. O Margaret, Margaret!
These your submissions to my low estate,
And cleavings to the fates of sunken Woodvil,
Write bitter things 'gainst my unworthiness:
Thou perfect pattern of thy slander'd sex,

Whom miseries of mine could never alienate,
Nor change of fortune shake; whom injuries,
And slights (the worst of injuries) which moved
Thy nature to return scorn with like scorn,
Then when you left in virtuous pride this house,
Could not so separate, but not in this
My day of shame, when all the world forsake me,
You only visit me, love, and forgive me.

 Marg. Dost yet remember the green arbour, John,
In the south gardens of my father's house,
Where we have seen the summer sun go down,
Exchanging true love's vows without restraint?
And that old wood, you call'd your wilderness,
And vow'd in sport to build a chapel in it,
There dwell

    " Like hermit poor
    In pensive place obscure."

And tell your Ave Maries by the curls
(Dropping like golden beads) of Margaret's hair;
And make confession seven times a day
Of every thought that stray'd from love and Margaret,
And I your saint the penance should appoint—
Believe me, sir, I will not now be laid
Aside, like an old fashion.

 John. O lady, poor and abject are my thoughts,
My pride is cured, my hopes are under clouds,
I have no part in any good man's love,
In all earth's pleasures portion have I none,
I fade and wither in my own esteem,
This earth holds not alive so poor a thing as I am.
I was not always thus.   (*Weeps.*)

 Marg. Thou noble nature,
Which lion-like didst awe the inferior creatures,
Now trampled on by beasts of basest quality,
My dear heart's lord, life's pride, soul-honour'd John;
Upon her knees (regard her poor request)
Your favourite, once-belovèd Margaret, kneels.

    John. What wouldst thou, lady, ever-honour'd Margaret?
    Marg. That John would think more nobly of himself,
More worthily of high heaven;
And not for one misfortune, child of chance,
No crime, but unforeseen, and sent to punish
The less offence with image of the greater,
Thereby to work the soul's humility,
(Which end hath happily not been frustrate quite)
O not for one offence mistrust heaven's mercy,
Nor quit thy hope of happy days to come—
John yet has many happy days to live;
To live and make atonement.
    John. Excellent lady,
Whose suit hath drawn this softness from my eyes,
Not the world's scorn, nor falling off of friends
Could ever do. Will you go with me, Margaret?
    Marg. (*rising*). Go whither, John?
    John. Go in with me,
And pray for the peace of our unquiet minds?
    Marg. That I will, John.   [*Exeunt.*

SCENE.—*An inner Apartment.*

JOHN *is discovered kneeling,* MARGARET *standing over him.*

    John (*rises*). I cannot bear
To see you waste that youth and excellent beauty
('Tis now the golden time of the day with you)
In tending such a broken wretch as I am.
    Marg. John will break Margaret's heart, if he speak so.
O sir, sir, sir, you are too melancholy,
And I must call it caprice. I am somewhat bold
Perhaps in this. But you are now my patient,
(You know you gave me leave to call you so)
And I must chide these pestilent humours from you.
    John. They are gone,—
Mark, love, how cheerfully I speak!

I can smile too, and I almost begin
To understand what kind of creature Hope is.
   Marg. Now this is better, this mirth becomes you, John.
   John. Yet tell me, if I overact my mirth,
(Being but a novice, I may fall into that error)
That were a sad indecency, you know.—
   Marg. Nay, never fear.
I will be mistress of your humours,
And you shall frown or smile by the book.
And herein I shall be most peremptory,
Cry "This shows well, but that inclines to levity,
This frown has too much of the Woodvil in it,
But that fine sunshine has redeem'd it quite."
   John. How sweetly Margaret robs me of myself!
   Marg. To give you in your stead a better self;
Such as you were, when these eyes first beheld
You mounted on your sprightly steed, White Margery,
Sir Rowland, my father's gift,
And all my maidens gave my heart for lost.
I was a young thing then, being newly come
Home from my convent education, where
Seven years I had wasted in the bosom of France:
Returning home true Protestant, you call'd me
Your little heretic nun. How timid-bashful
Did John salute his love, being newly seen.
Sir Rowland term'd it a rare modesty,
And praised it in a youth.
   John. Now Margaret weeps herself.

        A noise of bells heard.

   Marg. Hark the bells, John.
   John. Those are the church bells of St. Mary Ottery.
   Marg. I know it.
   John. Saint Mary Ottery, my native village
In the sweet shire of Devon.
Those are the bells.
   Marg. Wilt go to church, John?
   John. I have been there already.

Marg. How canst say thou hast been there already?
The bells are only now ringing for morning service, and
hast thou been at church already?

John. I left my bed betimes, I could not sleep,
And when I rose, I look'd (as my custom is)
From my chamber window, where I can see the sun rise;
And the first object I discern'd
Was the glistering spire of St. Mary Ottery.

Marg. Well, John,—

John. Then I remember'd, 'twas the Sabbath day,
Immediately a wish arose in my mind,
To go to church and pray with Christian people,
And then I check'd myself, and said to myself,
"Thou hast been a heathen, John, these two years past,
(Not having been at church in all that time)
And is it fit, that now for the first time
Thou should'st offend the eyes of Christian people
With a murderer's presence in the house of prayer?
Thou would'st but discompose their pious thoughts,
And do thyself no good: for how could'st thou pray,
With unwash'd hands, and lips unused to the offices?"
And then I at my own presumption smiled;
And then I wept that I should smile at all,
Having such cause of grief! I wept outright;
Tears, like a river, flooded all my face,
And I began to pray, and found I could pray;
And still I yearn'd to say my prayers in the church.
"Doubtless (said I) one might find comfort in it."
So stealing down the stairs, like one that fear'd detection,
Or was about to act unlawful business
At that dead time of dawn,
I flew to the church, and found the doors wide open
(Whether by negligence I knew not,
Or some peculiar grace to me vouchsafed,
For all things felt like mystery).

Marg. Yes.

John. So entering in, not without fear,
I pass'd into the family pew,

And covering up my eyes for shame,
And deep perception of unworthiness,
Upon the little hassock knelt me down,
Where I so oft had kneel'd,
A docile infant by Sir Walter's side;
And, thinking so, I wept a second flood
More poignant than the first;—
But afterwards was greatly comforted.
It seem'd, the guilt of blood was passing from me
Even in the act and agony of tears,
And all my sins forgiven.

THE WITCH.

A DRAMATIC SKETCH OF THE SEVENTEENTH CENTURY.

CHARACTERS.
Old Servant in the Family of SIR FRANCIS FAIRFORD.
STRANGER.

Servant. One summer night Sir Francis, as it chanced,
Was pacing to and fro in the avenue
That westward fronts our house,
Among those agèd oaks, said to have been planted
Three hundred years ago
By a neighb'ring prior of the Fairford name.
Being o'ertask'd in thought, he heeded not
The importunate suit of one who stood by the gate,
And begg'd an alms.
Some say he shoved her rudely from the gate
With angry chiding; but I can never think
(Our master's nature hath a sweetness in it)
That he could use a woman, an old woman,
With such discourtesy: but he refused her—
And better had he met a lion in his path
Than that old woman that night;
For she was one who practised the black arts,
And served the devil, being since burnt for witchcraft.
She look'd on him as one that meant to blast him,
And with a frightful noise
('Twas partly like a woman's voice,
And partly like the hissing of a snake),
She nothing said but this:—
(Sir Francis told the words)
  A mischief, mischief, mischief,
 And a nine-times-killing curse,
By day and by night, to the caitiff wight,
Who shakes the poor like snakes from his door,
 And shuts up the womb of his purse.

And still she cried—
    A mischief,
And a nine-fold-withering curse:
For that shall come to thee that will undo thee,
    Both all that thou fearest and worse.
So saying she departed,
Leaving Sir Francis like a man, beneath
Whose feet a scaffolding was suddenly falling;
So he described it.
    Str. A terrible curse! What followed?
    Serv. Nothing immediate, but some two months after
Young Philip Fairford suddenly fell sick,
And none could tell what ailed him; for he lay,
And pined, and pined, till all his hair fell off,
And he, that was full-flesh'd, became as thin
As a two-month's babe that has been starved in the nursing.
And sure I think
He bore his death-wound like a little child;
With such rare sweetness of dumb melancholy
He strove to clothe his agony in smiles,
Which he would force up in his poor pale cheeks,
Like ill-timed guests that had no proper dwelling there;
And, when they ask'd him his complaint, he laid
His hand upon his heart to show the place,
Where Susan came to him a-nights, he said,
And prick'd him with a pin.—
And thereupon Sir Francis call'd to mind
The beggar-witch that stood by the gateway
And begged an alms.
    Str. But did the witch confess?
    Serv. All this and more at her death.
    Str. I do not love to credit tales of magic.
Heaven's music, which is Order, seems unstrung,
And this brave world
(The Mystery of God) unbeautified,
Disorder'd, marr'd; where such strange things are acted.
                                        1799.

A BALLAD:

NOTING THE DIFFERENCE OF RICH AND POOR, IN THE WAYS OF A RICH MAN'S PALACE AND A POOR MAN'S WORKHOUSE.

To the tune of the "Old and Young Courtier."

In a costly palace Youth goes clad in gold;
In a wretched workhouse Age's limbs are cold:
There they sit, the old men by a shivering fire,
Still close and closer cowering, warmth is their desire.

In a costly palace, when the brave gallants dine,
They have store of good venison, with old canary wine,
With singing and music to heighten the cheer;
Coarse bits, with grudging, are the pauper's best fare.

In a costly palace, Youth is still carest
By a train of attendants which laugh at my young Lord's jest;
In a wretched workhouse the contrary prevails:
Does age begin to prattle?—no man heark'neth to his tales.

In a costly palace, if the child with a pin
Do but chance to prick a finger, straight the doctor is called in;
In a wretched workhouse, men are left to perish
For want of proper cordials, which their old age might cherish.

In a costly palace, Youth enjoys his lust;
In a wretched workhouse Age, in corners thrust,
Thinks upon the former days, when he was well to do,
Had children to stand by him, both friends and kinsmen too.

In a costly palace, Youth his temples hides
With a new devised peruke that reaches to his sides;

In a wretched workhouse Age's crown is bare,
With a few thin locks, just to fence out the cold air.

In peace, as in war, 'tis our young gallants' pride
To walk, each one i' the streets, with a rapier by his side,
That none to do them injury may have pretence;
Wretched Age, in poverty, must brook offence.

1800.

BALLAD, FROM THE GERMAN.

THE clouds are blackening, the storms threatening,
    And ever the forest maketh a moan;
Billows are breaking, the damsel's heart aching,
    Thus by herself she singeth alone
        Weeping right plenteously.

The world is empty, the heart is dead surely,
    In this world plainly all seemeth amiss;
To Thy breast, Holy One, take now Thy little one,
    I have had earnest of all earth's bliss,
        Living right lovingly.

1800.

HESTER.

WHEN maidens such as Hester die,
Their place ye may not well supply,
Though ye among a thousand try,
    With vain endeavour.

A month or more hath she been dead,
Yet cannot I by force be led
To think upon the wormy bed,
    And her together.

A springy motion in her gait,
A rising step, did indicate
Of pride and joy no common rate,
    That flush'd her spirit.

I know not by what name beside
I shall it call:—if 'twas not pride,
It was a joy to that allied,
    She did inherit.

Her parents held the Quaker rule,
Which doth the human feeling cool,
But she was train'd in Nature's school,
    Nature had blest her.

A waking eye, a prying mind,
A heart that stirs is hard to bind,
A hawk's keen sight ye cannot blind,
    Ye could not Hester.

My sprightly neighbour, gone before
To that unknown and silent shore,
Shall we not meet, as heretofore,
    Some summer morning,

When from thy cheerful eyes a ray
Hath struck a bliss upon the day,
A bliss that would not go away,
    A sweet forewarning?

1803.

A FAREWELL TO TOBACCO.

May the Babylonish curse
Straight confound my stammering verse,
If I can a passage see
In this word-perplexity,
Or a fit expression find,
Or a language to my mind,
(Still the phrase is wide or scant)
To take leave of thee, GREAT PLANT!
Or in any terms relate
Half my love, or half my hate:

For I hate, yet love, thee so,
That, whichever thing I show,
The plain truth will seem to be
A constrain'd hyperbole,
And the passion to proceed
More from a mistress than a weed.

   Sooty retainer to the vine,
Bacchus' black servant, negro-fine ;
Sorcerer, that makest us dote upon
Thy begrimed complexion,
And, for thy pernicious sake,
More and greater oaths to break
Than reclaimèd lovers take
'Gainst women : thou thy siege dost lay
Much too in the female way,
While thou suck'st the labouring breath
Faster than kisses or than death.

Thou in such a cloud dost bind us,
That our worst foes cannot find us,
And ill fortune, that would thwart us,
Shoots at rovers, shooting at us ;
While each man, thro' thy heightening steam,
Does like a smoking Etna seem,
And all about us does express
(Fancy and wit in richest dress)
A Sicilian fruitfulness.

   Thou through such a mist dost shew us,
That our best friends do not know us,
And, for those allowèd features,
Due to reasonable creatures
Liken'st us to fell Chimeras,
Monsters that, who see us, fear us ;
Worse than Cerberus or Geryon,
Or, who first loved a cloud, Ixion.

Bacchus we know, and we allow
His tipsy rites. But what art thou,
That but by reflex can'st show
What his deity can do,
As the false Egyptian spell
Aped the true Hebrew miracle?
Some few vapours thou may'st raise,
The weak brain may serve to amaze,
But to the reins and nobler heart
Can'st nor life nor heat impart.

Brother of Bacchus, later born,
The old world was sure forlorn,
Wanting thee, that aidest more
The god's victories than before
All his panthers, and the brawls
Of his piping Bacchanals.
These, as stale, we disallow,
Or judge of *thee* meant: only thou
His true Indian conquest art;
And, for ivy round his dart,
The reformèd god now weaves
A finer thyrsus of thy leaves.

Scent to match thy rich perfume
Chemic art did ne'er presume
Through her quaint alembic strain,
None so sovereign to the brain.
Nature, that did in thee excel,
Framed again no second smell.
Roses, violets, but toys
For the smaller sort of boys,
Or for greener damsels meant;
Thou art the only manly scent.

Stinking'st of the stinking kind,
Filth of the mouth and fog of the mind,
Africa, that brags her foyson,
Breeds no such prodigious poison,

A FAREWELL TO TOBACCO.

Henbane, nightshade, both together,
Hemlock, aconite——

    Nay, rather,
Plant divine, of rarest virtue;
Blisters on the tongue would hurt you,
'Twas but in a sort I blamed thee;
None e'er prosper'd who defamed thee;
Irony all, and feign'd abuse,
Such as perplex'd lovers use,
At a need, when, in despair
To paint forth their fairest fair,
Or in part but to express
That exceeding comeliness
Which their fancies doth so strike
They borrow language of dislike;
And, instead of Dearest Miss,
Jewel, Honey, Sweetheart, Bliss,
And those forms of old admiring,
Call her Cockatrice and Siren,
Basilisk, and all that's evil,
Witch, Hyena, Mermaid, Devil,
Ethiop, Wench, and Blackamoor,
Monkey, Ape, and twenty more;
Friendly Traitress, loving Foe,'
Not that she is truly so,
But no other way they know
A contentment to express,
Borders so upon excess,
That they do not rightly wot
Whether it be pain or not.

 Or, as men, constrain'd to part
With what's nearest to their heart,
While their sorrow's at the height,
Lose discrimination quite,
And their hasty wrath let fall,
To appease their frantic gall,

On the darling thing whatever,
Whence they feel it death to sever,
Though it be, as they, perforce,
Guiltless of the sad divorce.

For I must (nor let it grieve thee,
Friendliest of plants, that I must) leave thee.
For thy sake, TOBACCO, I
Would do anything but die,
And but seek to extend my days
Long enough to sing thy praise.
But, as she, who once hath been
A king's consort, is a queen
Ever after, nor will bate
Any tittle of her state,
Though a widow, or divorced,
So I, from thy converse forced,
The old name and style retain,
A right Katherine of Spain;
And a seat, too, 'mongst the joys
Of the blest Tobacco Boys;
Where, though I, by sour physician,
Am debarr'd the full fruition
Of thy favours, I may catch
Some collateral sweets, and snatch
Sidelong odours, that give life
Like glances from a neighbour's wife;
And still live in the by-places
And the suburbs of thy graces;
And in thy borders take delight,
An unconquer'd Canaanite.

1805.

LINES ON THE CELEBRATED PICTURE

BY LEONARDO DA VINCI; CALLED THE VIRGIN OF THE ROCKS.

WHILE young John runs to greet
The greater Infant's feet,
The mother standing by, with trembling passion
Of devout admiration,
Beholds the engaging mystic play, and pretty adoration;
Nor knows as yet the full event
Of those so low beginnings,
From whence we date our winnings,
But wonders at the intent
Of those new rites, and what that strange child-worship
    meant.

But at her side
An angel doth abide,
With such a perfect joy
As no dim doubts alloy,
An intuition,
A glory, an amenity,
Passing the dark condition
Of blind humanity,
As if he surely knew
All the blest wonders should ensue,
Or he had lately left the upper sphere,
And had read all the sovran schemes and divine riddles
    there.

The three following from " Poetry for Children," 1809.

THE THREE FRIENDS.

THREE young maids in friendship met;
Mary, Martha, Margaret.
Margaret was tall and fair,
Martha shorter by a hair;

If the first excell'd in feature,
Th' other's grace and ease were greater;
Mary, though to rival loth,
In their best gifts equall'd both.
They a due proportion kept;
Martha mourn'd if Margaret wept;
Margaret joy'd when any good
She of Martha understood;
And in sympathy for either
Mary was outdone by neither.
Thus far, for a happy space,
All three ran an even race,
A most constant friendship proving,
Equally beloved and loving;
All their wishes, joys, the same;
Sisters only not in name.

    Fortune upon each one smiled,
As upon a favourite child;
Well to do and well to see
Were the parents of all three;
Till on Martha's father crosses
Brought a flood of worldly losses,
And his fortunes rich and great
Changed at once to low estate;
Under which o'erwhelming blow
Martha's mother was laid low;
She a hapless orphan left,
Of maternal care bereft,
Trouble following trouble fast,
Lay in a sick bed at last.

    In the depth of her affliction
Martha now received conviction,
That a true and faithful friend
Can the surest comfort lend.
Night and day, with friendship tried,
Ever constant by her side

Was her gentle Mary found,
With a love that knew no bound;
And the solace she imparted
Saved her dying broken-hearted.

   In this scene of earthly things
Not one good unmixèd springs.
That which had to Martha proved
A sweet consolation, moved
Different feelings of regret
In the mind of Margaret.
She, whose love was not less dear,
Nor affection less sincere
To her friend, was, by occasion
Of more distant habitation,
Fewer visits forced to pay her,
When no other cause did stay her;
And her Mary living nearer,
Margaret began to fear her,
Lest her visits day by day
Martha's heart should steal away.
That whole heart she ill could spare her,
Where till now she'd been a sharer.
From this cause with grief she pined,
Till at length her health declined.
All her cheerful spirits flew,
Fast as Martha gather'd new;
And her sickness waxèd sore,
Just when Martha felt no more.

   Mary, who had quick suspicion
Of her alter'd friend's condition,
Seeing Martha's convalescence
Less demanded now her presence,
With a goodness, built on reason,
Changed her measures with the season;
Turn'd her steps from Martha's door,
Went where she was wanted more;

All her care and thoughts were set
Now to tend on Margaret.
Mary, living 'twixt the two,
From her home could oftener go,
Either of her friends to see,
Than they could together be.

Truth explain'd is to suspicion
Evermore the best physician.
Soon her visits had the effect;
All that Margaret did suspect,
From her fancy vanish'd clean;
She was soon what she had been,
And the colour she did lack,
To her faded cheek came back.
Wounds which love had made her feel,
Love alone had power to heal.

Martha, who the frequent visit
Now had lost, and sore did miss it,
With impatience waxèd cross,
Counted Margaret's gain her loss;
All that Mary did confer
On her friend, thought due to her.
In her girlish bosom rise
Little foolish jealousies,
Which into such rancour wrought,
She one day for Margaret sought;
Finding her by chance alone,
She began, with reasons shewn,
To insinuate a fear
Whether Mary was sincere;
Wish'd that Margaret would take heed
Whence her actions did proceed.
For herself, she'd long been minded
Not with outsides to be blinded;
All that pity and compassion,
She believed was affectation;

In her heart she doubted whether
Mary cared a pin for either.
She could keep whole weeks at distance,
And not know of their existence,
While all things remain'd the same;
But when some misfortune came,
Then she made a great parade
Of her sympathy and aid,—
Not that she did really grieve,
It was only *make-believe*,
And she cared for nothing, so
She might her fine feelings shew,
And get credit, on her part,
For a soft and tender heart.

   With such speeches, smoothly made,
She found methods to persuade
Margaret (who, being sore
From the doubts she'd felt before,
Was preparèd for mistrust)
To believe her reasons just;
Quite destroy'd that comfort glad,
Which in Mary late she had;
Made her, in experience' spite,
Think her friend a hypocrite,
And resolve, with cruel scoff,
To renounce and cast her off.

   See how good turns are rewarded!
She of both is now discarded,
Who to both had been so late
Their support in low estate,
All their comfort and their stay—
Now of both is cast away.
But the league her presence cherish'd,
Losing its best prop, soon perish'd;
She, that was a link to either,
To keep them and it together,

Being gone, the two (no wonder)
That were left, soon fell asunder;—
Some civilities were kept,
But the heart of friendship slept;
Love with hollow forms was fed,
But the life of love lay dead:—
A cold intercourse they held
After Mary was expell'd.

    Two long years did intervene
Since they'd either of them seen,
Or, by letter, any word
Of their old companion heard,—
When, upon a day, once walking,
Of indifferent matters talking,
They a female figure met;—
Martha said to Margaret,
"That young maid in face does carry
A resemblance strong of Mary."
Margaret, at nearer sight,
Own'd her observation right:
But they did not far proceed
Ere they knew 'twas she indeed.
She—but, ah! how changed they view her
From that person which they knew her;
Her fine face disease had scarr'd,
And its matchless beauty marr'd:—
But enough was left to trace
Mary's sweetness—Mary's grace.
When her eye did first behold them,
How they blush'd!—but, when she told them,
How on a sick-bed she lay
Months, while they had kept away,
And had no inquiries made
If she were alive or dead;—
How, for want of a true friend,
She was brought near to her end,

And was like so to have died,
With no friend at her bed-side;—
How the constant irritation,
Caused by fruitless expectation
Of their coming, had extended
The illness, when she might have mended,—
Then, O then, how did reflection
Come on them with recollection!
All that she had done for them,
How it did their fault condemn!

But sweet Mary, still the same,
Kindly eased them of their shame;
Spoke to them with accents bland,
Took them friendly by the hand;
Bound them both with promise fast,
Not to speak of troubles past;
Made them on the spot declare
A new league of friendship there;
Which, without a word of strife,
Lasted thenceforth long as life.
Martha now and Margaret
Strove who most should pay the debt
Which they owed her, nor did vary
Ever after from their Mary.

1809.

TO A RIVER IN WHICH A CHILD WAS DROWNED.

SMILING river, smiling river,
  On thy bosom sunbeams play;
Though they're fleeting, and retreating,
  Thou hast more deceit than they.

In thy channel, in thy channel,
  Choked with ooze and gravelly stones,
Deep immersèd, and unhearsèd,
  Lies young Edward's corse: his bones

Ever whitening, ever whitening,
  As thy waves against them dash :
What thy torrent, in the current,
  Swallow'd, now it helps to wash.

As if senseless, as if senseless
  Things had feeling in this case ;
What so blindly and unkindly
  It destroy'd, it now does grace.

1809.

QUEEN ORIANA'S DREAM.

"On a bank with roses shaded,
Whose sweet scent the violets aided,
Violets whose breath alone
Yields but feeble smell or none,
(Sweeter bed Jove ne'er reposed on
When his eyes Olympus closed on)
While o'erhead six slaves did hold
Canopy of cloth o' gold,
And two more did music keep,
Which might Juno lull to sleep,
Oriana who was queen
To the mighty Tamerlane,
That was lord of all the land
Between Thrace and Samarcand,
While the noon-tide fervour beam'd,
Mused herself to sleep and *dream'd.*"

Thus far, in magnific strain,
A young poet soothed his vein,
But he had nor prose nor numbers
To express a princess' slumbers.—
Youthful Richard had strange fancies,
Was deep versed in old romances,
And could talk whole hours upon
The great Cham and Prester John,—
Tell the field in which the Sophy
From the Tartar won a trophy—

What he read with such delight of,
Thought he could as easily write of—
But his over-young invention
Kept not pace with brave intention.
Twenty suns did rise and set,
And he could no further get;
But, unable to proceed,
Made a virtue out of need,
And, his labours wiselier deem'd of,
Did omit *what the queen dream'd of.*

1809.

TO T. L. H.—A CHILD.

MODEL of thy parent dear,
Serious infant worth a fear:
In thy unfaltering visage well
Picturing forth the son of TELL,
When on his forehead, firm and good,
Motionless mark, the apple stood;
Guileless traitor, rebel mild,
Convict unconscious, culprit child!
Gates that close with iron roar
Have been to thee thy nursery door;
Chains that chink in cheerless cells
Have been thy rattles and thy bells;
Walls contrived for giant sin
Have hemm'd thy faultless weakness in;
Near thy sinless bed black Guilt
Her discordant house hath built,
And fill'd it with her monstrous brood—
Sights, by thee not understood—
Sights of fear, and of distress,
That pass a harmless infant's guess!

But the clouds, that overcast
Thy young morning, may not last.
Soon shall arrive the rescuing hour,
That yields thee up to Nature's power.

Nature, that so late doth greet thee,
Shall in o'er-flowing measure meet thee.
She shall recompense with cost
For every lesson thou hast lost.
Then wandering up thy sire's loved hill,[1]
Thou shalt take thy airy fill
Of health and pastime. *Birds shall sing
For thy delight each May morning.*
'Mid new-yean'd lambkins thou shalt play,
Hardly less a lamb than they.
Then thy prison's lengthen'd bound
Shall be the horizon skirting round.
And, while thou fill'st thy lap with flowers,
To make amends for wintry hours,
The breeze, the sunshine, and the place,
Shall from thy tender brow efface
Each vestige of untimely care,
That sour restraint had graven there;
And on thy every look impress
A more excelling childishness.

So shall be thy days beguiled,
THORNTON HUNT, my favourite child.

1813.

TO MISS KELLY.

YOU are not, Kelly, of the common strain,
That stoop their pride and female honour down
To please that many-headed beast *the town*,
And vend their lavish smiles and tricks for gain;
By fortune thrown amid the actors' train,
You keep your native dignity of thought;
The plaudits that attend you come unsought,
As tributes due unto your natural vein.
Your tears have passion in them, and a grace
Of genuine freshness, which our hearts avow;

[1] Hampstead.

Your smiles are winds whose ways we cannot trace,
That vanish and return we know not how—
And please the better from a pensive face,
And thoughtful eye, and a reflecting brow.

ON THE SIGHT OF SWANS IN KENSINGTON GARDENS.

QUEEN-BIRD that sittest on thy shining nest
And thy young cygnets without sorrow hatchest,
And thou, thou other royal bird, that watchest
Lest the white mother wandering feet molest:
Shrined are your offspring in a crystal cradle,
Brighter than Helen's ere she yet had burst
Her shelly prison. They shall be born at first
Strong, active, graceful, perfect, swan-like, able
To tread the land or waters with security,
Unlike poor human births, conceived in sin,
In grief brought forth, both outwardly and in
Confessing weakness, error, and impurity.
Did heavenly creatures own succession's line,
The births of heaven like to yours would shine.

THE FAMILY NAME.

WHAT reason first imposed thee, gentle name,
Name that my father bore, and his sire's sire,
Without reproach? we trace our stream no higher;
And I, a childless man, may end the same.
Perchance some shepherd on Lincolnian plains,
In manners guileless as his own sweet flocks,
Received thee first amid the merry mocks
And arch allusions of his fellow swains.
Perchance from Salem's holier fields return'd,
With glory gotten on the heads abhorr'd
Of faithless Saracens, some martial lord
Took HIS meek title, in whose zeal he burn'd.
Whate'er the fount whence thy beginnings came,
No deed of mine shall shame thee, gentle name.

TO JOHN LAMB, ESQ., OF THE SOUTH-SEA HOUSE.

JOHN, you were figuring in the gay career
Of blooming manhood with a young man's joy,
When I was yet a little peevish boy—
Though time has made the difference disappear
Betwixt our ages, which *then* seemed so great—
And still by rightful custom you retain,
Much of the old authoritative strain,
And keep the elder brother up in state.
O! you do well in this. 'Tis man's worst deed
To let the "things that have been" run to waste,
And in the unmeaning present sink the past:
In whose dim glass even now I faintly read
Old buried forms, and faces long ago,
Which you, and I, and one more, only know.

TO MARTIN CHARLES BURNEY.

(*Prefixed to the Second Volume of Lamb's Collected Works*, 1818.)

FORGIVE me, BURNEY, if to thee these late
And hasty products of a critic pen,
Thyself no common judge of books and men,
In feeling of thy worth I dedicate.
My *verse* was offer'd to an older friend;
The humbler *prose* has fallen to thy share:
Nor could I miss the occasion to declare,
What spoken in thy presence must offend.
That, set aside some few caprices wild,
Those humorous clouds, that flit o'er brightest days,
In all my threadings of this worldly maze,
(And I have watch'd thee almost from a child,)
Free from self-seeking, envy, low design,
I have not found a whiter soul than thine.

WRITTEN AT CAMBRIDGE ON THE 15TH AUGUST, 1819.

I WAS not train'd in Academic bowers,
And to those learned streams I nothing owe
Which copious from those twin fair founts do flow;
Mine have been anything but studious hours.
Yet can I fancy, wandering 'mid thy towers,
Myself a nursling, Granta, of thy lap;
My brow seems tightening with the Doctor's cap,
And I walk *gowned;* feel unusual powers.
Strange forms of logic clothe my admiring speech,
Old Ramus' ghost is busy at my brain;
And my skull teems with notions infinite.
Be still, ye reeds of Camus, while I teach
Truths, which transcend the searching Schoolmen's vein,
And half had stagger'd that stout Stagirite!

TO THE AUTHOR OF POEMS, PUBLISHED UNDER THE NAME OF BARRY CORNWALL.

LET hate, or grosser heats, their foulness mask
Under the vizor of a borrow'd name;
Let things eschew the light deserving blame:
No cause hast thou to blush for thy sweet task.
"Marcian Colonna" is a dainty book;
And thy "Sicilian Tale" may boldly pass;
Thy "Dream" 'bove all, in which, as in a glass,
On the great world's antique glories we may look.
No longer then, as "lowly substitute,
Factor, or PROCTOR, for another's gains,"
Suffer the admiring world to be deceived;
Lest thou thyself, by self of fame bereaved,
Lament too late the lost prize of thy pains,
And heavenly tunes piped through an alien flute.

1820.

WORK.

Who first invented work, and bound the free
And holyday-rejoicing spirit down
To the ever-haunting importunity
Of business in the green fields, and the town—
To plough, loom, anvil, spade—and oh! most sad,
To that dry drudgery at the desk's dead wood?
Who but the Being unblest, alien from good,
Sabbathless Satan! he who his unglad
Task ever plies 'mid rotatory burnings,
That round and round incalculably reel—
For wrath divine hath made him like a wheel—
In that red realm from which are no returnings:
Where toiling, and turmoiling, ever and aye
He, and his thoughts, keep pensive working-day.

LEISURE.

They talk of time, and of time's galling yoke,
That like a mill-stone on man's mind doth press,
Which only works and business can redress:
Of divine Leisure such foul lies are spoke,
Wounding her fair gifts with calumnious stroke.
But might I, fed with silent meditation,
Assoiled live from that fiend Occupation—
Improbus Labor, which my spirits hath broke—
I'd drink of time's rich cup, and never surfeit:
Fling in more days than went to make the gem,
That crown'd the white top of Methusalem:
Yea on my weak neck take, and never forfeit,
Like Atlas bearing up the dainty sky,
The heaven-sweet burthen of eternity.

DEUS NOBIS HÆC OTIA FECIT.   1821.

TO J. S. KNOWLES, ESQ.

ON HIS TRAGEDY OF VIRGINIUS.

TWELVE years ago I knew thee, Knowles, and then
Esteemèd you a perfect specimen
Of those fine spirits warm-soul'd Ireland sends,
To teach us colder English how a friend's
Quick pulse should beat. I knew you brave, and plain,
Strong-sensed, rough-witted, above fear or gain;
But nothing further had the gift to espy.
Sudden you re-appear. With wonder I
Hear my old friend (turn'd Shakspeare) read a scene
Only to *his* inferior in the clean
Passes of pathos: with such fence-like art—
Ere we can see the steel, 'tis in our heart.
Almost without the aid language affords,
Your piece seems wrought. That huffing medium, *words*,
(Which in the modern Tamburlaines quite sway
Our shamed souls from their bias) in your play
We scarce attend to. Hastier passion draws
Our tears on credit: and we find the cause
Some two hours after, spelling o'er again
Those strange few words at ease, that wrought the pain.
Proceed, old friend; and, as the year returns,
Still snatch some new old story from the urns
Of long-dead virtue. We, that knew before
Your worth, may admire, we cannot love you more.
                                                1820.

IN THE ALBUM OF LUCY BARTON.

LITTLE Book, surnamed of *white*,
Clean as yet, and fair to sight,
Keep thy attribution right.

Never disproportion'd scrawl;
Ugly blot, that's worse than all;
On thy maiden clearness fall!

In each letter, here design'd,
Let the reader emblem'd find
Neatness of the owner's mind.

Gilded margins count a sin,
Let thy leaves attraction win
By the golden rules within;

Sayings fetch'd from sages old;
Laws which Holy Writ unfold,
Worthy to be graved in gold:

Lighter fancies not excluding;
Blameless wit, with nothing rude in
Sometimes mildly interluding.

Amid strains of graver measure:
Virtue's self hath oft her pleasure
In sweet Muses' groves of leisure.

Riddles dark, perplexing sense;
Darker meanings of offence;
What but *shades*—he banish'd hence.

Whitest thoughts in whitest dress,
Candid meanings, best express
Mind of quiet Quakeress.

1824.

TO THE EDITOR OF THE "EVERY-DAY BOOK."

I LIKE you, and your book, ingenious Hone!
　In whose capacious all-embracing leaves
The very marrow of tradition's shown;
　And all that history—much that fiction—weaves.

By every sort of taste your work is graced.
　Vast stores of modern anecdote we find,
With good old story quaintly interlaced—
　The theme as various as the reader's mind.

Rome's lie-fraught legends you so truly paint—
   Yet kindly,—that the half-turn'd Catholic
Scarcely forbears to smile at his own saint,
   And cannot curse the candid heretic.

Rags, relics, witches, ghosts, fiends, crowd your page;
   Our father's mummeries we well pleased behold,
And, proudly conscious of a purer age,
   Forgive some fopperies in the times of old.

Verse-honouring Phœbus, Father of bright *Days*,
   Must needs bestow on you both good and many,
Who, building trophies of his Children's praise,
   Run their rich Zodiac through, not missing any.

Dan Phœbus loves your book—trust me, friend Hone—
   The title only errs, he bids me say:
For while such art, wit, reading, there are shown,
   He swears, 'tis not a work of *every day*.
                                   1825.

THE YOUNG CATECHIST.[1]

WHILE this tawny Ethiop prayeth,
Painter, who is she that stayeth
By, with skin of whitest lustre,
Sunny locks, a shining cluster,
Saint-like seeming to direct him
To the Power that must protect him?
Is she of the Heaven-born Three,
Meek Hope, strong Faith, sweet Charity:
Or some Cherub?—
                They you mention
Far transcend my weak invention.
'Tis a simple Christian child,
Missionary young and mild,
From her stock of Scriptural knowledge,
Bible-taught without a college,

[1] A Picture by Henry Meyer, Esq.

Which by reading she could gather,
Teaches him to say OUR FATHER
To the common Parent, who
Colour not respects, nor hue.
White and black in Him have part,
Who looks not to the skin, but heart.

1827.

ANGEL HELP.[1]

THIS rare tablet doth include
Poverty with Sanctitude.
Past midnight this poor Maid hath spun,
And yet the work is not half done,
Which must supply from earnings scant
A feeble bed-rid parent's want.
Her sleep-charged eyes exemption ask,
And Holy hands take up the task;
Unseen the rock and spindle ply,
And do her earthly drudgery.
Sleep, saintly poor one, sleep, sleep on;
And, waking, find thy labours done.
Perchance she knows it by her dreams;
Her eye hath caught the golden gleams,
Angelic presence testifying,
That round her everywhere are flying;
Ostents from which she may presume,
That much of Heaven is in the room.
Skirting her own bright hair they run,
And to the sunny add more sun:
Now on that aged face they fix,
Streaming from the Crucifix;

[1] Suggested by a drawing in the possession of Charles Aders, Esq., in which is represented the legend of a poor female saint, who, having spun past midnight to maintain a bed-rid mother, has fallen asleep from fatigue, and angels are finishing her work. In another part of the chamber an angel is tending a lily, the emblem of purity.

The flesh-clogg'd spirit disabusing,
Death-disarming sleeps infusing,
Prelibations, foretastes high,
And equal thoughts to live or die.
Gardener bright from Eden's bower,
Tend with care that lily flower;
To its leaves and root infuse,
Heaven's sunshine, Heaven's dews.
'Tis a type, and 'tis a pledge,
Of a crowning privilege.
Careful as that lily flower,
This Maid must keep her precious dower;
Live a sainted Maid, or die
Martyr to virginity.

1827.

ON AN INFANT DYING AS SOON AS BORN.

I SAW where in the shroud did lurk
A curious frame of Nature's work.
A flow'ret crushèd in the bud,
A nameless piece of Babyhood,
Was in a cradle-coffin lying;
Extinct, with scarce the sense of dying;
So soon to exchange the imprisoning womb
For darker closets of the tomb!
She did but ope an eye, and put
A clear beam forth, then straight up shut
For the long dark: ne'er more to see
Through glasses of mortality.
Riddle of destiny, who can show
What thy short visit meant, or know
What thy errand here below?
Shall we say, that Nature blind
Check'd her hand, and changed her mind,
Just when she had exactly wrought
A finish'd pattern without fault?
Could she flag, or could she tire,

Or lack'd she the Promethean fire
(With her nine moons' long workings sicken'd)
That should thy little limbs have quicken'd?
Limbs so firm, they seem'd to assure
Life of health, and days mature:
Woman's self in miniature!
Limbs so fair, they might supply
(Themselves now but cold imagery)
The sculptor to make Beauty by.
Or did the stern-eyed Fate descry,
That babe, or mother, one must die;
So in mercy left the stock,
And cut the branch; to save the shock
Of young years widow'd; and the pain,
When Single State comes back again
To the lone man who, 'reft of wife,
Thenceforward drags a maimèd life?
The economy of Heaven is dark:
And wisest clerks have miss'd the mark,
Why Human Buds, like this, should fall,
More brief than fly ephemeral,
That has his day; while shrivell'd crones
Stiffen with age to stocks and stones;
And crabbed use the conscience sears
In sinners of an hundred years.
Mother's prattle, mother's kiss,
Baby fond, thou ne'er wilt miss.
Rites, which custom does impose,
Silver bells and baby clothes,
Coral redder than those lips,
Which pale death did late eclipse;
Music framed for infant's glee,
Whistle never tuned for thee;
Though thou want'st not, thou shalt have them,
Loving hearts were they which gave them.
Let not one be missing; nurse,
See them laid upon the hearse
Of infant slain by doom perverse

Why should kings and nobles have
Pictured trophies to their grave;
And we, churls, to thee deny
Thy pretty toys with thee to lie,
A more harmless vanity?

1828.

THE CHRISTENING.

ARRAY'D—a half-angelic sight—
In vests of pure Baptismal white,
The Mother to the Font doth bring
The little helpless nameless thing,
With hushes soft and mild caressing,
At once to get—a name and blessing.
Close by the Babe the Priest doth stand,
The Cleansing Water at his hand,
Which must assoil the soul within
From every stain of Adam's sin.
The Infant eyes the mystic scenes,
Nor knows what all this wonder means;
And now he smiles, as if to say
"I am a Christian made this day;"
Now frighted clings to Nurse's hold,
Shrinking from the water cold,
Whose virtues, rightly understood,
Are, as Bethesda's waters, good.
Strange words—the World, the Flesh, the Devil—
Poor Babe, what can it know of Evil?
But we must silently adore
Mysterious truths, and not explore.
Enough for him, in after-times,
When he shall read these artless rhymes,
If, looking back upon this day
With quiet conscience, he can say
"I have in part redeem'd the pledge
Of my Baptismal privilege;
And more and more will strive to flee
All which my Sponsors kind did then renounce for me."

1829.

IN THE ALBUM OF MISS ——.

I.

Such goodness in your face doth shine,
With modest look, without design,
That I despair, poor pen of mine
    Can e'er express it,
To give it words I feebly try;
My spirits fail me to supply
Befitting language for't, and I
    Can only bless it!

II.

But stop, rash verse! and don't abuse
A bashful Maiden's ear with news
Of her own virtues. She'll refuse
    Praise sung so loudly.
Of that same goodness you admire,
The best part is, she don't aspire
To praise—nor of herself desire
    To think too proudly.

                              1829.

THE GIPSY'S MALISON.

"Suck, baby, suck, mother's love grows by giving,
  Drain the sweet founts that only thrive by wasting;
Black manhood comes, when riotous guilty living
  Hands thee the cup that shall be death in tasting.

"Kiss, baby, kiss, mother's lips shine by kisses,
  Choke the warm breath that else would fall in blessings;
Black manhood comes, when turbulent guilty blisses
  Tend thee the kiss that poisons 'mid caressings.

"Hang, baby, hang, mother's love loves such forces,
  Strain the fond neck that bends still to thy clinging;

Black manhood comes, when violent lawless courses
Leave thee a spectacle in rude air swinging."

So sang a wither'd Beldam energetical,
And bann'd the ungiving door with lips prophetical.
                                                1829.

IN THE ALBUM OF A CLERGYMAN'S LADY.

AN Album is a Garden, not for show
Planted, but use; where wholesome herbs should grow.
A Cabinet of curious porcelain, where
No fancy enters, but what's rich or rare.
A Chapel, where mere ornamental things
Are pure as crowns of saints, or angels' wings.
A List of living friends: a holier Room
For names of some since mouldering in the tomb,
Whose blooming memories life's cold laws survive;
And, dead elsewhere, they here yet speak, and live.
Such, and so tender, should an Album be;
And, Lady, such I wish this book to thee.

IN THE AUTOGRAPH BOOK OF MRS. SERJEANT W——.

HAD I a power, Lady, to my will,
You should not want Hand Writings. I would fill
Your leaves with Autographs—resplendent names
Of Knights and Squires of old, and courtly Dames,
Kings, Emperors, Popes. Next under these should stand
The hands of famous lawyers—a grave band—
Who in their Courts of Law or Equity
Have best upheld Freedom and Property.
These should moot cases in your book, and vie
To show their reading and their Serjeantry.
But I have none of these; nor can I send
The notes by Bullen to her Tyrant penn'd

H

In her authentic hand; nor in soft hours
Lines writ by Rosamund in Clifford's bowers.
The lack of curious Signatures I moan,
And want the courage to subscribe my own.

IN THE ALBUM OF A VERY YOUNG LADY.

Joy to unknown Josepha who, I hear,
Of all good gifts, to Music most is given;
Science divine, which through the enraptured ear
Enchants the soul, and lifts it nearer Heaven.
Parental smiles approvingly attend
Her pliant conduct of the trembling keys,
And listening strangers their glad suffrage lend.
Most musical is Nature. Birds and bees,
All their sweet labour sing. The moaning winds
Rehearse a *lesson* to attentive minds,
In louder tones "Deep unto deep doth call;"
And there is music in the waterfall.

IN THE ALBUM OF A FRENCH TEACHER.

IMPLORED for verse, I send you what I can;
But you are so exact a Frenchwoman,
As I am told, Jemima, that I fear
To wound with English your Parisian ear,
And think I do your choice collection wrong
With lines not written in the Frenchman's tongue.
Had I a knowledge equal to my will,
With airy *Chansons* I your leaves would fill;
With *Fabliaux* that should emulate the vein
Of sprightly Gresset, or of La Fontaine;
Or *Scènes Comiques*, that should approach the air
Of your own favourite—renown'd Molière.
But at my suit the Muse of France looks sour,
And strikes me dumb! Yet, what is in my power
To testify respect for you, I pray,
Take in plain English—our rough Enfield way.

IN THE ALBUM OF MISS DAUBENY

I.

Some poets by poetic law
Have beauties praised, they never saw;
And sung of Kittys and of Nancys,
Whose charms but lived in their own fancies.
So I, to keep my Muse a-going,
That willingly would still be doing,
A Canzonet or two must try
In praise of—*pretty* Daubeny.

II.

But whether she indeed be comely,
Or only very good and homely,
Of my own eyes I cannot say;
I trust to Emma Isola.
But sure I think her voice is tuneful,
As smoothest birds that sing in June full;
For else would strangely disagree
The *flowing* name of—Daubeny.

III.

I hear that she a Book hath got—
As what young damsel now hath not,
In which they scribble favourite fancies,
Copied from poems or romances?
And prettiest draughts, of her design,
About the curious Album shine;
And therefore she shall have for me
The style of—*tasteful* Daubeny.

IV.

Thus far I have taken on believing:
But well I know without deceiving.
That in her heart she keeps alive still
Old school-day likings, which survive still

In spite of absence—worldly coldness—
And thereon can my Muse take boldness
To crown her other praises three
With praise of—*friendly* Daubeny.

IN THE ALBUM OF MRS. JANE TOWERS.

LADY Unknown, who crav'st from me Unknown
The trifle of a verse these leaves to grace,
How shall I find fit matter? with what face
Address a face that ne'er to me was shown?
Thy looks, tones, gestures, manners, and what not,
Conjecturing, I wonder in the dark.
I know thee only sister to Charles Clarke!
But at that name my cold Muse waxes hot,
And swears that thou art such a one as he,
Warm, laughter-loving, with a touch of madness,
Wild, glee-provoking, pouring oil of gladness
From frank heart, without guile.   And, if thou be
The pure reverse of this, and I mistake—
Demure one, I will like thee for his sake.

IN THE ALBUM OF CATHERINE ORKNEY.

CANADIA! boast no more the toils
Of hunters for the furry spoils;
Your whitest ermines are but foils
    To brighter Catherine Orkney.

That such a flower should ever burst
From climes with rigorous winter curst!—
We bless you that so kindly nurst
    This flower, this Catherine Orkney.

We envy not your proud display
Of lake, wood, vast Niagara:
Your greatest pride we've borne away,
    How spared you Catherine Orkney?

That Wolfe on Heights of Abraham fell,
To your reproach no more we tell:
Canadia, you repaid us well
    With rearing Catherine Orkney.

O Britain, guard with tenderest care
The charge allotted to your share:
You've scarce a native maid so fair,
    So good, as Catherine Orkney.

IN MY OWN ALBUM

FRESH clad from heaven in robes of white,
A young probationer of light,
Thou wert my soul, an Album bright,

A spotless leaf; but thought, and care,
And friend and foe, in foul or fair,
Have "written strange defeatures" there;

And Time with heaviest hand of all,
Like that fierce writing on the wall,
Hath stamp'd sad dates—he can't recall;

And error gilding worst designs—
Like speckled snake that strays and shines—
Betrays his path by crooked lines;

And vice hath left his ugly blot;
And good resolves, a moment hot,
Fairly began—but finish'd not;

And fruitless, late remorse doth trace—
Like Hebrew lore, a backward pace—
Her irrecoverable race.

Disjointed numbers; sense unknit;
Huge realms of folly, shreds of wit;
Compose the mingled mass of it.

My scalded eyes no longer brook
Upon this ink-blurred thing to look—
Go shut the leaves, and clasp the book.

TO BERNARD BARTON,

with a coloured print.[1]

When last you left your Woodbridge pretty,
To stare at sights, and see the City,
If I your meaning understood,
You wish'd a Picture, cheap, but good;
The colouring? decent; clear, not muddy;
To suit a Poet's quiet study,
Where Books and Prints for delectation
Hang, rather than vain ostentation.
The subject? what I pleased, if comely;
But something scriptural and homely:
A sober Piece, not gay or wanton,
For winter fire-sides to descant on;
The theme so scrupulously handled,
A Quaker might look on unscandal'd;
Such as might satisfy Ann Knight,
And classic Mitford just not fright.
Just such a one I've found, and send it;
If liked, I give—if not, but lend it.
The moral? nothing can be sounder.
The fable? 'tis its own expounder—
A Mother teaching to her Chit
Some good book, and explaining it.
He, silly urchin, tired of lesson,
His learning lays no mighty stress on,
But seems to hear not what he hears;
Thrusting his fingers in his ears,
Like Obstinate, that perverse funny one,
In honest parable of Bunyan.

---

[1] From the venerable and ancient Manufactory of Carrington Bowles; some of my readers may recognise it.

His working Sister, more sedate,
Listens; but in a kind of state,
The painter meant for steadiness,
But has a tinge of sullenness;
And, at first sight, she seems to brook
As ill her needle, as he his book.
This is the Picture. For the Frame—
'Tis not ill suited to the same;
Oak-carved, nor gilt, for fear of falling;
Old-fashion'd; plain, yet not appalling;
And sober, as the Owner's Calling.

SHE IS GOING.

For their elder sister's hair
Martha does a wreath prepare
Of bridal rose, ornate and gay:
To-morrow is the wedding day:
   She is going.

Mary, youngest of the three,
Laughing idler, full of glee,
Arm in arm does fondly chain her,
Thinking, poor trifler, to detain her—
   But she's going.

Vex not, maidens, nor regret
Thus to part with Margaret.
Charms like yours can never stay
Long within doors; and one day
   You'll be going.

TO A YOUNG FRIEND.

ON HER TWENTY-FIRST BIRTHDAY.

Crown me a cheerful goblet, while I pray
A blessing on thy years, young Isola;
Young, but no more a child. How swift have flown
To me thy girlish times, a woman grown

Beneath my heedless eyes! In vain I rack
My fancy to believe the almanack,
That speaks thee Twenty-One. Thou should'st have still
Remain'd a child, and at thy sovereign will
Gambol'd about our house, as in times past.
Ungrateful Emma, to grow up so fast,
Hastening to leave thy friends!—for which intent,
Fond Runagate, be this thy punishment.
After some thirty years, spent in such bliss
As this earth can afford, where still we miss
Something of joy entire, may'st thou grow old
As we whom thou hast left! That wish was cold.
O far more aged and wrinkled, till folks say,
Looking upon thee reverend in decay,
"This dame for length of days, and virtues rare,
With her respected Grandsire may compare."—
Grandchild of that respected Isola,
Thou should'st have had about thee on this day
Kind looks of Parents, to congratulate
Their Pride grown up to woman's grave estate.
But they have died, and left thee, to advance
Thy fortunes how thou may'st, and owe to chance
The friends which Nature grudged. And thou wilt find,
Or make such, Emma, if I am not blind
To thee and thy deservings. That last strain
Had too much sorrow in it. Fill again
Another cheerful goblet, while I say
"Health, and twice health, to our lost Isola."

TO THE SAME.

EXTERNAL gifts of fortune, or of face,
Maiden, in truth, thou hast not much to show;
Much fairer damsels have I known, and know,
And richer may be found in every place.
In thy *mind* seek thy beauty, and thy wealth.
Sincereness lodgeth there, the soul's best health.

O guard that treasure above gold or pearl,
Laid up secure from moths and worldly stealth—
And take my benison, plain-hearted girl.

HARMONY IN UNLIKENESS.

By Enfield lanes, and Winchmore's verdant hill,
Two lovely damsels cheer my lonely walk:
The fair Maria, as a vestal, still;
And Emma brown, exuberant in talk.
With soft and lady speech the first applies
The mild correctives that to grace belong
To her redundant friend, who her defies
With jest, and mad discourse, and bursts of song.
O differing pair, yet sweetly thus agreeing,
What music from your happy discord rises,
While your companion hearing each, and seeing,
Nor this, nor that, but both together, prizes;
This lesson teaching, which our souls may strike,
That harmonies may be in things unlike!

TO A CELEBRATED FEMALE PERFORMER IN "THE BLIND BOY."

Rare artist! who with half thy tools, or none,
Canst execute with ease thy curious art,
And press thy powerful'st meanings on the heart,
Unaided by the eye, expression's throne!
While each blind sense, intelligential grown
Beyond its sphere, performs the effect of sight:
Those orbs alone, wanting their proper might,
All motionless and silent seem to moan
The unseemly negligence of nature's hand,
That left them so forlorn. What praise is thine,
O mistress of the passions; artist fine!
Who dost our souls against our sense command,
Plucking the horror from a sightless face,
Lending to blank deformity a grace.

TO SAMUEL ROGERS, ESQ.

ROGERS, of all the men that I have known
But slightly, who have died, your Brother's loss
Touch'd me most sensibly. There came across
My mind an image of the cordial tone
Of your fraternal meetings, where a guest
I more than once have sat; and grieve to think,
That of that threefold cord one precious link
By Death's rude hand is sever'd from the rest.
Of our old Gentry he appear'd a stem—
A Magistrate who, while the evil-doer
He kept in terror, could respect the Poor,
And not for every trifle harass them,
As some, divine and laic, too oft do.
This man's a private loss, and public too.

TO CAROLINE MARIA APPLEBEE.

An Acrostic.

CAROLINE glides smooth in verse,
And is easy to rehearse;
Runs just like some crystal river
O'er its pebbly bed for ever.
Lines as harsh and quaint as mine
In their close at least will shine,
Nor from sweetness can decline,
Ending but with *Caroline*.

Maria asks a statelier pace—
"*Ave Maria*, full of grace!"
Romish rites before me rise,
Image-worship, sacrifice,
And well-meant but mistaken pieties.

Apple with *Bee* doth rougher run.
Paradise was lost by one;

Peace of mind would we regain,
Let us, like the other, strain
Every harmless faculty,
Bee-like at work in our degree,
Ever some sweet task designing,
Extracting still, and still refining.

TO CECILIA CATHERINE LAWTON.

An Acrostic.

Choral service, solemn chanting,
Echoing round cathedrals holy—
Can aught else on earth be wanting
In heaven's bliss to plunge us wholly?
Let us great *Cecilia* honour
In the praise we give unto them,
And the merit be upon her.

Cold the heart that would undo them,
And the solemn organ banish
That this sainted Maid invented.
Holy thoughts too quickly vanish,
Ere the expression can be vented.
Raise the song to *Catherine*,
In her torments most divine!
Ne'er by Christians be forgot—
Envied be—this Martyr's lot.

Lawton, who these *names* combinest,
Aim to emulate their praises;
Women were they, yet divinest
Truths they taught; and story raises
O'er their mouldering bones a Tomb,
Not to die till Day of Doom.

TO A LADY WHO DESIRED ME TO WRITE HER EPITAPH.

An Acrostic.

GRACE JOANNA here doth lie:
Reader, wonder not that I
Ante-date her hour of rest.
Can I thwart her wish exprest,
Even unseemly though the laugh

Jesting with an Epitaph?
On her bones the turf lie lightly,
And her rise again be brightly!
No dark stain be found upon her—
No, there will not, on mine honour—
Answer that at least I can.

Would that I, thrice happy man,
In as spotless garb might rise,
Light as she will climb the skies,
Leaving the dull earth behind,
In a car more swift than wind.
All her errors, all her failings,
(Many they were not) and ailings,
Sleep secure from Envy's railings.

ANOTHER,

TO HER YOUNGEST DAUGHTER.

LEAST daughter, but not least beloved, of *Grace!*
O frown not on a stranger, who from place
Unknown and distant these few lines hath penn'd.
I but report what thy Instructress Friend
So oft hath told us of thy gentle heart.
A pupil most affectionate thou art,

Careful to learn what elder years impart.
Louisa—Clare—by which name shall I call thee?

A prettier pair of names sure ne'er was found,
Resembling thy own sweetness in sweet sound.
Ever calm peace and innocence befall thee!

TRANSLATIONS.
From the Latin of Vincent Bourne.

I.

ON A SEPULCHRAL STATUE OF AN INFANT SLEEPING.

BEAUTIFUL Infant, who dost keep
Thy posture here, and sleep'st a marble sleep,
May the repose unbroken be,
Which the fine Artist's hand hath lent to thee,
While thou enjoy'st along with it
That which no art, or craft, could ever hit
Or counterfeit to mortal sense,
The heaven-infusèd sleep of Innocence!

II.

THE RIVAL BELLS.

A TUNEFUL challenge rings from either side
Of Thames' fair banks. Thy twice six Bells, Saint Bride,
Peal swift and shrill; to which more slow reply
The deep-toned eight of Mary Overy.
Such harmony from the contention flows,
That the divided ear no preference knows;
Betwixt them both disparting Music's State,
While one exceeds in number, one in weight.

III.

EPITAPH ON A DOG.

POOR Irus' faithful wolf-dog here I lie,
That wont to tend my old blind master's steps,

His guide and guard; nor, while my service lasted,
Had he occasion for that staff, with which
He now goes picking out his path in fear
Over the highways and crossings, but would plant
Safe in the conduct of my friendly string,
A firm foot forward still, till he had reach'd
His poor seat on some stone, nigh where the tide
Of passers-by in thickest confluence flow'd:
To whom with loud and passionate laments
From morn to eve his dark estate he wail'd.
Nor wail'd to all in vain: some here and there,
The well-disposed and good, their pennies gave.
I meantime at his feet obsequious slept;
Not all-asleep in sleep, but heart and ear
Prick'd up at his least motion, to receive
At his kind hand my customary crumbs,
And common portion in his feast of scraps;
Or when night warn'd us homeward, tired and spent
With our long day, and tedious beggary.
These were my manners, this my way of life,
Till age and slow disease me overtook,
And sever'd from my sightless master's side.
But lest the grace of so good deeds should die,
Through tract of years in mute oblivion lost,
This slender tomb of turf hath Irus rear'd,
Cheap monument of no ungrudging hand,
And with short verse inscribed it, to attest,
In long and lasting union to attest,
The virtues of the Beggar and his Dog.

IV.

THE BALLAD SINGERS.

WHERE seven fair Streets to one tall Column draw,[1]
Two Nymphs have ta'en their stand, in hats of straw;
Their yellower necks huge beads of amber grace,
And by their trade they're of the Sirens' race:

[1] Seven Dials.

With cloak loose-pinn'd on each, that has been red,
But long with dust and dirt discoloured
Belies its hue; in mud behind, before,
From heel to middle leg becrusted o'er.
One a small infant at the breast does bear;
And one in her right hand her tuneful ware,
Which she would vend. Their station scarce is taken,
When youths and maids flock round. His stall forsaken,
Forth comes a Son of Crispin, leathern-capt,
Prepared to buy a ballad, if one apt
To move his fancy offers. Crispin's sons
Have, from uncounted time, with ale and buns
Cherish'd the gift of *Song*, which sorrow quells;
And working single in their low-roof'd cells,
Oft cheat the tedium of a winter's night
With anthems warbled in the Muses' spight.
Who now hath caught the alarm? the Servant Maid
Hath heard a buzz at distance; and, afraid
To miss a note, with elbows red comes out.
Leaving his forge to cool, Pyracmon stout
Thrusts in his unwash'd visage. *He* stands by,
Who the hard trade of Porterage does ply,
With stooping shoulders. What cares he? he sees
The assembled ring, nor heeds his tottering knees,
But pricks his ears up with the hopes of song.
So, while the Bard of Rhodope his wrong
Bewail'd to Proserpine on Thracian strings,
The tasks of gloomy Orcus lost their stings,
And stone-vex'd Sysiphus forgets his load.
Hither and thither from the sevenfold road
Some cart or 'waggon crosses, which divides
The close-wedged audience; but, as when the tides
To ploughing ships gave way, the ship being past,
They re-unite, so these unite as fast,
The older Songstress hitherto hath spent
Her elocution in the argument
Of their great Song in *prose;* to wit, the woes
Which Maiden true to faithless Sailor owes—

Ah! "*Wandering He!*"—which now in loftier *verse*
Pathetic they alternately rehearse.
All gaping wait the event. This Critic opes
His right ear to the strain. The other hopes
To catch it better with his left. Long trade
It were to tell, how the deluded Maid
A victim fell. And now right greedily
All hands are stretching forth the songs to buy,
That are so tragical; which She, and She,
Deals out, and *sings the while*, nor can there be
A breast so obdurate here, that will hold back
His contribution from the gentle rack
Of Music's pleasing torture. Irus' self
The staff-propt beggar, his thin-gotten pelf
Brings out from pouch, where squalid farthings rest,
And boldly claims his ballad with the best.
An old Dame only lingers. To her purse
The penny sticks. At length, with harmless curse
"Give me," she cries. "I'll paste it on my wall,
While the wall lasts, to show what ills befall
Fond hearts, seduced from Innocency's way;
How Maidens fall, and Mariners betray."

V.

TO DAVID COOK, OF THE PARISH OF ST. MARGARET'S, WESTMINSTER, WATCHMAN.

FOR much good-natured verse received from thee,
A loving verse take in return from me.
"Good-morrow to my masters," is your cry;
And to our David, "twice as good," say I.
Not Peter's monitor, shrill chanticleer,
Crows the approach of dawn in notes more clear,
Or tells the hours more faithfully. While night
Fills half the world with shadows of affright,
You with your lantern, partner of your round,
Traverse the paths of Margaret's hallow'd bound.

The tales of ghosts which old wives' ears drink up,
The drunkard reeling home from tavern cup,
Nor prowling robber, your firm soul appal;
Arm'd with thy faithful staff thou slight'st them all.
But if the market-gardener chance to pass,
Bringing to town his fruit, or early grass,
The gentle salesman you with candour greet,
And with reit'rated "good-mornings" meet.
Announcing your approach by formal bell,
Of nightly weather you the changes tell;
Whether the Moon shines, or her head doth steep
In rain-portending clouds. When mortals sleep
In downy rest, you brave the snows and sleet
Of winter; and in alley, or in street,
Relieve your midnight progress with a verse.
What though fastidious Phœbus frown averse
On your didactic strain—indulgent Night
With caution hath seal'd up both ears of Spite,
And critics sleep while you in staves do sound
The praise of long-dead Saints, whose Days abound
In wintry months; but Crispin chief proclaim:
Who stirs not at that Prince of Cobblers' name?
Profuse in loyalty some couplets shine,
And wish long days to all the Brunswick line!
To youths and virgins they chaste lesson read;
Teach wives and husbands how their lives to lead;
Maids to be cleanly, footmen free from vice;
How death at last all ranks doth equalise;
And, in conclusion, pray good years befall,
With store of wealth, your "worthy masters all."
For this and other tokens of good-will,
On boxing-day may store of shillings fill
Your Christmas purse; no householder give less,
When at each door your blameless suit you press:
And what you wish to us (it is but reason)
Receive in turn—the compliments o' th' season!

VI.

ON A DEAF AND DUMB ARTIST.[1]

And hath thy blameless life become
A prey to the devouring tomb?
A more mute silence hast thou known,
A deafness deeper than thine own,
While Time was? and no friendly Muse,
That mark'd thy life, and knows thy dues,
Repair with quickening verse the breach,
And write thee into light and speech?
The Power, that made the Tongue, restrain'd
Thy lips from lies, and speeches feign'd;
Who made the Hearing, without wrong
Did rescue thine from Siren's song.
He let thee *see* the ways of men,
Which thou with pencil, not with pen,
Careful Beholder, down didst note,
And all their motley actions quote,
Thyself unstain'd the while. From look
Or gesture reading, more than *book*,
In letter'd pride thou took'st no part,
Contented with the Silent Art,
Thyself as silent. Might I be
As speechless, deaf, and good, as He!

VII.

NEWTON'S PRINCIPIA.

Great Newton's self, to whom the world's in debt,
Owed to School Mistress sage his Alphabet;
But quickly wiser than his Teacher grown,
Discover'd properties to her unknown;
Of A *plus* B, or *minus*, learn'd the use,
Known Quantities from unknown to educe;

[1] Benjamin Ferrers, died A.D. 1732.

And made—no doubt to that old dame's surprise—
The Christ-Cross-Row his ladder to the skies.
Yet, whatsoe'er Geometricians say,
Her Lessons were his true PRINCIPIA!

VIII.

THE HOUSEKEEPER.

THE frugal snail, with forecast of repose,
Carries his house with him, where'er he goes;
Peeps out—and if there comes a shower of rain,
Retreats to his small domicile amain.
Touch but a tip of him, a horn—'tis well—
He curls up in his sanctuary shell.
He's his own landlord, his own tenant; stay
Long as he will, he dreads no Quarter-day.
Himself he boards and lodges; both invites,
And feasts, himself; sleeps with himself o' nights.
He spares the upholsterer trouble to procure
Chattels; himself is his own furniture,
And his sole riches.   Wheresoe'er he roam—
Knock when you will—he's sure to be at home.

IX.

THE FEMALE ORATORS.

NIGH London's famous Bridge, a Gate more famed
Stands, or once stood, from old Belinus named,
So judged Antiquity; and therein wrongs
A name, allusive strictly to *two Tongues*.[1]
Her school hard by the Goddess Rhetoric opes,
And *gratis* deals to Oyster-wives her Tropes.
With Nereid green, green Nereid disputes,
Replies, rejoins, confutes, and still confutes.
One her coarse sense by metaphors expounds,
And one in literalities abounds;

[1] *Billingis* in the Latin.

In mood and figure these keep up the din :
Words multiply, and every word tells in.
Her hundred throats here bawling Slander strains ;
And unclothed Venus to her tongue gives reins
In terms, which Demosthenic force outgo,
And baldest jests of foul-mouth'd Cicero.
Right in the midst great Ate keeps her stand,
And from her sovereign station taints the land.
Hence Pulpits rail ; grave Senates learn to jar ;
Quacks scold ; and Billingsgate infects the Bar.

PINDARIC ODE TO THE TREAD-MILL.

I.

INSPIRE my spirit, Spirit of De Foe,
That sang the Pillory,
In loftier strains to show
A more sublime Machine
Than that, where thou wert seen,
With neck outstretch'd and shoulders ill awry,
Courting coarse plaudits from vile crowds below—
A most unseemly show.

II.

In such a place
Who could expose thy face,
Historiographer of deathless Crusoe !
That paint'st the strife
And all the naked ills of savage life,
Far above Rousseau ?
Rather myself had stood
In that ignoble wood,
Bare to the mob, on holy day or high day.
If nought else could atone
For waggish libel,
I swear on Bible,
I would have spared him for thy sake alone,
Man Friday !

III.

Our ancestors' were sour days,
Great Master of Romance !
A milder doom had fallen to thy chance
In our days :
Thy sole assignment
Some solitary confinement
(Not worth thy care a carrot),
Where in world-hidden cell
Thou thy own Crusoe might have acted well,
Only without the parrot ;
By sure experience taught to know,
Whether the qualms thou makest him feel were
    truly such or no.

IV.

But stay ! methinks in statelier measure—
A more companionable pleasure—
I see thy steps the mighty Tread-Mill trace,
(The subject of my song,
Delay'd however long),
And some of thine own race,
To keep thee company, thou bring'st with thee along.
There with thee go,
Link'd in like sentence,
With regulated pace and footing slow,
Each old acquaintance,
Rogue—harlot—thief—that live to future ages ;
Through many a laboured tome,
Rankly embalm'd in thy too natural pages.
Faith, friend De Foe, thou art quite at home !
Not one of thy great offspring thou dost lack,
From pirate Singleton to pilfering Jack,
Here Flandrian Moll her brazen incest brags ;
Vice-stript Roxana, penitent in rags,
There points to Amy, treading equal chimes,
The faithful handmaid to her faithless crimes.

V.

Incompetent my song to raise
To its just height thy praise,
Great Mill!
That by thy motion proper
(No thanks to wind, or sail, or working rill)
Grinding that stubborn corn, the Human will,
Turn'st out men's consciences,
That were begrimed before, as clean and sweet
As flour from purest wheat,
Into thy hopper.
All reformation short of thee but nonsense is,
Or human, or divine.

VI.

Compared with thee,
What are the labours of that Jumping Sect,
Which feeble laws connive at rather than respect?
Thou dost not bump,
Or jump,
But *walk* men into virtue; betwixt crime
And slow repentance giving breathing time,
And leisure to be good;
Instructing with discretion demi-reps
How to direct their steps.

VII.

Thou best Philosopher made out of wood!
Not that which framed the tub,
Where sate the Cynic cub,
With nothing in his bosom sympathetic;
But from those groves derived, I deem,
Where Plato nursed his dream
Of immortality;
Seeing that clearly
Thy system all is merely
Peripatetic.

Thou to thy pupils dost such lessons give
Of how to live
With temperance, sobriety, morality
(A new art),
That from thy school, by force of virtuous deeds,
Each Tyro now proceeds
A "Walking Stewart!"

EPICEDIUM.

GOING OR GONE.

I.

FINE merry franions,
Wanton companions,
My days are ev'n banyans
    With thinking upon ye;
How Death, that last stinger,
Finis-writer, end-bringer,
Has laid his chill finger,
    Or is laying on ye.

II.

There's rich Kitty Wheatley,
With footing it featly
That took me completely,
    She sleeps in the Kirk House;
And poor Polly Perkin,
Whose dad was still firking
The jolly ale firkin,
    She's gone to the Work-house:

III.

Fine Gard'ner, Ben Carter
(In ten counties no smarter),
Has ta'en his departure
    For Proserpine's orchards;

And Lily, postilion,
With cheeks of vermilion,
Is one of a million
    That fill up the churchyards;

IV.

And, lusty as Dido,
Fat Clemitson's widow
Flits now a small shadow
    By Stygian hid ford;
And good master Clapton
Has thirty years nap't on,
The ground he last hap't on,
    Intomb'd by fair Widford;

V.

And gallant Tom Dockwra,
Of Nature's finest crockery,
Now but thin air and mockery,
    Lurks by Avernus,
Whose honest grasp of hand
Still, while his life did stand,
At friend's or foe's command,
    Almost did burn us.

VI.

Roger de Coverley
Not more good man than he
Yet has he equally
    Push'd for Cocytus,
With drivelling Worral,
And wicked old Dorrell,
'Gainst whom I've a quarrel,
    Whose end might affright us!—

VII.

Kindly hearts have I known;
Kindly hearts, they are flown;

Here and there if but one
    Linger yet uneffaced,
Imbecile tottering elves,
Soon to be wreck'd on shelves,
These scarce are half themselves,
    With age and care crazed.

VIII.

But this day Fanny Hutton
Her last dress has put on;
Her fine lessons forgotten,
    She died, as the dunce died:
And prim Betsy Chambers,
Decay'd in her members,
No longer remembers
    Things as she once did;

IX.

And prudent Miss Wither
Not in jest now doth *wither*
And soon must go—whither
    Nor I well, nor you know;
And flaunting Miss Waller,
That soon must befall her,
Whence none can recall her,
    Though proud once as Juno!

THE WIFE'S TRIAL;
OR, THE INTRUDING WIDOW.

A Dramatic Poem,
Founded on Mr. Crabbe's Tale of the "Confidant."

CHARACTERS.

MR. SELBY, *a Wiltshire Gentleman.*
KATHERINE, *Wife to Selby.*
LUCY, *Sister to Selby.*
MRS. FRAMPTON, *a Widow.*
SERVANTS.

SCENO.—*At* MR. SELBY'S *House, or in the Grounds adjacent.*

SCENE.—*A Library.* MR. SELBY, KATHERINE.

Selby. Do not too far mistake me, gentlest wife;
I meant to chide your virtues, not yourself,
And those too with allowance. I have not
Been blest by thy fair side with five white years
Of smooth and even wedlock, now to touch
With any strain of harshness on a string
Hath yielded me such music. 'Twas the quality
Of a too grateful nature in my Katherine,
That to the lame performance of some vows,
And common courtesies of man to wife,
Attributing too much, hath sometimes seem'd
To esteem as favours, what in that blest union
Are but reciprocal and trivial dues,
As fairly yours as mine: 'twas this I thought
Gently to reprehend.
  Kath. In friendship's barter
The riches we exchange should hold some level,

And corresponding worth.   Jewels for toys
Demand some thanks thrown in.   You took me, sir,
To that blest haven of my peace, your bosom,
An orphan founder'd in the world's black storm.
Poor, you have made me rich ; from lonely maiden,
Your cherish'd and your full-accompanied wife.
   Selby. But to divert the subject : Kate, too fond
I would not wrest your meanings ; else that word
Accompanied, and full-accompanied too,
Might raise a doubt in some men, that their wives
Haply did think their company too long ;
And over-company, we know by proof,
Is worse than no attendance.
   Kath. I must guess,
You speak this of the Widow——
   Selby. 'Twas a bolt
At random shot ; but if it hit, believe me,
I am most sorry to have wounded you
Through a friend's side.   I know not how we have swerved
From our first talk.   I was to caution you
Against this fault of a too grateful nature :
Which, for some girlish obligations past,
In that relenting season of the heart,
When slightest favours pass for benefits
Of endless binding, would entail upon you
An iron slavery of obsequious duty
To the proud will of an imperious woman.
   Kath. The favours are not slight to her I owe.
   Selby. Slight or not slight, the tribute she exacts
Cancels all dues——   (*A voice within.*)
                        even now I hear her call you
In such a tone as lordliest mistresses
Expect a slave's attendance.   Prithee, Kate,
Let her expect a brace of minutes or so.
Say, you are busy.   Use her by degrees
To some less hard exactions.
   Kath. I conjure you,
Detain me not.   I will return——

Selby. Sweet wife,
Use thy own pleasure—   [*Exit* KATHERINE.
            but it troubles me.
A visit of three days, as was pretended,
Spun to ten tedious weeks, and no hint given
When she will go! I would this buxom Widow
Were a thought handsomer! I'd fairly try
My Katherine's constancy; make desperate love
In seeming earnest; and raise up such broils,
That she, not I, should be the first to warn
The insidious guest depart.

Re-enter KATHERINE.

            So soon return'd!
What was our Widow's will?
    Kath. A trifle, sir.
    Selby. Some toilet service—to adjust her head,
Or help to stick a pin in the right place——
    Kath. Indeed 'twas none of these.
    Selby. Or new vamp up
The tarnish'd cloak she came in. I have seen her
Demand such service from thee, as her maid,
Twice told to do it, would blush angry-red,
And pack her few clothes up. Poor fool! fond slave!
And yet my dearest Kate!—This day at least
(It is our wedding-day), we spend in freedom,
And will forget our Widow.—Philip, our coach—
Why weeps my wife? You know, I promised you
An airing o'er the pleasant Hampshire downs
To the blest cottage on the green hill-side
Where first I told my love. I wonder much
If the crimson parlour hath exchanged its hue
For colours not so welcome. Faded though it be,
It will not show less lovely than the tinge
Of this faint red, contending with the pale,
Where once the full-flush'd health gave to this cheek
An apt resemblance to the fruit's warm side

That bears my Katherine's name.—

                    Our carriage, Philip.

           Enter a Servant.

Now, Robin, what make you here?
  Serv. May it please you,
The coachman has driven out with Mistress Frampton.
  Selby. He had no orders——
  Serv. None, sir, that I know of,
But from the lady, who expects some letters
At the next post town.
  Selby. Go, Robin.   [*Exit Servant.*
               How is this?
  Kath. I came to tell you so, but feared your anger——
  Selby. It was ill done, though, of this Mistress Framp-
    ton—
This forward Widow. But a ride's poor loss
Imports not much. In to your chamber, love,
Where you with music may beguile the hour,
While I am tossing over dusty tomes,
Till our most reasonable friend returns.
  Kath. I am all obedience.   [*Exit* KATHERINE.
  Selby. Too obedient, Kate,
And to too many masters. I can hardly,
On such a day as this, refrain to speak
My sense of this injurious friend—this pest—
This household evil—this close-clinging fiend—
In rough terms to my wife. 'Death, my own servants
Controll'd above me! orders countermanded!
What next?
      [*Servant enters and announces the Sister.*

           Enter Lucy.

Sister! I know you are come to welcome
This day's return. 'Twas well done.
  Lucy. You seem ruffled.
In years gone by this day was used to be

The smoothest of the year.   Your honey turn'd
So soon to gall?

   Selby. Gall'd am I, and with cause,
And rid to death, yet cannot get a riddance,
Nay, scarce a ride, by this proud Widow's leave.

   Lucy. Something you wrote me of a Mistress Frampton.

   Selby. She came at first a meek admitted guest,
Pretending a short stay; her whole deportment
Seem'd as of one obliged.   A slender trunk,
The wardrobe of her scant and ancient clothing,
Bespoke no more.   But in few days her dress,
Her looks, were proudly changed.   And now she flaunts it
In jewels stolen or borrow'd from my wife;
Who owes her some strange service, of what nature
I must be kept in ignorance.   Katherine's meek
And gentle spirit cowers beneath her eye,
As spell-bound by some witch.

   Lucy. Some mystery hangs on it.
How bears she in her carriage towards yourself?

   Selby. As one who fears, and yet not greatly cares
For my displeasure.   Sometimes I have thought
A secret glance would tell me she could love,
If I but gave encouragement.   Before me
She keeps some moderation; but is never
Closeted with my wife, but in the end
I find my Katherine in briny tears.
From the small chamber where she first was lodged,
The gradual fiend, by specious wriggling arts,
Has now ensconced herself in the best part
Of this large mansion; calls the left wing her own;
Commands my servants, equipage.—I hear
Her hated tread.   What makes she back so soon?

         Enter MRS. FRAMPTON.

   Mrs. F. O, I am jolter'd, bruised, and shook to death
With your vile Wiltshire roads.   The villain Philip
Chose, on my conscience, the perversest tracks
And stoniest hard lanes in all the county,

Till I was fain get out, and so walk back,
My errand unperform'd at Andover.
    Lucy. And I shall love the knave for ever after (*aside*).
    Mrs. F. A friend with you!
    Selby. My eldest sister Lucy,
Come to congratulate this returning morn.—
Sister, my wife's friend, Mistress Frampton.
    Mrs. F. Pray,
Be seated. For your brother's sake, you are welcome.
I had thought this day to have spent in homely fashion
With the good couple, to whose hospitality
I stand so far indebted. But your coming
Makes it a feast.
    Lucy. She does the honours naturally——
    Selby. As if she were the mistress of the house—
                                           (*aside*).
    Mrs. F. I love to be at home with loving friends.
To stand on ceremony with obligations,
Is to restrain the obliger. That old coach, though,
Of yours jumbles one strangely.
    Selby. I shall order
An equipage soon, more easy to you, madam——
    Lucy. To drive her and her pride to Lucifer,
I hope he means (*aside*).
    Mrs. F. I must go trim myself; this humbled garb
Would shame a wedding feast. I have your leave
For a short absence?—and your Katherine——
    Selby. You'll find her in her closet——
    Mrs. F. Fare you well, then.
    Selby. How like you her assurance?
    Lucy. Even so well,
That if this Widow were my guest, not yours,
She should have coach enough, and scope to ride.
My merry groom should in a trice convey her
To Sarum Plain, and set her down at Stonehenge,
To pick her path through those antiques at leisure;
She should take sample of our Wiltshire flints.
O, be not lightly jealous! nor surmise

That to a wanton bold-faced thing like this
Your modest shrinking Katherine could impart
Secrets of any worth, especially
Secrets that touch'd your peace. If there be aught,
My life upon't, 'tis but some girlish story
Of a first love; which even the boldest wife
Might modestly deny to a husband's ear,
Much more your timid and too sensitive Katherine.

Selby. I think it is no more; and will dismiss
My further fears, if ever I have had such.

Lucy. Shall we go walk? I'd see your gardens, brother;
And how the new trees thrive, I recommended.
Your Katherine is engaged now——

Selby. I'll attend you. [*Exeunt.*

SCENE.—*Servants' Hall.*

Housekeeper, PHILIP, *and others, laughing.*

Housek. Our lady's guest, since her short ride, seems ruffled,
And somewhat in disorder. Philip, Philip,
I do suspect some roguery. Your mad tricks
Will some day cost you a good place, I warrant.

Phil. Good Mistress Jane, our serious housekeeper,
And sage duenna to the maids and scullions,
We must have leave to laugh; our brains are younger,
And undisturb'd with care of keys and pantries.
We are wild things.

Butler. Good Philip, tell us all.

All. Ay, as you live, tell, tell——

Phil. Mad fellows, you shall have it.
The Widow's bell rang lustily and loud——

Butl. I think that no one can mistake her ringing.

Waiting-maid. Our lady's ring is soft sweet music to it,
More of entreaty hath it than command.

Phil. I lose my story, if you interrupt thus.
The bell, I say, rang fiercely; and a voice

More shrill than bell, call'd out for "Coachman Philip."
I straight obey'd, as 'tis my name and office.
"Drive me," quoth she, "to the next market town,
Where I have hope of letters." I made haste,
Put to the horses, saw her fairly coach'd,
And drove her——
    Waiting-maid. ——By the straight high road to
        Andover,
I guess——
    Phil. Pray, warrant things within your knowledge,
Good Mistress Abigail; look to your dressings,
And leave the skill in horses to the coachman.
    Butl. He'll have his humour; best not interrupt him.
    Phil. 'Tis market-day, thought I; and the poor beasts,
Meeting such droves of cattle and of people,
May take a fright; so down the lane I trundled,
Where Goodman Dobson's crazy mare was founder'd,
And where the flints were biggest, and ruts widest,
By ups and downs, and such bone-cracking motions,
We flounder'd on a furlong, till my madam,
In policy to save the few joints left her,
Betook her to her feet, and there we parted.
    All. Ha! ha! ha!
    Butl. Hang her! 'tis pity such as she should ride.
    Waiting-maid. I think she is a witch; I have tired
        myself out
With sticking pins in her pillow; still she 'scapes them.
    Butl. And I with helping her to mum for claret,
But never yet could cheat her dainty palate.
    Housek. Well, well, she is the guest of our good Mistress,
And so should be respected. Though, I think,
Our Master cares not for her company,
He would ill brook we should express so much
By rude discourtesies and short attendance,
Being but servants. (*A bell rings furiously.*) 'Tis her
        bell speaks now;
Good, good, bestir yourselves: who knows who's wanted?
    Butl. But 'twas a merry trick of Philip Coachman.
                                                [*Exeunt.*

Scene.—*Mrs. Selby's Chamber.*

Mrs. Frampton, Katherine, *working.*

Mrs. F. I am thinking, child, how contrary our fates
Have traced our lots through life. Another needle,
This works untowardly. An heiress born
To splendid prospects, at our common school
I was as one above you all, not of you;
Had my distinct prerogatives, my freedoms,
Denied to you. Pray, listen——

Kath. I must hear
What you are pleased to speak!—How my heart sinks
    here! (*aside*).

Mrs. F. My chamber to myself, my separate maid,
My coach, and so forth.—Not that needle, simple one,
With the great staring eye fit for a Cyclops!
Mine own are not so blinded with their griefs,
But I could make a shift to thread a smaller.
A cable or a camel might go through this,
And never strain for the passage.

Kath. I will fit you.—
Intolerable tyranny! (*aside*).

Mrs. F. Quick! quick!
You were not once so slack.—As I was saying,
Not a young thing among ye but observed me
Above the mistress. Who but I was sought to
In all your dangers, all your little difficulties,
Your girlish scrapes? I was the scape-goat still,
To fetch you off; kept all your secrets; some,
Perhaps, since then——

Kath. No more of that, for mercy,
If you'd not have me, sinking at your feet,
Cleave the cold earth for comfort (*kneels*).

Mrs. F. This to me?
This posture to your friend had better suited
The orphan Katherine in her humble school-days,
To the *then* rich heiress, than the wife of Selby—
Of wealthy Mr. Selby—

To the poor Widow Frampton, sunk as she is.
Come, come,
'Twas something, or 'twas nothing, that I said;
I did not mean to fright you, sweetest bed-fellow!
You once were so, but Selby now engrosses you.
I'll make him give you up a night or so—
In faith I will—that we may lie and talk
Old tricks of school-days over.

   Kath. Hear me, madam——
   Mrs. F. Not by that name.   Your friend——
   Kath. My truest friend,
And saviour of my honour!
   Mrs. F. This sounds better;
You still shall find me such.
   Kath. That you have graced
Our poor house with your presence hitherto,
Has been my greatest comfort, the sole solace
Of my forlorn and hardly guess'd estate.
You have been pleased
To accept some trivial hospitalities,
In part of payment of a long arrear
I owe to you, no less than for my life.
   Mrs. F. You speak my services too large.
   Kath. Nay, less;
For what an abject thing were life to me
Without your silence on my dreadful secret!
And I would wish the league we have renew'd
Might be perpetual——
   Mrs. F. Have a care, fine madam! (*aside*).
   Kath. That one house still might hold us.   But my
      husband
Has shown himself of late——
   Mrs. F. How, Mistress Selby?
   Kath. Not, not impatient. You misconstrue him.
He honours, and he loves—nay, he must love—
The friend of his wife's youth.   But there are moods
In which——
   Mrs. F. I understand you;—in which husbands,

And wives that love, may wish to be alone,
To nurse the tender fits of new-born dalliance,
After a five years' wedlock.

 Kath. Was that well
Or charitably put? do these pale cheeks
Proclaim a wanton blood? this wasting form
Seem a fit theatre for Levity
To play his love-tricks on; and act such follies,
As even in Affection's first bland moon
Have less of grace than pardon in best wedlocks?
I was about to say that there are times,
When the most frank and sociable man
May surfeit on most loved society,
Preferring loneliness rather——

 Mrs. F. To my company——

 Kath. Ay, yours, or mine, or any one's. Nay, take
Not this unto yourself. Even in the newness
Of our first married loves 'twas sometimes so.
For solitude, I have heard my Selby say,
Is to the mind as rest to the corporal functions;
And he would call it oft, the *day's soft sleep.*

 Mrs. F. What is your drift? and whereto tends this speech,
Rhetorically labour'd?

 Kath. That you would
Abstain but from our house a month, a week:
I make request but for a single day.

 Mrs. F. A month, a week, a day! A single hour
Is every week, and month, and the long year,
And all the years to come! My footing here,
Slipt once, recovers never. From the state
Of gilded roofs, attendance, luxuries,
Parks, gardens, sauntering walks, or wholesome rides,
To the bare cottage on the withering moor,
Where I myself am servant to myself,
Or only waited on by blackest thoughts,
I sink, if this be so. No; here I sit.

 Kath. Then I am lost for ever!

   [*Sinks at her feet—curtain drops.*

SCENE.—*An Apartment, contiguous to the last.*
SELBY, *as if listening.*

Selby. The sounds have died away. What am I
changed to?
What do I here, listening like to an abject
Or heartless wittol, that must hear no good,
If he hear aught? "This shall to the ear of your husband."
It was the Widow's word. I guess'd some mystery,
And the solution with a vengeance comes.
What can my wife have left untold to me,
That must be told by proxy? I begin
To call in doubt the course of her life past
Under my very eyes. She hath not been good,
Not virtuous, not discreet; she hath not outrun
My wishes still with prompt and meek observance.
Perhaps she is not fair, sweet-voiced; her eyes
Not like the dove's; all this as well may be
As that she should entreasure up a secret
In the peculiar closet of her breast,
And grudge it to my ear. It is my right
To claim the halves in any truth she owns,
As much as in the babe I have by her:
Upon whose face henceforth I fear to look,
Lest I should fancy in its innocent brow
Some strange shame written.

Enter LUCY.

Sister, an anxious word with you.
From out that chamber, where my wife but now
Held talk with her encroaching friend, I heard
(Not of set purpose hearkening, but by chance)
A voice of chiding, answer'd by a tone
Of replication such as the meek dove
Makes when the kite has clutch'd her. The high Widow
Was loud and stormy. I distinctly heard
One threat pronounced—" Your husband shall know all."

I am no listener, sister; and I hold
A secret got by such unmanly shift,
The pitiful'st of thefts; but what mine ear,
I not intending it, receives perforce,
I count my lawful prize.   Some subtle meaning
Lurks in this fiend's behaviour; which, by force
Or fraud, I must make mine.
   Lucy. The gentlest means
Are still the wisest.   What if you should press
Your wife to a disclosure?
   Selby. I have tried
All gentler means; thrown out low hints, which, though
Merely suggestions still, have never fail'd
To blanch her cheek with fears.   Roughlier to insist
Would be to kill, where I but meant to heal.
   Lucy. Your own description gave that Widow out
As one not much precise, nor over coy
And nice to listen to a suit of love,
What if you feign'd a courtship, putting on
(To work the secret from her easy faith),
For honest ends, a most dishonest seeming?
   Selby. I see your drift, and partly meet your counsel.
But must it not in me appear prodigious—
To say the least, unnatural and suspicious—
To move hot love where I have shown cool scorn,
And undissembled looks of blank aversion?
   Lucy. Vain woman is the dupe of her own charms,
And easily credits the resistless power
That in besieging beauty lies, to cast down
The slight-built fortress of a casual hate.
   Selby. I am resolved——
   Lucy. Success attend your wooing!
   Selby. And I'll about it roundly, my wise sister.
                                               [*Exeunt.*

Scene.—*The Library.*

Mr. Selby.   Mrs. Frampton.

Selby. A fortunate encounter, Mistress Frampton.
My purpose was, if you can spare so much
From your sweet leisure, a few words in private.
    Mrs. F. What mean his alter'd tones? These looks
        to me,
Whose glances yet he has repell'd with coolness?
Is the wind changed? I'll veer about with it,
And meet him in all fashions (*aside*).
                    All my leisure,
Feebly bestow'd upon my kind friends here,
Would not express a tithe of the obligements
I every hour incur.
    Selby. No more of that.—
I know not why my wife hath lost of late
Much of her cheerful spirits.
    Mrs. F. It was my topic
To-day; and every day, and all day long,
I still am chiding with her. "Child," I said,
And said it pretty roundly—it may be
I was too peremptory—we elder school-fellows,
Presuming on the advantage of a year
Or two, which, in that tender time, seem'd much,
In after years, much like to elder sisters,
Are prone to keep the authoritative style,
When time has made the difference most ridiculous.
    Selby. The observation's shrewd.
    Mrs. F. "Child," I was saying,
"If some wives had obtain'd a lot like yours,"
And then perhaps I sigh'd, "they would not sit
In corners moping, like to sullen moppets,
That want their will, but dry their eyes, and look
Their cheerful husbands in the face,"—perhaps
I said, their Selbys,—" with proportion'd looks
Of honest joy."

Selby. You do suspect no jealousy?

Mrs. F. What is his import? Whereto tends his
    speech? (*aside*).
Of whom, or what, should she be jealous, sir?

Selby. I do not know; but women have their fancies;
And underneath a cold indifference,
Or show of some distaste, husbands have mask'd
A growing fondness for a female friend,
Which the wife's eye was sharp enough to see
Before the friend had wit to find it out.
You do not quit us soon?

Mrs. F. 'Tis as I find
Your Katherine profits by my lesson, sir.—
Means this man honest? Is there no deceit? (*aside*).

Selby. She cannot choose.—Well, well, I have been
    thinking,
And if the matter were to do again——

Mrs. F. What matter, sir?

Selby. This idle bond of wedlock;
These sour-sweet briars, fetters of harsh silk;
I might have made, I do not say a better,
But a more fit choice in a wife.

Mrs. F. The parch'd ground,
In hottest Julys, drinks not in the showers
More greedily than I his words! (*aside*).

Selby. My humour
Is to be frank and jovial; and that man
Affects me best, who most reflects me in
My most free temper.

Mrs. F. Were you free to choose,
As jestingly I'll put the supposition,
Without a thought reflecting on your Katherine,
What sort of woman would you make your choice?

Selby. I like your humour, and will meet your jest.
She should be one about my Katherine's age;
But not so old, by some ten years, in gravity.
One that would meet my mirth, sometimes outrun it;
No puling, pining moppet, as you said,

Nor moping maid, that I must still be teaching
The freedoms of a wife all her life after;
But one that, having worn the chain before
(And worn it lightly, as report gave out),
Enfranchised from it by her poor fool's death,
Took it not so to heart that I need dread
To die myself, for fear a second time
To wet a widow's eye.
    Mrs. F. Some widows, sir,
Hearing you talk so wildly, would be apt
To put strange misconstruction on your words,
As aiming at a Turkish liberty,
Where the free husband hath his several mates;
His Penseroso, his Allegro wife,
To suit his sober, or his frolic fit.
    Selby. How judge you of that latitude?
    Mrs. F.   As one,
In European customs bred, must judge. Had I
Been born a native of the liberal East,
I might have thought as they do. Yet I knew
A married man that took a second wife,
And (the man's circumstances duly weigh'd,
With all their bearings) the considerate world
Nor much approved, nor much condemn'd the deed.
    Selby. You move my wonder strangely. Pray, proceed.
    Mrs. F. An eye of wanton liking he had placed
Upon a widow, who liked him again,
But stood on terms of honourable love,
And scrupled wronging his most virtuous wife;
When to their ears a lucky rumour ran,
That this demure and saintly-seeming wife
Had a first husband living; with the which
Being question'd, she but faintly could deny.
"A priest indeed there was; some words had past,
But scarce amounting to a marriage rite.
Her friend was absent; she supposed him dead;
And, seven years parted, both were free to choose."
    Selby. What did the indignant husband? Did he not

With violent handlings stigmatise the cheek
Of the deceiving wife, who had entail'd
Shame on their innocent babe?
   Mrs. F. He neither tore
His wife's locks nor his own; but wisely weighing
His own offence with hers in equal poise,
And woman's weakness 'gainst the strength of man,
Came to a calm and witty compromise.
He coolly took his gay-faced widow home,
Made her his second wife; and still the first
Lost few or none of her prerogatives.
The servants call'd her mistress still; she kept
The keys, and had the total ordering
Of the house affairs; and, some slight toys excepted,
Was all a moderate wife would wish to be.
   Selby. A tale full of dramatic incident!—
And, if a man should put it in a play,
How should he name the parties?
   Mrs. F. The man's name
Through time I have forgot—the widow's too;—
But his first wife's first name, her maiden one,
Was—not unlike to *that* your Katherine bore,
Before she took the honour'd style of Selby.
   Selby. A dangerous meaning in your riddle lurks;
One knot is yet unsolved; that told, this strange
And most mysterious drama ends. The name
Of that first husband——

          Enter LUCY.

   Mrs. F. Sir, your pardon.
The allegory fits your private ear.
Some half-hour hence, in the garden's secret walk,
We shall have leisure.   *Exit.*
   Selby. Sister, whence come you?
   Lucy. From your poor Katherine's chamber, where she
      droops
In sad presageful thoughts, and sighs, and weeps,

And seems to pray by turns. At times she looks
As she would pour her secret in my bosom—
Then starts, as I have seen her, at the mention
Of some immodest act. At her request,
I left her on her knees.
    Selby. The fittest posture;
For great has been her fault to Heaven and me.
She married me with a first husband living,
Or not known not to be so, which, in the judgment
Of any but indifferent honesty,
Must be esteem'd the same. The shallow Widow,
Caught by my art, under a riddling veil
Too thin to hide her meaning, hath confess'd all.
Your coming in broke off the conference,
When she was ripe to tell the fatal *name*
That seals my wedded doom.
    Lucy. Was she so forward
To pour her hateful meanings in your ear
At the first hint?
    Selby. Her newly-flattered hopes
Array'd themselves at first in forms of doubt;
And with a female caution she stood off
Awhile, to read the meaning of my suit,
Which with such honest seeming I enforced,
That her cold scruples soon gave way; and now
She rests prepared, as mistress, or as wife,
To seize the place of her betrayèd friend—
My much offending, but more suffering, Katherine.
    Lucy. Into what labyrinth of fearful shapes
My simple project has conducted you!
Were but my wit as skilful to invent
A clue to lead you forth!—I call to mind
A letter, which your wife received from the Cape,
Soon after you were married, with some circumstances
Of mystery too,
    Selby. I well remember it.
That letter did confirm the truth (she said)
Of a friend's death, which she had long fear'd true,

But knew not for a fact. A youth of promise
She gave him out—a hot adventurous spirit—
That had set sail in quest of golden dreams,
And cities in the heart of Central Afric;
But named no names, nor did I care to press
My question further, in the passionate grief
She show'd at the receipt. Might this be he?
   Lucy. Tears were not all. When that first shower
      was past,
With claspèd hands she raised her eyes to Heaven,
As if in thankfulness for some escape,
Or strange deliverance, in the news implied,
Which sweeten'd that sad news.
   Selby. Something of that
I noted also——
   Lucy. In her closet once,
Seeking some other trifle, I espied
A ring, in mournful characters deciphering
The death of "Robert Halford, aged two
And twenty." Brother, I am not given
To the confident use of wagers, which I hold
Unseemly in a woman's argument;
But I am strangely tempted now to risk
A thousand pounds out of my patrimony,
(And let my future husband look to it,
If it be lost), that this immodest Widow
Shall name the name that tallies with that ring.
   Selby. That wager lost, I should be rich indeed—
Rich in my rescued Kate—rich in my honour,
Which now was bankrupt. Sister, I accept
Your merry wager, with an aching heart
For very fear of winning. 'Tis the hour
That I should meet my Widow in the walk,
The south side of the garden. On some pretence
Lure forth my Wife that way, that she may witness
Our seeming courtship. Keep us still in sight,
Yourselves unseen; and by some sign I'll give
(A finger held up, or a kerchief waved),

You'll know your wager won—then break upon us,
As if by chance.
  Lucy. I apprehend your meaning——
  Selby. And may you prove a true Cassandra here,
Though my poor acres smart for't, wagering sister.
[*Exeunt.*

Scene.—*Mrs. Selby's Chamber.*

Mrs. Frampton. Katherine.

  Mrs. F. Did I express myself in terms so strong?
  Kath. As nothing could have more affrighted me.
  Mrs. F. Think it a hurt friend's jest, in retribution
Of a suspected cooling hospitality.
And, for my staying here, or going hence
(Now I remember something of our argument),
Selby and I can settle that between us.
You look amazed. What if your husband, child,
Himself has courted me to stay?
  Kath. You move
My wonder and my pleasure equally.
  Mrs. F. Yes, courted me to stay, waived all objections,
Made it a favour to yourselves; not me,
His troublesome guest, as you surmised. Child, child,
When I recall his flattering welcome, I
Begin to think the burden of my presence
Was——
  Kath. What, for Heaven——
  Mrs. F. A little, little spice
Of jealousy—that's all—an honest pretext,
No wife need blush for. Say that you should see
(As oftentimes we widows take such freedoms,
Yet still on this side virtue), in a jest
Your husband pat me on the cheek, or steal
A kiss, while you were by,—not else, for virtue's sake.
  Kath. I could endure all this, thinking my husband
Meant it in sport——
  Mrs. F. But if in downright earnest

(Putting myself out of the question here)
Your Selby, as I partly do suspect,
Own'd a divided heart——

  Kath. My own would break——

  Mrs. F. Why, what a blind and witless fool it is,
That will not see its gains, its infinite gains——

  Kath. Gain in a loss!
Or mirth in utter desolation!

  Mrs. F. He doting on a face—suppose it mine,
Or any other's tolerably fair—
What need you care about a senseless secret?

  Kath. Perplex'd and fearful woman! I in part
Fathom your dangerous meaning. You have broke
The worse than iron band, fretting the soul,
By which you held me captive. Whether my husband
Is what you give him out, or your fool'd fancy
But dreams he is so, either way I am free.

  Mrs. F. It talks it bravely, blazons out its shame;
A very heroine while on its knees;
Rowe's Penitent, an absolute Calista!

  Kath. Not to thy wretched self these tears are falling;
But to my husband, and offended Heaven,
Some drops are due—and then I sleep in peace,
Relieved from frightful dreams, my dreams though sad.
                                      [*Exit.*

  Mrs. F. I have gone too far. Who knows but in this mood
She may forestall my story, win on Selby
By a frank confession?—and the time draws on
For our appointed meeting. The game's desperate
For which I play. A moment's difference
May make it hers or mine. I fly to meet him. [*Exit.*

        Scene.—*A Garden.*

    Mr. Selby. Mrs. Frampton.

  Selby. I am not so ill a guesser, Mistress Frampton,
Not to conjecture that some passages

In your unfinish'd story, rightly interpreted,
Glanced at my bosom's peace ;
       You knew my wife ?
 Mrs. F. Even from her earliest school-days.—What
  of that ?
Or how is she concern'd in my fine riddles,
Framed for the hour's amusement ?
 Selby. By my *hopes*
Of my new interest conceived in you,
And by the honest passion of my heart,
Which not obliquely I to you did hint ;
Come from the clouds of misty allegory,
And in plain language let me hear the worst.
Stand I disgraced, or no ?
 Mrs. F. Then, by *my* hopes
Of my new interest conceived in you,
And by the kindling passion in *my* breast,
Which through my riddles you had almost read,
Adjured so strongly, I will tell you all.
In her school years, then bordering on fifteen,
Or haply not much past, she loved a youth——
 Selby. My most ingenuous Widow——
 Mrs. F. Met him oft
By stealth, where I still of the party was——
 Selby. Prime confidant to all the school, I war-
  rant,
And general go-between—— (*aside*).
 Mrs. F. One morn he came
In breathless haste :—" The ship was under sail.
Or in few hours would be, that must convey
Him and his destinies to barbarous shores,
Where, should he perish by inglorious hands,
It would be consolation in his death'
To have call'd his Katherine *his*."
 Selby. Thus far the story
Tallies with what I hoped (*aside*).
 Mrs. F. Wavering between
The doubt of doing wrong, and losing him ;

And my dissuasions not o'er hotly urged,
Whom he had flatter'd with the bridemaid's part;—
   Selby. I owe my subtle widow, then, for this (*aside*).
   Mrs. F. Briefly, we went to church. The ceremony
Scarcely was huddled over, and the ring
Yet cold upon her finger, when they parted—
He to his ship; and we to school got back,
Scarce miss'd, before the dinner-bell could ring.
   Selby. And from that hour——
   Mrs. F. Nor sight, nor news of him,
For aught that I could hear, she e'er obtain'd.
   Selby. Like to a man that hovers in suspense
Over a letter just received, on which
The black seal hath impress'd its ominous token,
Whether to open it or no, so I
Suspended stand, whether to press my fate
Further, or check ill curiosity,
That tempts me to more loss.—the name, the name
Of this fine youth?
   Mrs. F. What boots it, if 'twere told?
   Selby. Now, by our loves,
And by my hopes of happier wedlocks, some day
To be accomplish'd, give to me his name!
   Mrs. F. 'Tis no such serious matter. It was—Huntingdon.
   Selby. How have three little syllables pluck'd from me
A world of countless hopes!—(*aside*). Evasive Widow!
   Mrs. F. How, sir! I like not this (*aside*).
   Selby. No, no, I meant
Nothing but good to thee. That other woman,
How shall I call her but evasive, false,
And treacherous?—by the trust I place in thee,
Tell me, and tell me truly, was the name
As you pronounced it?
   Mrs. F. Huntingdon—the name
Which his paternal grandfather assumed,
Together with the estates, of a remote
Kinsman; but our high-spirited youth——

Selby. Yes——

Mrs. F. Disdaining
For sordid pelf to truck the family honours,
At risk of the lost estates, resumed the old style,
And answer'd only to the name of——
Selby. What?
Mrs. F. Of Halford.
Selby. A Huntingdon to Halford changed so soon!
Why, then, I see a witch hath her good spells
As well as bad, and can by a backward charm
Unruffle the foul storm she has just been raising.
                      [*Aside. He makes the signal.*
My frank, fair-spoken Widow! let this kiss,
Which yet aspires no higher, speak my thanks,
Till I can think on greater.

        Enter LUCY *and* KATHERINE.

Mrs. F. Interrupted!
Selby. My sister here! and see, where with her comes
My serpent gliding in an angel's form,
To taint the new-born Eden of our joys.
Why should we fear them? We'll not stir a foot,
Nor coy it for their pleasures. [*He courts the Widow.*
Lucy (*to* KATHERINE). This, your free
And sweet ingenuous confession binds me
For ever to you; and it shall go hard
But it shall fetch you back your husband's heart,
That now seems blindly straying: or, at worst,
In me you have still a sister.—Some wives, brother,
Would think it strange to catch their husbands thus
Alone with a trim widow; but your Katherine
Is arm'd, I think, with patience.
Kath. I am fortified
With knowledge of self-faults to endure worse wrongs,
If they be wrongs, than he can lay upon me;
Even to look on, and see him sue in earnest,
As now I think he does it but in seeming,
To that ill woman.

                L

Selby. Good words, gentle Kate,
And not a thought irreverent of our Widow.
Why, 'twere unmannerly at any time,
But most uncourteous on our wedding-day,
When we should show most hospitable.—Some wine.
                              [*Wine is brought.*
I am for sports. And now I do remember,
The old Egyptians at their banquets placed
A charnel sight of dead men's skulls before them,
With images of cold mortality,
To temper their fierce joys when they grew rampant.
I like the custom well: and ere we crown
With freer mirth the day, I shall propose,
In calmest recollection of our spirits,
We drink the solemn "Memory of the Dead."
   Mrs. F. Or the supposed dead (*aside to him*).
   Selby.   Pledge me, good wife—(*she fills*).
Nay, higher yet, till the brimm'd cup swell o'er.
   Kath. I catch the awful import of your words;
And, though I could accuse you of unkindness,
Yet as your lawful and obedient wife,
While that name lasts (as I perceive it fading,
Nor I much longer may have leave to use it),
I calmly take the office you impose;
And on my knees, imploring their forgiveness,
Whom I in heaven or earth may have offended,
Exempt from starting tears, and woman's weakness,
I pledge you, sir—The Memory of the Dead!
                           [*She drinks kneeling.*
   Selby. 'Tis gently and discreetly said, and like
My former loving Kate.
   Mrs. F. Does he relent? (*aside*).
   Selby. That ceremony past, we give the day
To unabated sport. And, in requital
Of certain stories, and quaint allegories,
Which my rare Widow hath been telling to me,
To raise my morning mirth, if she will lend
Her patient hearing, I will here recite

A Parable; and, the more to suit her taste,
The scene is laid in the East.
   Mrs. F. I long to hear it.—
Some tale, to fit his wife (*aside*).
   Kath. Now comes my TRIAL.
   Lucy. The hour of your deliverance is at hand,
If I presage right. Bear up, gentlest sister.
   Selby. "The Sultan Haroun"—Stay—O now I have it—
"The Caliph Haroun in his orchards had
A fruit-tree, bearing such delicious fruits,
That he reserved them for his proper gust;
And through the palace it was death proclaim'd
To any one that should purloin the same."
   Mrs. F. A heavy penance for so light a fault——
   Selby. Pray you, be silent, else you put me out.
"A crafty page, that for advantage watch'd,
Detected in the act a brother page,
Of his own years, that was his bosom-friend;
And thenceforth he became that other's lord,
And like a tyrant he demean'd himself,—
Laid forced exactions on his fellow's purse;
And when that poor means fail'd, held o'er his head
Threats of impending death in hideous forms;
Till the small culprit on his nightly couch
Dream'd of strange pains, and felt his body writhe
In tortuous pangs around the impaling stake."
   Mrs. F. I like not this beginning——
   Selby. Pray you attend.
"The Secret, like a night-hag, rid his sleeps,
And took the youthful pleasures from his days,
And chased the youthful smoothness from his brow,
That from a rose-cheek'd boy he waned and waned
To a pale skeleton of what he was;
And would have died, but for one lucky chance."
   Kath. Oh!
   Mrs. F. Your wife—she faints—some cordial—smell
     to this.
   Selby. Stand off. My sister best will do that office.

Mrs. F. Are all his tempting speeches come to
  this? (*aside*).
Selby. What ail'd my wife?
Kath. A warning faintness, sir,
Seized on my spirits when you came to where
You said "a lucky chance." I am better now.
Please you go on.
Selby. The sequel shall be brief.
Kath. But, brief or long, I feel my fate hangs on
  it (*aside*).
Selby. "One morn the Caliph, in a covert hid,
Close by an arbour where the two boys talk'd
(As oft we read that Eastern sovereigns
Would play the eaves-dropper, to learn the truth
Imperfectly received from mouths of slaves),
O'erheard their dialogue; and heard enough
To judge aright the cause, and know his cue.
The following day a Cadi was despatch'd
To summon both before the judgment-seat;
The lickerish culprit, almost dead with fear,
And the informing friend, who readily,
Fired with fair promises of large reward,
And Caliph's love, the hateful truth disclosed."
Mrs. F. What did the Caliph to the offending boy,
That had so grossly err'd?
Selby. His sceptred hand
He forth in token of forgiveness stretch'd
And clapp'd his cheeks, and courted him with gifts,
And he became once more his favourite page.
Mrs. F. But for that other——
Selby. He dismissed him straight,
From dreams of grandeur and of Caliph's love,
To the bare cottage on the withering moor,
Where friends, turn'd fiends, and hollow confidants,
And widows, hide, who in a husband's ear
Pour baneful truths, but tell not all the truth;
And told him not that Robin Halford died
Some moons before *his* marriage-bells were rung.

Too near dishonour hast thou trod, dear wife,
And on a dangerous cast our fates were set ;
But Heaven, that will'd our wedlock to be blest,
Hath interposed to save it gracious too.
Your penance is—to dress your cheek in smiles,
And to be once again my merry Kate.—
Sister, your hand ;
Your wager won, makes me a happy man ;
Though poorer, Heaven knows, by a thousand pounds.
The sky clears up after a dubious day.—
Widow, your hand. I read a penitence
In this dejected brow ; and in this shame
Your fault is buried. You shall in with us,
And, if it please you, taste our nuptial fare ;
For, till this moment, I can joyful say,
Was never truly Selby's Wedding Day.

[In a leaf of a quarto edition of the "*Lives of the Saints*, written in Spanish by the learned and reverend father Alfonso Villegas, Divine of the Order of St. Dominick, set forth in English by John Heigham, Anno 1630," bought at a Catholic bookshop in Duke Street, Lincoln's Inn Fields, I found, carefully inserted, a painted flower, seemingly coeval with the book itself; and did not for some time discover that it opened in the middle, and was the cover to a very humble draught of a Saint Anne, with the Virgin and Child; doubtless the performance of some poor but pious Catholic, whose meditations it assisted.]

O LIFT with reverent hand that tarnish'd flower,
That shrines beneath her modest canopy
Memorials dear to Romish piety;
Dim specks, rude shapes of Saints: in fervent hour
The work perchance of some meek devotee,
Who, poor in worldly treasures to set forth
The sanctities she worshipp'd to their worth,
In this imperfect tracery might see
Hints, that all Heaven did to her sense reveal.
Cheap gifts best fit poor givers. We are told
Of the love mite, the cup of water cold,
That in their way approved the offerer's zeal.
True love shows costliest, where the means are scant;
And, in their reckoning, they *abound*, who *want*.

IN THE ALBUM OF ROTHA QUILLINAN.

A PASSING glance was all I caught of thee,
In my own Enfield haunts at random roving.
Old friends of ours were with thee, faces loving;
Time short: and salutations cursory,
Though deep and hearty. The familiar name
Of you, yet unfamiliar, raised in me
Thoughts—what the daughter of that man should be
Who call'd our Wordsworth friend. My thoughts did
    frame

A growing Maiden, who, from day to day
Advancing still in stature, and in grace,
Would all her lonely father's griefs efface,
And his paternal cares with usury pay.
I still retain the phantom, as I can;
And call the gentle image—Quillinan.

TO DORA WORDSWORTH,

ON BEING ASKED BY HER FATHER TO WRITE IN HER ALBUM.

An album is a banquet: from the store,
In his intelligential orchard growing,
Your sire might heap your board to overflowing;
One shaking of the tree—'twould ask no more
To set a salad forth, more rich than that
Which Evelyn [1] in his princely cookery fancied:
Or that more rare, by Eve's neat hands enhanced,
Where a pleased guest, the angelic virtue sat.
But like the all-grasping founder of the feast,
Whom Nathan to the sinning king did tax,
From his less wealthy neighbours he exacts;
Spares his own flocks, and takes the poor man's beast.
Obedient to his bidding, lo, I am,
A zealous, meek, *contributory*—Lamb.

IN THE ALBUM OF EDITH SOUTHEY.

In Christian world MARY the garland wears!
REBECCA sweetens on a Hebrew's ear;
Quakers for pure PRISCILLA are more clear;
And the light Gaul by amorous NINON swears.
Among the lesser lights how LUCY shines!
What air of fragrance ROSAMOND throws around!
How like a hymn doth sweet CECILIA sound!
Of MARTHAS, and of ABIGAILS, few lines

---

[1] *Acetaria*, a discourse on Sallets, by J. E., 1706.

Have bragg'd in verse. Of coarsest household stuff
Should homely JOAN be fashioned. But can
You BARBARA resist, or MARIAN?
And is not CLARE for love excuse enough?
Yet, by my faith in numbers, I profess,
These all, than Saxon EDITH, please me less.
1833.

THE SELF-ENCHANTED.

I HAD sense in dreams of a beauty rare,
Whom Fate had spell-bound, and rooted there,
Stooping, like some enchanted theme,
Over the marge of that crystal stream,
Where the blooming Greek, to Echo blind,
With self-love fond, had to waters pined.
Ages had waked, and ages slept,
And that bending posture still she kept:
For her eyes she may not turn away,
Till a fairer object shall pass that way—
Till an image more beauteous this world can show,
Than her own which she sees in the mirror below.

Pore on, fair creature! for ever pore,
Nor dream to be disenchanted more;
For vain is expectance, and wish is vain,
Till a new Narcissus can come again.
1832.

TO A FRIEND, ON HIS MARRIAGE.

What makes a happy wedlock? What has fate
Not given to thee in thy well-chosen mate?
Good sense—good humour;—these are trivial things,
Dear M——, that each trite encomiast sings.
But she hath these, and more. A mind exempt
From every low-bred passion, where contempt,
Nor envy, nor detraction, ever found
A harbour yet; an understanding sound;

TO LOUISA M————.

Just views of right and wrong; perception full
Of the deform'd, and of the beautiful,
In life and manners; wit above her sex,
Which, as a gem, her sprightly converse decks;
Exuberant fancies, prodigal of mirth,
To gladden woodland walk, or winter hearth;
A noble nature, conqueror in the strife
Of conflict with a hard discouraging life,
Strengthening the veins of virtue, past the power
Of those whose days have been one silken hour,
Spoil'd fortune's pamper'd offspring; a keen sense
Alike of benefit, and of offence.
With reconcilement quick, that instant springs
From the charged heart with nimble angel wings;
While grateful feelings, like a signet sign'd
By a strong hand, seem burnt into her mind.
If these, dear friend, a dowry can confer
Richer than land, thou hast them all in her;
And beauty, which some hold the chiefest boon,
Is in thy bargain for a make-weight thrown.

1833.

TO LOUISA M————,

Whom I used to call "Monkey."

Louisa, serious grown and mild,
I knew you once a romping child,
Obstreperous much and very wild.

Then you would clamber up my knees,
And strive with every art to tease,
When every art of yours could please.

These things would scarce be proper now,
But they are gone, I know not how,
And woman's written on your brow.

Time draws his finger o'er the scene;
But I cannot forget between
The Thing to me you once have been;

Each sportive sally, wild escape,—
The scoff, the banter, and the jape,—
And antics of my gamesome Ape.

FREE THOUGHTS ON SEVERAL EMINENT COMPOSERS.

Some cry up Haydn, some Mozart,
Just as the whim bites; for my part,
I do not care a farthing candle
For either of them, or for Handel.—
Cannot a man live free and easy,
Without admiring Pergolesi?
Or through the world with comfort go
That never heard of Doctor Blow?
So help me Heaven, I hardly have;
And yet I eat, and drink, and shave,
Like other people, if you watch it,
And know no more of stave or crotchet
Than did the primitive Peruvians;
Or those old ante-queer-diluvians
That lived in the unwash'd world with Jubal,
Before that dirty blacksmith Tubal,
By stroke on anvil, or by summat,
Found out, to his great surprise, the gamut.
I care no more for Cimarosa
Than he did for Salvator Rosa,
Being no painter; and bad luck
Be mine, if I can bear that Gluck!
Old Tycho Brahe, and modern Herschel,
Had something in them; but who's Purcel?
The devil with his foot so cloven,
For aught I care, may take Beethoven;

And, if the bargain does not suit,
I'll throw him Weber in to boot!
There's not the splitting of a splinter
To choose 'twixt him last named, and Winter.
Of Doctor Pepusch old Queen Dido
Knew just as much, God knows, as I do.
I would not go four miles to visit
Sebastian Bach (or Batch, which is it?)
No more I would for Bononcini.
As for Novello, or Rossini,
I shall not say a word to grieve 'em,
Because they're living; so I leave 'em.

TO MARGARET W——.

MARGARET, in happy hour
Christen'd from that humble flower
   Which we a daisy call!
May thy pretty namesake be
In all things a type of thee,
   And image thee in all.

Like *it* you show a modest face,
An unpretending native grace;—
   The tulip, and the pink,
The china and the damask rose,
And every flaunting flower that blows,
   In the comparing shrink.

Of lowly fields you think no scorn;
Yet gayest gardens would adorn,
   And grace, wherever set.
Home-seated in your lonely bower,
Or wedded—a transplanted flower—
   I bless you, Margaret!

October 8, 1834.

ROSAMUND GRAY.

Chapter I.

It was noontide. The sun was very hot. An old gentlewoman sat spinning in a little arbour at the door of her cottage. She was blind; and her granddaughter was reading the Bible to her. The old lady had just left her work, to attend to the story of Ruth.

"Orpah kissed her mother-in-law; but Ruth clave unto her." It was a passage she could not let pass without a *comment.* The moral she drew from it was not very *new*, to be sure. The girl had heard it a hundred times before—and a hundred times more she could have heard it, without suspecting it to be tedious. Rosamund loved her grandmother.

The old lady loved Rosamund too; and she had reason for so doing. Rosamund was to her at once a child and a servant. She had only *her* left in the world. They two lived together.

They had once known better days. The story of Rosamund's parents, their failure, their folly, and distresses, may be told another time. Our tale hath grief enough in it.

It was now about a year and a half since old Margaret Gray had sold off all her effects, to pay the debts of Rosamund's father—just after the mother had died of a broken heart; for her husband had fled his country to hide his shame in a foreign land. At that period the old lady retired to a small cottage, in the village of Widford, in Hertfordshire.

Rosamund, in her thirteenth year, was left destitute, without fortune or friends; she went with her grandmother. In all this time she had served her faithfully and lovingly.

Old Margaret Gray, when she first came into these parts, had eyes, and could see. The neighbours said, they had been dimmed by weeping: be that as it may, she was latterly grown quite blind. "God is very good to us, child; I can *feel* you yet." This she would sometimes say; and we need not wonder to hear, that Rosamund clave unto her grandmother.

Margaret retained a spirit unbroken by calamity. There was a principle *within*, which it seemed as if no outward circumstances could reach. It was a *religious* principle, and she had taught it to Rosamund; for the girl had mostly resided with her grandmother from her earliest years. Indeed she had taught her all that she knew herself and the old lady's knowledge did not extend a vast way.

Margaret had drawn her maxims from observation; and a pretty long experience in life had contributed to make her, at times, a little *positive;* but Rosamund never argued with her grandmother.

Their library consisted chiefly in a large family Bible, with notes and expositions by various learned expositors from Bishop Jewell downwards.

This might never be suffered to lie about like other books—but was kept constantly wrapped up in a handsome case of green velvet, with gold tassels—the only relic of departed grandeur they had brought with them to the cottage—everything else of value had been sold off for the purpose above-mentioned.

This Bible Rosamund, when a child, had never dared to open without permission; and even yet, from habit, continued the custom. Margaret had parted with none of her *authority;* indeed it was never exerted with much harshness; and happy was Rosamund, though a girl grown, when she could obtain leave to read her Bible. It was a treasure too valuable for an indiscriminate use; and Margaret still pointed out to her granddaughter *where to read*.

Besides this, they had the "Complete Angler, or Contemplative Man's Recreation," with cuts—"Pilgrim's Progress," the first part—a "Cookery Book," with a few dry sprigs of rosemary and lavender stuck here and there between the leaves (I suppose, to point to some of the old lady's most favourite receipts) and there was "Wither's Emblems," an old book, and quaint. The old-fashioned pictures in this last book were among the first exciters of the infant Rosamund's curiosity. Her contemplation had fed upon them in rather older years.

Rosamund had not read many books besides these; or if any, they had been only occasional companions: these were to Rosamund as old friends, that she had long known. I know not, whether the peculiar cast of her mind might not be traced, in part, to a tincture she had received, in early life, from Walton, and Wither, from John Bunyan, and her Bible.

Rosamund's mind was pensive and reflective, rather than what passes usually for *clever* or *acute*. From a child she was remarkably shy and thoughtful—this was taken for stupidity and want of feeling; and the child has been sometimes whipped for being a *stubborn thing*, when her little heart was almost bursting with affection.

Even now her grandmother would often reprove her, when she found her too grave or melancholy; give her sprightly lectures about good humour and rational mirth; and not unfrequently fall a crying herself, to the great discredit of her lecture. Those tears endeared her the more to Rosamund.

Margaret would say, "Child, I love you to cry, when I think you are only remembering your poor dear father and mother—I would have you think about them sometimes—it would be strange if you did not—but I fear,

Rosamund, I fear, girl, you sometimes think too deeply about your own situation and poor prospects in life. When you do so, you do wrong—remember the naughty rich man in the parable. He never had any good thoughts about God, and his religion: and that might have been your case."

Rosamund, at these times, could not reply to her: she was not in the habit of *arguing* with her grandmother; so she was quite silent on these occasions—or else the girl knew well enough herself, that she had only been sad to think of the desolate condition of her best friend, to see her, in her old age, so infirm and blind. But she had never been used to make excuses, when the old lady said she was doing wrong.

The neighbours were all very kind to them. The veriest rustics never passed them without a bow, or a pulling off of the hat—some show of courtesy, awkward indeed, but affectionate—with a "good morrow, madam," or "young madam," as it might happen.

Rude and savage natures, who seem born with a propensity to express contempt for anything that looks like prosperity, yet felt respect for its declining lustre.

The farmers, and better sort of people (as they are called) all promised to provide for Rosamund, when her grandmother should die. Margaret trusted in God, and believed them.

She used to say, "I have lived many years in the world, and have never known people, *good people,* to be left without some friend; a relation, a benefactor, a *something.* God knows our wants—that it is not good for man or woman to be alone; and he always sends us an helpmate, a leaning-place, a *somewhat.*" Upon this sure ground of experience, did Margaret build her trust in Providence.

Chapter II.

ROSAMUND had just made an end of her story (as I was about to relate) and was listening to the application of the moral (which said application she was old enough to have made herself, but her grandmother still continued to treat her in many respects as a child, and Rosamund was in no haste to lay claim to the title of womanhood) when a young gentleman made his appearance, and interrupted them.

It was young Allan Clare, who had brought a present of peaches, and some roses, for Rosamund.

He laid his little basket down on a seat of the arbour; and in a respectful tone of voice, as though he were addressing a parent, inquired of Margaret, "how she did."

The old lady seemed pleased with his attentions—answered his inquiries by saying, that "her cough was less troublesome a nights, but she had not yet got rid of it, and probably she never might; but she did not like to tease young people with an account of her infirmities."

A few kind words passed on either side, when young Clare, glancing a tender look at the girl, who had all this time been silent, took leave of them with saying, "I shall bring *Elinor* to see you in the evening."

When he was gone, the old lady began to prattle.

"That is a sweet dispositioned youth, and I *do* love him dearly, I must say it—there is such a modesty in all he says or does—he should not come here so often, to be sure, but I don't know how to help it; there is so much goodness in him, I can't find in my heart to forbid him. But, Rosamund, girl, I must tell you beforehand; when you grow older Mr. Clare must be no companion for *you*—while you were both so young, it was all very well—but the time is coming, when folks will think harm of it, if a rich young gentleman, like Mr. Clare, comes so often to our poor cottage. Dost hear, girl? why don't you answer? come, I did not mean to say anything to hurt you—speak to me, Rosamund—nay, I must not have you be sullen—I don't love people that are sullen."

And in this manner was this poor soul running on, unheard and unheeded, when it occurred to her that possibly the girl might not be *within hearing*.

M

And true it was, that Rosamund had slunk away at the first mention of Mr. Clare's good qualities: and when she returned, which was not till a few minutes after Margaret had made an end of her fine harangue, it is certain her cheeks *did* look very *rosy*. That might have been from the heat of the day or from exercise, for she had been walking in the garden.

Margaret, we know, was blind; and, in this case, it was lucky for Rosamund that she was so, or she might have made some not unlikely surmises.

I must not have my reader infer from this, that I at all think it likely, a young maid of fourteen would fall in love without asking her grandmother's leave—the thing itself is not to be conceived.

To obviate all suspicions, I am disposed to communicate a little anecdote of Rosamund.

A month or two back her grandmother had been giving her the strictest prohibitions, in her walks, not to go near a certain spot, which was dangerous from the circumstance of a huge overgrown oak-tree spreading its prodigious arms across a deep chalk-pit, which they partly concealed.

To this fatal place Rosamund came one day—female curiosity, we know, is older than the flood—let us not think hardly of the girl, if she partook of the sexual failing.

Rosamund ventured farther and farther—climbed along one of the branches—approached the forbidden chasm—her foot slipped—she was not killed—but it was by a mercy she escaped—other branches intercepted her fall—and with a palpitating heart she made her way back to the cottage.

It happened that evening, that her grandmother was in one of her best humours, caressed Rosamund, talked of old times, and what a blessing it was they two found a shelter in their little cottage, and in conclusion told Rosamund "she was a good girl, and God would one day reward her for her kindness to her old blind grandmother."

This was more than Rosamund could bear. Her morning's disobedience came fresh in her mind, she felt she did not deserve all this from Margaret, and at last burst into a fit of crying, and made confession of her fault. The old gentlewoman kissed and forgave her.

Rosamund never went near that naughty chasm again.

Margaret would never have heard of this, if Rosamund had not told of it herself. But this young maid had a delicate moral sense, which would not suffer her to take advantage of her grandmother, to deceive her, or conceal anything from her, though Margaret was old, and blind, and easy to be imposed upon.

Another virtuous *trait* I recollect of Rosamund, and, now I am in the vein, I will tell it.

Some, I know, will think these things trifles—and they are so—but if these *minutiæ* make my reader better acquainted with Rosamund, I am content to abide the imputation.

These promises of character, hints, and early indications of a *sweet nature*, are to me more dear, and choice in the selection, than any of those pretty wild flowers, which this young maid, this virtuous Rosamund, has ever gathered in a fine May morning, to make a posy to place in the bosom of her old blind friend.

Rosamund had a very just notion of drawing, and would often employ her talent in making sketches of the surrounding scenery.

On a landscape, a larger piece than she had ever yet attempted, she had now been working for three or four months. She had taken great pains with it, given much time to it, and it was nearly finished. For *whose* particular inspection it was designed, I will not venture to conjecture. We know it could not have been for her grandmother's.

One day she went out on a short errand, and left her landscape on the table. When she returned, she found it *gone*.

Rosamund from the first suspected some mischief, but

held her tongue. At length she made the fatal discovery. Margaret, in her absence, had laid violent hands on it; not knowing what it was, but taking it for some waste paper, had torn it in half, and with one half of this elaborate composition had twisted herself up—a thread-paper!

Rosamund spread out her hands at sight of the disaster, gave her grandmother a roguish smile, but said not a word. She knew the poor soul would only fret, if she told her of it,—and when once Margaret was set a-fretting for other people's misfortunes, the fit held her pretty long.

So Rosamund that very afternoon began another piece of the same size and subject; and Margaret, to her dying day, never dreamed of the mischief she had unconsciously done.

Chapter III.

ROSAMUND GRAY was the most beautiful young creature that eyes ever beheld. Her face had the sweetest expression in it—a gentleness—a modesty—a timidity—a certain charm—a grace without a name.

There was a sort of melancholy mingled in her smile. It was not the thoughtless levity of a girl—it was not the restrained simper of premature womanhood—it was something which the poet Young might have remembered, when he composed that perfect line,

"Soft, modest, melancholy, female, fair."

She was a mild-eyed maid, and everybody loved her. Young Allan Clare, when but a boy, sighed for her.

Her yellow hair fell in bright and curling clusters, like

"those hanging locks
Of young Apollo."

Her voice was trembling and musical. A graceful diffidence pleaded for her whenever she spake—and, if she said but little, that little found its way to the heart.

Young, and artless, and innocent, meaning no harm, and thinking none; affectionate, as a smiling infant—playful, yet unobtrusive, as a weaned lamb—everybody loved her. Young Allan Clare, when but a boy, sighed for her.

The moon is shining in so brightly at my window, where I write, that I feel it is a crime not to suspend my employment awhile to gaze at her.

See how she glideth, in maiden honour, through the clouds, who divide on either side to do her homage.

Beautiful vision!—as I contemplate thee, an internal harmony is communicated to my mind, a moral brightness, a tacit analogy of mental purity; a calm like *that* we ascribe in fancy to the favoured inhabitants of thy fairy regions, "argent fields."

I marvel not, O moon, that heathen people, in the "olden times," did worship thy deity—Cynthia, Diana, Hecate. Christian Europe invokes thee not by these names now—her idolatry is of a blacker stain; Belial is her God—she worships Mammon.

False things are told concerning thee, fair Planet—For I will ne'er believe, that thou canst take a perverse pleasure in distorting the brains of us poor mortals. Lunatics! moon-struck! Calumny invented, and Folly took up, these names. I would hope better things from thy mild aspect and benign influences.

Lady of Heaven, thou lendest thy pure lamp to light the way to the Virgin Mourner, when she goes to seek the tomb where her Warrior Lover lies.

Friend of the distressed, thou speakest only *peace* to the lonely sufferer, who walks forth in the placid evening, beneath thy gentle light, to chide at fortune, or to complain of changed friends, or unhappy loves.

Do I dream, or doth not even now a heavenly calm descend from thee into my bosom, as I meditate on the chaste loves of Rosamund and her Clare?

Chapter IV.

Allan Clare was just two years older than Rosamund. He was a boy of fourteen, when he first became acquainted with her—it was soon after she had come to reside with her grandmother at Widford.

He met her by chance one day, carrying a pitcher in her hand, which she had been filling from a neighbouring well—the pitcher was heavy, and she seemed to be bending with its weight.

Allan insisted on carrying it for her—for he thought it a sin, that a delicate young maid, like her, should be so employed, and he stand idle by.

Allan had a propensity to do little kind offices for everybody—but at sight of Rosamund Gray his first fire was kindled—his young mind seemed to have found an object, and his enthusiasm was from that time forth awakened. His visits, from that day, were pretty frequent at the cottage.

He was never happier than when he could get Rosamund to walk out with him. He would make her admire the scenes he admired—fancy the wild flowers he fancied—watch the clouds he was watching—and not unfrequently repeat to her poetry, which he loved, and make her love it.

On their return, the old lady, who considered them yet as but children, would bid Rosamund fetch Mr. Clare a glass of her currant wine, a bowl of new milk, or some cheap dainty, which was more welcome to Allan than the costliest delicacies of a prince's court.

The boy and girl, for they were no more at that age, grew fond of each other—more fond than either of them suspected.

>"They would sit and sigh,
>And look upon each other, and conceive
>Not what they ail'd; yet something they did ail,
>And yet were well—and yet they were not well;
>And what was their disease, they could not tell."

And thus,
> "In this first garden of their simpleness
> They spent their childhood."

A circumstance had lately happened, which in some sort altered the nature of their attachment.

Rosamund was one day reading the tale of "Julia de Roubigné,"—a book which young Clare had lent her—

Allan was standing by, looking over her, with one hand thrown round her neck, and a finger of the other pointing to a passage in Julia's third letter.

"Maria! in my hours of visionary indulgence, I have sometimes painted to myself a *husband*—no matter whom —comforting me amidst the distresses, which fortune had laid upon us. I have smiled upon him through my tears; tears, not of anguish, but of tenderness;—our children were playing around us, unconscious of misfortune; we had taught them to be humble, and to be happy; our little shed was reserved to us, and their smiles to cheer it. I have imagined the luxury of such a scene, and affliction became a part of my dream of happiness."

The girl blushed as she read, and trembled—she had a sort of confused sensation, that Allan was noticing her —yet she durst not lift her eyes from the book, but continued reading, scarce knowing what she read.

Allan guessed the cause of her confusion. Allan trembled too—his colour came and went—his feelings became impetuous—and, flinging both arms round her neck, he kissed his young favourite.

Rosamund was vexed, and pleased, soothed and frightened, all in a moment—a fit of tears came to her relief.

Allan had indulged before in these little freedoms, and Rosamund had thought no harm of them—but from this time the girl grew timid and reserved—distant in her manner, and careful of her behaviour, in Allan's presence —not seeking his society, as before, but rather shunning it—delighting more to feed upon his idea in absence.

Allan too, from this day, seemed changed: his manner became, though not less tender, yet more respectful and diffident—his bosom felt a throb it had till now not known, in the society of Rosamund—and, if he was less familiar with her than in former times, that charm of delicacy had superadded a grace to Rosamund, which, while he feared, he loved.

There is a *mysterious character*, heightened indeed by fancy and passion, but not without foundation in reality and observation, which true lovers have ever imputed to the object of their affections. This character Rosamund had now acquired with Allan—something *angelic, perfect, exceeding nature.*

Young Clare dwelt very near to the cottage. He had lost his parents, who were rather wealthy, early in life; and was left to the care of a sister, some ten years older than himself.

Elinor Clare was an excellent young lady—discreet, intelligent, and affectionate. Allan revered her as a parent, while he loved her as his own familiar friend. He told all the little secrets of his heart to her—but there was *one*, which he had hitherto unaccountably concealed from her—namely, the extent of his regard for Rosamund.

Elinor knew of his visits to the cottage, and was no stranger to the persons of Margaret and her granddaughter. She had several times met them, when she has been walking with her brother—a civility usually passed on either side—but Elinor avoided troubling her brother with any unseasonable questions.

Allan's heart often beat, and he had been going to tell his sister *all*—but something like shame (false or true, I shall not stay to inquire) had hitherto kept him back—still the secret, unrevealed, hung upon his conscience like a crime—for his temper had a sweet and noble frankness in it, which bespake him yet a virgin from the world.

There was a fine openness in his countenance—the character of it somewhat resembled Rosamund's—except that more fire and enthusiasm were discernible in Allan's —his eyes were of a darker blue than Rosamund's—his hair was of a chestnut colour—his cheeks ruddy, and tinged with brown. There was a cordial sweetness in Allan's smile, the like to which I never saw in any other face.

Elinor had hitherto connived at her brother's attachment to Rosamund. Elinor, I believe, was something of a physiognomist, and thought she could trace in the countenance and manner of Rosamund qualities which no brother of hers need be ashamed to love.

The time was now come when Elinor was desirous of knowing her brother's favourite more intimately — an opportunity offered of breaking the matter to Allan.

The morning of the day in which he carried his present of fruit and flowers to Rosamund, his sister had observed him more than usually busy in the garden, culling fruit with a nicety of choice not common to him.

She came up to him, unobserved, and, taking him by the arm, inquired, with a questioning smile—"What are you doing, Allan? and who are those peaches designed for?"

"For Rosamund Gray," he replied; and his heart seemed relieved of a burthen, which had long oppressed it.

"I have a mind to become acquainted with your handsome friend—will you introduce me, Allan? I think I should like to go and see her this afternoon."

"Do go, do go, Elinor—you don't know what a good creature she is—and old blind Margaret, you will like *her* very much."

His sister promised to accompany him after dinner; and they parted. Allan gathered no more peaches, but hastily cropping a few roses to fling into his basket, went away with it half filled, being impatient to announce to Rosamund the coming of her promised visitor.

Chapter V.

When Allan returned home, he found an invitation had been left for him, in his absence, to spend that evening with a young friend, who had just quitted a public school in London, and was come to pass one night in his father's house at Widford, previous to his departure the next morning for Edinburgh University.

It was Allan's bosom friend—they had not met for some months—and it was probable, a much longer time must intervene, before they should meet again.

Yet Allan could not help looking a little blank, when he first heard of the invitation. This was to have been an important evening. But Elinor soon relieved her brother, by expressing her readiness to go alone to the cottage.

"I will not lose the pleasure I promised myself, whatever you may determine upon, Allan—I will go by myself, rather than be disappointed."

"Will you, will you, Elinor?"

Elinor promised to go—and I believe, Allan, on a second thought, was not very sorry to be spared the awkwardness of introducing two persons to each other, both so dear to him, but either of whom might happen not much to fancy the other.

At times, indeed, he was confident that Elinor *must* love Rosamund, and Rosamund *must* love Elinor—but there were also times in which he felt misgivings—it was an event he could scarce hope for very joy!

Allan's *real presence* that evening was more at the cottage than at the house where his *bodily semblance* was visiting—his friend could not help complaining of a certain absence of mind, a *coldness* he called it.

It might have been expected, and in the course of things predicted, that Allan would have asked his friend some questions, of what had happened since their last meeting, what his feelings were on leaving school, the probable time when they should meet again, and a hundred natural questions, which friendship is most lavish of at such times; but nothing of all this ever occurred to Allan—they did not even settle the method of their future correspondence.

The consequence was, as might have been expected, Allan's friend thought him much altered, and, after his departure, sat down to compose a doleful sonnet about a "faithless friend." I do not find that he ever finished it—indignation, or a dearth of rhymes, causing him to break off in the middle.

Chapter VI.

In my catalogue of the little library at the cottage, I forgot to mention a book of Common Prayer. My reader's fancy might easily have supplied the omission—old ladies of Margaret's stamp (God bless them) may as well be without their spectacles, or their elbow chair, as their prayer-book—I love them for it.

Margaret's was a handsome octavo, printed by Baskerville, the binding red, and fortified with silver at the edges. Out of this book it was their custom every afternoon to read the proper psalms appointed for the day.

The way they managed was this: they took verse by verse—Rosamund *read* her little portion, and Margaret repeated hers, in turn, from memory—for Margaret could say all the psalter by heart, and a good part of the Bible besides. She would not unfrequently put the girl right, when she stumbled or skipped. This Margaret imputed to giddiness—a quality, which Rosamund was by no means remarkable for—but old ladies, like Margaret, are not, in all instances, alike discriminative.

They had been employed in this manner just before Miss Clare arrived at the cottage. The psalm they had been reading, was the hundred and fourth—Margaret was naturally led by it into a discussion of the works of creation.

There had been *thunder* in the course of the day—an occasion of instruction which the old lady never let pass—she began—

"Thunder has a very awful sound—some say, God Almighty is angry whenever it thunders—that it is the voice of God speaking to us—for my part, I am not afraid of it——."

And in this manner the old lady was going on to particularise, as usual, its beneficial effects, in clearing the air, destroying of vermin, etc., when the entrance of Miss Clare put an end to her discourse.

Rosamund received her with respectful tenderness—and, taking her grandmother by the hand, said with great sweetness, "Miss Clare is come to see you, grandmother."

"I beg pardon, lady—I cannot *see* you—but you are heartily welcome—is your brother with you, Miss Clare? I don't hear him."

"He could not come, madam, but he sends his love by me."

"You have an excellent brother, Miss Clare—but pray do us the honour to take some refreshment—Rosamund——"

And the old lady was going to give directions for a bottle of her currant wine—when Elinor, smiling, said "she was come to drink a dish of tea with her, and expected to find no ceremony."

"After tea I promise myself a walk with *you*, Rosamund, if your grandmother can spare you——" Rosamund looked at her grandmother.

"O for that matter, I should be sorry to debar the girl from any pleasure—I am sure it's lonesome enough for her to be with *me* always—and, if Miss Clare will take you out, child, I shall do very well by myself till you return—it will not be the first time, you know, that I have been left here alone—some of the neighbours will be dropping in by-and-by—or if *not*, I shall take no harm."

Rosamund had all the simple manners of a child—she kissed her grandmother, and looked happy.

All tea-time the old lady's discourse was little more than a panegyric on young Clare's good qualities. Elinor looked at her young friend, and smiled. Rosamund was beginning to look grave—but there was a cordial sunshine in the face of Elinor, before which any clouds of reserve that had been gathering on Rosamund's, soon brake away.

"Does your grandmother ever go out, Rosamund?"

Margaret prevented the girl's reply by saying,—"My dear young lady, I am an old woman, and very infirm—Rosamund takes me a few paces beyond the door sometimes—but I walk very badly—I love best to sit in our little arbour, when the sun shines—I yet can feel it warm and cheerful—and, if I lose the beauties of the season, I can still remember them with pleasure, and rejoice that younger eyes than mine can see and enjoy them—I shall be very happy if you and Rosamund can take delight in this fine summer evening."

"I shall want to rob you of Rosamund's company now and then, if we like one another. I had hoped to have seen *you*, madam, at our house. I don't know whether we could not make room for you to come and live with us—what say you to it?—Allan would be proud to tend you, I am sure; and Rosamund and I should be nice company."

Margaret was all unused to such kindnesses, and wept—Margaret had a great spirit—yet she was not above accepting an obligation from a worthy person—there was a delicacy in Miss Clare's manner—she could have no interest, but pure goodness, to induce her to make the offer—at length the old lady spake from a full heart.

"Miss Clare, this little cottage received us in our distress—it gave us shelter when we had *no home*—we have praised God in it—and, while life remains, I think I shall never part from it—Rosamund does everything for me——"

"And will do, grandmother, as long as I live"—and then Rosamund fell a-crying.

"You are a good girl, Rosamund, and, if you do but find friends when I am dead and gone, I shall want no better accommodation while I live—but God bless you, lady, a thousand times for your kind offer."

Elinor was moved to tears, and, affecting a sprightliness, bade Rosamund prepare for her walk. The girl put on her white silk bonnet; and Elinor thought she never beheld so lovely a creature.

They took leave of Margaret, and walked out together —they rambled over all Rosamund's favourite haunts— through many a sunny field—by secret glade or woodwalk, where the girl had wandered so often with her beloved Clare.

Who now so happy as Rosamund? She had ofttimes heard Allan speak with great tenderness of his sister— she was now rambling, arm in arm, with that very sister, the "vaunted sister" of her friend, her beloved Clare.

Not a tree, not a bush, scarce a wild flower in their path, but revived in Rosamund some tender recollection, a conversation perhaps, or some chaste endearment. Life, and a new scene of things, were now opening before her —she was got into a fairy-land of uncertain existence.

Rosamund was too happy to talk much—but Elinor was delighted with her, when she *did* talk: the girl's remarks were suggested, most of them, by the passing scene—and they betrayed, all of them, the liveliness of present impulse :—her conversation did not consist in a comparison of vapid feeling, and interchange of sentiment lip-deep—it had all the freshness of young sensation in it.

Sometimes they talked of Allan.

"Allan is very good," said Rosamund, "very good *indeed* to my grandmother—he will sit with her, and hear her stories, and read to her, and try to divert her a hundred ways. I wonder sometimes he is not tired. She talks him to death!"

"Then you confess, Rosamund, that the old lady *does* tire *you* sometimes."

"O no, I did not mean *that*—it's very different—I am used to all her ways, and I can humour her, and please her, and I ought to do it, for she is the only friend I ever had in the world."

The new friends did not conclude their walk till it was late, and Rosamund began to be apprehensive about the old lady, who had been all this time alone.

On their return to the cottage, they found that Margaret had been somewhat impatient—old ladies, *good old ladies*, will be so at times—age is timorous, and suspicious of danger, where no danger is.

Besides, it was Margaret's bedtime, for she kept very good hours—indeed, in the distribution of her meals, and sundry other particulars, she resembled the livers in the antique world, more than might well beseem a creature of this.

So the new friends parted for that night, Elinor having made Margaret promise to give Rosamund leave to come and see her the next day.

Chapter VII.

Miss Clare, we may be sure, made her brother very happy when she told him of the engagement she had made for the morrow, and how delighted she had been with his handsome friend.

Allan, I believe, got little sleep that night. I know not, whether joy be not a more troublesome bed-fellow than grief—hope keeps a body very wakeful, I know.

Elinor Clare was the best good creature—the least selfish human being I ever knew—always at work for other people's good, planning other people's happiness—continually forgetful to consult for her own personal gratifications, except, indirectly, in the welfare of another, while her parents lived, the most attentive of daughters—

since they died, the kindest of sisters—I never knew but *one* like her.

It happens that I have some of this young lady's *letters* in my possession, I shall present my reader with one of them—it was written a short time after the death of her mother, and addressed to a cousin, a dear friend of Elinor's, who was then on the point of being married to Mr. Beaumont of Staffordshire, and had invited Elinor to assist at her nuptials. I will transcribe it with minute fidelity.

Elinor Clare to Maria Leslie.

WIDFORD, *July the* —, 17—.

Health, innocence, and beauty, shall be thy bridesmaids, my sweet cousin. I have no heart to undertake the office. Alas! what have I to do in the house of feasting?

Maria! I fear, lest my griefs should prove obtrusive. Yet bear with me a little—I have recovered already a share of my former spirits.

I fear more for Allan than myself. The loss of two such parents, with so short an interval, bears very heavy on him. The boy *hangs* about me from morning till night. He is perpetually forcing a smile into his poor pale cheeks —you know the sweetness of his smile, Maria.

To-day, after dinner, when he took his glass of wine in his hand, he burst into tears, and would not, or could not then, tell me the reason—afterwards he told me— "he had been used to drink mamma's health after dinner, and *that* came in his head, and made him cry." I feel the claims the boy has upon me—I perceive that I am living to *some end*—and the thought supports me.

Already I have attained to a state of complacent feelings—my mother's lessons were not thrown away upon her Elinor.

In the visions of last night her spirit seemed to stand at my bedside—a light, as of noonday, shone upon the room—she opened my curtains—she smiled upon me with the same placid smile as in her lifetime. I felt no fear.

"Elinor," she said, "for my sake take care of young Allan," —and I awoke with calm feelings.

Maria! shall not the meeting of blessed spirits, think you, be something like this? I think, I could even now behold my mother without dread—I would ask pardon of her for all my past omissions of duty, for all the little asperities in my temper, which have so often grieved her gentle spirit when living. Maria! I think she would not turn away from me.

Oftentimes a feeling, more vivid than memory, brings her before me—I see her sit in her old elbow chair, her arms folded upon her lap, a tear upon her cheek, that seems to upbraid her unkind daughter for some inattention—I wipe it away—and kiss her honoured lips.

Maria! when I have been fancying all this, Allan will come in, with his poor eyes red with weeping, and taking me by the hand, destroy the vision in a moment.

I am prating to you, my sweet cousin, but it is the prattle of the heart, which Maria loves. Besides, whom have I to talk to of these things, but you—you have been my counsellor in times past, my companion, and sweet familiar friend. Bear with me a little—I mourn the "cherishers of my infancy."

I sometimes count it a blessing, that my father did not prove the *survivor*. You know something of his story. You know there was a foul tale current, it was the busy malice of that bad man, S——, which helped to spread it abroad—you will recollect the active good nature of our friends W—— and T——; what pains they took to undeceive people—with the better sort their kind labours prevailed; but there was still a party, who shut their ears. You know the issue of it. My father's great spirit bore up against it for some time—my father never was a *bad* man —but that spirit was broken at the last, and the greatly-injured man was forced to leave his old paternal dwelling in Staffordshire—for the neighbours had begun to point at him. Maria! I have *seen* them *point* at him, and have been ready to drop.

In this part of the country, where the slander had not reached he sought a retreat—and he found a still more grateful asylum in the daily solicitudes of the best of wives.

"An enemy hath done this," I have heard him say—and at such times my mother would speak to him so soothingly of forgiveness, and long-suffering, and the bearing of injuries with patience; would heal all his wounds with so gentle a touch;—I have seen the old man weep like a child.

The gloom that beset his mind, at times betrayed him into scepticism—he has doubted if there be a Providence! I have heard him say, "GOD has built a brave world, but methinks he has left his creatures to bustle in it *how they may*."

At such times he could not endure to hear my mother talk in a religious strain. He would say, "Woman, have done—you confound, you perplex me, when you talk of these matters, and for one day at least unfit me for the business of life."

I have seen her look at him—O GOD, Maria! such a *look!* it plainly spake, that she was willing to have shared her precious hope with the partner of her earthly cares—but she found a repulse.

Deprived of such a wife, think you the old man could have long endured his existence? or what consolation would his wretched daughter have had to offer him, but silent and imbecile tears?

My sweet cousin, you will think me tedious—and I am so—but it does me good to talk these matters over. And do not you be alarmed for me—my sorrows are subsiding into a deep and sweet resignation. I shall soon be sufficiently composed, I know it, to participate in my friend's happiness.

Let me call her, while yet I may, my own Maria Leslie! Methinks, I shall not like you by any other name. Beaumont! Maria Beaumont! it hath a strange sound with it, I shall never be reconciled to this name—

but do not you fear—Maria Leslie shall plead with me for Maria Beaumont.

And now, my sweet friend, God love you, and your
ELINOR CLARE.

I find in my collection, several letters, written soon after the date of the preceding, and addressed all of them to Maria Beaumont. I am tempted to make some short extracts from these—my tale will suffer interruption by them—but I was willing to preserve whatever memorials I could of Elinor Clare.

From Elinor Clare to Maria Beaumont.
(AN EXTRACT.)

——I have been strolling out for half an hour in the fields; and my mind has been occupied by thoughts, which Maria has a right to participate. I have been bringing my *mother* to my recollection. My heart ached with the remembrance of infirmities, that made her closing years of life so sore a trial to her.

I was concerned to think that our family differences have been one source of disquiet to her. I am sensible that *this last* we are apt to exaggerate after a person's death; and surely, in the main, there was considerable harmony among the members of our little family, still I was concerned to think, that we ever gave her gentle spirit disquiet.

I thought on years back—on all my parents' friends—the H——s, the F——s, on D——, S——, and on many a merry evening in the fire-side circle, in that comfortable back parlour—it is never used now.

Oh, ye *Matravises*[1] of the age, ye know not what ye lose, in despising these petty topics of endeared remembrance, associated circumstances of past times; ye know not the throbbings of the heart, tender yet affectionately familiar, which accompany the dear and honoured names of *father* or of *mother*.

[1] This name will be explained presently.

Maria! I thought on all these things; my heart ached at the review of them—it yet aches, while I write this—but I am never so satisfied with my train of thoughts, as when they run upon these subjects; the tears they draw from us, meliorate and soften the heart, and keep fresh within us that memory of dear friends dead, which alone can fit us for a readmission to their society hereafter.

From another Letter.

——I had a bad dream this morning, that Allan was dead; and who, of all persons in the world, do you think, put on mourning for him? Why, *Matravis*. This alone might cure me of superstitious thoughts, if I were inclined to them; for why should Matravis *mourn* for us, or our family? *Still* it was pleasant to awake, and find it but a dream. Methinks something like an awakening from an ill dream shall the Resurrection from the dead be. Materially different from our accustomed scenes, and ways of life, the *World to come* may possibly not be; still it is represented to us under the notion of a *Rest*, a *Sabbath*, a state of bliss.

From another Letter.

——Methinks, you and I should have been born under the same roof, sucked the same milk, conned the same hornbook, thumbed the same Testament, together: —for we have been more than sisters, Maria!

Something will still be whispering to me, that I shall one day be inmate of the same dwelling with my cousin, partaker with her in all the delights, which spring from mutual good offices, kind words, attentions in sickness and in health,—conversation, sometimes innocently trivial, and at others profitably serious;—books read and commented on, together; meals eat, and walks taken, together, —and conferences, how we may best do good to this poor person or that, and wean our spirits from the world's *cares*, without divesting ourselves of its *charities*. What a picture I have drawn, Maria!—and none of all these things may ever come to pass.

From another Letter.

——Continue to write to me, my sweet cousin. Many good thoughts, resolutions, and proper views of things, pass through the mind in the course of the day, but are lost for want of committing them to paper. Seize them, Maria, as they pass, these Birds of Paradise, that show themselves and are gone, and make a grateful present of the precious fugitives to your friend.

To use a homely illustration, just rising in my fancy,—shall the good housewife take such pains in pickling and preserving her worthless fruits, her walnuts, her apricots, and quinces—and is there not much *spiritual housewifery* in treasuring up our mind's best fruits,—our heart's meditations in its most favoured moments?

This said simile is much in the fashion of the old Moralisers, such as I conceive honest Baxter to have been, such as Quarles and Wither were, with their curious, serio-comic, quaint emblems. But they sometimes reach the heart, when a more elegant simile rests in the fancy.

Not low and mean, like these, but beautifully familiarised to our conceptions, and condescending to human thoughts and notions, are all the discourses of our LORD—conveyed in parable, or similitude, what easy access do they win to the heart, through the medium of the delighted imagination! speaking of heavenly things in fable, or in simile, drawn from earth, from objects *common, accustomed*.

Life's business, with such delicious little interruptions as our correspondence affords, how pleasant it is!—why can we not paint on the dull paper our whole feelings, exquisite as they rise up?

From another Letter.

——I had meant to have left off at this place; but, looking back, I am sorry to find too gloomy a cast tincturing my last page—a representation of life false and unthankful. Life is *not* all vanity and disappointment—it hath much of evil in it, no doubt; but to those who do not misuse it, it affords comfort, *temporary* comfort, much—much that endears us to it, and dignifies it—many true and good feelings, I trust, of which we need not be ashamed—hours of tranquillity and hope. But the morning was dull and overcast, and my spirits were under a cloud. I feel my error.

Is it no blessing, that we two love one another so dearly—that Allan is left me—that you are settled in life—that worldly affairs go smooth with us both—above all, that our lot hath fallen to us in a Christian country? Maria! these things are not little. I will consider life as a long feast, and not forget to say grace.

From another Letter.

——Allan has written to me—you know, he is on a visit at his old tutor's in Gloucestershire—he is to return home on Thursday—Allan is a dear boy—he concludes his letter, which is very affectionate throughout, in this manner—

"Elinor, I charge you to learn the following stanza by heart—

> The monarch may forget his crown,
>   That on his head an hour hath been;
> The bridegroom may forget his bride
>   Was made his wedded wife yestreen,
> The mother may forget her child,
>   That smiles so sweetly on her knee:
> But I'll remember thee, Glencairn,
>   And all that thou hast done for me.

The lines are in Burns—you know, we read him for the first time together at Margate—and I have been used to refer them to you, and to call you, in my mind, *Glencairn*—for you were always very, very good to me. I had a thousand failings, but you would love me in spite of them all. I am going to drink your health."

I shall detain my reader no longer from the narrative.

Chapter VIII.

They had but four rooms in the cottage. Margaret slept in the biggest room upstairs, and her granddaughter in a kind of closet adjoining, where she could be within hearing, if her grandmother should call her in the night.

The girl was often disturbed in that manner—two or three times in a night she has been forced to leave her bed, to fetch her grandmother's cordials, or do some little service for her—but she knew, that Margaret's ailings were *real* and pressing, and Rosamund never complained—never suspected, that her grandmother's requisitions had anything unreasonable in them.

The night she parted with Miss Clare, she had helped Margaret to bed, as usual—and, after saying her prayers, as the custom was, kneeling by the old lady's bed-side, kissed her grandmother, and wished her a good-night—Margaret blessed her, and charged her to go to bed directly. It was her customary injunction, and Rosamund had never dreamed of disobeying.

So she retired to her little room. The night was warm and clear—the moon very bright—her window commanded a view of *scenes* she had been tracing in the day-time with Miss Clare.

All the events of the day past, the occurrences of their walk arose in her mind. She fancied she should like to retrace those scenes—but it was now nine o'clock, a late hour in the village.

Still she fancied it would be very charming; and then her grandmother's injunction came powerfully to her recollection—she sighed and turned from the window—and walked up and down her little room.

Ever, when she looked at the window, the wish returned. It was not so *very late*. The neighbours were yet about, passing under the window to their homes; she thought, and thought again, till her sensations became vivid, even to painfulness—her bosom was aching to give them vent.

The village clock struck ten! the neighbours ceased to pass under the window! Rosamund, stealing downstairs, fastened the latch behind her, and left the cottage.

One, that knew her, met her, and observed her with some surprise. Another recollects having wished her a good-night. Rosamund never returned to the cottage!

An old man, that lay sick in a small house adjoining to Margaret's, testified the next morning, that he had plainly heard the old creature calling for her granddaughter. All the night long she made her moan, and ceased not to call upon the name of Rosamund. But no Rosamund was there—the voice died away, but not till near daybreak.

When the neighbours came to search in the morning, Margaret was missing! She had *straggled* out of bed, and made her way into Rosamund's room—worn out with fatigue and fright, when she found the girl not there, she had laid herself down to die—and, it is thought, she died *praying*—for she was discovered in a kneeling posture, her arms and face extended on the pillow, where Rosamund had slept the night before—a smile was on her face in death.

Chapter IX.

Fain would I draw a veil over the transactions of that night—but I cannot—grief, and burning shame, forbid me to be silent—black deeds are about to be made public, which reflect a stain upon our common nature.

Rosamund, enthusiastic, and improvident, wandered unprotected to a distance from her guardian doors; through lonely glens, and woodwalks, where she had rambled many a *day* in safety; till she arrived at a shady copse, out of the hearing of any human habitation.

Matravis met her.——" Flown with insolence and wine," returning home late at night, he passed that way!

Matravis was a very ugly man. Sallow-complexioned! and, if hearts can wear that colour, his heart was sallow-complexioned also.

A young man with *gray* deliberation! cold and systematic in all his plans; and all his plans were evil. His very lust was systematic.

He would brood over his bad purposes for such a dreary length of time, that it might have been expected, some solitary check of conscience must have intervened to save him from commission. But that *light from heaven* was extinct in his dark bosom.

Nothing that is great, nothing that is amiable, existed for this unhappy man. He feared, he envied, he suspected; but he never loved. The sublime and beautiful in nature, the excellent and becoming in morals, were things placed beyond the capacity of his sensations. He loved not poetry—nor ever took a lonely walk to meditate —never beheld virtue, which he did not try to disbelieve, or female beauty and innocence, which he did not lust to contaminate.

A sneer was perpetually upon his face, and malice *grinning* at his heart. He would say the most ill-natured things, with the least remorse of any man I ever knew. This gained him the reputation of a wit—other *traits* got him the reputation of a villain.

And this man formerly paid his court to Elinor Clare! with what success I leave my readers to determine. It was not in Elinor's nature to despise any living thing— but in the estimation of this man, to be rejected was to be *despised;* and Matravis *never forgave*.

He had long turned his eyes upon Rosamund Gray. To steal from the bosom of her friends the jewel they prized so much, the little ewe lamb they held so dear, it was a scheme of delicate revenge, and Matravis had a twofold motive for accomplishing this young maid's ruin.

Often had he met her in her favourite solitudes, but found her ever cold and inaccessible. Of late the girl had avoided straying far from her own home, in the fear of meeting him—but she had never told her fears to Allan.

Matravis had, till now, been content to be a villain within the limits of the law—but, on the present occasion, hot fumes of wine, co-operating with his deep desire of revenge, and the insolence of an unhoped meeting, overcame his customary prudence, and Matravis rose, at once, to an audacity of glorious mischief.

Late at night he met her, a lonely, unprotected virgin—no friend at hand—no place near of refuge.

Rosamund Gray, my soul is exceeding sorrowful for thee—I loathe to tell the hateful circumstances of thy wrongs—Night and silence were the only witnesses of this young maid's disgrace—Matravis fled.

Rosamund, polluted and disgraced, wandered, an abandoned thing, about the fields and meadows till daybreak. Not caring to return to the cottage, she sat herself down before the gate of Miss Clare's house—in a stupor of grief.

Elinor was just rising, and had opened the windows of her chamber, when she perceived her desolate young friend. She ran to embrace her—she brought her into the house—she took her to her bosom—she kissed her—she spake to her; but Rosamund could not speak.

Tidings came from the cottage. Margaret's death was an event which could not be kept concealed from Rosamund. When the sweet maid heard of it, she languished, and fell sick; she never held up her head after that time.

If Rosamund had been a *sister*, she could not have been kindlier treated, than by her two friends.

Allan had prospects in life; might, in time, have married into any of the first families in Hertfordshire; but Rosamund Gray, humbled though she was, and put to shame, had yet a charm for *him;* and he would have been content to share his fortunes with her yet, if Rosamund would have lived to be his companion.

But this was not to be, and the girl soon after died.

She expired in the arms of Elinor—quiet, gentle, as she lived—thankful, that she died not among strangers—and expressing by signs, rather than words, a gratitude for the most trifling services, the common offices of humanity. She died uncomplaining; and this young maid, this untaught Rosamund, might have given a lesson to the grave philosopher in death.

Chapter X.

I was but a boy, when these events took place. All the village remember the story, and tell of Rosamund Gray and old blind Margaret.

I parted from Allan Clare on that disastrous night, and set out for Edinburgh the next morning, before the facts were commonly known; I heard not of them—and it was four months before I received a letter from Allan.

"His heart," he told me, "was gone from him; for his sister had died of a phrenzy fever!" not a word of Rosamund in the letter—I was left to collect her story from sources which may one day be explained.

I soon after quitted Scotland, on the death of my father, and returned to my native village. Allan had left the place, and I could gain no information, whether he were dead or living.

I passed the *cottage*. I did not dare to look that way, or to inquire *who* lived there. A little dog, that had been Rosamund's, was yelping in my path. I laughed aloud like one mad, whose mind had suddenly gone from him; I stared vacantly around me, like one alienated from common perceptions.

But I was young at that time, and the impression became gradually weakened, as I mingled in the business of life. It is now *ten years* since these events took place, and I sometimes think of them as unreal. Allan Clare was a dear friend to me; but there are times, when Allan and his sister, Margaret and her granddaughter, appear like personages of a dream—an idle dream.

Chapter XI.

Strange things have happened unto me—I seem scarce awake—but I will re-collect my thoughts, and try to give an account of what hath befallen me in the few last weeks.

Since my father's death our family have resided in London. I am in practice as a surgeon there. My mother died two years after we left Widford.

A month or two ago I had been busying myself in drawing up the above narrative, intending to make it public. The employment had forced my mind to dwell upon *facts*, which had begun to fade from it; the memory of old times became vivid, and more vivid—I felt a strong desire to revisit the scenes of my native village—of the young loves of Rosamund and her Clare.

A kind of dread had hitherto kept me back; but I was restless now, till I had accomplished my wish. I set out one morning to walk—I reached Widford about eleven in the forenoon—after a slight breakfast at my Inn—where I was mortified to perceive, the old landlord did not know me again—(old Thomas Billet—he has often made angle rods for me when a child)—I rambled over all my accustomed haunts.

Our old house was vacant, and to be sold. I entered, unmolested, into the room that had been my bed-chamber. I kneeled down on the spot where my little bed had stood—I felt like a child—I prayed like one—it seemed as though old times were to return again; I looked round involuntarily, expecting to see some face I knew—but all was naked and mute. The bed was gone. My little pane of painted window, through which I loved to look at the sun, when I awoke in a fine summer's morning, was taken out, and had been replaced by one of common glass.

I visited, by turns, every chamber—they were all desolate and unfurnished, one excepted, in which the owner had left a harpsichord, probably to be sold—I touched the keys—I played some old Scottish tunes, which had delighted me when a child. Past associations revived with the music—blended with a sense of *unreality*, which at last became too powerful—I rushed out of the room to give vent to my feelings.

I wandered, scarce knowing where, into an old wood, that stands at the back of the house—we called it the *wilderness*. A well-known *form* was missing, that used to meet me in this place—it was thine, Ben Moxam—the kindest, gentlest, politest, of human beings, yet was he nothing higher than a gardener in the family. Honest creature, thou didst never pass me in my childish rambles, without a soft speech, and a smile. I remember thy good-natured face. But there is one thing, for which I can never forgive thee, Ben Moxam; that thou didst join with an old maiden aunt of mine in a cruel plot, to lop away the hanging branches of the old fir-trees. I remember them sweeping to the ground.

I have often left my childish sports to ramble in this place—its glooms and its solitude had a mysterious charm for my young mind, nurturing within me that love of quietness and lonely thinking, which have accompanied me to maturer years.

In this *wilderness* I found myself after a ten years' absence. Its stately fir-trees were yet standing, with all their luxuriant company of underwood—the squirrel was there, and the melancholy cooings of the wood-pigeon, all was as I had left it—my heart softened at the sight—it seemed, as though my character had been suffering a *change*, since I forsook these shades.

My parents were both dead; I had no counsellor left, no experience of age to direct me, no sweet voice of reproof. The Lord had taken away my *friends*, and I knew not where he had laid them. I paced round the wilderness, seeking a comforter. I prayed, that I might be restored to that *state of innocence*, in which I had wandered in those shades.

Methought, my request was heard; for it seemed, as

though the stains of manhood were passing from me, and I were relapsing into the purity and simplicity of childhood. I was content to have been moulded into a perfect child. I stood still, as in a trance. I dreamed that I was enjoying a personal intercourse with my heavenly Father; and, extravagantly, put off the shoes from my feet—for the place where I stood, I thought, was holy ground.

This state of mind could not last long; and I returned, with languid feelings, to my Inn. I ordered my dinner—green peas and a sweetbread—it had been a favourite dish with me in my childhood—I was allowed to have it on my birthdays. I was impatient to see it come upon table—but, when it came, I could scarce eat a mouthful; my tears choked me. I called for wine—I drank a pint and a half of red wine—and not till then had I dared to visit the churchyard, where my parents were interred.

The *cottage* lay in my way—Margaret had chosen it for that very reason, to be near the church—for the old lady was regular in her attendance on public worship—I passed on—and in a moment found myself among the tombs.

I had been present at my father's burial, and knew the spot again—my mother's funeral I was prevented by illness from attending—a plain stone was placed over the grave, with their initials carved upon it—for they both occupied one grave.

I prostrated myself before the spot; I kissed the earth that covered them—I contemplated, with gloomy delight, the time when I should mingle my dust with theirs—and kneeled, with my arms incumbent on the grave-stone, in a kind of mental prayer—for I could not speak.

Having performed these duties, I arose with quieter feelings, and felt leisure to attend to indifferent objects. Still I continued in the churchyard, reading the various inscriptions, and moralising on them with that kind of levity, which will not unfrequently spring up in the mind, in the midst of deep melancholy.

I read of nothing but careful parents, loving husbands, and dutiful children. I said jestingly, where be all the *bad* people buried? Bad parents, bad husbands, bad children—what cemeteries are appointed for these? do they not sleep in consecrated ground? or is it but a pious fiction, a generous oversight, in the survivors, which thus tricks out men's epitaphs when dead, who in their lifetime discharged the offices of life, perhaps, but lamely? Their failings, with their reproaches, now sleep with them in the grave. *Man wars not with the dead.* It is a *trait* of human nature, for which I love it.

I had not observed, till now, a little group assembled at the other end of the churchyard; it was a company of children, who were gathered round a young man, dressed in black, sitting on a gravestone.

He seemed to be asking them questions—probably, about their learning—and one little dirty ragged-headed fellow was clambering up his knees to kiss him. The children had been eating black cherries—for some of the stones were scattered about, and their mouths were smeared with them.

As I drew near them, I thought I discerned in the stranger a mild benignity of countenance, which I had somewhere seen before—I gazed at him more attentively.

It was Allan Clare! sitting on the grave of his sister.

I threw my arms about his neck. I exclaimed "Allan," —he turned his eyes upon me—he knew me—we both wept aloud—it seemed as though the interval, since we parted, had been as nothing—I cried out, "Come, and tell me about these things."

I drew him away from his little friends—he parted with a show of reluctance from the churchyard—Margaret and her granddaughter lay buried there, as well as his sister—I took him to my Inn—secured a room, where we might be private—ordered fresh wine—scarce knowing what I did, I danced for joy.

Allan was quite overcome, and taking me by the hand he said, "This repays me for all."

It was a proud day for me—I had found a friend I thought dead—earth seemed to me no longer valuable, than as it contained *him;* and existence a blessing no longer than while I should live to be his comforter.

I began at leisure, to survey him with more attention. Time, and grief, had left few traces of that fine *enthusiasm* which once burned in his countenance—his eyes had lost their original fire, but they retained an uncommon sweetness, and, whenever they were turned upon me, their smile pierced to my heart.

"Allan, I fear you have been a sufferer." He replied not, and I could not press him further. I could not call the dead to life again.

So we drank, and told old stories—and repeated old poetry—and sung old songs—as if nothing had happened. We sat till very late—I forgot that I had purposed returning to town that evening—to Allan all places were alike—I grew noisy, he grew cheerful—Allan's old manners, old enthusiasm, were returning upon him—we laughed, we wept, we mingled our tears, and talked extravagantly.

Allan was my bedfellow that night—and we lay awake, planning schemes of living together under the same roof, entering upon similar pursuits;—and praising GOD that we had met.

I was obliged to return to town the next morning, and Allan proposed to accompany me. "Since the death of his sister," he told me, "he had been a wanderer."

In the course of our walk, he unbosomed himself without reserve—told me many particulars of his way of life for the last nine or ten years, which I do not feel myself at liberty to divulge.

Once, on my attempting to cheer him, when I perceived him over thoughtful, he replied to me in these words:

"Do not regard me as unhappy, when you catch me in these moods. I am never more happy than at times, when by the cast of my countenance men judge me most miserable.

"My friend, the events which have left this sadness behind them are of no recent date. The melancholy, which comes over me with the recollection of them, is not hurtful, but only tends to soften and tranquillise my mind, to detach me from the restlessness of human pursuits.

"The stronger I feel this detachment, the more I find myself drawn heavenward to the contemplation of spiritual objects.

"I love to keep old friendships alive and warm within me, because I expect a renewal of them in the *World of Spirits*.

"I am a wandering and unconnected thing on the earth. I have made no new friendships, that can compensate me for the loss of the old—and the more I know mankind, the more does it become necessary for me to supply their loss by little images, recollections, and circumstances, of past pleasures.

"I am sensible that I am surrounded by a multitude of very worthy people, plain-hearted souls, sincere, and kind. But they have hitherto eluded my pursuit, and will continue to bless the little circle of their families and friends, while I must remain a stranger to them.

"Kept at a distance by mankind, I have not ceased to love them—and could I find the cruel persecutor, the malignant instrument of GOD's judgments on me and mine, I think I would forgive, and try to love him too.

"I have been a quiet sufferer. From the beginning of my calamities it was given to me, not to see the hand of man in them. I perceived a mighty arm, which none but myself could see, extended over me. I gave my heart to the Purifier, and my will to the Sovereign Will of the Universe. The irresistible wheels of destiny passed on in their everlasting rotation,—and I suffered myself to be carried along with them, without complaining."

Chapter XII.

ALLAN told me, that for some years past, feeling himself disengaged from every personal tie, but not alienated from human sympathies, it had been his taste, his *humour* he called it, to spend a great portion of his time in *hospitals* and *lazar-houses*.

He had found a *wayward pleasure*, he refused to name it a virtue, in tending a description of people, who had long ceased to expect kindness or friendliness from mankind, but were content to accept the reluctant services, which the oftentimes unfeeling instruments and servants of these well-meant institutions deal out to the poor sick people under their care.

It is not medicine,—it is not broths and coarse meats, served up at a stated hour with all the hard formalities of a prison,—it is not the scanty dole of a bed to die on —which dying man requires from his species.

Looks, attentions, consolations,—in a word, *sympathies*, are what a man most needs in this awful close of mortal sufferings. A kind look, a smile, a drop of cold water to the parched lip—for these things a man shall bless you in death.

And these better things than cordials did Allan love to administer—to stay by a bedside the whole day, when something disgusting in a patient's distemper has kept the very nurses at a distance—to sit by, while the poor wretch got a little sleep—and be there to smile upon him when he awoke—to slip a guinea, now and then, into the hands of a nurse or attendant—these things have been to Allan as *privileges*, for which he was content to live, choice marks, and circumstances, of his Maker's goodness to him.

And I do not know whether occupations of this kind be not a spring of purer and nobler delight (certainly instances of a more disinterested virtue) than ariseth from what are called Friendships of Sentiment.

Between two persons of liberal education, like opinions, and common feelings, oftentimes subsists a Vanity of Sentiment, which disposes each to look upon the other as the only being in the universe worthy of friendship, or capable of understanding it,—themselves they consider as the solitary receptacles of all that is delicate in feeling, or stable in attachment :—when the odds are, that under every green hill, and in every crowded street, people of equal worth are to be found, who do more good in their generation, and make less noise in the doing of it.

It was in consequence of these benevolent propensities I have been describing, that Allan oftentimes discovered considerable inclinations in favour of my way of life, which I have before mentioned as being that of a surgeon. He would frequently attend me on my visits to patients; and I began to think, that he had serious intentions of making my profession his study.

He was present with me at a scene—a *death-bed* scene —I shudder, when I do but think of it.

Chapter XIII.

I WAS sent for the other morning to the assistance of a gentleman, who had been wounded in a duel,—and his wounds by unskilful treatment had been brought to a dangerous crisis.

The uncommonness of the name, which was *Matravis*, suggested to me, that this might possibly be no other than Allan's old enemy. Under this apprehension, I did what I could to dissuade Allan from accompanying me— but he seemed bent upon going, and even pleased himself with the notion, that it might lie within his ability to do the unhappy man some service. So he went with me.

When we came to the house, which was in Soho Square, we discovered that it was indeed the man—the identical Matravis, who had done all that mischief in times past—but not in a condition to excite any other sensation than pity in a heart more hard than Allan's.

Intense pain had brought on a delirium—we perceived this on first entering the room—for the wretched man was raving to himself—talking idly in mad, unconnected sentences,—that yet seemed, at times, to have a reference to *past facts.*

One while he told us his dream. "He had lost his way on a great heath, to which there seemed no end—it was cold, cold, cold—and dark, very dark—an old woman in leading-strings, *blind,* was groping about for a guide"—and then he frightened me,—for he seemed disposed to be *jocular,* and sung a song about an "old woman clothed in grey," and said "he did not believe in a devil."

Presently he bid us "not tell Allan Clare"—Allan was hanging over him at that very moment, sobbing. I could not resist the impulse, but cried out, "*This* is Allan Clare—Allan Clare is come to see you, my dear sir." The wretched man did not hear me, I believe, for he turned his head away, and began talking of *charnel houses,* and *dead men,* and "whether they knew anything that passed, in their coffins."

Matravis died that night.

CURIOUS FRAGMENTS,

EXTRACTED FROM A COMMON-PLACE BOOK, WHICH BELONGED TO ROBERT BURTON, THE FAMOUS AUTHOR OF THE "ANATOMY OF MELANCHOLY."

EXTRACT I.

I DEMOCRITUS Junior have put my finishing pen to a tractate *De Melancholia*, this day, December 5, 1620. First, I blesse the Trinity, which hath given me health to prosecute my worthlesse studies thus far, and make supplication with a *Laus Deo*, if in any case these my poor labours may be found instrumental to weede out black melancholy, carking cares, harte-grief, from the mind of man. *Sed hoc magis volo quam expecto.*

I turn now to my book, *i nunc liber, goe forth, my brave Anatomy, child of my brain-sweat*, and yee, *candidi lectores*, lo! here I give him up to you, even do with him what you please, my masters. Some, I suppose, will applaud, commend, cry him up (these are my friends) hee is a *flos rarus*, forsooth, a none-such, a Phœnix (concerning whom see *Plinius* and *Mandeuille*, though *Fienus de monstris* doubteth at large of such a bird, whom *Montaltus* confuting argueth to have been a man *malæ scrupulositatis*, of a weak and cowardlie faith : *Christopherus a Vega* is with him in this). Others again will blame, hiss, reprehende in many things, cry down altogether, my collections, for crude, inept, putid, *post cœnam scripta, Coryate could write better upon a full meal*, verbose, inerudite, and not sufficiently abounding in authorities, *dogmata*, sentences, of learneder writers which have been before me, when as that first named sort clean otherwise judge of my labours to bee nothing else but a *messe of opinions*, a vortex attracting indiscriminate, gold, pearls, hay, straw, wood, excrement, an exchange, tavern, marte, for foreigners to congregate, Danes, Swedes, Hollanders, Lombards, so many strange faces, dresses, salutations, languages, all which *Wolfius* behelde with great contente upon the Venetian Rialto, as he describes diffusedly in his book the world's Epitome, which *Sannazar* so bepraiseth, *e contra* our Polydore can see nothing in it; they call me singular, a pedant, fantastic, words of reproach in this age, which is all too neoteric and light for my humour.

One cometh to me sighing, complaining. He expected universal remedies in my Anatomy; so many cures as there are distemperatures among men. I have not put his affection in my cases. Hear you his case. My fine Sir is a lover, an *inamorato*, a Pyramus, a Romeo; he walks seven years disconsolate, moping, becauset he cannot enjoy his miss, *insanus amor* is his melancholy, the man is mad; *delirat*, he dotes; all this while his Glycera is rude, spiteful, not to be entreated, churlish, spits at him, yet exceeding fair, gentle eyes (which is a beauty), hair lustrous and *smiling*, the trope is none of mine, *Æneas Sylvius* hath *crines ridentes*—in conclusion she is wedded to his rival, a boore, a *Corydon*, a rustic, *omnino ignarus, he can scarce construe Corderius*, yet haughty, fantastic, *opiniatre*. The lover travels, goes into foreign parts, peregrinates, *amoris ergo*, sees manners, customs, not English, converses with pilgrims, lying travellers, monks, hermits, those cattle, pedlars, travelling gentry, *Egyptians*, natural wonders, unicorns (though *Aldobrandus* will have them to be figments), satyrs, semi-viri, apes, monkeys, baboons, curiosities artificial, *pyramides*, Virgilius his tombe, relicks, bones, which are nothing but ivory as *Melancthon* judges, though *Cornutus* leaneth to think them bones of dogs, cats (why not men?), which subtill priests vouch to have been saints, martyrs, *heu Pietas!* By that time he has ended his course, *fugit hora*, seven other years are expired, gone by, time is he should return, he taketh ship for Britaine, much desired of his friends, *favebant venti, Neptune is curteis*, after some weekes at sea he landeth, rides post to town, greets his family, kinsmen, *compotores, those jokers his friends that were wont to tipple with him at alehouses;* these wonder now to see the change, *quantum mutatus, the man is quite another thing*, he is disenthralled, manumitted, he wonders what so bewitched him, he can now both see, hear, smell, handle, converse with his mistress, single by reason of the death of his rival, a widow having children, grown willing, prompt, amorous, shewing no such great dislike to second nuptials, hee might have her for asking, no such thing, his mind is changed, he loathes his former meat, had liever eat ratsbane, aconite, his humour is to die a batchelour; marke the conclusion. In this humour of celibate seven other years are consumed in idleness, sloth, world's pleasures, which fatigue, satiate, induce wearinesse, vapours, *tædium vitæ:* When upon a day, behold a wonder, *redit Amor*, the man is as sick as ever, he is commenced lover upon the old stock, walks with his hand thrust into his bosom for negligence, moping he leans his head, face yellow, beard flowing and incomposite, eyes sunken, *anhelus, breath wheezy and asthmatical, by reason of over-much sighing:* society he abhors, solitude is but a hell, what shall he doe? all this while his mistresse is forward, coming, *amantissima, ready to jump at once into his mouth*, her he hateth, feels disgust when she is but mentioned, thinks her ugly, old, a painted Jezabeel, Alecto, Megara, and Tisiphone all at once, a Corinthian Lais, a strumpet, only not handsome; that which he affecteth so much, that which drives him mad, distracted, phrenetic, beside himself, is no beauty which lives, nothing *in rerum naturâ* (so he might entertain a hope of a cure), but something *which is not*, can never be, a certain *fantastic opinion or notional image* of his mistresse, *that which she was*, and that which hee thought her to be, in former times, how beautiful! torments him, frets him, follows him, makes him that he wishes to die.

This Caprichio, *Sir Humourous*, hee cometh to me to

be cured. I counsel marriage with his mistresse, according to Hippocrates his method, together with milk diet, herbs, aloes, and wild parsley, good in such cases, though Avicenna preferreth some sort of wild fowl, teals, widgeons, becca ficos, which men in Sussex eat. He flies out in a passion, ho! ho; and falls to calling me names, dizzard, ass, lunatic, moper, Bedlamite, Pseudo-Democritus. I smile in his face, bidding him be patient, tranquil, to no purpose, he still rages, I think this man must fetch his remedies from Utopia, Fairy Land, Islands in the Moone, etc.

EXTRACT II.

* * * Much disputacyons of fierce wits amongst themselves, in logomachies, subtle controversies, many dry blows given on either side, contentions of learned men, or such as would be so thought, as *Bodinus de Periodis* saith of such an one, *arrident amici ridet mundus*, in English, this man his cronies they cocker him up, they flatter him, he would fayne appear somebody, meanwhile the world thinks him no better than a dizzard, a ninny, a sophist * * *

* * * Philosophy running mad, madness philosophising, much idle-learned inquiries, what truth is? and no issue, fruit, of all these noises, only huge books are written, and who is the wiser? * * * * Men sitting in the Doctor's chair, we marvel how they got there, being *homines intellectus pulverulenti*, as *Trincauellius* notes; they care not so they may raise a dust to smother the eyes of their oppugners; *homines parvulissimi* as *Lemnius*, whom *Alcuin* herein taxeth of a crude Latinism; dwarfs, minims, the least little men, these spend their time, and 'tis odds but they lose their time and wits too into the bargain, chacing of nimble and retiring Truth. Her they prosecute, her still they worship, *libant*, they make libations, spilling the wine, as those old Romans in their sacrificials, *Cerealia, May-games:* Truth is the game all these hunt after, to the extreme perturbacyon and drying up of the moistures, *humidum radicale exsiccant*, as *Galen*, in his counsels to one of these wear-wits, brain-moppers, spunges, saith. * * * and for all this *nunquam metam attingunt*, and how should they? they bowle awry, shooting beside the marke; whereas it should appear, that *Truth absolute* on this planet of ours, is scarcely to be found, but in her stede *Queene opinion* predominates, governs, whose shifting and ever mutable *Lampas*, me seemeth, is man's destinie to follow, she præcurseth, she guideth him, before his uncapable eyes she frisketh her tender lights, which entertayne the child-man, untill what time his sight be strong to endure the vision of *Very Truth*, which is in the heavens, the vision which is beatifical, as *Anianus* expounds in his argument against certain mad wits which helde God to be corporeous; these were dizzards, fools, *gothamites*. * * * but and if *Very Truth* be extant indeede on earth, as some hold she it is which actuates men's deeds, purposes, ye may in vaine look for her in the learned universities, halls, colleges. Truth is no Doctoresse, she taketh no degrees at Paris or Oxford, amongst great clerks, disputants, subtile Aristotles, men *nodosi ingenii*, *able to take Lully by the chin*, but oftentimes to such an one as myself, an *Idiota* or common person, *no great things*, melancholising in woods where waters are, quiet places by rivers, fountains, whereas the silly man expecting no such matter, thinketh only how best to delectate and refresh his mynde continually with *Natura* her pleasant scenes, woods, waterfalls, or *Art* her statelier gardens, parks, terraces, *Belvideres*, on a sudden the goddesse herself *Truth* has appeared, with a shyning lyghte and a sparklyng countenance, so as yee may not be able lightly to resist her. * * * *

EXTRACT IV.

This morning, May 2, 1602, having first broken my fast upon eggs and cooling salades, mallows, water-cresses, those herbes, according to *Villanovus* his prescription, who disallows the use of meat in a morning as gross, fat, hebetant, *feral*, altogether fitter for wild beasts than men, *e contra* commendeth this herb-diete for gentle, humane, active, conducing to contemplation in most men, I betook myselfe to the nearest fields. (Being in London I commonly dwell in the *suburbes,* as airiest, quietest, *loci musis propriores,* free from noises of caroches, waggons, mechanick and base workes, workshoppes, also sights, pageants, spectacles of outlandish birds, fishes, crocodiles, *Indians,* mermaids, adde quarrels, fightings, wranglings of the mobbe, *plebs,* the rabble, duellos with fists, *proper to this island,* at which the stiletto'd and secrete *Italian* laughs :) withdrawing myselfe from these buzzing and illiterate vanities, with a *bezo las manos* to the citty, I begin to inhale, draw in, snuff up, as horses *dilatis naribus* snort the fresh aires, with exceeding great delight, when suddenly there crosses me a procession sad, heavy, dolorous, tristfull, melancholick, able to change mirth into dolour, and overcast a clearer atmosphere than possibly the neighbourhoods of so great a city can afford. An old man, a poore man, deceased, is borne on men's shoulders to a poore buriall, without solemnities of hearse, mourners, plumes, *mutæ personæ, those personate actors that will weep if yee show them a piece of silver ;* none of those customed civilities of children, kinsfolk, *dependants,* following the coffin ; he died a poore man, his friends *assessores opum, those cronies of his that stuck by him so long as he had a penny,* now leave him, forsake him, shun him, desert him : they think it much to follow his putrid and stinking carcase to the grave ; his children, if he had any, for commonly the case stands thus, this poore man his son dies before him, he survives poore, indigent, base, dejected, miserable, etc., or if he have any which survive him, *sua negotia agunt,* they mind their own business, forsooth, cannot, will not, find time, leisure, *inclination, extremum munus perficere,* to follow to the pit their old indulgent father, which loved them, stroked them, caressed them, cockering them up, *quantum potuit,* as farre as his means extended, while they were babes, chits, *minims,* hee may rot in his grave, lie stinking in the sun, *for them,* have no buriall at all, they care not. *O nefas!* Chiefly I noted the coffin to have been *without a pall,* nothing but a few planks of cheapest wood that could be had, *naked,* having none of the ordinary *symptomata* of a funerall, those *locularii* which bare the body, having on diversely, coloured coats, *and none black;* (one of these reported the deceased to have been an almsman seven yeares, a pauper, harboured and fed in the workhouse of St. Giles in the fields, to whose proper burying ground he was now going for interment). All which when I behelde, hardly I refrained from weeping, and incontinently I fell to musing: "If this man had been rich, a *Crœsus,* a *Crassus,* or as rich as *Whittington,* what pompe, charge, lavish cost, expenditure of rich buriall, *ceremoniall-obsequies, obsequious ceremonies,* had been thought too good for such an one; what store of panegyricks, elogies, funeral orations, etc., some beggarly poetaster, worthy to be beaten for his ill rimes, crying him up, hee was rich, generous, bountiful, polite, learned, *a Mæcenas,* while as in very deede he was nothing lesse : what weeping, sighing, sorrowing, honing, complaining, kinsmen, friends, relatives, fourtieth cousins, poor relatives, lamenting for the deceased; hypocriticall heirs, sobbing, striking their breasts (they care not if he had died a year ago); so many clients dependants, flatterers, *parasites, cunning Gnathoes,* tramping on foot after the hearse, all their care is, who shall stand fairest with the successour; he meantime (like enough) spurns them from him, spits at them, treads them under his foot, will have nought to do with any such cattle. I think him in the right: *Hæc sunt majora gravitate Heracliti. These follies are enough to give crying Heraclitus a fit of the spleene.*

HYPOCHONDRIACUS.

By myself walking,
To myself talking,
When as I ruminate
On my untoward fate,
Scarcely seem I
Alone sufficiently,
Black thoughts continually
Crowding my privacy;
They come unbidden,
Like foes at a wedding,
Thrusting their faces
In better guests' places,
Peevish and malecontent,
Clownish, impertinent,
Dashing the merriment:
So in like fashions
Dim cogitations
Follow and haunt me,
Striving to daunt me,
In my heart festering,
In my ears whispering,
"Thy friends are treacherous,
Thy foes are dangerous,
Thy dreams ominous."

Fierce Anthropophagi,
Spectra, Diaboli,
What scared St. Anthony,
Hobgoblins, Lemures,

Dreams of Antipodes,
Night-riding Incubi
Troubling the fantasy,
All dire illusions
Causing confusions;
Figments heretical,
Scruples fantastical,
Doubts diabolical;
Abaddon vexeth me,
Mahu perplexeth me,
Lucifer teareth me—
*Jesu! Maria! liberate nos ab his
diris tentationibus Inimici.*

RECOLLECTIONS OF CHRIST'S HOSPITAL.

To comfort the desponding parent with the thought that, without diminishing the stock which is imperiously demanded to furnish the more pressing and homely wants of our nature, he has disposed of one or more perhaps out of a numerous offspring, under the shelter of a care scarce less tender than the paternal, where not only their bodily cravings shall be supplied, but that mental *pabulum* is also dispensed, which HE hath declared to be no less necessary to our sustenance, who said that "not by bread alone man can live;" for this Christ's Hospital unfolds her bounty. Here neither, on the one hand, are the youth lifted up above their family, which we must suppose liberal though reduced; nor, on the other hand, are they liable to be depressed below its level by the mean habits and sentiments which a common charity-school generates. It is, in a word, an Institution to keep those who have yet held up their heads in the world from sinking; to keep alive the spirit of a decent household, when poverty was in danger of crushing it; to assist those who are the most willing, but not always the most able, to assist themselves; to separate a child from his family for a season, in order to render him back hereafter, with feelings and habits more congenial to it, than he could even have attained by remaining at home in the bosom of it. It is a preserving and renovating principle, an antidote for the *res angusta domi*, when it presses, as it always does, most heavily upon the most ingenuous natures.

This is Christ's Hospital; and whether its character

would be improved by confining its advantages to the very lowest of the people, let those judge who have witnessed the looks, the gestures, the behaviour, the manner of their play with one another, their deportment towards strangers, the whole aspect and physiognomy of that vast assemblage of boys on the London foundation, who freshen and make alive again with their sports the else mouldering cloisters of the old Grey Friars—which strangers who have never witnessed, if they pass through Newgate Street, or by Smithfield, would do well to go a little out of their way to see.

For the Christ's Hospital boy feels that he is no charity-boy; he feels it in the antiquity and regality of the foundation to which he belongs; in the usage which he meets with at school, and the treatment he is accustomed to out of its bounds; in the respect, and even kindness, which his well-known garb never fails to procure him in the streets of the metropolis; he feels it in his education, in that measure of classical attainments, which every individual at that school, though not destined to a learned profession, has it in his power to procure, attainments which it would be worse than folly to put it in the reach of the labouring classes to acquire; he feels it in the numberless comforts, and even magnificences, which surround him; in his old and awful cloisters, with their traditions; in his spacious schoolrooms, and in the well-ordered, airy, and lofty rooms where he sleeps; in his stately dining-hall, hung round with pictures, by Verrio, Lely, and others, one of them surpassing in size and grandeur almost any other in the kingdom;[1] above all, in the very extent and magnitude of the body to which he belongs, and the consequent spirit, the intelligence, and public conscience, which is the result of so many various yet wonderfully combining members. Compared with

[1] By Verrio, representing James the Second on his throne, surrounded by his courtiers (all curious portraits), receiving the mathematical pupils at their annual presentation, a custom still kept up on New Year's Day at Court.

this last-named advantage, what is the stock of information (I do not here speak of book-learning, but of that knowledge which boy receives from boy), the mass of collected opinions, the intelligence in common, among the few and narrow members of an ordinary boarding-school.

The Christ's Hospital or Blue-coat boy has a distinctive character of his own, as far removed from the abject qualities of a common charity-boy as it is from the disgusting forwardness of a lad brought up at some other of the public schools. There is *pride* in it, accumulated from the circumstances which I have described as differencing him from the former; and there is a *restraining modesty*, from a sense of obligation and dependence, which must ever keep his deportment from assimilating to that of the latter. His very garb, as it is antique and venerable, feeds his self-respect; as it is a badge of dependence, it restrains the natural petulance of that age from breaking out into overt acts of insolence. This produces silence and a reserve before strangers, yet not that cowardly shyness which boys mewed up at home will feel; he will speak up when spoken to, but the stranger must begin the conversation with him. Within his bounds he is all fire and play; but in the streets he steals along with all the self-concentration of a young monk. He is never known to mix with other boys, they are a sort of laity to him. All this proceeds, I have no doubt, from the continual consciousness which he carries about him of the difference of his dress from that of the rest of the world; with a modest jealousy over himself, lest, by over-hastily mixing with common and secular playfellows, he should commit the dignity of his cloth. Nor let any one laugh at this; for, considering the propensity of the multitude, and especially of the small multitude, to ridicule anything unusual in dress—above all, where such peculiarity may be construed by malice into a mark of disparagement—this reserve will appear to be nothing more than a wise instinct in the Blue-coat boy. That it is neither pride nor rusticity, at least that it has none of the offensive qualities of either, a stranger may soon satisfy himself by putting a question to any of these boys: he may be sure of an answer couched in terms of plain civility, neither loquacious nor embarrassed. Let him put the same question to a parish-boy, or to one of the trencher-caps in the —— cloisters, and the impudent reply of the one shall not fail to exasperate any more than the certain servility, and mercenary eye to reward, which he will meet with in the other, can fail to depress and sadden him.

The Christ's Hospital boy is a religious character. His school is eminently a religious foundation; it has its peculiar prayers, its services at set times, its graces, hymns, and anthems, following each other in an almost monastic closeness of succession. This religious character in him is not always untinged with superstition. That is not wonderful, when we consider the thousand tales and traditions which must circulate with undisturbed credulity, amongst so many boys, that have so few checks to their belief from any intercourse with the world at large; upon whom their equals in age must work so much, their elders so little. With this leaning towards an over-belief in matters of religion, which will soon correct itself when he comes out into society, may be classed a turn for romance above most other boys. This is to be traced in the same manner to their excess of society with each other, and defect of mingling with the world. Hence the peculiar avidity with which such books as the Arabian Nights' Entertainments, and others of a still wilder cast, are, or at least were in my time, sought for by the boys. I remember when some half-dozen of them set off from school, without map, card, or compass, on a serious expedition to find out *Philip Quarll's Island*.

The Christ's Hospital boy's sense of right and wrong is peculiarly tender and apprehensive. It is even apt to run out into ceremonial observances, and to impose a yoke upon itself beyond the strict obligations of the moral law. Those who were contemporaries with me at that School thirty years ago, will remember with what more than Judaic rigour the eating of the fat of certain boiled meats[1] was interdicted. A boy would have blushed, as at the exposure of some heinous immorality, to have been detected eating that forbidden portion of his allowance of animal food, the whole of which, while he was in health, was little more than sufficient to allay his hunger. The same, or even greater, refinement was shown in the rejection of certain kinds of sweet-cake. What gave rise to these supererogatory penances, these self-denying ordinances, I could never learn;[2] they certainly argue no defect of the conscientious principle. A little excess in that article is not undesirable in youth, to make allowance for the inevitable waste which comes in maturer years. But in the less ambiguous line of duty, in those directions of the moral feelings which cannot be mistaken or depreciated, I will relate what took place in the year 1785, when Mr. Perry, the steward, died. I must be pardoned for taking my instances from my own times. Indeed the vividness of my recollections, while I am upon this subject, almost brings back those times; they are present to me still. But I believe that in the years which have elapsed since the period which I speak of, the character of the Christ's Hospital boy is very little changed. Their situation in point of many comforts is improved; but that which I ventured before to term the *public conscience* of the school, the pervading moral sense, of which every mind partakes, and to which so many individual minds contribute, remains, I believe, pretty much

[1] Under the denomination of *gags*.
[2] I am told that the late steward, Mr. Hathaway, who evinced on many occasions a most praiseworthy anxiety to promote the comfort of the boys, had occasion for all his address and perseverance to eradicate the first of these unfortunate prejudices, in which he at length happily succeeded, and thereby restored to one half of the animal nutrition of the school those honours which painful superstition and blind zeal had so long conspired to withhold from it.

the same as when I left it. I have seen within this twelvemonth almost the change which has been produced upon a boy of eight or nine years of age, upon being admitted into that school; how, from a pert young coxcomb, who thought that all knowledge was comprehended within his shallow brains, because a smattering of two or three languages and one or two sciences were stuffed into him by injudicious treatment at home, by a mixture with the wholesome society of so many schoolfellows, in less time than I have spoken of, he has sunk to his own level, and is contented to be carried on in the quiet orb of modest self-knowledge in which the common mass of that unpresumptuous assemblage of boys seem to move; from being a little unfeeling mortal, he has got to feel and reflect. Nor would it be a difficult matter to show how, at a school like this, where the boy is neither entirely separated from home, nor yet exclusively under its influence, the best feelings, the filial for instance, are brought to a maturity which they could not have attained under a completely domestic education; how the relation of parent is rendered less tender by unremitted association, and the very awfulness of age is best apprehended by some sojourning amidst the comparative levity of youth; how absence, not drawn out by too great extension into alienation or forgetfulness, puts an edge upon the relish of occasional intercourse, and the boy is made the better *child* by that which keeps the force of that relation from being felt as perpetually pressing on him; how the substituted paternity, into the care of which he is adopted, while in everything substantial it makes up for the natural, in the necessary omission of individual fondness and partialities, directs the mind only the more strongly to appreciate that natural and first tie, in which such weaknesses are the bond of strength, and the appetite which craves after them betrays no perverse palate. But these speculations rather belong to the question of the comparative advantage of a public over a private education in general. I must get back to my favourite school; and to that which took place when our old and good steward died.

And I will say,. that when I think of the frequent instances which I have met with in children, of a hard-heartedness, a callousness, and insensibility to the loss of relations, even of those who have begot and nourished them, I cannot but consider it as a proof of something in the peculiar conformation of that school, favourable to the expansion of the best feelings of our nature, that, at the period which I am noticing, out of five hundred boys there was not a dry eye to be found among them, nor a heart that did not beat with genuine emotion. Every impulse to play, until the funeral day was past, seemed suspended throughout the school; and the boys, lately so mirthful and sprightly, were seen pacing their cloisters alone, or in sad groups standing about, few of them without some token, such as their slender means could provide, a black riband or something to denote respect and a sense of their loss. The time itself was a time of anarchy, a time in which all authority (out of school-hours) was abandoned. The ordinary restraints were for those days superseded; and the gates, which at other times kept us in, were left without watchers. Yet, with the exception of one or two graceless boys at most, who took advantage of that suspension of authorities to *skulk out*, as it was called, the whole body of that great school kept rigorously within their bounds, by a voluntary self-imprisonment; and they who broke bounds, though they escaped punishment from any master, fell into a general disrepute among us, and, for that which at any other time would have been applauded and admired as a mark of spirit, were consigned to infamy and reprobation; so much *natural government* have gratitude and the principles of reverence and love, and so much did a respect to their dead friend prevail with these Christ's Hospital boys above any fear which his presence among them when living could ever produce. And if the impressions which were made on my mind so long ago are to be trusted, very richly did their steward deserve this tribute. It is a pleasure to me even now to call to mind his portly form, the regal awe which he always contrived to inspire, in spite of a tenderness and even weakness of nature that would have enfeebled the reins of discipline in any other master; a yearning of tenderness towards those under his protection, which could make five hundred boys at once feel towards him each as to their individual father. He had faults, with which we had nothing to do; but, with all his faults, indeed, Mr. Perry was a most extraordinary creature. Contemporary with him, and still living, though he has long since resigned his occupation, will it be impertinent to mention the name of our excellent upper grammar-master, the Rev. James Boyer? He was a disciplinarian, indeed, of a different stamp from him whom I have just described; but, now the terrors of the rod, and of a temper a little too hasty to leave the more nervous of us quite at our ease to do justice to his merits in those days, are long since over, ungrateful were we if we should refuse our testimony to that unwearied assiduity with which he attended to the particular improvement of each of us. Had we been the offspring of the first gentry in the land, he could not have been instigated by the strongest views of recompense and reward to have made himself a greater slave to the most laborious of all occupations than he did for us sons of charity, from whom, or from our parents, he could expect nothing. He has had his reward in the satisfaction of having discharged his duty, in the pleasurable consciousness of having advanced the respectability of that institution to which, both man and boy, he was attached; in the honours to which so many of his pupils have successfully aspired at both our Universities; and in the staff with which the Governors of the Hospital at the close of his hard labours, with the highest expressions of the obligations the school lay under to him, unanimously voted to present him.

I have often considered it among the felicities of the constitution of this school, that the offices of steward and schoolmaster are kept distinct; the strict business of education alone devolving upon the latter, while the former has the charge of all things out of school, the control of the provisions, the regulation of meals, of dress, of play, and the ordinary intercourse of the boys. By this division of management, a superior respectability must attach to the teacher while his office is unmixed with any of these lower concerns. A still greater advantage over the construction of common boarding-schools is to be found in the settled salaries of the masters, rendering them totally free of obligation to any individual pupil or his parents. This never fails to have its effect at schools where each boy can reckon up to a hair what profit the master derives from him, where he views him every day in the light of a caterer, a provider for the family, who is to get so much by him in each of his meals. Boys will see and consider these things; and how much must the sacred character of preceptor suffer in their minds by these degrading associations! The very bill which the pupil carries home with him at Christmas, eked out, perhaps, with elaborate though necessary minuteness, instructs him that his teachers have other ends than the mere love to learning in the lessons which they give him; and though they put into his hands the fine sayings of Seneca or Epictetus, yet they themselves are none of those disinterested pedagogues to teach philosophy *gratis*. The master, too, is sensible that he is seen in this light; and how much this must lessen that affectionate regard to the learners which alone can sweeten the bitter labour of instruction, and convert the whole business into unwelcome and uninteresting task-work, many preceptors that I have conversed with on the subject are ready, with a sad heart, to acknowledge. From this inconvenience the settled salaries of the masters of this school in great measure exempt them; while the happy custom of choosing masters (indeed every officer of the establishment) from those who have received their education there, gives them an interest in advancing the character of the school, and binds them to observe a tenderness and a respect to the children, in which a stranger, feeling that independence which I have spoken of might well be expected to fail.

In affectionate recollections of the place where he was bred up, in hearty recognitions of old schoolfellows met with again after the lapse of years, or in foreign countries, the Christ's Hospital boy yields to none; I might almost say he goes beyond most other boys. The very compass and magnitude of the school, its thousand bearings, the space it takes up in the imagination beyond the ordinary schools, impresses a remembrance, accompanied with an elevation of mind, that attends him through life. It is too big, too affecting an object, to pass away quickly from his mind. The Christ's Hospital boy's friends at school are commonly his intimates through life. For me, I do not know whether a constitutional imbecility does not incline me too obstinately to cling to the remembrances of childhood; in an inverted ratio to the usual sentiments of mankind, nothing that I have been engaged in since seems of any value or importance, compared to the colours which imagination gave to everything then. I belong to no *body corporate* such as I then made a part of.—And here before I close, taking leave of the general reader, and addressing myself solely to my old schoolfellows, that were contemporaries with me from the year 1782 to 1789, let me have leave to remember some of those circumstances of our school, which they will not be unwilling to have brought back to their minds.

And first, let us remember, as first in importance in our childish eyes, the young men (as they almost were) who, under the denomination of *Grecians*, were waiting the expiration of the period when they should be sent, at the charges of the Hospital, to one or other of our Universities, but more frequently to Cambridge. These youths, from their superior acquirements, their superior age and stature, and the fewness of their numbers (for seldom above two or three at a time were inaugurated into that high order), drew the eyes of all, and especially of the younger boys, into a reverent observance and admiration. How tall they used to seem to us!—how stately would they pace along the cloisters!—while the play of the lesser boys was absolutely suspended, or its boisterousness at least allayed, at their presence! Not that they ever beat or struck the boys—that would have been to have demeaned themselves—the dignity of their persons alone insured them all respect. The task of blows, of corporal chastisement, they left to the common monitors, or heads of wards, who it must be confessed, in our time had rather too much licence allowed them to oppress and misuse their inferiors; and the interference of the Grecian, who may be considered as the spiritual power, was not unfrequently called for, to mitigate by its mediation, the heavy unrelenting arm of this temporal power, or monitor. In fine, the Grecians were the solemn Muftis of the school. Æras were computed from their time;—it used to be said, such or such a thing was done when S—— or T—— was Grecian.

As I ventured to call the Grecians the Muftis of the school, the king's boys,[1] as their character then was, may well pass for the Janisaries. They were the terror of all the other boys; bred up under that hardy sailor, as well as excellent mathematician, and co-navigator with Captain Cook, William Wales. All his systems were adapted to fit them for the rough element which they were destined to encounter. Frequent and severe punishments, which were expected to be borne with more than Spartan fortitude, came to be considered less as inflictions of disgrace than as trials of obstinate endurance. To make his boys hardy, and to give them early sailor-habits, seemed to be his only aim; to this everything was subordinate. Moral obliquities, indeed, were sure of receiving their full recompense, for no occasion of laying on the lash was ever let slip; but the effects expected to

[1] The mathematical pupils, bred up to the sea, on the foundation of Charles the Second.

be produced from it were something very different from contrition or mortification. There was in William Wales a perpetual fund of humour, a constant glee about him, which, heightened by an inveterate provincialism of North-country dialect, absolutely took away the sting from his severities. His punishments were a game at patience, in which the master was not always worst contented when he found himself at times overcome by his pupil. What success this discipline had, or how the effects of it operated upon the after-lives of these king's boys, I cannot say: but I am sure that, for the time, they were absolute nuisances to the rest of the school. Hardy, brutal, and often wicked, they were the most graceless lump in the whole mass: older and bigger than the other boys (for, by the system of their education they were kept longer at school by two or three years than any of the rest, except the Grecians), they were a constant terror to the younger part of the school; and some who may read this, I doubt not, will remember the consternation into which the juvenile fry of us were thrown, when the cry was raised in the cloisters, that *the First Order was coming*—for so they termed the first form or class of those boys. Still these sea-boys answered some good purposes in the school. They were the military class among the boys, foremost in athletic exercises, who extended the fame of the prowess of the school far and near: and the apprentices in the vicinage, and sometimes the butchers' boys in the neighbouring market, had sad occasion to attest their valour.

The time would fail me if I were to attempt to enumerate all those circumstances, some pleasant, some attended with some pain, which seen through the mist of distance, come sweetly softened to the memory. But I must crave leave to remember our transcending superiority in those invigorating sports, leap-frog, and basting the bear; our delightful excursions in the summer holidays to the New River, near Newington, where, like otters, we would live the long day in the water, never caring for dressing ourselves when we had once stripped; our savoury meals afterwards, when we came home almost famished with staying out all day without our dinners; our visits at other times to the Tower, where, by ancient privilege, we had free access to all the curiosities; our solemn processions through the City at Easter, with the Lord Mayor's largess of buns, wine, and a shilling, with the festive questions and civic pleasantries of the dispensing Aldermen, which were more to us than all the rest of the banquet; our stately suppings in public, where the well-lighted hall, and the confluence of well-dressed company who came to see us, made the whole look more like a concert or assembly, than a scene of a plain bread and cheese collation; the annual orations upon St. Matthew's day, in which the senior scholar, before he had done, seldom failed to reckon up, among those who had done honour to our school by being educated in it, the names of those accomplished critics and Greek scholars, Joshua Barnes and Jeremiah Markland (I marvel they left out Camden while they were about it). Let me have leave to remember our hymns and anthems, and well-toned organ; the doleful tune of the burial anthem chanted in the solemn cloisters, upon the seldom-occurring funeral of some schoolfellow; the festivities at Christmas, when the richest of us would club our stock to have a gaudy day, sitting round the fire, replenished to the height with logs, and the penniless, and he that could contribute nothing, partook in all the mirth, and in some of the substantialities of the feasting; the carol sung by night at that time of the year, which, when a young boy, I have so often lain awake to hear from seven (the hour of going to bed) till ten, when it was sung by the older boys and monitors, and have listened to it, in their rude chanting, till I have been transported in fancy to the fields of Bethlehem, and the song which was sung at that season by angels' voices to the shepherds.

Nor would I willingly forget any of those things which administered to our vanity. The hem-stitched bands, and town-made shirts, which some of the most fashionable among us wore; the town-girdles, with buckles of silver, or shining stone; the badges of the sea-boys; the cots, or superior shoe-strings of the monitors; the medals of the markers (those who were appointed to hear the Bible read in the wards on Sunday morning and evening), which bore on their obverse in silver, as certain parts of our garments carried in meaner metal, the countenance of our Founder, that godly and royal child, King Edward the Sixth, the flower of the Tudor name—the young flower that was untimely cropped as it began to fill our land with its early odours—the boy-patron of boys—the serious and holy child who walked with Cranmer and Ridley—fit associate, in those tender years, for the bishops and future martyrs of our Church, to receive, or (as occasion sometimes proved) to give instruction.

"But ah! what means the silent tear?
Why, e'en mid joy, my bosom heave?
Ye long lost scenes, enchantments dear!
Lo! how I linger o'er your grave.

"—— Fly then, ye hours of rosy hue,
And bear away the bloom of years!
And quick succeed, ye sickly crew
Of doubts and sorrows, pains and fears!

"Still will I ponder Fate's unaltered plan,
Nor, tracing back the child, forget that I am man."[1]

---

[1] Lines meditated in the cloisters of Christ's Hospital, in the *Poetics* of Mr. George Dyer.

ON THE TRAGEDIES OF SHAKSPERE.

CONSIDERED WITH REFERENCE TO THEIR FITNESS FOR STAGE REPRESENTATION.

TAKING a turn the other day in the Abbey, I was struck with the affected attitude of a figure, which I do not remember to have seen before, and which upon examination proved to be a whole-length of the celebrated Mr. Garrick. Though I would not go so far with some good Catholics abroad as to shut players altogether out of consecrated ground, yet I own I was not a little scandalised at the introduction of theatrical airs and gestures into a place set apart to remind us of the saddest realities. Going nearer, I found inscribed under this harlequin figure the following lines :—

> To paint fair Nature, by divine command,
> Her magic pencil in his glowing hand,
> A Shakspere rose : then, to expand his fame
> Wide o'er this breathing world, a Garrick came.
> Though sunk in death the forms the Poet drew,
> The Actor's genius made them breathe anew ;
> Though, like the bard himself, in night they lay,
> Immortal Garrick call'd them back to-day :
> And till Eternity with power sublime
> Shall mark the mortal hour of hoary Time,
> Shakspere and Garrick like twin-stars shall shine,
> And earth irradiate with a beam divine.

It would be an insult to my readers' understandings to attempt anything like a criticism on this farrago of false thoughts and nonsense. But the reflection it led me into was a kind of wonder, how, from the days of the actor here celebrated to our own, it should have been the fashion to compliment every performer in his turn, that has had the luck to please the town in any of the great characters of Shakspere, with a notion of possessing a *mind congenial with the poet's ;* how people should come thus unaccountably to confound the power of originating poetical images and conceptions with the faculty of being able to read or recite the same when put into words ;[1] or what connection that absolute mastery over the heart and soul of man, which a great dramatic poet possesses, has with those low tricks upon the eye and ear, which a player by observing a few general effects, which some common passion, as grief, anger, etc., usually has upon the gestures and exterior, can easily compass. To know the internal workings and movements of a great mind, of an Othello or a Hamlet, for instance, the *when* and the *why* and the *how far* they should be moved ; to what pitch a passion is becoming ; to give the reins and to pull in the curb exactly at the moment when the drawing in or the slacking is most graceful ; seems to demand a reach of intellect of a vastly different extent from that which is employed upon the bare imitation of the signs of these passions in the countenance or gesture, which signs are usually observed to be most lively and emphatic in the weaker sort of minds, and which signs can after all but indicate some passion, as I said before, anger, or grief, generally ; but of the motives and grounds of the passion, wherein it differs from the same passion in low and vulgar natures, of these the actor can give no more idea by his face or gesture than the eye (without a metaphor) can speak, or the muscles utter intelligible sounds. But such is the instantaneous nature of the impressions which

---

[1] It is observable that we fall into this confusion only in *dramatic* recitations. We never dream that the gentleman who reads Lucretius in public with great applause, is therefore a great poet and philosopher ; nor do we find that Tom Davies, the bookseller, who is recorded to have recited the *Paradise Lost* better than any man in England in his day (though I cannot help thinking there must be some mistake in this tradition) was therefore, by his intimate friends, set upon a level with Milton.

we take in at the eye and ear at a playhouse, compared with the slow apprehension oftentimes of the understanding in reading, that we are apt not only to sink the play-writer in the consideration which we pay to the actor, but even to identify in our minds in a perverse manner, the actor with the character which he represents. It is difficult for a frequent play-goer to disembarrass the idea of Hamlet from the person and voice of Mr. K. We speak of Lady Macbeth, while we are in reality thinking of Mrs. S. Nor is this confusion incidental alone to unlettered persons, who, not possessing the advantage of reading, are necessarily dependent upon the stage-player for all the pleasure which they can receive from the drama, and to whom the very idea of *what an author is* cannot be made comprehensible without some pain and perplexity of mind: the error is one from which persons otherwise not meanly lettered, find it almost impossible to extricate themselves.

Never let me be so ungrateful as to forget the very high degree of satisfaction which I received some years back from seeing for the first time a tragedy of Shakspere performed, in which these two great performers sustained the principal parts. It seemed to embody and realise conceptions which had hitherto assumed no distinct shape. But dearly do we pay all our life afterwards for this juvenile pleasure, this sense of distinctness. When the novelty is past, we find to our cost that, instead of realising an idea, we have only materialised and brought down a fine vision to the standard of flesh and blood. We have let go a dream, in quest of an unattainable substance.

How cruelly this operates upon the mind, to have its free conceptions thus cramped and pressed down to the measure of a strait-lacing actuality, may be judged from that delightful sensation of freshness, with which we turn to those plays of Shakspere which have escaped being performed, and to those passages in the acting plays of the same writer which have happily been left out in the performance. How far the very custom of hearing anything *spouted*, withers and blows upon a fine passage, may be seen in those speeches from *Henry the Fifth*, etc., which are current in the mouths of school-boys from their being to be found in *Enfield Speakers*, and such kind of books. I confess myself utterly unable to appreciate that celebrated soliloquy in *Hamlet*, beginning "To be or not to be," or to tell whether it be good, bad, or indifferent, it has been so handled and pawed about by declamatory boys and men, and torn so inhumanly from its living place and principle of continuity in the play, till it is become to me a perfect dead member.

It may seem a paradox, but I cannot help being of opinion that the plays of Shakspere are less calculated for performance on a stage than those of almost any other dramatist whatever. Their distinguished excellence is a reason that they should be so. There is so much in them, which comes not under the province of acting, with which eye, and tone, and gesture, have nothing to do.

The glory of the scenic art is to personate passion, and the turns of passion; and the more coarse and palpable the passion is, the more hold upon the eyes and ears of the spectators the performer obviously possesses. For this reason, scolding scenes, scenes where two persons talk themselves into a fit of fury, and then in a surprising manner talk themselves out of it again, have always been the most popular upon our stage. And the reason is plain, because the spectators are here most palpably appealed to, they are the proper judges in this war of words, they are the legitimate ring that should be formed round such "intellectual prize-fighters." Talking is the direct object of the imitation here. But in the best dramas, and in Shakspere above all, how obvious it is, that the form of *speaking*, whether it be in soliloquy or dialogue, is only a medium, and often a highly artificial one, for putting the reader or spectator into possession of that knowledge of the inner structure and workings of mind in a character, which he could otherwise never have arrived at *in that form of composition* by any gift short of intuition. We do here as we do with novels written in the *epistolary form*. How many improprieties, perfect solecisms in letter-writing, do we put up with in "Clarissa" and other books, for the sake of the delight which that form upon the whole gives us.

But the practice of stage representation reduces everything to a controversy of elocution. Every character, from the boisterous blasphemings of Bajazet to the shrinking timidity of womanhood, must play the orator. The love-dialogues of *Romeo and Juliet*, those silver-sweet sounds of lovers' tongues by night; the more intimate and sacred sweetness of nuptial colloquy between an Othello or a Posthumus with their married wives, all those delicacies which are so delightful in the reading, as when we read of those youthful dalliances in Paradise—

> As beseem'd
> Fair couple link'd in happy nuptial league,
> Alone:

by the inherent fault of stage representation, how are these things sullied and turned from their very nature by being exposed to a large assembly; when such speeches as Imogen addresses to her lord, come drawling out of the mouth of a hired actress, whose courtship, though nominally addressed to the personated Posthumus, is manifestly aimed at the spectators, who are to judge of her endearments and her returns of love.

The character of Hamlet is perhaps that by which, since the days of Betterton, a succession of popular performers have had the greatest ambition to distinguish themselves. The length of the part may be one of their reasons. But for the character itself, we find it in a play, and therefore we judge it a fit subject of dramatic representation. The play itself abounds in maxims and reflections beyond any other, and therefore we consider it as a proper vehicle for conveying moral instruction. But Hamlet himself—what does he suffer meanwhile by being dragged forth as a public schoolmaster, to give lectures to the crowd! Why, nine parts in ten of what Hamlet does, are transactions between himself and his moral sense, they are the effusions of his solitary musings, which he retires to holes and corners and the most sequestered parts of the palace to pour forth; or rather, they are the silent meditations with which his bosom is bursting, reduced to *words* for the sake of the reader, who must else remain ignorant of what is passing there. These profound sorrows, these light-and-noise-abhorring ruminations, which the tongue scarce dares utter to deaf walls and chambers, how can they be represented by a gesticulating actor, who comes and mouths them out before an audience, making four hundred people his confidants at once? I say not that it is the fault of the actor so to do; he must pronounce them *ore rotundo*, he must accompany them with his eye, he must insinuate them into his auditory by some trick of eye, tone, or gesture, or he fails. *He must be thinking all the while of his appearance, because he knows that all the while the spectators are judging of it.* And this is the way to represent the shy, negligent, retiring Hamlet.

It is true that there is no other mode of conveying a vast quantity of thought and feeling to a great portion of the audience, who otherwise would never learn it for themselves by reading, and the intellectual acquisition gained this way may, for aught I know, be inestimable; but I am not arguing that *Hamlet* should not be acted, but how much *Hamlet* is made another thing by being acted. I have heard much of the wonders which Garrick performed in this part; but as I never saw him, I must have leave to doubt whether the representation of such a character came within the province of his art. Those who tell me of him, speak of his eye, of the magic of his eye, and of his commanding voice: physical properties, vastly desirable in an actor, and without which he can never insinuate meaning into an auditory,—but what have they to do with Hamlet? what have they to do with intellect? In fact, the things aimed at in theatrical representation, are to arrest the spectator's eye upon the form and the gesture, and so to gain a more favourable hearing to what is spoken: it is not what the character is, but how he looks; not what he says, but how he speaks it. I see no reason to think that if the play of Hamlet were written over again by some such writer as Banks or Lillo, retaining the process of the story, but totally omitting all the poetry of it, all the divine features of Shakspere, his stupendous intellect; and only taking care to give us enough of passionate dialogue, which Banks or Lillo were never at a loss to furnish; I see not how the effect could be much different upon an audience, nor how the actor has it in his power to represent Shakspere to us differently from his representation of Banks or Lillo. Hamlet would still be a youthful accomplished prince, and must be gracefully personated; he might be puzzled in his mind, wavering in his conduct, seemingly cruel to Ophelia, he might see a ghost, and start at it, and address it kindly when he found it to be his father; all this in the poorest and most homely language of the servilest creeper after nature that ever consulted the palate of an audience; without troubling Shakspere for the matter; and I see not but there would be room for all the power which an actor has, to display itself. All the passions and changes of passion might remain; for those are much less difficult to write or act than is thought; it is a trick easy to be attained, it is but rising or falling a note or two in the voice, a whisper with a significant foreboding look to announce its approach, and so contagious the counterfeit appearance of any emotion is, that let the words be what they will, the look and tone shall carry it off and make it pass for deep skill in the passions.

It is common for people to talk of Shakspere's plays being *so natural*, that everybody can understand him. They are natural indeed, they are grounded deep in nature, so deep that the depth of them lies out of the reach of most of us. You shall hear the same persons say that *George Barnwell* is very natural, and *Othello* is very natural, that they are both very deep; and to them they are the same kind of thing. At the one they sit and shed tears, because a good sort of young man is tempted by a naughty woman to commit *a trifling peccadillo*, the murder of an uncle or so,[1] that is all, and so comes to an untimely end, which is *so moving;* and at the other, because a blackamoor in a fit of jealousy kills his innocent white wife: and the odds are that ninety-nine out of a hundred would willingly behold the same catastrophe happen to both the heroes, and have thought the rope more due to Othello than to Barnwell. For of the texture of Othello's mind, the inward construction marvellously laid open with all its strengths and weaknesses, its heroic confidences and its human misgivings, its agonies of hate springing from the depths of love, they see no more than the spectators at a cheaper rate, who pay their pennies apiece to look through the man's telescope in Leicester Fields, see into the inward plot and topography of the moon. Some dim thing or other they see, they see an actor personating a passion, of grief, or anger, for instance, and they recognise it as a copy of the usual external effects of such passions; or at least as being true to *that symbol of the emotion which passes current at the theatre for it*, for it is often no more than that: but of the grounds of the passion, its correspondence to a great or heroic nature, which is the only worthy object of tragedy,

---

[1] If this note could hope to meet the eye of any of the Managers, I would entreat and beg of them, in the name of both the galleries, that this insult upon the morality of the common people of London should cease to be eternally repeated in the holiday weeks. Why are the 'Prentices of this famous and well-governed city, instead of an amusement, to be treated over and over again with a nauseous sermon of George Barnwell? Why *at the end of their vistas* are we to place the *gallows?* Were I an uncle, I should not much like a nephew of mine to have such an example placed before his eyes. It is really making uncle-murder too trivial to exhibit it as done upon such slight motives;—it is attributing too much to such characters as Millwood; it is putting things into the heads of good young men, which they would never otherwise have dreamed of. Uncles that think anything of their lives, should fairly petition the Chamberlain against it.

—that common auditors know anything of this, or can have any such notions dinned into them by the mere strength of an actor's lungs,—that apprehensions foreign to them should be thus infused into them by storm, I can neither believe, nor understand how it can be possible.

We talk of Shakspere's admirable observation of life, when we should feel that not from a petty inquisition into those cheap and every-day characters which surrounded him, as they surround us, but from his own mind, which was, to borrow a phrase of Ben Jonson's, the very "sphere of humanity," he fetched those images of virtue and of knowledge, of which every one of us recognising a part, think we comprehend in our natures the whole; and oftentimes mistake the powers which he positively creates in us for nothing more than indigenous faculties of our own minds, which only waited the application of corresponding virtues in him to return a full and clear echo of the same.

To return to Hamlet.—Among the distinguishing features of that wonderful character, one of the most interesting (yet painful) is that soreness of mind which makes him treat the intrusions of Polonius with harshness, and that asperity which he puts on in his interviews with Ophelia. These tokens of an unhinged mind (if they be not mixed in the latter case with a profound artifice of love, to alienate Ophelia by affected discourtesies, so to prepare her mind for the breaking off of that loving intercourse, which can no longer find a place amidst business so serious as that which he has to do) are parts of his character, which to reconcile with our admiration of Hamlet, the most patient consideration of his situation is no more than necessary; they are what we *forgive afterwards,* and explain by the whole of his character, but *at the time* they are harsh and unpleasant. Yet such is the actor's necessity of giving strong blows to the audience, that I have never seen a player in this character, who did not exaggerate and strain to the utmost these ambiguous features,—these temporary deformities in the character. They make him express a vulgar scorn at Polonius which utterly degrades his gentility, and which no explanation can render palatable; they make him show contempt, and curl up the nose at Ophelia's father,—contempt in its very grossest and most hateful form; but they get applause by it: it is natural, people say; that is, the words are scornful, and the actor expresses scorn, and that they can judge of: but why so much scorn, and of that sort, they never think of asking.

So to Ophelia.—All the Hamlets that I have ever seen, rant and rave at her as if she had committed some great crime, and the audience are highly pleased, because the words of the part are satirical, and they are enforced by the strongest expression of satirical indignation of which the face and voice are capable. But then, whether Hamlet is likely to have put on such brutal appearances to a lady whom he loved so dearly, is never thought on. The truth is, that in all such deep affections as had subsisted between Hamlet and Ophelia, there is a stock of *supererogatory love* (if I may venture to use the expression), which in any great grief of heart, especially where that which preys upon the mind cannot be communicated, confers a kind of indulgence upon the grieved party to express itself, even to its heart's dearest object, in the language of a temporary alienation; but it is not alienation, it is a distraction purely, and so it always makes itself to be felt by that object: it is not anger, but grief assuming the appearance of anger,—love awkwardly counterfeiting hate, as sweet countenances when they try to frown: but such sternness and fierce disgust as Hamlet is made to show, is no counterfeit, but the real face of absolute aversion,—of irreconcilable alienation. It may be said he puts on the madman; but then he should only so far put on this counterfeit lunacy as his own real distraction will give him leave; that is, incompletely, imperfectly; not in that confirmed, practised way, like a master of his art, or as Dame Quickly would say, "like one of those harlotry players."

I mean no disrespect to any actor, but the sort of pleasure which Shakspere's plays give in the acting seems to me not at all to differ from that which the audience receive from those of other writers; and, *they being in themselves essentially so different from all others*, I must conclude that there is something in the nature of acting which levels all distinctions. And in fact, who does not speak indifferently of the *Gamester* and of *Macbeth* as fine stage performances, and praise the Mrs. Beverley in the same way as the Lady Macbeth of Mrs. S.? Belvidera, and Calista, and Isabella, and Euphrasia, are they less liked than Imogen, or than Juliet, or than Desdemona? Are they not spoken of and remembered in the same way? Is not the female performer as great (as they call it) in one as in the other? Did not Garrick shine, and was he not ambitious of shining in every drawling tragedy that his wretched day produced,—the productions of the Hills and the Murphys and the Browns,—and shall he have that honour to dwell in our minds for ever as an inseparable concomitant with Shakspere? A kindred mind! O who can read that affecting sonnet of Shakspere which alludes to his profession as a player :—

> Oh for my sake do you with Fortune chide,
> The guilty goddess of my harmful deeds,
> That did not better for my life provide
> Than public means which public manners breeds—
> Thence comes it that my name receives a brand;
> And almost thence my nature is subdued
> To what it works in, like the dyer's hand——

Or that other confession ;—

> Alas! 'tis true, I have gone here and there,
> And made myself a motley to the view,
> Gored mine own thoughts, sold cheap what is most dear—

Who can read these instances of jealous self-watchfulness in our sweet Shakspere, and dream of any congeniality between him and one that, by every tradition of him, appears to have been as mere a player as ever existed;

to have had his mind tainted with the lowest player's vices,—envy and jealousy, and miserable cravings after applause; one who in the exercise of his profession was jealous even of the women-performers that stood in his way; a manager full of managerial tricks and stratagems and finesse: that any resemblance should be dreamed of between him and Shakspere,—Shakspere who, in the plenitude and consciousness of his own powers, could with that noble modesty, which we can neither imitate nor appreciate, express himself thus of his own sense of his own defects:—

> Wishing me like to one more rich in hope,
> Featured like him, like him with friends possess'd:
> Desiring *this man's art, and that man's scope.*

I am almost disposed to deny to Garrick the merits of being an admirer of Shakspere. A true lover of his excellences he certainly was not; for would any true lover of them have admitted into his matchless scenes such ribald trash as Tate and Cibber, and the rest of them, that

> With their darkness durst affront his light,

have foisted into the acting plays of Shakspere? I believe it impossible that he could have had a proper reverence for Shakspere, and have condescended to go through that interpolated scene in *Richard the Third*, in which Richard tries to break his wife's heart by telling her he loves another woman, and says, "if she survives this she is immortal." Yet I doubt not he delivered this vulgar stuff with as much anxiety of emphasis as any of the genuine parts: and for acting, it is as well calculated as any. But we have seen the part of Richard lately produce great fame to an actor by his manner of playing it, and it lets us into the secret of acting, and of popular judgments of Shakspere derived from acting. Not one of the spectators who have witnessed Mr. C.'s exertions in that part, but has come away with a proper conviction that Richard is a very wicked man, and kills little children in their beds, with something like the pleasure which the giants and ogres in children's books are represented to have taken in that practice ; moreover, that. he is very close and shrewd, and devilish cunning, for you could see that by his eye.

But is in fact this the impression we have in reading the Richard of Shakspere ? Do we feel anything like disgust, as we do at that butcher-like representation of him that passes for him on the stage ? A horror at his crimes blends with the effect which we feel, but how is it qualified, how is it carried off, by the rich intellect which he displays, his resources, his wit, his buoyant spirits, his vast knowledge and insight into characters, the poetry of his part—not an atom of all which is made perceivable in Mr. C.'s way of acting it. Nothing but his crimes, his actions, is visible ; they are prominent and staring ; the murderer stands out, but where is the lofty genius, the man of vast capacity,—the profound, the witty, accomplished Richard ?

The truth is, the characters of Shakspere are so much the objects of meditation rather than of interest or curiosity as to their actions, that while we are reading any of his great criminal characters,—Macbeth, Richard, even Iago,—we think not so much of the crimes which they commit, as of the ambition, the aspiring spirit, the intellectual activity which prompts them to overleap those moral fences. Barnwell is a wretched murderer ; there is a certain fitness between his neck and the rope ; he is the legitimate heir to the gallows ; nobody who thinks at all can think of any alleviating circumstances in his case to make him a fit object of mercy. Or to take an instance from the higher tragedy, what else but a mere assassin is Glenalvon ! Do we think of anything but of the crime which he commits, and the rack which he deserves ? That is all which we really think about him. Whereas in corresponding characters in Shakspere so little do the actions comparatively affect us, that while the impulses, the inner mind in all its perverted greatness, solely seems real and is exclusively attended to, the crime is comparatively nothing. But when we see these things represented, the acts which they do are comparatively everything, their impulses nothing. The state of sublime emotion into which we are elevated by those images of night and horror which Macbeth is made to utter, that solemn prelude with which he entertains the time till the bell shall strike which is to call him to murder Duncan,—when we no longer read it in a book, when we have given up that vantage-ground of abstraction which reading possesses over seeing, and come to see a man in his bodily shape before our eyes actually preparing to commit a murder, if the acting be true and impressive, as I have witnessed it in Mr. K.'s performance of that part, the painful anxiety about the act, the natural longing to prevent it while it yet seems unperpetrated, the too close pressing semblance of reality, give a pain and an uneasiness which totally destroy all the delight which the words in the book convey, where the deed doing never presses upon us with the painful sense of presence: it rather seems to belong to history,—to something past and inevitable, if it has anything to do with time at all. The sublime images, the poetry alone, is that which is present to our minds in the reading.

So to see Lear acted,—to see an old man tottering about the stage with a walking-stick, turned out of doors by his daughters in a rainy night, has nothing in it but what is painful and disgusting. We want to take him into shelter and relieve him. That is all the feeling which the acting of Lear ever produced in me. But the Lear of Shakspere cannot be acted. The contemptible machinery by which they mimic the storm which he goes out in, is not more inadequate to represent the horrors of the real elements, than any actor can be to represent Lear: they might more easily propose to personate the Satan of Milton upon a stage, or one of Michael Angelo's terrible figures. The greatness of Lear is not in corporal dimension, but in intellectual: the explosions of his passion are terrible as a volcano: they are storms turning up and disclosing to the bottom that sea his mind, with all its vast riches. It is his mind which is laid bare. This case of flesh and blood seems too insignificant to be thought on; even as he himself neglects it. On the stage we see nothing but corporal infirmities and weakness, the impotence of rage; while we read it, we see not Lear, but we are Lear,—we are in his mind, we are sustained by a grandeur which baffles the malice of daughters and storms; in the aberrations of his reason, we discover a mighty irregular power of reasoning, immethodised from the ordinary purposes of life, but exerting its powers, as the wind blows where it listeth, at will upon the corruptions and abuses of mankind. What have looks, or tones, to do with that sublime identification of his age with that of the *heavens themselves*, when in his reproaches to them for conniving at the injustice of his children, he reminds them that "they themselves are old?" What gestures shall we appropriate to this? What has the voice or the eye to do with such things? But the play is beyond all art, as the tamperings with it show: it is too hard and stony; it must have love-scenes, and a happy ending. It is not enough that Cordelia is a daughter, she must shine as a lover too. Tate has put his hook in the nostrils of this Leviathan, for Garrick and his followers, the showmen of scene, to draw the mighty beast about more easily. A happy ending!—as if the living martyrdom that Lear had gone through,—the flaying of his feelings alive, did not make a fair dismissal from the stage of life the only decorous thing for him. If he is to live and be happy after, if he could sustain this world's burden after, why all this pudder and preparation,—why torment us with all this unnecessary sympathy? As if the childish pleasure of getting his gilt robes and sceptre again could tempt him to act over again his misused station,—as if at his years, and with his experience, anything was left but to die.

Lear is essentially impossible to be represented on a

stage. But how many dramatic personages are there in Shakspere, which though more tractable and feasible (if I may so speak) than Lear, yet from some circumstance, some adjunct to their character, are improper to be shown to our bodily eye. *Othello,* for instance. Nothing can be more soothing, more flattering to the nobler parts of our natures, than to read of a young Venetian lady of highest extraction, through the force of love and from a sense of merit in him whom she loved, laying aside every consideration of kindred, and country, and colour, and wedding with a *coal-black Moor*—(for such he is represented, in the imperfect state of knowledge respecting foreign countries in those days, compared with our own, or in compliance with popular notions, though the Moors are now well enough known to be by many shades less unworthy of white woman's fancy)—it is the perfect triumph of virtue over accidents, of the imagination over the senses. She sees Othello's colour in his mind. But upon the stage, when the imagination is no longer the ruling faculty, but we are left to our poor unassisted senses, I appeal to every one that has seen *Othello* played, whether he did not, on the contrary, sink Othello's mind in his colour; whether he did not find something extremely revolting in the courtship and wedded caresses of Othello and Desdemona; and whether the actual sight of the thing did not over-weigh all that beautiful compromise which we make in reading;—and the reason it should do so is obvious, because there is just so much reality presented to our senses as to give a perception of disagreement, with not enough of belief in the internal motives,—all that which is unseen,—to overpower and reconcile the first and obvious prejudices.[1] What we

[1] The error of supposing that because Othello's colour does not offend us in the reading, it should also not offend us in the seeing, is just such a fallacy as supposing that an Adam and Eve in a picture shall affect us just as they do in the poem. But in the poem we for a while have Paradisaical senses given us, which vanish when we see a man and his wife without clothes in the picture. The painters themselves feel this, as is apparent by the

see upon a stage is body and bodily action; what we are conscious of in reading is almost exclusively the mind, and its movements: and this, I think, may sufficiently account for the very different sort of delight with which the same play so often affects us in the reading and the seeing.

It requires little reflection to perceive, that if those characters in Shakspere which are within the precincts of nature, have yet something in them which appeals too exclusively to the imagination, to admit of their being made objects to the senses without suffering a change and a diminution,—that still stronger the objection must lie against representing another line of characters, which Shakspere has introduced to give a wildness and a supernatural elevation to his scenes, as if to remove them still further from that assimilation to common life in which their excellence is vulgarly supposed to consist. When we read the incantations of those terrible beings the Witches in *Macbeth*, though some of the ingredients of their hellish composition savour of the grotesque, yet is the effect upon us other than the most serious and appalling that can be imagined? Do we not feel spell-bound as Macbeth was? Can any mirth accompany a sense of their presence? We might as well laugh under a consciousness of the principle of Evil himself being truly and really present with us. But attempt to bring these beings on to a stage, and you turn them instantly into so many old women, that men and children are to laugh at. Contrary to the old saying, that "seeing is believing," the sight actually destroys the faith: and the mirth in which we indulge at their expense, when we see these creatures upon a stage, seems to be a sort of indemnification which we make to ourselves for the terror which

---

awkward shifts they have recourse to, to make them look not quite naked; by a sort of prophetic anachronism antedating the invention of fig-leaves. So in the reading of the play, we see with Desdemona's eyes; in the seeing of it, we are forced to look with our own.

they put us in when reading made them an object of belief,—when we surrendered up our reason to the poet, as children to their nurses and their elders; and we laugh at our fears, as children who thought they saw something in the dark, triumph when the bringing in of a candle discovers the vanity of their fears. For this exposure of supernatural agents upon a stage is truly bringing in a candle to expose their own delusiveness. It is the solitary taper and the book that generates a faith in these terrors: a ghost by chandelier light, and in good company, deceives no spectators,—a ghost that can be measured by the eye, and his human dimensions made out at leisure. The sight of a well-lighted house, and a well-dressed audience, shall arm the most nervous child against any apprehensions: as Tom Brown says of the impenetrable skin of Achilles with his impenetrable armour over it, "Bully Dawson would have fought the devil with such advantages."

Much has been said, and deservedly, in reprobation of the vile mixture which Dryden has thrown into the *Tempest:* doubtless without some such vicious alloy, the impure ears of that age would never have sate out to hear so much innocence of love as is contained in the sweet courtship of Ferdinand and Miranda. But is the *Tempest* of Shakspere at all a subject for stage representation? It is one thing to read of an enchanter, and to believe the wondrous tale while we are reading it; but to have a conjuror brought before us in his conjuring-gown, with his spirits about him, which none but himself and some hundred of favoured spectators before the curtain are supposed to see, involves such a quantity of the *hateful incredible*, that all our reverence for the author cannot hinder us from perceiving such gross attempts upon the senses to be in the highest degree childish and inefficient Spirits and fairies cannot be represented, they cannot even be painted,—they can only be believed. But the elaborate and anxious provision of scenery, which the luxury of the age demands, in these cases works a quite contrary effect to what is intended. That which in comedy, or plays of familiar life, adds so much to the life of the imitation, in plays which appeal to the higher faculties, positively destroys the illusion which it is introduced to aid. A parlour or a drawing-room,—a library opening into a garden,—a garden with an alcove in it,—a street, or the piazza of Covent Garden does well enough in a scene; we are content to give as much credit to it as it demands; or rather, we think little about it,—it is little more than reading at the top of a page, "Scene, a Garden;" we do not imagine ourselves there, but we readily admit the imitation of familiar objects. But to think by the help of painted trees and caverns, which we know to be painted, to transport our minds to Prospero, and his island and his lonely cell;[1] or by the aid of a fiddle dexterously thrown in, in an interval of speaking, to make us believe that we hear those supernatural noises of which the isle was full:— the Orrery Lecturer at the Haymarket might as well hope, by his musical glasses cleverly stationed out of sight behind his apparatus, to make us believe that we do indeed hear the crystal spheres ring out that chime, which if it were to inwrap our fancy long, Milton thinks,

> Time would run back and fetch the age of gold,
> And speckled vanity
> Would sicken soon and die,
> And leprous Sin would melt from earthly mould;
> Yea Hell itself would pass away,
> And leave its dolorous mansions to the peering day.

The Garden of Eden, with our first parents in it, is not more impossible to be shown on a stage, than the Enchanted Isle, with its no less interesting and innocent first settlers.

The subject of Scenery is closely connected with that

---

[1] It will be said these things are done in pictures. But pictures and scenes are very different things. Painting is a word of itself, but in scene-painting there is the attempt to deceive; and there is the discordancy, never to be got over, between painted scenes and real people.

of the Dresses, which are so anxiously attended to on our stage. I remember the last time I saw *Macbeth* played, the discrepancy I felt at the changes of garment which he varied,—the shiftings and re-shiftings, like a Romish priest at mass. The luxury of stage-improvements, and the importunity of the public eye, require this. The coronation robe of the Scottish monarch was fairly a counterpart to that which our King wears when he goes to the Parliament-house,—just so full and cumbersome, and set out with ermine and pearls. And if things must be represented, I see not what to find fault with in this. But in reading, what robe are we conscious of? Some dim images of royalty—a crown and sceptre, may float before our eyes, but who shall describe the fashion of it? Do we see in our mind's eye what Webb or any other robe-maker could pattern? This is the inevitable consequence of imitating everything, to make all things natural. Whereas the reading of a tragedy is a fine abstraction. It presents to the fancy just so much of external appearances as to make us feel that we are among flesh and blood, while by far the greater and better part of our imagination is employed upon the thoughts and internal machinery of the character. But in acting, scenery, dress, the most contemptible things, call upon us to judge of their naturalness.

Perhaps it would be no bad similitude, to liken the pleasure which we take in seeing one of these fine plays acted, compared with that quiet delight which we find in the reading of it, to the different feelings with which a reviewer, and a man that is not a reviewer, reads a fine poem. The accursed critical habit,—the being called upon to judge and pronounce, must make it quite a different thing to the former. In seeing these plays acted, we are affected just as judges. When Hamlet compares the two pictures of Gertrude's first and second husband, who wants to see the pictures? But in the acting, a miniature must be lugged out; which we know not to be the picture, but only to show how finely a miniature may be represented. This shewing of everything, levels all things: it makes tricks, bows, and curtseys, of importance. Mrs. S. never got more fame by anything than by the manner in which she dismisses the guests in the banquet-scene in *Macbeth:* it is as much remembered as any of her thrilling tones or impressive looks. But does such a trifle as this enter into the imaginations of the reader of that wild and wonderful scene? Does not the mind dismiss the feasters as rapidly as it can? Does it care about the gracefulness of the doing it? But by acting, and judging of acting, all these non-essentials are raised into an importance, injurious to the main interest of the play.

I have confined my observations to the tragic parts of Shakspere. It would be no very difficult task to extend the inquiry to his comedies; and to show why Falstaff, Shallow, Sir Hugh Evans, and the rest are equally incompatible with stage representation. The length to which this Essay has run, will make it, I am afraid, sufficiently distasteful to the Amateurs of the Theatre, without going any deeper into the subject at present.

CHARACTERS OF DRAMATIC WRITERS,

CONTEMPORARY WITH SHAKSPERE.

WHEN I selected for publication, in 1808, Specimens of English Dramatic Poets who lived about the time of Shakspere, the kind of extracts which I was anxious to give were, not so much passages of wit and humour, though the old plays are rich in such, as scenes of passion, sometimes of the deepest quality, interesting situations, serious descriptions, that which is more nearly allied to poetry than to wit, and to tragic rather than to comic poetry. The plays which I made choice of were, with few exceptions, such as treat of human life and manners, rather than masques and Arcadian pastorals, with their train of abstractions, unimpassioned deities, passionate mortals—Claius, and Medorus, and Amintas, and Amarillis. My leading design was, to illustrate what may be called the moral sense of our ancestors. To shew in what manner they felt, when they placed themselves by the power of imagination in trying circumstances, in the conflicts of duty and passion, or the strife of contending duties; what sort of loves and enmities theirs were; how their griefs were tempered, and their full-swoln joys abated: how much of Shakspere shines in the great men his contemporaries, and how far in his divine mind and manners he surpassed them and all mankind. I was also desirous to bring together some of the most admired scenes of Fletcher and Massinger, in the estimation of the world the only dramatic poets of that age entitled to be considered after Shakspere, and, by exhibiting them in the same volume with the more impressive scenes of old Marlowe, Heywood, Tourneur, Webster, Ford, and others, to shew what we had slighted, while beyond all proportion we had been crying up one or two favourite names. From the desultory criticisms which accompanied that publication I have selected a few which I thought would best stand by themselves, as requiring least immediate reference to the play or passage by which they were suggested.

CHRISTOPHER MARLOWE.

Lust's Dominion, or the Lascivious Queen.—This tragedy is in King Cambyses' vein; rape, and murder, and superlatives; "huffing braggart puft lines," such as the play-writers anterior to Shakspere are full of, and Pistol but coldly imitates.

Tamburlaine the Great, or the Scythian Shepherd.— The lunes of Tamburlaine are perfect midsummer madness. Nebuchadnezzar's are mere modest pretensions compared with the thundering vaunts of this Scythian Shepherd. He comes in, drawn by conquered kings, and reproaches these *pampered jades of Asia* that they can *draw but twenty miles a day.* Till I saw this passage with my own eyes, I never believed that it was any thing more than a pleasant burlesque of mine ancient's. But I can assure my readers that it is soberly set down in a play, which their ancestors took to be serious.

Edward the Second.—In a very different style from mighty *Tamburlaine* is the tragedy of *Edward the Second.* The reluctant pangs of abdicating royalty in Edward furnished hints which Shakspere scarcely improved in his *Richard the Second*; and the death-scene of Marlowe's king moves pity and terror beyond any scene ancient or modern with which I am acquainted.

The Rich Jew of Malta.—Marlowe's Jew does not approach so near to Shakspere's as his Edward the Second does to Richard the Second. Barabas is a mere monster brought in with a large painted nose to please the rabble. He kills in sport, poisons whole nunneries, invents infernal machines. He is just such an exhibition as a century or two earlier might have been played before the Londoners " by the royal command," when a general pillage and massacre of the Hebrews had been previously resolved on in the cabinet. It is curious to see a superstition wearing out. The idea of a Jew, which our pious ancestors contemplated with so much horror, has nothing in it now revolting. We have tamed the claws of the beast, and pared its nails, and now we take it to our arms, fondle it, write plays to flatter it; it is visited by princes, affects a taste, patronises the arts, and is the only liberal and gentlemanlike thing in Christendom.

Doctor Faustus.—The growing horrors of Faustus' last scene are awfully marked by the hours and half-hours as they expire, and bring him nearer and nearer to the exactment of his dire compact. It is indeed an agony and a fearful colluctation. Marlowe is said to have been tainted with atheistical positions, to have denied God and the Trinity. To such a genius the history of Faustus must have been delectable food: to wander in fields where curiosity is forbidden to go, to approach the dark gulf near enough to look in, to be busied in speculations which are the rottenest part of the core of the fruit that fell from the tree of knowledge.[1] Barabas the Jew, and Faustus the conjurer, are offsprings of a mind which at least delighted to dally with interdicted subjects. They both talk a language which a believer would have been tender of putting into the mouth of a character though but in fiction. But the holiest minds have sometimes not thought it reprehensible to counterfeit impiety in the person of another, to bring Vice upon the stage speaking her own dialect; and, themselves being armed with an unction of self-confident impunity, have not scrupled to

---

[1] Error, entering into the world with Sin among us poor Adamites, may be said to spring from the tree of knowledge itself, and from the rotten kernels of that fatal apple.—*Howell's Letters.*

handle and touch that familiarly which would be death to others. Milton in the person of Satan has started speculations hardier than any which the feeble armoury of the atheist ever furnished; and the precise, strait-laced Richardson has strengthened Vice, from the mouth of Lovelace, with entangling sophistries and abstruse pleas against her adversary Virtue, which Sedley, Villiers, and Rochester wanted depth of libertinism enough to have invented.

Thomas Decker.

Old Fortunatus.—The humour of a frantic lover, in the scene where Orleans to his friend Galloway defends the passion with which himself, being a prisoner in the English king's court, is enamoured to frenzy of the king's daughter Agripyna, is done to the life. Orleans is as passionate an inamorata as any which Shakspere ever drew. He is just such another adept in Love's reasons. The sober people of the world are with him

——A swarm of fools
Crowding together to be counted wise.

He talks "pure Biron and Romeo," he is almost as poetical as they, quite as philosophical, only a little madder. After all, Love's sectaries are a reason unto themselves. We have gone retrograde to the noble heresy, since the days when Sidney proselyted our nation to this mixed health and disease; the kindliest symptom, yet the most alarming crisis in the ticklish state of youth; the nourisher and the destroyer of hopeful wits; the mother of twin births, wisdom and folly, valour and weakness; the servitude above freedom; the gentle mind's religion; the liberal superstition.

The Honest Whore.—There is in the second part of this play, where Bellafront, a reclaimed harlot, recounts some of the miseries of her profession, a simple picture of honour and shame, contrasted without violence, and expressed without immodesty, which is worth all the *strong*

lines against the harlot's profession with which both parts of this play are offensively crowded. A satirist is always to be suspected who, to make vice odious, dwells upon all its acts and minutest circumstances with a sort of relish and retrospective fondness. But so near are the boundaries of panegyric and invective, that a worn-out sinner is sometimes found to make the best declaimer against sin. The same high-seasoned descriptions, which in his unregenerate state served but to inflame his appetites, in his new province of a moralist will serve him, a little turned, to expose the enormity of those appetites in other men. When Cervantes with such proficiency of fondness dwells upon the Don's library, who sees not that he has been a great reader of books of knight-errantry—perhaps was at some time of his life in danger of falling into those very extravagances which he ridiculed so happily in his hero?

JOHN MARSTON.

Antonio and Mellida.—The situation of Andrugio and Lucio, in the first part of this tragedy, where Andrugio Duke of Genoa banished his country, with the loss of a son supposed drowned, is cast upon the territory of his mortal enemy the Duke of Venice, with no attendants but Lucio an old nobleman, and a page — resembles that of Lear and Kent in that king's distresses. Andrugio, like Lear, manifests a kinglike impatience, a turbulent greatness, an affected resignation. The enemies which he enters lists to combat, "Despair and mighty Grief and sharp Impatience," and the forces which he brings to vanquish them, "cornets of horse," etc., are in the boldest style of allegory. They are such a "race of mourners" as the "infection of sorrows loud" in the intellect might beget on some "pregnant cloud" in the imagination. The prologue to the second part, for its passionate earnestness, and for the tragic note of preparation which it sounds, might have preceded one of those old tales of Thebes or Pelops' line, which Milton has so highly commended, as free from the common error of the poets in his day, of "intermixing comic stuff with tragic sadness and gravity, brought in without discretion corruptly to gratify the people." It is as solemn a preparative as the "warning voice which he who saw the Apocalypse heard cry."

What you Will.—O I shall ne'er forget how he went cloath'd. Act I. Scene 1.—To judge of the liberality of these notions of dress, we must advert to the days of Gresham, and the consternation which a phenomenon habited like the merchant here described would have excited among the flat round caps and cloth stockings upon 'Change, when those "original arguments or tokens of a citizen's vocation were in fashion, not more for thrift and usefulness than for distinction and grace." The blank uniformity to which all professional distinctions in apparel have been long hastening, is one instance of the decay of symbols among us, which, whether it has contributed or not to make us a more intellectual, has certainly made us a less imaginative people. Shakspere knew the force of signs: a "malignant and a turban'd Turk." This "meal-cap miller," says the author of *God's Revenge against Murder*, to express his indignation at an atrocious outrage committed by the miller Pierot upon the person of the fair Marieta.

Author Unknown.

The Merry Devil of Edmonton.—The scene in this delightful comedy, in which Jerningham, "with the true feeling of a zealous friend," touches the griefs of Mounchensey, seems written to make the reader happy. Few of our dramatists or novelists have attended enough to this. They torture and wound us abundantly. They are economists only in delight. Nothing can be finer, more gentlemanlike, and nobler, than the conversation and compliments of these young men. How delicious is

Raymond Mounchensey's forgetting, in his fears, that Jerningham has a "Saint in Essex;" and how sweetly his friend reminds him! I wish it could be ascertained, which there is some grounds for believing, that Michael Drayton was the author of this piece. It would add a worthy appendage to the renown of that Panegyrist of my native Earth; who has gone over her soil, in his Polyolbion, with the fidelity of a herald, and the painful love of a son; who has not left a rivulet, so narrow that it may be stept over, without honourable mention; and has animated hills and streams with life and passion beyond the dreams of old mythology.

Thomas Heywood.

A Woman Killed with Kindness.—Heywood is a sort of *prose* Shakspere. His scenes are to the full as natural and affecting. But we miss *the poet*, that which in Shakspere always appears out and above the surface of *the nature*. Heywood's characters in this play, for instance, his country gentlemen, etc., are exactly what we see, but of the best kind of what we see, in life. Shakspere makes us believe, while we are among his lovely creations, that they are nothing but what we are familiar with, as in dreams new things seem old; but we awake, and sigh for the difference.

The English Traveller.—Heywood's preface to this play is interesting, as it shews the heroic indifference about the opinion of posterity, which some of these great writers seem to have felt. There is a magnanimity in authorship as in everything else. His ambition seems to have been confined to the pleasure of hearing the players speak his lines while he lived. It does not appear that he ever contemplated the possibility of being read by after ages. What a slender pittance of fame was motive sufficient to the production of such plays as the *English Traveller,* the *Challenge for Beauty,* and the *Woman Killed with Kindness!* Posterity is bound to take care that a writer loses nothing by such a noble modesty.

Thomas Middleton and William Rowley.

A Fair Quarrel.—The insipid levelling morality to which the modern stage is tied down, would not admit of such admirable passions as these scenes are filled with. A puritanical obtuseness of sentiment, a stupid infantile goodness, is creeping among us, instead of the vigorous passions, and virtues clad in flesh and blood, with which the old dramatists present us. Those noble and liberal casuists could discern in the differences, the quarrels, the animosities of men, a beauty and truth of moral feeling, no less than in the everlastingly inculcated duties of forgiveness and atonement. With us, all is hypocritical meekness. A reconciliation-scene, be the occasion never so absurd, never fails of applause. Our audiences come to the theatre to be complimented on their goodness. They compare notes with the amiable characters in the play, and find a wonderful sympathy of disposition between them. We have a common stock of dramatic morality, out of which a writer may be supplied without the trouble of copying it from originals within his own breast. To know the boundaries of honour, to be judiciously valiant, to have a temperance which shall beget a smoothness in the angry swellings of youth, to esteem life as nothing when the sacred reputation of a parent is to be defended, yet to shake and tremble under a pious cowardice when that ark of an honest confidence is found to be frail and tottering, to feel the true blows of a real disgrace blunting that sword which the imaginary strokes of a supposed false imputation had put so keen an edge upon but lately: to do, or to imagine this done in a feigned story, asks something more of a moral sense, somewhat a greater delicacy of perception in questions of right and wrong, than goes to the writing of two or three hackneyed sentences about the laws of honour as opposed to the laws of the land, or a commonplace against duelling. Yet such things would stand a writer nowadays in far better stead than Captain Agar and his conscientious honour; and he would be considered as a far better teacher of morality than old Rowley or Middleton, if they were living.

WILLIAM ROWLEY.

A New Wonder; a Woman Never Vext.—The old play-writers are distinguished by an honest boldness of exhibition, they shew everything without being ashamed. If a reverse in fortune is to be exhibited, they fairly bring us to the prison-grate and the alms-basket. A poor man on our stage is always a gentleman, he may be known by a peculiar neatness of apparel, and by wearing black. Our delicacy in fact forbids the dramatising of distress at all. It is never shewn in its essential properties; it appears but as the adjunct of some virtue, as something which is to be relieved, from the approbation of which relief the spectators are to derive a certain soothing of self-referred satisfaction. We turn away from the real essences of things to hunt after their relative shadows, moral duties; whereas, if the truth of things were fairly represented, the relative duties might be safely trusted to themselves, and moral philosophy lose the name of a science.

THOMAS MIDDLETON.

The Witch.—Though some resemblance may be traced between the charms in *Macbeth*, and the incantations in this play, which is supposed to have preceded it, this coincidence will not detract much from the originality of Shakspere. His witches are distinguished from the witches of Middleton by essential differences. These are creatures to whom man or woman, plotting some dire mischief, might resort for occasional consultation. Those originate deeds of blood, and begin bad impulses to men. From the moment that their eyes first meet with Macbeth's, he is spell-bound. That meeting sways his destiny. He can never break the fascination. These witches can hurt the body, those have power over the soul. Hecate in Middleton has a son, a low buffoon: the hags of Shakspere have neither child of their own, nor seem to be descended from any parent. They are foul anomalies, of whom we know not whence they are sprung, nor whether they have beginning or ending. As they are without human passions, so they seem to be without human relations. They come with thunder and lightning, and vanish to airy music. This is all we know of them. Except Hecate, they have no *names;* which heightens their mysteriousness. The names, and some of the properties, which the other author has given to his hags, excite smiles. The Weïrd Sisters are serious things. Their presence cannot co-exist with mirth. But, in a lesser degree, the witches of Middleton are fine creations. Their power, too, is, in some measure, over the mind. They raise jars, jealousies, strifes, "like a thick scurf" over life.

WILLIAM ROWLEY,—THOMAS DECKER,—JOHN FORD, etc.

The Witch of Edmonton.—Mother Sawyer, in this wild play, differs from the hags of both Middleton and Shakspere. She is the plain traditional old woman witch of our ancestors; poor, deformed, and ignorant; the terror of villages, herself amenable to a justice. That should be a hardy sheriff, with the power of the county at his heels, that would lay hands upon the Weïrd Sisters. They are of another jurisdiction. But upon the common and received opinion, the author (or authors) have engrafted strong fancy. There is something frightfully earnest in her invocations to the Familiar.

CYRIL TOURNEUR.

The Revengers' Tragedy.—The reality and life of the dialogue, in which Vindici and Hippolito first tempt their mother, and then threaten her with death for consenting to the dishonour of their sister, passes any scenical illusion I ever felt. I never read it but my ears tingle, and I feel a hot blush overspread my cheeks, as if I were presently about to proclaim such malefactions of myself as the brothers here rebuke in their unnatural parent, in words more keen and dagger-like than those which Hamlet speaks to his mother. Such power has the passion of shame truly personated, not only to strike guilty creatures unto the soul, but to "appal" even those that are "free."

JOHN WEBSTER.

The Duchess of Malfy.—All the several parts of the dreadful apparatus with which the death of the Duchess is ushered in, the waxen images which counterfeit death, the wild masque of madmen, the tomb-maker, the bellman, the living person's dirge, the mortification by degrees,—are not more remote from the conceptions of ordinary vengeance, than the strange character of suffering which they seem to bring upon their victim is out of the imagination of ordinary poets. As they are not like inflictions of this life, so her language seems not of this world. She has lived among horrors till she is become "native and endowed unto that element." She speaks the dialect of despair; her tongue has a smatch of Tartarus and the souls in bale. To move a horror skilfully, to touch a soul to the quick, to lay upon fear as much as it can bear, to wean and weary a life till it is ready to drop, and then step in with mortal instruments to take its last forfeit: this only a Webster can do. Inferior geniuses may "upon horror's head horrors accumulate," but they cannot do this. They mistake quantity for quality; they "terrify babes with painted devils;" but they know not how a soul is to be moved. Their terrors want dignity, their affrightments are without decorum.

The White Devil, or Vittoria Corombona.—This White Devil of Italy sets off a bad cause so speciously, and pleads with such an innocence-resembling boldness, that we seem to see that matchless beauty of her face which inspires such gay confidence into her, and are ready to expect, when she has done her pleadings, that her very judges, her accusers, the grave ambassadors who sit as spectators, and all the court, will rise and make proffer to defend her in spite of the utmost conviction of her guilt; as the Shepherds in *Don Quixote* make proffer to follow the beautiful Shepherdess Marcela, "without making any profit of her manifest resolution made there in their hearing."

> So sweet and lovely does she make the shame,
> Which, like a canker in the fragrant rose,
> Does spot the beauty of her budding name!

I never saw anything like the funeral dirge in this play, for the death of Marcello, except the ditty which reminds Ferdinand of his drowned father in the *Tempest*. As that is of the water, watery; so this is of the earth, earthy. Both have that intenseness of feeling, which seems to resolve itself into the element which it contemplates.

In a note on the *Spanish Tragedy* in the Specimens, I have said that there is nothing in the undoubted plays of Jonson which would authorise us to suppose that he could have supplied the additions to *Hieronymo*. I suspected the agency of some more potent spirit. I thought that Webster might have furnished them. They seemed full of that wild, solemn, preternatural cast of grief which bewilders us in the Duchess of Malfy. On second consideration, I think this a hasty criticism. They are more like the overflowing griefs and talking distraction of Titus Andronicus. The sorrows of the Duchess set inward; if she talks, it is little more than soliloquy imitating conversation in a kind of bravery.

JOHN FORD.

The Broken Heart.—I do not know where to find, in any play, a catastrophe so grand, so solemn, and so surprising as in this. This is indeed, according to Milton, to describe high passions and high actions. The fortitude of the Spartan boy, who let a beast gnaw out his bowels till he died without expressing a groan, is a faint bodily image of this dilaceration of the spirit, and exenteration of the inmost mind, which Calantha, with a holy violence against her nature, keeps closely covered, till the last duties of a wife and a queen are fulfilled. Stories of martyrdom are but of chains and the stake; a little bodily suffering. These torments

> On the purest spirits prey,
> As on entrails, joints, and limbs,
> With answerable pains, but more intense.

What a noble thing is the soul in its strengths and in its weaknesses! Who would be less weak than Calantha? Who can be so strong? The expression of this transcendent scene almost bears us in imagination to Calvary and the Cross; and we seem to perceive some analogy between the scenical sufferings which we are here contemplating, and the real agonies of that final completion to which we dare no more than hint a reference. Ford was of the first order of poets. He sought for sublimity, not by parcels, in metaphors or visible images, but directly where she has her full residence in the heart of man; in the actions and sufferings of the greatest minds. There is a grandeur of the soul above mountains, seas, and the elements. Even in the poor perverted reason of Giovanni and Annabella, in the play[1] which stands at the head of the modern collection of the works of this author, we discern traces of that fiery particle, which, in the irregular starting from out the road of beaten action, discovers something of a right line even in obliquity, and shews hints of an improveable greatness in the lowest descents and degradations of our nature.

[1] *'Tis Pity she is a Whore.*

Fulke Greville, Lord Brooke.

Alaham, Mustapha.—The two tragedies of Lord Brooke, printed among his poems, might with more propriety have been termed political treatises than plays. Their author has strangely contrived to make passion, character, and interest, of the highest order, subservient to the expression of state dogmas and mysteries. He is nine parts Machiavel and Tacitus, for one part Sophocles or Seneca. In this writer's estimate of the powers of the mind, the understanding must have held a most tyrannical pre-eminence. Whether we look into his plays, or his most passionate love-poems, we shall find all frozen and made rigid with intellect. The finest movements of the human heart, the utmost grandeur of which the soul is capable, are essentially comprised in the actions and speeches of Cælica and Camena. Shakspere, who seems to have had a peculiar delight in contemplating womanly perfection, whom for his many sweet images of female excellence all women are in an especial manner bound to love, has not raised the ideal of the female character higher than Lord Brooke, in these two women, has done. But it requires a study equivalent to the learning of a new language to understand their meaning when they speak. It is indeed hard to hit:

> Much like thy riddle, Samson, in one day
> Or seven though one should musing sit.

It is as if a being of pure intellect should take upon him to express the emotions of our sensitive natures. There would be all knowledge, but sympathetic expressions would be wanting.

Ben Jonson.

The Case is Altered.—The passion for wealth has worn out much of its grossness in tract of time. Our ancestors certainly conceived of money as able to confer a distinct gratification in itself, not considered simply as a symbol of wealth. The old poets, when they introduce a miser, make him address his gold as his mistress; as something to be seen, felt, and hugged; as capable of satisfying two of the senses at least. The substitution of a thin, unsatisfying medium in the place of the good old tangible metal, has made avarice quite a Platonic affection in comparison with the seeing, touching, and handling pleasures of the old Chrysophilites. A bank note can no more satisfy the touch of a true sensualist in this passion, than Creusa could return her husband's embrace in the shades. See the Cave of Mammon in Spenser; Barabas' contemplation of his wealth in the *Rich Jew of Malta;* Luke's raptures in the *City Madam;* the idolatry and absolute gold-worship of the miser Jaques in this early comic production of Ben Jonson's. Above all hear Guzman, in that excellent old translation of the *Spanish Rogue,* expatiate on the "ruddy cheeks of your golden ruddocks, your Spanish pistolets, your plump and full-faced Portuguese, and your clear-skinned pieces of eight of Castile," which he and his fellows the beggars kept secret to themselves, and did privately enjoy in a plentiful manner. "For to have them, to pay them away, is not to enjoy them; to enjoy them, is to have them lying by us; having no other need of them than to use them for the clearing of the eye-sight, and the comforting of our senses. These we did carry about with us, sewing them in some patches of our doublets near unto the heart, and as close to the skin as we could handsomely quilt them in, holding them to be restorative."

Poetaster.—This Roman play seems written to confute those enemies of Ben in his own days and ours, who have said that he made a pedantical use of his learning. He has here revived the whole Court of Augustus, by a learned spell. We are admitted to the society of the illustrious dead. Virgil, Horace, Ovid, Tibullus, converse in our own tongue more finely and poetically than they were used to express themselves in their native Latin.

Nothing can be imagined more elegant, refined, and courtlike, than the scenes between this Louis the Fourteenth of antiquity and his literati. The whole essence and secret of that kind of intercourse is contained therein. The economical liberality by which greatness, seeming to waive some part of its prerogative, takes care to lose none of the essentials; the prudential liberties of an inferior, which flatter by commanded boldness and soothe with complimentary sincerity. These, and a thousand beautiful passages from his *New Inn*, his *Cynthia's Revels*, and from those numerous court-masques and entertainments which he was in the daily habit of furnishing, might be adduced to shew the poetical fancy and elegance of mind of the supposed rugged old bard.

Alchemist.—The judgment is perfectly overwhelmed by the torrent of images, words, and book-knowledge, with which Epicure Mammon (Act II. Scene 2) confounds and stuns his incredulous hearer. They come pouring out like the successive falls of Nilus. They "doubly redouble strokes upon the foe." Description outstrides proof. We are made to believe effects before we have testimony for their causes. If there is no one image which attains the height of the sublime, yet the confluence and assemblage of them all produces a result equal to the grandest poetry. The huge Xerxean army countervails against single Achilles. Epicure Mammon is the most determined offspring of its author. It has the whole "matter and copy of the father—eye, nose, lip, the trick of his frown." It is just such a swaggerer as contemporaries have described old Ben to be. Meercraft, Bobadil, the Host of the New Inn, have all his image and superscription. But Mammon is arrogant pretension personified. Sir Samson Legend, in Love for Love, is such another lying, overbearing character, but he does not come up to Epicure Mammon. What a "towering bravery" there is in his sensuality! he affects no pleasure under a Sultan. It is as if "Egypt with Assyria strove in luxury."

GEORGE CHAPMAN.

Bussy D'Ambois, Byron's Conspiracy, Byron's Tragedy, etc. etc.—Webster has happily characterised the "full and heightened style" of Chapman, who, of all the English play-writers, perhaps approaches nearest to Shakspere in the descriptive and didactic, in passages which are less purely dramatic. He could not go out of himself, as Shakspere could shift at pleasure, to inform and animate other existences, but in himself he had an eye to perceive and a soul to embrace all forms and modes of being. He would have made a great epic poet, if indeed he has not abundantly shewn himself to be one; for his Homer is not so properly a translation as the stories of Achilles and Ulysses re-written. The earnestness and passion which he has put into every part of these poems, would be incredible to a reader of mere modern translations. His almost Greek zeal for the glory of his heroes can only be paralleled by that fierce spirit of Hebrew bigotry, with which Milton, as if personating one of the zealots of the old law, clothed himself when he sat down to paint the acts of Samson against the uncircumcised. The great obstacle to Chapman's translations being read, is their unconquerable quaintness. He pours out in the same breath the most just and natural, and the most violent and crude expressions. He seems to grasp at whatever words come first to hand while the enthusiasm is upon him, as if all other must be inadequate to the divine meaning. But passion (the all in all in poetry) is everywhere present, raising the low, dignifying the mean, and putting sense into the absurd. He makes his readers glow, weep, tremble, take any affection which he pleases, be moved by words, or in spite of them, be disgusted and overcome their disgust.

FRANCIS BEAUMONT.—JOHN FLETCHER.

Maid's Tragedy.—One characteristic of the excellent old poets is, their being able to bestow grace upon subjects which naturally do not seem susceptible of any. I will mention two instances. Zelmane in the *Arcadia* of Sidney, and Helena in the *All's Well that Ends Well* of Shakspere. What can be more unpromising at first sight, than the idea of a young man disguising himself in woman's attire, and passing himself off for a woman among women; and that for a long space of time? Yet Sir Philip has preserved so matchless a decorum, that neither does Pyrocles' manhood suffer any stain for the effeminacy of Zelmane, nor is the respect due to the princesses at all diminished when the deception comes to be known. In the sweetly constituted mind of Sir Philip Sidney, it seems as if no ugly thought or unhandsome meditation could find a harbour. He turned all that he touched into images of honour and virtue. Helena in Shakspere is a young woman seeking a man in marriage. The ordinary rules of courtship are reversed, the habitual feelings are crossed. Yet with such exquisite address this dangerous subject is handled, that Helena's forwardness loses her no honour; delicacy dispenses with its laws in her favour, and nature, in her single case, seems content to suffer a sweet violation. Aspatia, in the *Maid's Tragedy*, is a character equally difficult, with Helena, of being managed with grace. She too is a slighted woman, refused by the man who had once engaged to marry her. Yet it is artfully contrived, that while we pity we respect her, and she descends without degradation. Such wonders true poetry and passion can do, to confer dignity upon subjects which do not seem capable of it. But Aspatia must not be compared at all points with Helena; she does not so absolutely predominate over her situation but she suffers some diminution, some abatement of the full lustre of the female character, which Helena never does. Her character has many degrees of sweetness, some of delicacy; but it has weakness, which, if we do not despise, we are sorry for. After all, Beaumont and Fletcher were but an inferior sort of Shakesperes and Sidneys.

Philaster.—The character of Bellario must have been extremely popular in its day. For many years after the date of *Philaster's* first exhibition on the stage, scarce a play can be found without one of these women pages in it, following in the train of some pre-engaged lover, calling on the gods to bless her happy rival (his mistress), whom no doubt she secretly curses in her heart, giving rise to many pretty *equivoques* by the way on the confusion of sex, and either made happy at last by some surprising turn of fate, or dismissed with the joint pity of the lovers and the audience. Donne has a copy of verses to his mistress, dissuading her from a resolution which she seems to have taken up from some of these scenical representations, of following him abroad as a page. It is so earnest, so weighty, so rich in poetry, in sense, in wit, and pathos, that it deserves to be read as a solemn close in future to all such sickly fancies as he there deprecates.

JOHN FLETCHER.

Thierry and Theodoret.—The scene where Ordella offers her life a sacrifice, that the king of France may not be childless, I have always considered as the finest in all Fletcher, and Ordella to be the most perfect notion of the female heroic character, next to Calantha in the *Broken Heart*. She is a piece of sainted nature. Yet noble as the whole passage is, it must be confessed that the manner of it, compared with Shakspere's finest scenes, is faint and languid. Its motion is circular, not progressive. Each line revolves on itself in a sort of separate orbit. They do not join into one another like a running-hand. Fletcher's ideas moved slow; his versification, though sweet, is tedious, it stops at every turn; he lays line upon line, making up one after the other, adding image to image so deliberately, that we see their junctures. Shakspere mingles everything, runs line into line, embarrasses sentences and metaphors; before one idea has burst its shell, another is hatched and clamorous for disclosure. Another striking difference between Fletcher and Shakspere, is the fondness of the former for unnatural and violent situations. He seems to have thought that nothing great could be produced in an ordinary way. The chief incidents in some of his most admired tragedies shew this.[1] Shakspere had nothing of this contortion in his mind, none of that craving after violent situations, and flights of strained and improbable virtue, which I think always betrays an imperfect moral sensibility. The wit of Fletcher is excellent,[2] like his serious scenes, but there is something strained and far-fetched in both. He is too mistrustful of Nature, he always goes a little on one side of her. Shakspere chose her without a reserve: and had riches, power, understanding, and length of days, with her, for a dowry.

Faithful Shepherdess.—If all the parts of this delightful pastoral had been in unison with its many innocent scenes and sweet lyric intermixtures, it had been a poem fit to vie with *Comus* or the *Arcadia*, to have been put into the hands of boys and virgins, to have made matter for young dreams, like the loves of Hermia and Lysander. But a spot is on the face of this Diana. Nothing short of infatuation could have driven Fletcher upon mixing with this "blessedness" such an ugly deformity as Cloe, the wanton shepherdess! If Cloe was meant to set off Clorin by contrast, Fletcher should have known that such weeds by juxtaposition do not set off, but kill sweet flowers.

PHILIP MASSINGER.—THOMAS DECKER.

The Virgin Martyr.—This play has some beauties of so very high an order, that with all my respect for Massinger, I do not think he had poetical enthusiasm capable of rising up to them. His associate Decker, who wrote

[1] *Wife for a Month, Cupid's Revenge, Double Marriage*, etc.
[2] *Wit without Money*, and his comedies generally.

Old Fortunatus, had poetry enough for anything. The very impurities which obtrude themselves among the sweet pieties of this play, like Satan among the Sons of Heaven, have a strength of contrast, a raciness, and a glow, in them, which are beyond Massinger. They are to the religion of the rest what Caliban is to Miranda.

PHILIP MASSINGER.—THOMAS MIDDLETON.— WILLIAM ROWLEY.

Old Law.—There is an exquisiteness of moral sensibility, making one's eyes to gush out tears of delight, and a poetical strangeness in the circumstances of this sweet tragi-comedy, which are unlike anything in the dramas which Massinger wrote alone. The pathos is of a subtler edge. Middleton and Rowley, who assisted in it, had both of them finer geniuses than their associate.

JAMES SHIRLEY

Claims a place amongst the worthies of this period, not so much for any transcendent talent in himself, as that he was the last of a great race, all of whom spoke nearly the same language, and had a set of moral feelings and notions in common. A new language, and quite a new turn of tragic and comic interest, came in with the Restoration.

SPECIMENS

FROM THE WRITINGS OF FULLER,

THE CHURCH HISTORIAN.

THE writings of Fuller are usually designated by the title of quaint, and with sufficient reason; for such was his natural bias to conceits, that I doubt not upon most occasions it would have been going out of his way to have expressed himself out of them. But his wit is not always a *lumen siccum*, a dry faculty of surprising; on the contrary, his conceits are oftentimes deeply steeped in human feeling and passion. Above all, his way of telling a story, for its eager liveliness, and the perpetual running commentary of the narrator happily blended with the narration, is perhaps unequalled.

As his works are now scarcely perused but by antiquaries, I thought it might not be unacceptable to my readers to present them with some specimens of his manner, in single thoughts and phrases; and in some few passages of greater length, chiefly of a narrative description. I shall arrange them as I casually find them in my book of extracts, without being solicitous to specify the particular work from which they are taken.

Pyramids.—"The Pyramids themselves, doting with age, have forgotten the names of their founders."

Virtue in a short person.—"His soul had but a short diocese to visit, and therefore might the better attend the effectual informing thereof."

Intellect in a very tall one.—" Oft times such who are built four stories high, are observed to have little in their cock-loft."

Naturals.—" Their heads sometimes so little, that there is no room for wit; sometimes so long, that there is no wit for so much room."

Negroes.—" The image of God cut in ebony."

School-divinity.—" At the first it will be as welcome to thee as a prison, and their very solutions will seem knots unto thee."

Mr. Perkins, the Divine.—" He had a capacious head, with angles winding and roomy enough to lodge all controversial intricacies."

The same.—"He would pronounce the word *Damn* with such an emphasis as left a doleful echo in his auditors' ears a good while after."

Judges in capital cases.—" O let him take heed how he strikes, that hath a dead hand."

Memory.—" Philosophers place it in the rear of the head, and it seems the mine of memory lies there, because there men naturally dig for it, scratching it when they are at a loss."

Fancy.—" It is the most boundless and restless faculty of the soul; for while the Understanding and the Will are kept, as it were, *in libera custodia* to their objects of *verum et bonum*, the Fancy is free from all engagements: it digs without spade, sails without ship, flies without wings, builds without charges, fights without bloodshed; in a moment striding from the centre to the circumference of the world; by a kind of omnipotency creating and annihilating things in an instant; and things divorced in Nature are married in Fancy as in a lawless place."

Infants.—" Some, admiring what motives to mirth infants meet with in their silent and solitary smiles, have resolved, how truly I know not, that then they converse with angels; as indeed such cannot among mortals find any fitter companions."

Music.—" Such is the sociableness of music, it conforms itself to all companies both in mirth and mourning; complying to improve that passion with which it finds the auditors most affected. In a word, it is an invention which might have beseemed a son of Seth to have been the father thereof: though better it was that Cain's great grandchild should have the credit first to find it, than the world the unhappiness longer to have wanted it."

St. Monica.—"Drawing near her death, she sent most pious thoughts as harbingers to heaven, and her soul saw a glimpse of happiness through the chinks of her sickness-broken body."[1]

Mortality.—"To smell to a turf of fresh earth is wholesome for the body, no less are thoughts of mortality cordial to the soul."

Virgin.—"No lording husband shall at the same time command her presence and distance; to be always near in constant attendance, and always to stand aloof in awful observance."

Elder Brother.—"Is one who made haste to come into the world to bring his parents the first news of male posterity, and is well rewarded for his tidings."

Bishop Fletcher.—"His pride was rather on him than in him, as only gait and gesture deep, not sinking to his heart, though causelessly condemned for a proud man, as who was a *good hypocrite*, and far more humble than he appeared."

Masters of Colleges.—"A little allay of dulness in a Master of a College makes him fitter to manage secular affairs."

The Good Yeoman.—"Is a gentleman in ore, whom the next age may see refined."

Good Parent.—"For his love, therein, like a well-drawn picture, he eyes all his children alike."

Deformity in Children.—"This partiality is tyranny,

---

[1] The soul's dark cottage, batter'd and decay'd,
  Lets in new lights through chinks which time has made.
  WALLER.

when parents despise those that are deformed; *enough to break those whom God had bowed before."*

Good Master.—" In correcting his servant he becomes not a slave to his own passion. Not cruelly making new *indentures* of the flesh of his apprentice. He is tender of his servant in sickness and age. If crippled in his service, his house is his hospital. Yet how many throw away those dry bones, out of the which themselves have sucked the marrow!"

Good Widow.—" If she can speak but little good of him [her dead husband] she speaks but little of him. So handsomely folding up her discourse, that his virtues are shewn outwards, and his vices wrapped up in silence; as counting it barbarism to throw dirt on his memory who hath moulds cast on his body."

Horses.—" These are men's wings, wherewith they make such speed. A generous creature a horse is, sensible in some sort of honour; and made most handsome by that which deforms men most—pride."

Martyrdom.—" Heart of oak hath sometimes warped a little in the scorching heat of persecution. Their want of true courage herein cannot be excused. Yet many censure them for surrendering up their forts after a long siege, who would have yielded up their own at the first summons. Oh! there is more required to make one valiant, than to call Cranmer or Jewel coward; as if the fire in Smithfield had been no hotter than what is painted in the Book of Martyrs."

Text of St. Paul.—"St. Paul saith, let not the sun go down on your wrath, to carry news to the antipodes in another world of thy revengeful nature. Yet let us take the Apostle's meaning rather than his words, with all possible speed to depose our passion; not understanding him so literally, that we may take leave to be angry till sunset: then might our wrath lengthen with the days; and men in Greenland, where the day lasts above a quarter of a year, have plentiful scope for revenge."[1]

[1] This whimsical prevention of a consequence which no one

Bishop Brownrig.—"He carried learning enough *in numerato* about him in his pockets for any discourse, and had much more at home in his chests for any serious dispute."

Modest Want.—"Those that with diligence fight against poverty, though neither conquer till death makes it a drawn battle; expect not but prevent their craving of thee: for God forbid the heavens should never rain, till the earth first opens her mouth; seeing *some grounds will sooner burn than chap.*"

Death-bed Temptations.—"The devil is most busy on the last day of his term; and a tenant to be outed cares not what mischief he doth."

Conversation.—"Seeing we are civilised Englishmen, let us not be naked savages in our talk."

Wounded Soldier.—"Halting is the stateliest march of a soldier; and 'tis a brave sight to see the flesh of an ancient as torn as his colours."

Wat Tyler.—"*A misogrammatist;* if a good Greek word may be given to so barbarous a rebel."

Heralds.—"Heralds new mould men's names,—taking from them, adding to them, melting out all the liquid letters, torturing mutes to make them speak, and making vowels dumb,—to bring it to a fallacious *homonomy* at the last, that their names may be the same with those noble houses they pretend to."

Antiquarian Diligence.—"It is most worthy observation, with what diligence he [Camden] inquired after ancient places, making hue and cry after many a city which was run away, and by certain marks and tokens pursuing to find it; as by the situation on the Roman highways, by just distance from other ancient cities, by

would have thought of deducing,—setting up an absurdum on purpose to hunt it down,—placing guards as it were at the very outposts of possibility,—gravely giving out laws to insanity and prescribing moral fences to distempered intellects, could never have entered into a head less entertainingly constructed than that of Fuller, or Sir Thomas Browne, the very air of whose style the conclusion of this passage most aptly imitates.

some affinity of name, by tradition of the inhabitants, by Roman coins digged up, and by some appearance of ruins. A broken urn is a whole evidence; or an old gate still surviving, out of which the city is run out. Besides, commonly some new spruce town not far off is grown out of the ashes thereof, which yet hath so much natural affection as dutifully to own those reverend ruins for her mother."

Henry de Essex.—" He is too well known in our English Chronicles, being Baron of Raleigh, in Essex, and Hereditary Standard Bearer of England. It happened in the reign of this king [Henry II.] there was a fierce battle fought in Flintshire, at Coleshall, between the English and Welsh, wherein this Henry de Essex *animum et signum simul abjecit,* betwixt traitor and coward, cast away both his courage and banner together, occasioning a great overthrow of English. But he that had the baseness to do, had the boldness to deny the doing of so foul a fact; until he was challenged in combat by Robert de Momford, a knight, eye-witness thereof, and by him overcome in a duel. Whereupon his large inheritance was confiscated to the king, and he himself, *partly thrust, partly going into a convent, hid his head in a cowl, under which, betwixt shame and sanctity, he blushed out the remainder of his life.*"[1]—*Worthies.* Article, "Bedfordshire."

[1] The fine imagination of Fuller has done what might have been pronounced impossible: it has given an interest, and a holy character, to coward infamy. Nothing can be more beautiful than the concluding account of the last days, and expiatory retirement, of poor Henry de Essex. The address with which the whole of this little story is told is most consummate: the charm of it seems to consist in a perpetual balance of antitheses not too violently opposed, and the consequent activity of mind in which the reader is kept: —"Betwixt traitor and coward"—"baseness to do, boldness to deny"—" partly thrust, partly going, into a convent"—"betwixt shame and sanctity." The reader by this artifice is taken into a kind of partnership with the writer,—his judgment is exercised in settling the preponderance,—he feels as if he were consulted as to the issue. But the modern historian flings at once the dead weight of his own judgment into the scale, and settles the matter.

Sir Edward Harwood, Knt.—"I have read of a bird, which hath a face like, and yet will prey upon, a man; who coming to the water to drink, and finding there by reflection, that he had killed one like himself, pineth away by degrees, and never afterwards enjoyeth itself.[1] Such in some sort the condition of Sir Edward. This accident, that he had killed one in a private quarrel, put period to his carnal mirth, and was a covering to his eyes all the days of his life. No possible provocations could afterwards tempt him to a duel; and no wonder that one's conscience loathed that whereof he had surfeited. He refused all challenges with more honour than others accepted them; it being well known, that he would set his foot as far in the face of his enemy as any man alive."—*Worthies.* Art. "Lincolnshire."

Decayed Gentry.—"It happened in the reign of King James, when Henry Earl of Huntingdon was Lieutenant of Leicestershire, that a labourer's son in that county was pressed into the wars; as I take it, to go over with Count Mansfield. The old man at Leicester requested his son might be discharged, as being the only staff of his age, who by his industry maintained him and his mother. The Earl demanded his name, which the man for a long time was loth to tell (as suspecting it a fault

---

[1] I do not know where Fuller read of this bird; but a more awful and affecting story, and moralising of a story, in Natural History, or rather in that Fabulous Natural History, where poets and mythologists found the Phœnix and the Unicorn, and "other strange fowl," is nowhere extant. It is a fable which Sir Thomas Browne, if he had heard of it, would have exploded among his Vulgar Errors; but the delight which he would have taken in the discussing of its probabilities, would have shown that the *truth of the fact*, though the avowed object of his search, was not so much the motive which put him upon the investigation, as those hidden affinities and poetical analogies,—those *essential verities* in the application of strange fable, which made him linger with such reluctant delay among the last fading lights of popular tradition; and not seldom to conjure up a superstition, that had been long extinct, from its dusty grave, to inter it himself with greater ceremonies and solemnities of burial.

for so poor a man to confess the truth), at last he told his name was Hastings. "Cousin Hastings," said the Earl, "we cannot all be top branches of the tree, though we all spring from the same root; your son, my kinsman, shall not be pressed." So good was the meeting of modesty in a poor, with courtesy in an honourable person, and gentry I believe in both. And I have reason to believe that some who justly own the surnames and blood of Bohuns, Mortimers, and Plantagenets (though ignorant of their own extractions), are hid in the heap of common people, where they find that under a thatched cottage, which some of their ancestors could not enjoy in a leaded castle,—contentment, with quiet and security."—*Worthies.* Art., "Of Shire-Reeves or Shiriffes."

Tenderness of Conscience in a Tradesman.—"Thomas Curson, born in Allhallows, Lombard Street, armourer, dwelt without Bishopsgate. It happened that a stage-player borrowed a rusty musket, which had lain long leger in his shop: now though his part were comical, he therewith acted an unexpected tragedy, killing one of the standers by, the gun casually going off on the stage, which he suspected not to be charged. O the difference of divers men in the tenderness of their consciences; some are scarce touched with a wound, whilst others are wounded with a touch therein. This poor armourer was highly afflicted therewith, though done against his will, yea without his knowledge, in his absence, by another, out of mere chance. Hereupon he resolved to give all his estate to pious uses: no sooner had he gotten a round sum, but presently he posted with it in his apron to the Court of Aldermen, and was in pain till by their direction he had settled it for the relief of poor in his own and other parishes, and disposed of some hundreds of pounds accordingly, as I am credibly informed by the then churchwardens of the said parish. Thus as he conceived himself casually (though at a great distance) to have occasioned the death of one, he was the immediate and direct cause of giving a comfortable living to many."

Burning of Wickliffe's Body by Order of the Council of Constance.—"Hitherto [A.D. 1428] the corpse of John Wickliffe had quietly slept in his grave about forty-one years after his death, till his body was reduced to bones, and his bones almost to dust. For though the earth in the chancel of Lutterworth, in Leicestershire, where he was interred, hath not so quick a digestion with the earth of Acoldama, to consume flesh in twenty-four hours, yet such the appetite thereof, and all other English graves, to leave small reversions of a body after so many years. But now such the spleen of the Council of Constance, as they not only cursed his memory as dying an obstinate heretic, but ordered that his bones (with this charitable caution,—if it may be discerned from the bodies of other faithful people) to be taken out of the ground, and thrown far off from any Christian burial. In obedience hereunto, Rich. Fleming, Bishop of Lincoln, Diocesan of Lutterworth, sent his officers (vultures with a quick sight, scent, at a dead carcase) to ungrave him. Accordingly to Lutterworth they come, Sumner, Commissary, Official, Chancellor, Proctors, Doctors, and their servants (so that the remnant of the body would not hold out a bone amongst so many hands), take what was left out of the grave, and burnt them to ashes, and cast them into Swift, a neighbouring brook, running hard by. *Thus this brook has conveyed his ashes into Avon, Avon into Severn, Severn into the narrow seas, they into the main ocean; and thus the ashes of Wickliffe are the emblem of his doctrine, which now is dispersed all the world over.*"[1]—*Church History.*

---

[1] The concluding period of this most lively narrative I will not call a conceit: it is one of the grandest conceptions I ever met with. One feels the ashes of Wickliffe gliding away out of the reach of the Sumners, Commissaries, Officials, Proctors, Doctors, and all the puddering rout of executioners of the impotent rage of the baffled Council: from Swift into Avon, from Avon into Severn, from Severn into the narrow seas, from the narrow seas into the main ocean, where they become the emblem of his doctrine, "dispersed all the world over." Hamlet's tracing the body of Cæsar

to the clay that stops a beer-barrel, is a no less curious pursuit of "ruined mortality;" but it is in an inverse ratio to this: it degrades and saddens us, for one part of our nature at least; but this expands the whole of our nature, and gives to the body a sort of ubiquity,—a diffusion, as far as the actions of its partner can have reach or influence.

I have seen this passage smiled at, and set down as a quaint conceit of old Fuller. But what is not a conceit to those who read it in a temper different from that in which the writer composed it? The most pathetic parts of poetry to cold tempers seem and are nonsense, as divinity was to the Greeks foolishness. When Richard II., meditating on his own utter annihilation as to royalty, cries out,

> "O that I were a mockery king of snow,
> To melt before the sun of Bolingbroke,"

if we have been going on pace for pace with the passion before, this sudden conversion of a strong-felt metaphor into something to be actually realised in nature, like that of Jeremiah, "Oh! that my head were waters, and mine eyes a fountain of tears," is strictly and strikingly natural; but come unprepared upon it, and it is a conceit: and so is a "head" turned into "waters."

ON THE
GENIUS AND CHARACTER OF HOGARTH;

WITH SOME REMARKS ON A PASSAGE IN THE WRITINGS OF THE LATE MR. BARRY.

ONE of the earliest and noblest enjoyments I had when a boy was in the contemplation of those capital prints by Hogarth, the *Harlot's* and *Rake's Progresses*, which, along with some others, hung upon the walls of a great hall in an old-fashioned house in ——shire, and seemed the solitary tenants (with myself) of that antiquated and life-deserted apartment.

Recollection of the manner in which those prints used to affect me, has often made me wonder, when I have heard Hogarth described as a mere comic painter, as one whose chief ambition was to *raise a laugh*. To deny that there are throughout the prints which I have mentioned circumstances introduced of a laughable tendency, would be to run counter to the common notions of mankind; but to suppose that in their *ruling character* they appeal chiefly to the risible faculty, and not first and foremost to the very heart of man, its best and most serious feelings, would be to mistake no less grossly their aim and purpose. A set of severer Satires (for they are not so much Comedies, which they have been likened to, as they are strong and masculine Satires) less mingled with any thing of mere fun, were never written upon paper, or graven upon copper. They resemble Juvenal, or the satiric touches in *Timon of Athens*.

I was pleased with the reply of a gentleman, who being asked which book he esteemed most in his library, answered,—"Shakspere:" being asked which he esteemed next best, replied—"Hogarth." His graphic representations are indeed books: they have the teeming, fruitful, suggestive meaning of *words*. Other pictures we look at,—his prints we read.

In pursuance of this parallel, I have sometimes entertained myself with comparing the *Timon of Athens* of Shakspere (which I have just mentioned) and Hogarth's *Rake's Progress* together. The story, the moral, in both is nearly the same. The wild course of riot and extravagance, ending in the one with driving the Prodigal from the society of men into the solitude of the deserts, and in the other with conducting the Rake through his several stages of dissipation into the still more complete desolations of the mad-house, in the play and in the picture are described with almost equal force and nature. The levee of the Rake, which forms the subject of the second plate in the series, is almost a transcript of Timon's levee in the opening scene of that play. We find a dedicating poet, and other similar characters, in both.

The concluding scene in the *Rake's Progress* is perhaps superior to the last scenes of *Timon*. If we seek for something of kindred excellence in poetry, it must be in the scenes of Lear's beginning madness, where the King and the Fool and the Tom-o'-Bedlam conspire to produce such a medley of mirth checked by misery, and misery rebuked by mirth; where the society of those "strange bed-fellows" which misfortunes have brought Lear acquainted with, so finely sets forth the destitute state of the monarch, while the lunatic bans of the one, and the disjointed sayings and wild but pregnant allusions of the other, so wonderfully sympathise with that confusion, which they seem to assist in the production of, in the senses of that "child-changed father."

In the scene in Bedlam, which terminates the *Rake's Progress*, we find the same assortment of the ludicrous

T

with the terrible. Here is desperate madness, the overturning of originally strong thinking faculties, at which we shudder, as we contemplate the duration and pressure of affliction which it must have asked to destroy such a building;—and here is the gradual hurtless lapse into idiocy, of faculties, which at their best of times never having been strong, we look upon the consummation of their decay with no more of pity than is consistent with a smile. The mad taylor, the poor driveller that has gone out of his wits (and truly he appears to have had no great journey to go to get past their confines) for the love of *Charming Betty Careless*,—these half-laughable, scarce-pitiable objects take off from the horror which the principal figure would of itself raise, at the same time that they assist the feeling of the scene by contributing to the general notion of its subject:—

> Madness, thou chaos of the brain,
> What art, that pleasure giv'st, and pain?
> Tyranny of Fancy's reign!
> Mechanic Fancy, that can build
> Vast labyrinths and mazes wild,
> With rule disjointed, shapeless measure,
> Fill'd with horror, fill'd with pleasure!
> Shapes of horror, that would even
> Cast doubts of mercy upon heaven.
> Shapes of pleasure, that, but seen,
> Would split the shaking sides of spleen.[1]

Is it carrying the spirit of comparison to excess to remark, that in the poor kneeling weeping female, who accompanies her seducer in his sad decay, there is something analogous to Kent, or Caius, as he delights rather to be called, in *Lear*,—the noblest pattern of virtue which even Shakspere has conceived,—who follows his royal master in banishment, that had pronounced *his* banishment, and forgetful at once of his wrongs and dignities, taking on himself the disguise of a menial, retains his fidelity to the figure, his loyalty to the carcase, the shadow, the shell and empty husk of Lear?

---

[1] Lines inscribed under the plate.

In the perusal of a book, or of a picture, much of the impression which we receive depends upon the habit of mind which we bring with us to such perusal. The same circumstance may make one person laugh, which shall render another very serious; or in the same person the first impression may be corrected by after-thought. The misemployed incongruous characters at the *Harlot's Funeral*, on a superficial inspection, provoke to laughter; but when we have sacrificed the first emotion to levity, a very different frame of mind succeeds, or the painter has lost half his purpose. I never look at that wonderful assemblage of depraved beings, who, without a grain of reverence or pity in their perverted minds, are performing the sacred exteriors of duty to the relics of their departed partner in folly, but I am as much moved to sympathy from the very want of it in them, as I should be by the finest representation of a virtuous death-bed surrounded by real mourners, pious children, weeping friends,—perhaps more by the very contrast. What reflections does it not awake, of the dreadful heartless state in which the creature (a female too) must have lived, who in death wants the accompaniment of one genuine tear. That wretch who is removing the lid of the coffin to gaze upon the corpse with a face which indicates a perfect negation of all goodness or womanhood—the hypocrite parson and his demure partner—all the fiendish group—to a thoughtful mind present a moral emblem more affecting than if the poor friendless carcase had been depicted as thrown out to the woods, where wolves had assisted at its obsequies, itself furnishing forth its own funeral banquet.

It is easy to laugh at such incongruities as are met together in this picture,—incongruous objects being of the very essence of laughter,—but surely the laugh is far different in its kind from that thoughtless species to which we are moved by mere farce and grotesque. We laugh when Ferdinand Count Fathom, at the first sight of the white cliffs of Britain, feels his heart yearn with filial fondness towards the land of his progenitors, which he is coming to fleece and plunder,—we smile at the exquisite irony of the passage,—but if we are not led on by such passages to some more salutary feeling than laughter, we are very negligent perusers of them in book or picture.

It is the fashion with those who cry up the great Historical School in this country, at the head of which Sir Joshua Reynolds is placed, to exclude Hogarth from that school, as an artist of an inferior and vulgar class. Those persons seem to me to confound the painting of subjects in common or vulgar life with the being a vulgar artist. The quantity of thought which Hogarth crowds into every picture, would alone *unvulgarise* every subject which he might choose. Let us take the lowest of his subjects, the print called *Gin Lane*. Here is plenty of poverty and low stuff to disgust upon a superficial view; and accordingly, a cold spectator feels himself immediately disgusted and repelled. I have seen many turn away from it, not being able to bear it. The same persons would perhaps have looked with great complacency upon Poussin's celebrated picture of the *Plague at Athens*.[1] Disease and Death and bewildering Terror, in *Athenian garments* are endurable, and come, as the delicate critics express it, within the "limits of pleasurable sensation." But the scenes of their own St. Giles', delineated by their own countryman, are too shocking to think of. Yet if we could abstract our minds from the fascinating colours of the picture, and forget the coarse execution (in some respects) of the print, intended as it was to be a cheap plate, accessible to the poorer sort of people, for whose instruction it was done, I think we could have no hesitation in conferring the palm of superior genius upon Hogarth, comparing this work of his with Poussin's picture. There is more of imagination in it—that power which draws all things to one,—which makes things animate and inanimate, beings with their attributes,

[1] At the late Mr. Hope's, in Cavendish Square.

subjects and their accessories, take one colour, and serve to one effect. Every thing in the print, to use a vulgar expression, *tells*. Every part is full of "strange images of death." It is perfectly amazing and astounding to look at. Not only the two prominent figures, the woman and the half-dead man, which are as terrible as any thing which Michael Angelo ever drew, but every thing else in the print contributes to bewilder and stupefy,—the very houses, as I heard a friend of mine express it, tumbling all about in various directions, seem drunk— seem absolutely reeling from the effect of that diabolical spirit of frenzy which goes forth over the whole composition.—To show the poetical and almost prophetical conception in the artist, one little circumstance may serve. Not content with the dying and dead figures, which he has strewed in profusion over the proper scene of the action, he shews you what (of a kindred nature) is passing beyond it. Close by the shell, in which, by the direction of the parish beadle, a man is depositing his wife, is an old wall, which, partaking of the universal decay around it, is tumbling to pieces. Through a gap in this wall are seen three figures, which appear to make a part in some funeral procession which is passing by on the other side of the wall, out of the sphere of the composition. This extending of the interest beyond the bounds of the subject could only have been conceived by a great genius. Shakspere, in his description of the painting of the Trojan War, in his *Tarquin and Lucrece*, has introduced a similar device, where the painter made a part stand for the whole:—

> For much imaginary work was there,
> Conceit deceitful, so compact, so kind,
> That for Achilles' image stood his spear,
> Grip'd in an armed hand; himself behind
> Was left unseen, save to the eye of mind:
> A hand, a foot, a face, a leg, a head,
> Stood for the whole to be imagined.

This he well calls *imaginary work*, where the spectator

must meet the artist in his conceptions half way; and it is peculiar to the confidence of high genius alone to trust so much to spectators or readers. Lesser artists shew every thing distinct and full, as they require an object to be made out to themselves before they can comprehend it.

When I think of the power displayed in this (I will not hesitate to say) sublime print, it seems to me the extreme narrowness of system alone, and of that rage for classification, by which, in matters of taste at least, we are perpetually perplexing instead of arranging our ideas, that would make us concede to the work of Poussin above mentioned, and deny to this of Hogarth, the name of a grand serious composition.

We are for ever deceiving ourselves with names and theories. We call one man a great historical painter, because he has taken for his subjects kings or great men, or transactions over which time has thrown a grandeur. We term another the painter of common life, and set him down in our minds for an artist of an inferior class, without reflecting whether the quantity of thought shewn by the latter may not much more than level the distinction which their mere choice of subjects may seem to place between them; or whether, in fact, from that very common life a great artist may not extract as deep an interest as another man from that which we are pleased to call history.

I entertain the highest respect for the talents and virtues of Reynolds, but I do not like that his reputation should overshadow and stifle the merits of such a man as Hogarth, nor that to mere names and classifications we should be content to sacrifice one of the greatest ornaments of England.

I would ask the most enthusiastic admirer of Reynolds, whether, in the countenances of his *Staring* and *Grinning Despair*, which he has given us for the faces of Ugolino and dying Beaufort, there be anything comparable to the expression which Hogarth has put into the face of his broken-down rake in the last plate but one of the *Rake's*

Progress,[1] where a letter from the manager is brought to him to say that his play "will not do?" Here all is easy, natural, undistorted, but withal what a mass of woe is here accumulated!—the long history of a mis-spent life is compressed into the countenance as plainly as the series of plates before had told it; here is no attempt at Gorgonian looks which are to freeze the beholder, no grinning at the antique bed-posts, no face-making, or consciousness of the presence of spectators in or out of the picture, but grief kept to a man's self, a face retiring from notice with the shame which great anguish sometimes brings with it, —a final leave taken of hope,—the coming on of vacancy and stupefaction,—a beginning alienation of mind looking like tranquillity. Here is matter for the mind of the beholder to feed on for the hour together,—matter to feed and fertilise the mind. It is too real to admit one thought about the power of the artist who did it. —When we compare the expression in subjects which so fairly admit of comparison, and find the superiority so clearly to remain with Hogarth, shall the mere contemptible difference of the scene of it being laid in the one case in our Fleet or King's Bench Prison, and in the other in the State Prison of Pisa, or the bedroom of a cardinal, or that the subject of the one has never been authenticated, and the other is matter of history,— so weigh down the real points of the comparison, as to induce us to rank the artist who has chosen the one scene or subject (though confessedly inferior in that which constitutes the soul of his art) in a class from which we exclude the better genius (who has happened to make choice of the other) with something like disgrace?[2]

[1] The first perhaps in all Hogarth for serious expression. That which comes next to it, I think, is the jaded morning countenance of the debauchée in the second plate of the *Marriage Alamode*, which lectures on the vanity of pleasure as audibly as any thing in Ecclesiastes.

[2] Sir Joshua Reynolds, somewhere in his lectures, speaks of the *presumption* of Hogarth in attempting the grand style in painting, by which he means his choice of certain Scripture subjects.

The Boys under Demoniacal Possession of Raphael and Dominichino, by what law of classification are we bound to assign them to belong to the great style in painting, and to degrade into an inferior class the Rake of Hogarth when he is the Madman in the Bedlam scene? I am sure he is far more impressive than either. It is a face which no one that has seen can easily forget. There is the stretch of human suffering to the utmost endurance, severe bodily pain brought on by strong mental agony, the frightful obstinate laugh of madness,— yet all so unforced and natural, that those who never were witness to madness in real life, think they see nothing but what is familiar to them in this face. Here are no tricks of distortion, nothing but the natural face of agony. This is high tragic painting, and we might as well deny to Shakspere the honours of a great tragedian, because he has interwoven scenes of mirth with the serious business of his plays, as refuse to Hogarth the same praise for the two concluding scenes of the *Rake's Progress*, because of the Comic Lunatics [1] which he has thrown into the

Hogarth's excursions into Holy Land were not very numerous, but what he has left us in this kind have at least this merit, that they have expression of *some sort or other* in them,—the *Child Moses before Pharaoh's Daughter*, for instance: which is more than can be said of Sir Joshua Reynold's *Repose in Egypt*, painted for Macklin's Bible, where for a Madonna he has substituted a sleepy, insensible, unmotherly girl, one so little worthy to have been selected as the Mother of the Saviour, that she seems to have neither heart nor feeling to entitle her to become a mother at all. But indeed the race of Virgin Mary painters seems to have been cut up, root and branch, at the Reformation. Our artists are too good Protestants to give life to that admirable commixture of maternal tenderness with reverential awe and wonder approaching to worship, with which the Virgin Mothers of L. da Vinci and Raphael (themselves by their divine countenances inviting men to worship) contemplate the union of the two natures in the person of their Heaven-born Infant.

[1] There are of madmen, as there are of tame,
All-humour'd not alike. We have here some
So apish and fantastic, play with a feather;
And though 'twould grieve a soul to see God's image
So blemish'd and defac'd, yet do they act

one, or the Alchymist that he has introduced in the other, who is paddling in the coals of his furnace, keeping alive the flames of vain hope within the very walls of the prison to which the vanity has conducted him, which have taught the darker lesson of extinguished hope to the desponding figure who is the principal person of the scene.

It is the force of these kindly admixtures, which assimilates the scenes of Hogarth and of Shakspere to the drama of real life, where no such thing as pure tragedy is to be found; but merriment and infelicity, ponderous crime and feather-light vanity, like twi-formed births, disagreeing complexions of one intertexture, perpetually unite to shew forth motley spectacles to the world. Then it is that the poet or painter shews his art, when in the selection of these comic adjuncts he chooses such circumstances as shall relieve, contrast with, or fall into, without forming a violent opposition to, his principal object. Who sees not that the Grave-digger in *Hamlet*, the Fool in *Lear*, have a kind of correspondency to, and fall in with, the subjects which they seem to interrupt, while the comic stuff in *Venice Preserved*, and the doggerel nonsense of the Cook and his poisoning associates in the *Rollo* of Beaumont and Fletcher, are pure, irrelevant, impertinent discords,—as bad as the quarrelling dog and cat under the table of the *Lord and the Disciples at Emmaus* of Titian?

Not to tire the reader with perpetual reference to prints which he may not be fortunate enough to possess, it may be sufficient to remark, that the same tragic cast of expression and incident, blended in some instances with a greater alloy of comedy, characterises his other great work, the *Marriage Alamode*, as well as those less elabor-

> Such antic and such pretty lunacies,
> That, spite of sorrow, they will make you smile.
> Others again we have, like angry lions,
> Fierce as wild bulls, untamable as flies.
> *Honest Whore.*

ate exertions of his genius, the prints called *Industry* and *Idleness*, the *Distrest Poet*, etc., forming, with the *Harlot's* and *Rake's Progresses*, the most considerable if not the largest class of his productions,—enough surely to rescue Hogarth from the imputation of being a mere buffoon, or one whose general aim was only to *shake the sides*.

There remains a very numerous class of his performances, the object of which must be confessed to be principally comic. But in all of them will be found something to distinguish them from the droll productions of Bunbury and others. They have this difference, that we do not merely laugh at, we are led into long trains of reflection by them. In this respect they resemble the characters of Chaucer's *Pilgrims*, which have strokes of humour in them enough to designate them for the most part as comic, but our strongest feeling still is wonder at the comprehensiveness of genius which could crowd, as poet and painter have done, into one small canvas so many diverse yet co-operating materials.

The faces of Hogarth have not a mere momentary interest, as in caricatures, or those grotesque physiognomies which we sometimes catch a glance of in the street, and, struck with their whimsicality, wish for a pencil and the power to sketch them down; and forget them again as rapidly,—but they are permanent abiding ideas. Not the sports of nature, but her necessary eternal classes. We feel that we cannot part with any of them, lest a link should be broken.

It is worthy of observation, that he has seldom drawn a mean or insignificant countenance.[1] Hogarth's mind was eminently reflective; and, as it has been well observed of Shakspere, that he has transfused his own poetical

---

[1] If there are any of that description, they are in his *Strolling Players*, a print which has been cried up by Lord Orford as the richest of his productions, and it may be, for what I know, in the mere lumber, the properties, and dead furniture of the scene, but in living character and expression it is (for Hogarth) lamentably poor and wanting; it is perhaps the only one of his performances at which we have a right to feel disgusted.

character into the persons of his drama (they are all more or less *poets*) Hogarth has impressed a *thinking character* upon the persons of his canvas. This remark must not be taken universally. The exquisite idiotism of the little gentleman in the bag and sword beating his drum in the print of the *Enraged Musician*, would of itself rise up against so sweeping an assertion. But I think it will be found to be true of the generality of his countenances. The knife-grinder and Jew flute-player in the plate just mentioned may serve as instances instead of a thousand. They have intense thinking faces, though the purpose to which they are subservient by no means required it; but indeed it seems as if it was painful to Hogarth to contemplate mere vacancy or insignificance.

This reflection of the artist's own intellect from the faces of his characters, is one reason why the works of Hogarth, so much more than those of any other artist are objects of meditation. Our intellectual natures love the mirror which gives them back their own likenesses. The mental eye will not bend long with delight upon vacancy.

Another line of eternal separation between Hogarth and the common painters of droll or burlesque subjects, with whom he is often confounded, is the sense of beauty, which in the most unpromising subjects seems never wholly to have deserted him. "Hogarth himself," says Mr. Coleridge,[1] from whom I have borrowed this observation, speaking of a scene which took place at Ratzeburg, "never drew a more ludicrous distortion, both of attitude and physiognomy, than this effect occasioned: nor was there wanting beside it one of those beautiful female faces which the same Hogarth, *in whom the satirist never extinguished that love of beauty which belonged to him as a poet*, so often and so gladly introduces as the central figure in a crowd of humorous deformities, which figure (such is the power of true genius) neither acts nor is meant to act as a contrast: but diffuses through all, and

[1] *The Friend*, No. XVI.

over each of the group, a spirit of reconciliation and human kindness; and even when the attention is no longer consciously directed to the cause of this feeling, still blends its tenderness with our laughter : and *thus prevents the instructive merriment at the whims of nature, or the foibles or humours of our fellow-men, from degenerating into the heart-poison of contempt or hatred.*" To the beautiful females in Hogarth, which Mr. C. has pointed out, might be added, the frequent introduction of children (which Hogarth seems to have taken a particular delight in) into his pieces. They have a singular effect in giving tranquillity and a portion of their own innocence to the subject. The baby riding in its mother's lap in the *March to Finchley* (its careless innocent face placed directly behind the intriguing time-furrowed countenance of the treason-plotting French priest) perfectly sobers the whole of that tumultuous scene. The boy mourner winding up his top with so much unpretending insensibility in the plate of the *Harlot's Funeral* (the only thing in that assembly that is not a hypocrite) quiets and soothes the mind that has been disturbed at the sight of so much depraved man and woman kind.

I had written thus far, when I met with a passage in the writings of the late Mr. Barry, which, as it falls in with the *vulgar notion* respecting Hogarth, which this Essay has been employed in combating, I shall take the liberty to transcribe, with such remarks as may suggest themselves to me in the transcription; referring the reader for a full answer to that which has gone before.

"Notwithstanding Hogarth's merit does undoubtedly entitle him to an honourable place among the artists, and that his little compositions, considered as so many dramatic representations, abounding with humour, character, and extensive observations on the various incidents of low, faulty, and vicious life, are very ingeniously brought together, and frequently tell their own story with more facility than is often found in many of the elevated and more noble inventions of Rafaelle, and other great men ; yet it must be honestly confessed, that in what is called knowledge of the figure, foreigners have justly observed, that Hogarth is often so raw and unformed, as hardly to deserve the name of an artist. But this capital defect is not often perceivable, as examples of the naked and of elevated nature but rarely occur in his subjects, which are for the most part filled with characters that in their nature tend to deformity; besides, his figures are small, and the junctures, and other difficulties of drawing that might occur in their limbs, are artfully concealed with their clothes, rags, etc. But what would atone for all his defects, even if they were twice told, is his admirable fund of invention, ever inexhaustible in its resources; and his satyr, which is always sharp and pertinent, and often highly moral, was (except in a few instances, where he weakly and meanly suffered his integrity to give way to his envy) seldom or never employed in a dishonest or unmanly way. Hogarth has been often imitated in his satirical vein, sometimes in his humorous; but very few have attempted to rival him in his moral walk. The line of art pursued by my very ingenious predecessor and brother academician, Mr. Penny, is quite distinct from that of Hogarth, and is of a much more delicate and superior relish; he attempts the heart, and reaches it, whilst Hogarth's general aim is only to shake the sides; in other respects no comparison can be thought of, as Mr. Penny has all that knowledge of the figure and academical skill, which the other wanted. As to Mr. Bunbury, who had so happily succeeded in the vein of humour and caricature, he has for some time past altogether relinquished it, for the more amiable pursuit of beautiful nature: this, indeed, is not to be wondered at, when we recollect that he has, in Mrs. Bunbury, so admirable an exemplar of the most finished grace and beauty continually at his elbow. But (to say all that occurs to me on this subject) perhaps it may be reasonably doubted, whether the being much conversant with Hogarth's method of exposing meanness, deformity, and vice, in many of his works, is not rather a dangerous, or, at least, a worthless pursuit; which, if it does not find a false relish and a love of and search after satyr and buffoonery in the spectator, is at least not unlikely to give him one. Life is short; and the little leisure of it is much better laid out upon that species of art which is employed about the amiable and the admirable, as it is more likely to be attended with better and nobler consequences to ourselves. These two pursuits in art may be compared with two sets of people with whom we might associate; if we give ourselves up to the Foots, the Kenricks, etc., we shall be continually busied and paddling in whatever is ridiculous, faulty, and vicious in life; whereas there are those to be found, with whom we should be in the constant pursuit and study of all that gives a value and a dignity to human nature." [Account of a Series of Pictures in the Great Room of the Society of Arts, Manufactures, and Commerce, at the Adelphi, by James Barry, R. A. Professor of Painting to the Royal Academy; reprinted in the last quarto edition of his works.]

"—— it must be honestly confessed, that in what is called knowledge of the figure, foreigners have justly observed," etc.

It is a secret well known to the professors of the art and mystery of criticism, to insist upon what they do not find in a man's works, and to pass over in silence what they do. That Hogarth did not draw the naked figure so well as Michael Angelo might be allowed, especially as " examples of the naked," as Mr. Barry acknowledges, "rarely (he might almost have said never) occur in his subjects;" and that his figures under their draperies do not discover all the fine graces of an Antinous or an Apollo, may be conceded likewise; perhaps it was more suitable to his purpose to represent the average forms of mankind in the mediocrity (as Mr. Burke expresses it) of the age in which he lived: but that his figures in general, and in his best subjects, are so glaringly incorrect as is here insinuated, I dare trust my own eye so far as positively to deny the fact. And there is one part of the figure in which Hogarth is allowed to have excelled, which these foreigners seem to have overlooked, or perhaps calculating from its proportion to the whole (a seventh or an eighth, I forget which) deemed it of trifling importance; I mean the human face; a small part, reckoning by geographical inches, in the map of man's body, but here it is that the painter of expression must condense the wonders of his skill, even at the expense of neglecting the "jonctures and other difficulties of drawing in the limbs," which it must be a cold eye that in the interest so strongly demanded by Hogarth's countenances, has leisure to survey and censure.

"The line of art pursued by my very ingenious predecessor and brother academician, Mr. Penny."

The first impression caused in me by reading this passage, was an eager desire to know who this Mr. Penny was. This great surpasser of Hogarth in the "delicacy of his relish," and the "line which he pursued," where is he, what are his works, what has he to shew? In vain

I tried to recollect, till by happily putting the question to a friend who is more conversant in the works of the illustrious obscure than myself, I learned that he was the painter of a *Death of Wolfe* which missed the prize the year that the celebrated picture of West on the same subject obtained it; that he also made a picture of the *Marquis of Granby relieving a Sick Soldier ;* moreover, that he was the inventor of two pictures of *Suspended and Restored Animation*, which I now remember to have seen in the Exhibition some years since, and the prints from which are still extant in good men's houses. This then I suppose is the line of subjects in which Mr. Penny was so much superior to Hogarth. I confess I am not of that opinion. The relieving of poverty by the purse, and the restoring a young man to his parents by using the methods prescribed by the Humane Society, are doubtless very amiable subjects, pretty things to teach the first rudiments of humanity; they amount to about as much instruction as the stories of good boys that give away their custards to poor beggar-boys in children's books. But, good God! is this *milk for babes* to be set up in opposition to Hogarth's moral scenes, his *strong meat for men?* As well might we prefer the fulsome verses upon their own goodness, to which the gentlemen of the Literary Fund annually sit still with such shameless patience to listen, to the satires of Juvenal and Persius; because the former are full of tender images of Worth relieved by Charity, and Charity stretching out her hand to rescue sinking Genius, and the theme of the latter is men's crimes and follies with their black consequences— forgetful meanwhile of those strains of moral pathos, those sublime heart-touches, which these poets (in *them* chiefly shewing themselves poets) are perpetually darting across the otherwise appalling gloom of their subject—consolatory remembrancers, when their pictures of guilty mankind have made us even to despair for our species, that there is such a thing as virtue and moral dignity in the world, that her unquenchable spark is not utterly out

—refreshing admonitions, to which we turn for shelter from the too great heat and asperity of the general satire.

And is there nothing analogous to this in Hogarth? nothing which "attempts and reaches the heart?"—no aim beyond that of "shaking the sides?"—If the kneeling ministering female in the last scene of the *Rake's Progress*, the Bedlam scene, of which I have spoken before, and have dared almost to parallel it with the most absolute idea of Virtue which Shakspere has left us, be not enough to disprove the assertion; if the sad endings of the Harlot and the Rake, the passionate heart-bleeding entreaties for forgiveness which the adulterous wife is pouring forth to her assassinated and dying lord in the last scene but one of the *Marriage Alamode*,—if these be not things to touch the heart, and dispose the mind to a meditative tenderness: is there nothing sweetly conciliatory in the mild, patient face and gesture with which the wife seems to allay and ventilate the feverish, irritated feelings of her poor, poverty-distracted mate (the true copy of the *genus irritabile*) in the print of the *Distrest Poet?* or if an image of maternal love be required, where shall we find a sublimer view of it than in that aged woman in *Industry and Idleness* (plate V.) who is clinging with the fondness of hope not quite extinguished to her brutal, vice-hardened child, whom she is accompanying to the ship which is to bear him away from his native soil, of which he has been adjudged unworthy: in whose shocking face every trace of the human countenance seems obliterated, and a brute beast's to be left instead, shocking and repulsive to all but her who watched over it in its cradle before it was so sadly altered, and feels it must belong to her while a pulse by the vindictive laws of his country shall be suffered to continue to beat in it. Compared with such things, what is Mr. Penny's "knowledge of the figure and academical skill which Hogarth wanted?"

With respect to what follows concerning another gentleman, with the congratulations to him on his escape out of the regions of "humour and caricatura," in which it appears he was in danger of travelling side by side with Hogarth, I can only congratulate my country that Mrs. Hogarth knew *her* province better than by disturbing her husband at his pallette to divert him from that universality of subject, which has stamped him perhaps, next to Shakspere, the most inventive genius which this island has produced, into the "amiable pursuit of beautiful nature," *i.e.* copying *ad infinitum* the individual charms and graces of Mrs. H——.

"Hogarth's method of exposing meanness, deformity, and vice, paddling in whatever is ridiculous, faulty, and vicious."

A person unacquainted with the works thus stigmatised, would be apt to imagine that in Hogarth there was nothing else to be found but subjects of the coarsest and most repulsive nature. That his imagination was naturally unsweet, and that he delighted in raking into every species of moral filth. That he preyed upon sore places only, and took a pleasure in exposing the unsound and rotten parts of human nature;—whereas, with the exception of some of the plates of the *Harlot's Progress*, which are harder in their character than any of the rest of his productions (the *Stages of Cruelty* I omit as mere worthless caricaturas, foreign to his general habits, the offspring of his fancy in some wayward humour), there is scarce one of his pieces where vice is most strongly satirised, in which some figure is not introduced upon which the moral eye may rest satisfied; a face that indicates goodness, or perhaps mere good humouredness and carelessness of mind (negation of evil) only, yet enough to give a relaxation to the frowning brow of satire, and keep the general air from tainting. Take the mild, supplicating posture of patient Poverty in the poor woman that is persuading the pawnbroker to accept her clothes in pledge, in the plate of *Gin Lane*, for an instance. A little does it, a little of the *good* nature overpowers a world of *bad.* One cordial, honest laugh of a Tom Jones absolutely clears the atmosphere that was reeking with the black, putrifying breathings of a hypocrite Blifil. One homely, expostulating shrug from Strap warms the whole air which the suggestions of a gentlemanly ingratitude from his friend Random had begun to freeze. One "Lord bless us!" of Parson Adams upon the wickedness of the times, exorcises and purges off the mass of iniquity which the world-knowledge of even a Fielding could cull out and rake together. But of the severer class of Hogarth's performances, enough, I trust, has been said to shew that they do not merely shock and repulse; that there is in them the "scorn of vice" and the "pity" too; something to touch the heart, and keep alive the sense of moral beauty; the "lacrymæ rerum," and the sorrowing by which the heart is made better. If they be bad things, then is satire and tragedy a bad thing; let us proclaim at once an age of gold, and sink the existence of vice and misery in our speculations; let us

—— wink, and shut our apprehensions up
From common sense of what men were and are :

let us *make believe* with the children that everybody is good and happy; and, with Dr. Swift, write panegyrics upon the world.

But that larger half of Hogarth's works which were painted more for entertainment than instruction (though such was the suggestiveness of his mind, that there is always something to be learned from them) his humorous scenes,—are they such as merely to disgust and set us against our species?

The confident assertions of such a man as I consider the late Mr. Barry to have been, have that weight of authority in them which staggers, at first hearing, even a long, preconceived opinion. When I read his pathetic admonition concerning the shortness of life, and how much better the little leisure of it were laid out upon "that species of art which is employed about the amiable and the admirable;" and Hogarth's "method" proscribed as a "dangerous or worthless pursuit," I began to think there was something in it; that I might have been indulging all my life a passion for the works of this artist, to the utter prejudice of my taste and moral sense; but my first convictions gradually returned, a world of good-natured English faces came up one by one to my recollection, and a glance at the matchless *Election Entertainment*, which I have the happiness to have hanging up in my parlour, subverted Mr. Barry's whole theory in an instant.

In that inimitable print (which in my judgment as far exceeds the more known and celebrated *March to Finchley*, as the best comedy exceeds the best farce that ever was written) let a person look till he be saturated, and when he is done wondering at the inventiveness of genius which could bring so many characters (more than thirty distinct classes of face) into a room, and set them down at table together, or otherwise dispose them about, in so natural a manner, engage them in so many easy sets and occupations, yet all partaking of the spirit of the occasion which brought them together, so that we feel that nothing but an election time could have assembled them; having no central figure or principal group (for the hero of the piece, the Candidate, is properly set aside in the levelling indistinction of the day, one must look for him to find him), nothing to detain the eye from passing from part to part, where every part is alike instinct with life,—for here are no furniture-faces, no figures brought in to fill up the scene like stage choruses, but all *dramatis personæ :* when he shall have done wondering at all these faces so strongly charactered, yet finished with the accuracy of the finest miniature; when he shall have done admiring the numberless appendages of the scene, those gratuitous doles which rich genius flings into the heap when it has already done enough, the over-measure which it delights in giving, as if it felt its stores were exhaustless; the dumb rhetoric of the scenery—for tables, and chairs, and joint-stools in Hogarth are living and significant things; the witticisms that are expressed by words (all artists but Hogarth have failed when they have endeavoured to combine two mediums of expression, and have introduced words into their pictures), and the unwritten numberless little allusive pleasantries that are scattered about; the work that is going on in the scene, and beyond it, as is made visible to the "eye of mind," by the mob which chokes up the doorway, and the sword that has forced an entrance before its master: when he shall have sufficiently admired this wealth of genius, let him fairly say what is the *result* left on his mind. Is it an impression of the vileness and worthlessness of his species? or is not the general feeling which remains, after the individual faces have ceased to act sensibly on his mind, a *kindly one in favour of his species?* was not the general air of the scene wholesome? did it do the heart hurt to be among it? Something of a riotous spirit to be sure is there, some worldly-mindedness in some of the faces, a Doddingtonian smoothness which does not promise any superfluous degree of sincerity in the fine gentleman who has been the occasion of calling so much good company together: but is not the general cast of expression in the faces, of the good sort? do they not seem cut out of the *good old rock*, substantial English honesty? would one fear treachery among characters of their expression? or shall we call their honest mirth and seldom-returning relaxation by the hard names of vice and profligacy? That poor country fellow, that is grasping his staff (which, from that difficulty of feeling themselves at home which poor men experience at a feast, he has never parted with since he came into the room), and is enjoying with a relish that seems to fit all the capacities of his soul the slender joke which that facetious wag, his neighbour, is practising upon the gouty gentleman, whose eyes the effort to suppress pain has made as round as rings—does it shock the "dignity of human nature" to look at that man, and to sympathise with him in the seldom-heard joke which has unbent his careworn, hardworking visage, and drawn iron smiles from it? or with that full-hearted cobbler, who is honouring with the grasp of an honest fist the unused palm of that annoyed patrician, whom the license of the time has seated next him.

I can see nothing "dangerous" in the contemplation of such scenes as this, or the *Enraged Musician*, or the *Southwark Fair*, or twenty other pleasant prints which come crowding in upon my recollection, in which the restless activities, the diversified bents and humours, the blameless peculiarities of men, as they deserve to be called, rather than their "vices and follies," are held up in a laughable point of view. All laughter is not of a dangerous or soul-hardening tendency. There is the petrifying sneer of a demon which excludes and kills Love, and there is the cordial laughter of a man which implies and cherishes it. What heart was ever made the worse by joining in a hearty laugh at the simplicities of Sir Hugh Evans or Parson Adams, where a sense of the ridiculous mutually kindles and is kindled by a perception of the amiable? That tumultuous harmony of singers that are roaring out the words, "The world shall bow to the Assyrian throne," from the opera of *Judith*, in the third plate of the series, called the *Four Groups of Heads;* which the quick eye of Hogarth must have struck off in the very infancy of the rage for sacred oratorios in this country, while "Music yet was young;" when we have done smiling at the deafening distortions, which these tearers of devotion to rags and tatters, these takers of Heaven by storm, in their boisterous mimicry of the occupation of angels, are making,—what unkindly impression is left behind, or what more of harsh or contemptuous feeling, that when we quietly leave Uncle Toby and Mr. Shandy riding their hobby-horses about the room? The conceited, long-backed Sign-painter, that with all the self-applause of a Raphael or Corregio (the twist of body which his conceit has thrown him into has something of the Corregiesque in it) is contemplating the picture of a bottle which he is drawing from an actual bottle that hangs beside him, in the print of *Beer Street*, —while we smile at the enormity of the self-delusion, can we help loving the good humour and self-complacency of the fellow? would we willingly wake him from his dream?

I say not that all the ridiculous subjects of Hogarth have necessarily something in them to make us like them; some are indifferent to us, some in their natures repulsive, and only made interesting by the wonderful skill and truth to nature in the painter; but I contend that there is in most of them that sprinkling of the better nature, which, like holy water, chases away and disperses the contagion of the bad. They have this in them besides, that they bring us acquainted with the every-day human face,—they give us skill to detect those gradations of sense and virtue (which escape the careless or fastidious observer) in the countenances of the world about us; and prevent that disgust at common life, that *tædium quotidianarum formarum*, which an unrestricted passion for ideal forms and beauties is in danger of producing. In this, as in many other things, they are analogous to the best novels of Smollett or Fielding.

ON THE
POETICAL WORKS OF GEORGE WITHER.

THE poems of G. Wither are distinguished by a hearty homeliness of manner, and a plain moral speaking. He seems to have passed his life in one continued act of an innocent self-pleasing. That which he calls his *Motto* is a continued self-eulogy of two thousand lines, yet we read it to the end without any feeling of distaste, almost without a consciousness that we have been listening all the while to a man praising himself. There are none of the cold particles in it, the hardness and self-ends which render vanity and egotism hateful. He seems to be praising another person, under the mask of self; or rather we feel that it was indifferent to him where he found the virtue which he celebrates; whether another's bosom, or his own, were its chosen receptacle. His poems are full, and this in particular is one downright confession, of a generous self-seeking. But by self he sometimes means a great deal,—his friends, his principles, his country, the human race.

Whoever expects to find in the satirical pieces of this writer any of those peculiarities which pleased him in the satires of Dryden or Pope, will be grievously disappointed. Here are no high-finished characters, no nice traits of individual nature, few or no personalities. The game run down is coarse general vice, or folly as it appears in classes. A liar, a drunkard, a coxcomb, is *stript and whipt;* no Shaftesbury, no Villiers, or Wharton, is curiously anatomised, and read upon. But to a well-natured mind there is a charm of moral sensibility running through them which amply compensates the want of those luxuries. Wither seems everywhere bursting with a love of goodness, and a hatred of all low and base actions. At this day it is hard to discover what parts in the poem here particularly alluded to, *Abuses Stript and Whipt*, could have occasioned the imprisonment of the author. Was Vice in High Places more suspicious than now? had she more power? or more leisure to listen after ill reports? That a man should be convicted of a libel when he named no names but Hate, and Envy, and Lust, and Avarice, is like one of the indictments in the *Pilgrim's Progress*, where Faithful is arraigned for having "railed on our noble Prince Beelzebub, and spoken contemptibly of his honourable friends, the Lord Old Man, the Lord Carnal Delight, and the Lord Luxurious." What unlucky jealousy could have tempted the great men of those days to appropriate such innocent abstractions to themselves?

Wither seems to have contemplated to a degree of idolatry his own possible virtue. He is for ever anticipating persecution and martyrdom; fingering, as it were, the flames, to try how he can bear them. Perhaps his premature defiance sometimes made him obnoxious to censures, which he would otherwise have slipped by.

The homely versification of these Satires is not likely to attract in the present day. It is certainly not such as we should expect from a poet "soaring in the high region of his fancies with his garland and his singing robes about him;"[1] nor is it such as he has shewn in his *Philarete*, and in some parts of his *Shepherds Hunting*. He seems to have adopted this dress with voluntary humility, as fittest for a moral teacher, as our divines choose sober gray or black; but in their humility consists their sweetness. The deepest tone of moral feeling in them (though all throughout is weighty, earnest and passionate) is in those pathetic injunctions against shed-

[1] Milton.

ding of blood in quarrels, in the chapter entitled *Revenge*. The story of his own forbearance, which follows, is highly interesting. While the Christian sings his own victory over Anger, the Man of Courage cannot help peeping out to let you know, that it was some higher principle than *fear* which counselled this forbearance.

Whether encaged, or roaming at liberty, Wither never seems to have abated a jot of that free spirit, which sets its mark upon his writings, as much as a predominant feature of independence impresses every page of our late glorious Burns; but the elder poet wraps his proof-armour closer about him, the other wears his too much outwards; he is thinking too much of annoying the foe, to be quite easy within; the spiritual defences of Wither are a perpetual source of inward sunshine, the magnanimity of the modern is not without its alloy of soreness, and a sense of injustice, which seems perpetually to gall and irritate. Wither was better skilled in the "sweet uses of adversity," he knew how to extract the "precious jewel" from the head of the "toad," without drawing any of the "ugly venom" along with it. The prison notes of Wither are finer than the wood notes of most of his poetical brethren. The description in the Fourth Eglogue of his *Shepherds Hunting* (which was composed during his imprisonment in the Marshalsea) of the power of the Muse to extract pleasure from common objects, has been oftener quoted, and is more known, than any part of his writings. Indeed the whole Eglogue is in a strain so much above not only what himself, but almost what any other poet has written, that he himself could not help noticing it; he remarks, that his spirits had been raised higher than they were wont "through the love of poesy." The praises of Poetry have been often sung in ancient and in modern times; strange powers have been ascribed to it of influence over animate and inanimate auditors; its force over fascinated crowds has been acknowledged; but, before Wither, no one ever celebrated its power *at home*, the wealth and the strength which this divine gift confers upon its possessor. Fame, and that too after death, was all which hitherto the poets had promised themselves from their art. It seems to have been left to Wither to discover that poetry was a present possession, as well as a rich reversion; and that the Muse had promise of both lives, of this, and of that which was to come.

The *Mistress of Philarete* is in substance a panegyric protracted through several thousand lines in the mouth of a single speaker, but diversified, so as to produce an almost dramatic effect, by the artful introduction of some ladies, who are rather auditors than interlocutors in the scene; and of a boy, whose singing furnishes pretence for an occasional change of metre: though the seven syllable line, in which the main part of it is written, is that in which Wither has shewn himself so great a master, that I do not know that I am always thankful to him for the exchange.

Wither has chosen to bestow upon the lady whom he commends, the name of Arete, or Virtue; and, assuming to himself the character of Philarete, or Lover of Virtue, there is a sort of propriety in that heaped measure of perfections, which he attributes to this partly real, partly allegorical, personage. Drayton before him had shadowed his mistress under the name of Idea, or Perfect Pattern, and some of the old Italian love-strains are couched in such religious terms as to make it doubtful, whether it be a mistress, or Divine Grace, which the poet is addressing.

In this poem (full of beauties) there are two passages of pre-eminent merit. The first is where the lover, after a flight of rapturous commendation, expresses his wonder why all men that are about his mistress, even to her very servants, do not view her with the same eyes that he does.

> Sometimes I do admire
> All men burn not with desire:
> Nay, I muse her servants are not
> Pleading love; but O! they dare not.
> And I therefore wonder, why

They do not grow sick and die.
Sure they would do so, but that,
By the ordinance of fate,
There is some concealed thing,
So each gazer limiting,
He can see no more of merit,
Than beseems his worth and spirit.
For in her a grace there shines,
That o'er-daring thoughts confines,
Making worthless men despair
To be loved of one so fair.
Yea, the destinies agree,
Some *good judgments* blind should be,
And not gain the power of knowing
Those rare beauties in her growing.
Reason doth as much imply :
For, if every judging eye,
Which beholdeth her, should there
Find what excellencies are,
All, o'ercome by those perfections,
Would be captive to affections.
So, in happiness unblest,
She for lovers should not rest.

The other is, where he has been comparing her beauties to gold, and stars, and the most excellent things in nature; and, fearing to be accused of hyperbole, the common charge against poets, vindicates himself by boldly taking upon him, that these comparisons are no hyperboles; but that the best things in nature do, in a lover's eye, fall short of those excellencies which he adores in her.

What pearls, what rubies can
Seem so lovely fair to man,
As her lips whom he doth love,
When in sweet discourse they move,
Or her lovelier teeth, the while
She doth bless him with a smile ?
Stars indeed fair creatures be ;
Yet amongst us where is he
Joys not more the whilst he lies
Sunning in his mistress' eyes,
Than in all the glimmering light
Of a starry winter's night ?
Note the beauty of an eye——
And if aught you praise it by

> Leave such passion in your mind,
> Let my reason's eye be blind.
> Mark if ever red or white
> Anywhere gave such delight,
> As when they have taken place
> In a worthy woman's face.
>
> *   *   *   *
>
> I must praise her as I may,
> Which I do mine own rude way,
> Sometime setting forth her glories
> By unheard of allegories——etc.

To the measure in which these lines are written, the wits of Queen Anne's days contemptuously gave the name of Namby Pamby, in ridicule of Ambrose Philips, who has used it in some instances, as in the lines on Cuzzoni, to my feeling at least, very deliciously; but Wither, whose darling measure it seems to have been, may shew, that in skilful hands it is capable of expressing the subtilest movements of passion. So true it is, which Drayton seems to have felt, that it is the poet who modifies the metre, not the metre the poet; in his own words, that

> It's possible to climb;
> To kindle, or to slake;
> Altho' in Skelton's rhime.[1]

---

[1] A long line is a line we are long repeating. In the *Shepherds Hunting* take the following—

> If thy verse doth bravely tower,
> *As she makes wing, she gets power;*
> Yet the higher she doth soar,
> She's affronted still the more,
> 'Till she to the high'st hath past,
> Then she rests with fame at last.

What longer measure can go beyond the majesty of this! what Alexandrine is half so long in pronouncing, or expresses *labour slowly but strongly surmounting difficulty* with the life with which it is done in the second of these lines? or what metre could go beyond these, from *Philarete*—

> Her true beauty leaves behind
> Apprehensions in my mind
> Of more sweetness, than all art
> Or inventions can impart.
> *Thoughts too deep to be express'd,*
> *And too strong to be suppress'd.*

THE LONDONER.

To the Editor of the Reflector.

MR. REFLECTOR—I was born under the shadow of St. Dunstan's steeple, just where the conflux of the eastern and western inhabitants of this twofold city meet and jostle in friendly opposition at Temple Bar. The same day which gave me to the world, saw London happy in the celebration of her great annual feast. This I cannot help looking upon as a lively omen of the future great good-will which I was destined to bear toward the city, resembling in kind that solicitude which every Chief Magistrate is supposed to feel for whatever concerns her interests and well-being. Indeed I consider myself in some sort a speculative Lord Mayor of London: for though circumstances unhappily preclude me from the hope of ever arriving at the dignity of a gold chain and Spital Sermon, yet thus much will I say of myself in truth, that Whittington with his Cat (just emblem of vigilance and a furred gown) never went beyond me in affection, which I bear to the citizens.

I was born, as you have heard, in a crowd. This has begot in me an entire affection for that way of life, amounting to an almost insurmountable aversion from solitude and rural scenes. This aversion was never interrupted or suspended, except for a few years in the younger part of my life, during a period in which I had set my affections upon a charming young woman. Every man while the passion is upon him, is for a time at least addicted to groves and meadows and purling streams. During this short period of my existence, I contracted just familiarity enough with rural *objects* to understand tolerably well ever after the *poets*, when they declaim in such passionate terms in favour of a country life.

For my own part, now the fit is past, I have no hesitation in declaring, that a mob of happy faces crowding up at the pit door of Drury Lane Theatre, just at the hour of six, gives me ten thousand sincerer pleasures, than I could ever receive from all the flocks of silly sheep that ever whitened the plains of Arcadia or Epsom Downs.

This passion for crowds is nowhere feasted so full as in London. The man must have a rare *recipe* for melancholy, who can be dull in Fleet Street. I am naturally inclined to hypochondria, but in London it vanishes, like all other ills. Often, when I have felt a weariness or distaste at home, have I rushed out into her crowded Strand, and fed my humour, till tears have wetted my cheek for unutterable sympathies with the multitudinous moving picture, which she never fails to present at all hours, like the scenes of a shifting pantomime.

The very deformities of London, which give distaste to others, from habit do not displease me. The endless succession of shops where *Fancy mis-called Folly* is supplied with perpetual gauds and toys, excite in me no puritanical aversion. I gladly behold every appetite supplied with its proper food. The obliging customer, and the obliged tradesman—things which live by bowing, and things which exist but for homage—do not affect me with disgust; from habit I perceive nothing but urbanity, where other men, more refined, discover meanness: I love the very smoke of London, because it has been the medium most familiar to my vision. I see grand principles of honour at work in the dirty ring which encompasses two combatants with fists, and principles of no less eternal justice in the detection of a pick-pocket. The salutary astonishment with which an execution is surveyed, convinces me more forcibly than a hundred volumes of abstract polity, that the universal instinct of man in all ages has leaned to order and good government.

Thus an art of extracting morality from the commonest incidents of a town life, is attained by the same well-natured alchemy, with which the Foresters of Arden, in a beautiful country,

> Found tongues in trees, books in the running brooks,
> Sermons in stones, and good in everything.

Where has spleen her food but in London? Humour, Interest, Curiosity, suck at her measureless breasts without a possibility of being satiated. Nursed amid her noise, her crowds, her beloved smoke, what have I been doing all my life, if I have not lent out my heart with usury to such scenes!—I am, Sir, your faithful servant,

A LONDONER.

ON BURIAL SOCIETIES; AND THE CHARACTER OF AN UNDERTAKER.

To the Editor of the Reflector.

MR. REFLECTOR—I was amused the other day with having the following notice thrust into my hand by a man who gives out bills at the corner of Fleet Market. Whether he saw any prognostics about me, that made him judge such a notice seasonable, I cannot say; I might perhaps carry in a countenance (naturally not very florid) traces of a fever which had not long left me. Those fellows have a good instinctive way of guessing at the sort of people that are likeliest to pay attention to their papers.

"BURIAL SOCIETY.

"A favourable opportunity now offers to any person, of either sex, who would wish to be buried in a genteel manner, by paying one shilling entrance, and twopence per week for the benefit of the stock. Members to be free in six months. The money to be paid at Mr. Middleton's, at the sign of the *First* and the *Last*, Stonecutter's Street, Fleet Market. The deceased to be furnished as follows:—A strong elm coffin, covered with superfine black, and finished with two rows, all round, close drove, best japanned nails, and adorned with ornamental drops, a handsome plate of inscription, Angel above, and Flower beneath, and four pair of handsome handles, with wrought gripes; the coffin to be well pitched, lined, and ruffled with fine crape; a handsome crape shroud, cap, and pillow. For use, a handsome velvet pall, three gentlemen's cloaks, three crape hatbands, three hoods and scarfs, and six pair of gloves; two porters equipped to attend the funeral, a man to attend the same with band and gloves; also, the burial fees paid, if not exceeding one guinea."

"Man," says Sir Thomas Browne, "is a noble animal, splendid in ashes, and pompous in the grave." Whoever drew up this little advertisement, certainly understood this appetite in the species, and has made abundant provision for it. It really almost induces a *tædium vitæ* upon one to read it. Methinks I could be willing to die, in death to be so attended. The two rows all round close-drove best black japanned nails,—how feelingly do they invite and almost irresistibly persuade us to come and be fastened down! what aching head can resist the temptation to repose, which the crape shroud, the cap, and the pillow present? what sting is there in death, which the handles with wrought gripes are not calculated to pluck away? what victory in the grave, which the drops and the velvet pall do not render at least extremely disputable? but above all, the pretty emblematic plate with the Angel above and the Flower beneath, takes me mightily.

The notice goes on to inform us, that though the society has been established but a very few years, upwards of eleven hundred persons have put down their names. It is really an affecting consideration to think of so many poor people, of the industrious and hard-working class (for none but such would be possessed of such a generous forethought) clubbing their twopences to save the reproach of a parish funeral. Many a poor fellow, I dare sware, has that Angel and Flower kept from the *Angel* and *Punchbowl*, while, to provide himself a bier, he has curtailed himself of *beer*. Many a savoury morsel has the living body been deprived of, that the lifeless one might be served up in a richer state to the worms. And sure, if the body could understand the actions of the soul, and entertain generous

x

notions of things, it would thank its provident partner, that she had been more solicitous to defend it from dishonours at its dissolution, than careful to pamper it with good things in the time of its union. If Cæsar were chiefly anxious at his death how he might die most decently, every Burial Society may be considered as a club of Cæsars.

Nothing tends to keep up, in the imaginations of the poorer sort of people, a generous horror of the workhouse more than the manner in which pauper funerals are conducted in this metropolis. The coffin nothing but a few naked planks, coarsely put together,—the want of a pall (that decent and well-imagined veil, which, hiding the coffin that hides the body, keeps that which would shock us at two removes from us), the coloured coats of the men that are hired, at cheap rates, to carry the body,—altogether give the notion of the deceased having been some person of an ill-life and conversation, some one who may not claim the entire rites of Christian burial,—one by whom some parts of the sacred ceremony would be desecrated if they should be bestowed upon him. I meet these meagre processions sometimes in the street. They are sure to make me out of humour and melancholy all the day after. They have a harsh and ominous aspect.

If there is anything in the prospectus issued from Mr. Middleton's, Stonecutter's Street, which pleases me less than the rest, it is to find that the six pair of gloves are to be returned, that they are only lent, or, as the bill expresses it, for use, on the occasion. The hood, scarfs, and hatbands, may properly enough be given up after the solemnity: the cloaks no gentleman would think of keeping; but a pair of gloves, once fitted on, ought not in courtesy to be re-demanded. The wearer should certainly have the fee-simple of them. The cost would be but trifling, and they would be a proper memorial of the day. This part of the Proposal wants reconsidering. It is not conceived in the same liberal way of thinking as the rest. I am also a little doubtful whether the limit, within which the burial fee is made payable, should not be extended to thirty shillings.

Some provision too ought undoubtedly to be made in favour of those well-intentioned persons and well-wishers to the fund, who, having all along paid their subscriptions regularly, are so unfortunate as to die before the six months, which would entitle them to their freedom, are quite completed. One can hardly imagine a more distressing case than that of a poor fellow lingering on in a consumption till the period of his freedom is almost in sight, and then finding himself going with a velocity which makes it doubtful whether he shall be entitled to his funeral honours: his quota to which he nevertheless squeezes out, to the diminution of the comforts which sickness demands. I think, in such cases, some of the contribution-money ought to revert. With some such modifications, which might easily be introduced, I see nothing in these Proposals of Mr. Middleton which is not strictly fair and genteel; and heartily recommend them to all persons of moderate incomes, in either sex, who are willing that this perishable part of them should quit the scene of its mortal activities, with as handsome circumstances as possible.

Before I quit the subject, I must guard my readers against a scandal, which they may be apt to take at the place whence these Proposals purport to be issued. From the sign of the *First* and the *Last*, they may conclude that Mr. Middleton is some publican, who, in assembling a club of this description at his house, may have a sinister end of his own, altogether foreign to the solemn purpose for which the club is pretended to be instituted. I must set them right by informing them that the issuer of these Proposals is no publican, though he hangs out a sign, but an honest superintendent of funerals, who, by the device of a Cradle and a Coffin, connecting both ends of human existence together, has most ingeniously contrived to insinuate, that the framers of these *first* and *last* receptacles of mankind divide this our life betwixt them, and that all that passes from the midwife to the undertaker may, in strict propriety, *go for nothing:* an awful and instructive lesson to human vanity.

Looking over some papers lately that fell into my hands by chance, and appear to have been written about the beginning of the last century, I stumbled, among the rest, upon the following short Essay, which the writer calls "*The Character of an Undertaker.*" It is written with some stiffness and peculiarities of style, but some parts of it, I think, not unaptly characterise the profession to which Mr. Middleton has the honour to belong. The writer doubtless had in his mind the entertaining character of Sable, in Steele's excellent comedy of the *Funeral*.

Character of an Undertaker.

"He is master of the ceremonies at burials and mourning assemblies, grand marshal at funeral processions, the only true yeoman of the body, over which he exercises a dictatorial authority from the moment that the breath has taken leave to that of its final commitment to the earth. His ministry begins where the physician's, the lawyer's, and the divine's, end. Or if some part of the functions of the latter run parallel with his, it is only *in ordine ad spiritualia*. His temporalities remain unquestioned. He is arbitrator of all questions of honour which may concern the defunct; and upon slight inspection will pronounce how long he may remain in this upper world with credit to himself, and when it will be prudent for his reputation that he should retire. His determination in these points is peremptory and without appeal. Yet, with a modesty peculiar to his profession, he meddles not out of his own sphere. With the good or bad actions of the deceased in his lifetime he has nothing to do. He leaves the friends of the dead man to form their own conjectures as to the place to which the departed spirit is gone. His care is only about the exuviæ. He concerns not himself even about the body, as it is a structure of parts internal, and a wonderful microcosm. He leaves such curious speculations to the anatomy professor. Or, if anything, he is averse to such wanton inquiries, as delighting rather that the parts which he has care of should be returned to their kindred dust in as handsome and unmutilated condition as possible; that the grave should have its full and unimpaired tribute,—a complete and just carcase. Nor is he only careful to provide for the body's entireness, but for its accommodation and ornament. He orders the fashion of its clothes, and designs the symmetry of its dwelling. Its vanity has an innocent survival in him. He is bed-maker to the dead. The pillows which he lays never rumple. The day of interment is the theatre in which he displays the mysteries of his art. It is hard to describe what he is, or rather to tell what he is not, on that day: for, being neither kinsman, servant, nor friend, he is all in turns; a transcendant, running through all those relations. His office is to supply the place of self-agency in the family, who are presumed incapable of it through grief. He is eyes, and ears, and hands, to the whole household. A draught of wine cannot go round to the mourners, but he must minister it. A chair may hardly be restored to its place by a less solemn hand than his. He takes upon himself all functions, and is a sort of ephemeral major-domo! He distributes his attentions among the company assembled according to the degree of affliction, which he calculates from the degree of kin to the deceased; and marshals them accordingly in the procession. He himself is of a sad and tristful countenance; yet such as (if well examined) is not without some show of patience and resignation at bottom: prefiguring, as it were, to the friends of the deceased, what their grief shall be when the hand of Time shall have softened and taken down the bitterness of their first anguish; so handsomely can he fore-shape and anticipate the work of Time. Lastly, with his wand, as with another divining rod, he calculates the depth of earth at which the bones of the dead man may rest, which he ordinarily contrives may be at such a distance from the surface of this earth, as may frustrate the profane attempts of such as would violate his repose, yet sufficiently on this side the centre to give his friends hopes of an easy and practicable resurrection. And here we leave him, casting in dust to dust, which is the last friendly office that he *undertakes* to do."

Begging your pardon for detaining you so long among "graves, and worms, and epitaphs,"—I am, Sir, your humble servant,

MORITURUS.

ON THE DANGER OF CONFOUNDING MORAL WITH PERSONAL DEFORMITY;

WITH A HINT TO THOSE WHO HAVE THE FRAMING OF ADVERTISEMENTS FOR APPREHENDING OFFENDERS.

To the Editor of the Reflector.

MR. REFLECTOR—There is no science in their pretensions to which mankind are more apt to commit grievous mistakes, than in the supposed very obvious one of physiognomy. I quarrel not with the principles of this science, as they are laid down by learned professors; much less am I disposed, with some people, to deny its existence altogether as any inlet of knowledge that can be depended upon. I believe that there is, or may be, an art to "read the mind's construction in the face." But, then, in every species of *reading*, so much depends upon the eyes of the reader; if they are blear, or apt to dazzle, or inattentive, or strained with too much attention, the optic power will infallibly bring home false reports of what it reads. How often do we say, upon a cursory glance at a stranger, what a fine open countenance he has, who, upon second inspection, proves to have the exact features of a knave. Nay, in much more intimate acquaintances, how a delusion of this kind shall continue for months, years, and then break up all at once.

Ask the married man, who has been so but for a short space of time, if those blue eyes where, during so many years of anxious courtship, truth, sweetness, serenity, seemed to be written in characters which could not be misunderstood—ask him if the characters which they now convey be exactly the same?—if for truth he does not *read* a dull virtue (the mimic of constancy) which changes not, only because it wants the judgment to make a preference?—if for sweetness he does not *read* a stupid habit of looking pleased at everything;—if for serenity he does not *read* animal tranquillity, the dead pool of the heart, which no breeze of passion can stir into health? Alas! what is this book of the countenance good for, which when we have read so long, and thought that we understood its contents, there comes a countless list of heart-breaking errata at the end!

But these are the pitiable mistakes to which love alone is subject. I have inadvertently wandered from my purpose, which was to expose quite an opposite blunder, into which we are no less apt to fall, through hate. How ugly a person looks upon whose reputation some awkward aspersion hangs, and how suddenly his countenance clears up with his character. I remember being persuaded of a man whom I had conceived an ill opinion of, that he had a very bad set of teeth; which, since I have had better opportunities of being acquainted with his face and facts, I find to have been the very reverse of the truth. *That crooked old woman,* I once said, speaking of an ancient gentlewoman, whose actions did not square altogether with my notions of the rule of right. The unanimous surprise of the company before whom I uttered these words, soon convinced me that I had confounded mental with bodily obliquity, and that there was nothing tortuous about the old lady but her deeds.

This humour of mankind to deny personal comeliness to those with whose moral attributes they are dissatisfied, is very strongly shewn in those advertisements, which stare us in the face from the walls of every street, and, with the tempting bait which they hang forth, stimulate at once cupidity and an abstract love of justice in the breast of every passing peruser; I mean, the advertisements offering rewards for the apprehension of absconded culprits, strayed apprentices, bankrupts who have conveyed away their effects, debtors that have run away from their bail. I observe, that in exact proportion to the indignity with which the prosecutor, who is commonly the framer of the advertisement, conceives he has been treated, the personal pretensions of the fugitive are denied, and his defects exaggerated.

A fellow, whose misdeeds have been directed against the public in general, and in whose delinquency no individual shall feel himself particularly interested, generally meets with fair usage. A coiner or a smuggler shall get off tolerably well. His beauty, if he has any, is not much underrated, his deformities are not much magnified. A runaway apprentice, who excites perhaps the next least degree of spleen in his prosecutor, generally escapes with a pair of bandy legs; if he has taken anything with him in his flight, a hitch in his gait is generally superadded. A bankrupt, who has been guilty of withdrawing his effects, if his case be not very atrocious, commonly meets with mild usage. But a debtor who has left his bail in jeopardy, is sure to be described in characters of unmingled deformity. Here the personal feelings of the bail, which may be allowed to be somewhat poignant, are admitted to interfere; and, as wrath and revenge commonly strike in the dark, the colours are laid on with a grossness which I am convinced must often defeat its own purpose. The fish that casts an inky cloud about him that his enemies may not find him, cannot more obscure himself by that device than the blackening representations of these angry advertisers must inevitably serve to cloak and screen the persons of those who have injured them from detection. I have before me at this moment one of these bills, which runs thus:—

"Fifty Pounds Reward.

"Run away from his bail, John Tomkins, formerly resident in Princes Street, Soho, but lately of Clerkenwell. Whoever shall apprehend, or cause to be apprehended and lodged in one of his Majesty's jails, the said John Tomkins, shall receive the above reward. He is a thickset, sturdy man, about five foot six inches high, halts in his left leg, with a stoop in his gait, with coarse red hair, nose short and cocked up, with little gray eyes, one of them bears the effect of a blow which he has lately received, with a pot belly, speaks with a thick and disagreeable voice, goes shabbily dressed, had on when he went away, a greasy shag greatcoat with rusty yellow buttons."

Now, although it is not out of the compass of possibility that John Tomkins aforesaid may comprehend in his agreeable person all the above-mentioned aggregate of charms; yet, from my observation of the manner in which these advertisements are usually drawn up, though I have not the pleasure of knowing the gentleman, yet would I lay a wager, that an advertisement to the following effect would have a much better chance of apprehending and laying by the heels this John Tomkins than the above description, although penned by one who, from the good services which he appears to have done for him, has not improbably been blessed with some years of previous intercourse with the said John. Taking, then, the above advertisement to be true, or nearly so, down to the words "left leg" inclusive (though I have some doubt if the blemish there implied amount to a positive lameness, or be perceivable by any but the nearest friends of John) I would proceed thus:—

—"Leans a little forward in his walk, his hair thick and inclining to auburn, his nose of the middle size, a little turned up at the end, lively hazel eyes (the contusion, as its effects are probably gone off by this time, I judge better omitted), inclines to be corpulent, his voice thick but pleasing, especially when he sings, had on a decent shag greatcoat with yellow buttons."

Now, I would stake a considerable wager (though by no means a positive man) that some such mitigated description would lead the beagles of the law into a much surer track for finding this ungracious varlet, than to set them upon a false scent after fictitious ugliness and fictitious shabbiness; though, to do those gentlemen justice, I have no doubt their experience has taught them in all such cases to abate a great deal of the deformity which they are instructed to expect; and has discovered to them, that the Devil's agents upon this earth, like their master, are far less ugly in reality than they are painted.

I am afraid, Mr. Reflector, that I shall be thought to have gone wide of my subject, which was to detect the practical errors of physiognomy, properly so called; whereas I have introduced physical defects, such as lameness, the effects of accidents upon a man's person, his wearing apparel, etc., as circumstances on which the eye of dislike, looking askance, may report erroneous conclusions to the understanding. But if we are liable, through a kind, or an unkind passion, to mistake so grossly concerning things so exterior and palpable, how much more are we likely to err respecting those nicer and less perceptible hints of character in a face, whose detection constitutes the triumph of the physiognomist?

To revert to those bestowers of unmerited deformity, the framers of advertisements for the apprehension of delinquents, a sincere desire of promoting the ends of public justice induces me to address a word to them on the best means of attaining those ends. I will endeavour to lay down a few practical, or rather negative, rules for their use, for my ambition extends no further than to arm them with cautions against the self-defeating of their own purposes:—

1. Imprimis, then, Mr. Advertiser! If the culprit whom you are willing to recover be one to whom in times past you have shewn kindness, and been disposed

to think kindly of him yourself, but he has deceived your trust, and has run away, and left you with a load of debt to answer for him,—sit down calmly, and endeavour to behold him through the spectacles of memory rather than of present conceit. Image to yourself, before you pen a tittle of his description, the same plausible, good-looking man who took you in; and try to put away from your mind every intrusion of that deceitful spectre which perpetually obtrudes itself in the room of your former friend's known visage. It will do you more credit to have been deceived by such a one; and depend upon it, the traitor will convey to the eyes of the world in general much more of that first idea which you formed (perhaps in part erroneous) of his physiognomy, than of that frightful substitute which you have suffered to creep in upon your mind and usurp upon it; a creature which has no archetype except in your own brain.

2. If you be a master that have to advertise a runaway apprentice, though the young dog's faults are known only to you, and no doubt his conduct has been aggravating enough, do not presently set him down as having crooked ankles. He may have a good pair of legs, and run away notwithstanding. Indeed, the latter does rather seem to imply the former.

3. If the unhappy person against whom your laudable vengeance is directed be a thief, think that a thief may have a good nose, good eyes, good ears. It is indispensable to his profession that he be possessed of sagacity, foresight, vigilance; it is more than probable, then, that he is endued with the bodily types or instruments of these qualities to some tolerable degree of perfectness.

4. If petty larceny be his offence, I exhort you, do not confound meanness of crime with diminutiveness of stature. These things have no connection. I have known a tall man stoop to the basest action, a short man aspire to the height of crime, a fair man be guilty of the foulest actions, etc.

5. Perhaps the offender has been guilty of some

atrocious and aggravated murder. Here is the most difficult case of all. It is above all requisite, that such a daring violator of the peace and safety of society should meet with his reward, a violent and ignominious death. But how shall we get at him? Who is there among us, that has known him before he committed the offence, that shall take upon him to say he can sit down coolly and pen a dispassionate description of a murderer? The tales of our nursery,—the reading of our youth,—the ill-looking man that was hired by the Uncle to despatch the Children in the Wood,—the grim ruffians who smothered the babes in the Tower,—the black and beetle-browed assassin of Mrs. Ratcliffe,—the shag-haired villain of Mr. Monk Lewis,—the Tarquin tread, and mill-stone dropping eyes, of Murder in Shakspere,—the exaggerations of picture and of poetry,—what we have read and what we have dreamed of,—rise up and crowd in upon us such eye-scaring portraits of the man of blood, that our pen is absolutely forestalled; we commence poets when we should play the part of strictest historians, and the very blackness of horror which the deed calls up, serves as a cloud to screen the doer. The fiction is blameless, it is accordant with those wise prejudices with which nature has guarded our innocence, as with impassable barriers, against the commission of such appalling crimes; but, meantime, the criminal escapes; or if,—owing to that wise abatement in their expectation of deformity, which, as I hinted at before, the officers of pursuit never fail to make, and no doubt in cases of this sort they make a more than ordinary allowance,—if, owing to this or any accident, the offender is caught and brought to his trial, who that has been led out of curiosity to witness such a scene, has not with astonishment reflected on the difference between a real committer of a murder, and the idea of one which he has been collecting and heightening all his life out of books, dreams, etc. The fellow, perhaps, is a sleek, smug-looking man, with light hair and eye-brows,—the latter by no means jutting out or like a crag,—and with none of those marks which our fancy had pre-bestowed upon him.

I find I am getting unawares too serious; the best way on such occasions is, to leave off, which I shall do by generally recommending to all prosecuting advertisers not to confound crimes with ugliness; or rather, to distinguish between that physiognomical deformity, which I am willing to grant always accompanies crime, and mere *physical ugliness,*—which signifies nothing, is the exponent of nothing, and may exist in a good or bad person indifferently.

CRITO.

ON THE INCONVENIENCES RESULTING FROM BEING HANGED

To the Editor of the Reflector.

SIR—I am one of those unhappy persons whose misfortunes, it seems, do not entitle them to the benefit of pure pity. All that is bestowed upon me of that kindest alleviator of human miseries, comes dashed with a double portion of contempt. My griefs have nothing in them that is felt as sacred by the bystanders. Yet is my affliction in truth of the deepest grain. The heaviest task that was ever given to mortal patience to sustain. Time, that wears out all other sorrows, can never modify or soften mine. Here they must continue to gnaw, as long as that fatal mark——

Why was I ever born? Why was innocence in my person suffered to be branded with a stain which was appointed only for the blackest guilt? What had I done, or my parents, that a disgrace of mine should involve a whole posterity in infamy? I am almost tempted to believe, that, in some pre-existent state, crimes to which this sublunary life of mine hath been as much a stranger as the babe that is newly born into it, have drawn down upon me this vengeance, so disproportionate to my actions on this globe.

My brain sickens, and my bosom labours to be delivered of the weight that presses upon it, yet my conscious pen shrinks from the avowal. But out it must——

O, Mr. Reflector! guess at the wretch's misery who now writes this to you, when, with tears and burning blushes, he is obliged to confess, that he has been—— HANGED——

Methinks I hear an involuntary exclamation burst from you, as your imagination presents to you fearful images of your correspondent unknown,—*hanged!*

Fear not, Mr. Editor. No disembodied spirit has the honour of addressing you. I am flesh and blood, an unfortunate system of bones, muscles, sinews, arteries, like yourself.

Then, I presume, you mean to be pleasant—That expression of yours, Mr. Correspondent, must be taken somehow in a metaphorical sense——

In the plainest sense, without trope or figure—Yes, Mr. Editor! this neck of mine has felt the fatal noose,—these hands have tremblingly held up the corroborative prayer-book,—these lips have sucked the moisture of the last consolatory orange,—this tongue has chanted the doleful cantata which no performer was ever called upon to repeat,—this face has had the veiling night-cap drawn over it——

But for no crime of mine.—Far be it from me to arraign the justice of my country, which, though tardy, did at length recognise my innocence. It is not for me to reflect upon judge or jury, now that eleven years have elapsed since the erroneous sentence was pronounced. Men will always be fallible, and perhaps circumstances did appear at the time a little strong——

Suffice it to say, that after hanging four minutes (as the spectators were pleased to compute it,—a man that is being strangled, I know from experience, has altogether a different measure of time from his friends who are breathing leisurely about him,—I suppose the minutes lengthen as time approaches eternity, in the same manner as the miles get longer as you travel northward—), after hanging four minutes, according to the best calculation of the bystanders, a reprieve came, and I was cut DOWN——

Really I am ashamed of deforming your pages with these technical phrases—if I knew how to express my meaning shorter——

But to proceed.—My first care after I had been brought to myself by the usual methods (those methods that are so interesting to the operator and his assistants, who are pretty numerous on such occasions,—but which no patient was ever desirous of undergoing a second time for the benefit of science), my first care was to provide myself with an enormous stock or cravat to hide the place—you understand me;—my next care was to procure a residence as distant as possible from that part of the country where I had suffered. For that reason I chose the metropolis, as the place where wounded honour (I had been told) could lurk with the least danger of exciting inquiry, and stigmatised innocence had the best chance of hiding her disgrace in a crowd. I sought out a new circle of acquaintance, and my circumstances happily enabling me to pursue my fancy in that respect, I endeavoured, by mingling in all the pleasures which the town affords, to efface the memory of what I had undergone.

But, alas! such is the portentous and all-pervading chain of connection which links together the head and members of this great community, my scheme of lying perdu was defeated almost at the outset. A countryman of mine, whom a foolish lawsuit had brought to town, by chance met me, and the secret was soon blazoned about.

In a short time, I found myself deserted by most of those who had been my intimate friends. Not that any guilt was supposed to attach to my character. My officious countryman, to do him justice, had been candid enough to explain my perfect innocence. But, somehow or other, there is a want of strong virtue in mankind. We have plenty of the softer instincts, but the heroic character is gone. How else can I account for it, that of all my numerous acquaintance, among whom I had the honour of ranking sundry persons of education, talents, and worth, scarcely here and there one or two could be found, who had the courage to associate with a man that had been hanged.

Those few who did not desert me altogether, were persons of strong but coarse minds; and from the absence of all delicacy in them I suffered almost as much as from the superabundance of a false species of it in the others. Those who stuck by me were the jokers, who thought themselves entitled by the fidelity which they had shewn towards me to use me with what familiarity they pleased. Many and unfeeling are the jests that I have suffered from these rude (because faithful) Achateses. As they passed me in the streets, one would nod significantly to his companion and say, pointing to me, "smoke his cravat," and ask me if I had got a wen, that I was so solicitous to cover my neck. Another would inquire, What news from * * * Assizes? (which you may guess, Mr. Editor, was the scene of my shame), and whether the sessions was like to prove a maiden one? A third would offer to ensure me from drowning. A fourth would tease me with inquiries how I felt when I was swinging, whether I had not something like a blue flame dancing before my eyes? A fifth took a fancy never to call me anything but *Lazarus*. And an eminent bookseller and publisher,—who, in his zeal to present the public with new facts, had he lived in those days, I am confident, would not have scrupled waiting upon the person himself last mentioned, at the most critical period of his existence, to solicit a *few facts relative to resuscitation*,—had the modesty to offer me * * guineas per sheet, if I would write, in his Magazine, a physiological account of my feelings upon coming to myself.

But these were evils which a moderate fortitude might have enabled me to struggle with. Alas! Mr. Editor, the women,—whose good graces I had always most assiduously cultivated, from whose softer minds I had hoped a more delicate and generous sympathy than I found in the men,—the women began to shun me—this was the unkindest blow of all.

But is it to be wondered at? How couldst thou imagine, wretchedest of beings, that that tender creature Serephina would fling her pretty arms about that neck which previous circumstances had rendered infamous? That she would put up with the refuse of the rope, the leavings of the cord? Or that any analogy could subsist between the knot which binds true lovers, and the knot which ties malefactors?

I can forgive that pert baggage Flirtilla, who, when I complimented her one day on the execution which her eyes had done, replied, that, to be sure, Mr. * * was a judge of those things. But from thy more exalted mind, Celestina, I expected a more unprejudiced decision.

The person whose true name I conceal under this appellation, of all the women that I was ever acquainted with, had the most manly turn of mind, which she had improved by reading and the best conversation. Her understanding was not more masculine than her manners and whole disposition were delicately and truly feminine. She was the daughter of an officer who had fallen in the service of his country, leaving his widow and Celestina, an only child, with a fortune sufficient to set them above want, but not to enable them to live in splendour. I had the mother's permission to pay my addresses to the young lady, and Celestina seemed to approve of my suit.

Often and often have I poured out my overcharged soul in the presence of Celestina, complaining of the hard and unfeeling prejudices of the world, and the sweet maid has again and again declared, that no irrational prejudice should hinder her from esteeming every man according to his intrinsic worth. Often has she repeated the consolatory assurance, that she could never consider as essentially ignominious an *accident*, which was indeed to be deprecated, but which might have happened to the most innocent of mankind. Then would she set forth some illustrious example, which her reading easily furnished, of a Phocion or a Socrates unjustly condemned; of a Raleigh or a Sir Thomas More, to whom late posterity had done justice; and by soothing my fancy with some such agreeable parallel, she would make me almost to triumph in my disgrace, and convert my shame into glory.

In such entertaining and instructive conversations the time passed on, till I importunately urged the mistress of my affections to name a day for our union. To this she obligingly consented, and I thought myself the happiest of mankind. But how was I surprised one morning on the receipt of the following billet from my charmer:—

Sir—You must not impute it to levity, or to a worse failing, ingratitude, if, with anguish of heart, I feel myself compelled by irresistible arguments to recall a vow which I fear I made with too little consideration. I never can be yours. The reasons of my decision, which is final, are in my own breast, and you must everlastingly remain a stranger to them. Assure yourself that I can never cease to esteem you as I ought.   Celestina.

At the sight of this paper, I ran in frantic haste to Celestina's lodgings, where I learned, to my infinite mortification, that the mother and daughter were set off on a journey to a distant part of the country, to visit a relation, and were not expected to return in less than four months.

Stunned by this blow, which left me without the courage to solicit an explanation by letter, even if I had known where they were (for the particular address was industriously concealed from me), I waited with impatience the termination of the period, in the vain hope that I might be permitted to have a chance of softening the harsh decision by a personal interview with Celestina after her return. But before three months were at an end, I learned from the newspapers, that my beloved had —given her hand to another!

Heart-broken as I was, I was totally at a loss to account for the strange step which she had taken; and it was not till some years after that I learned the true reason from a female relation of hers, to whom it seems Celestina had confessed in confidence, that it was no demerit of mine that had caused her to break off the match so abruptly, nor any preference which she might feel for any other person, for she preferred me (she was pleased to say) to all mankind; but when she came to lay the matter closer to her heart, she found that she never should be able to bear the sight (I give you her very words as they were detailed to me by her relation) the sight of a man in a nightcap, who had appeared on a public platform, it would lead to such a disagreeable association of ideas! And to this punctilio I was sacrificed.

To pass over an infinite series of minor mortifications, to which this last and heaviest might well render me callous, behold me here, Mr. Editor! in the thirty-seventh year of my existence (the twelfth, reckoning from my re-animation), cut off from all respectable connections, rejected by the fairer half of the community,—who in my case alone seemed to have laid aside the characteristic pity of their sex; punished because I was once punished unjustly; suffering for no other reason than because I once had the misfortune to suffer without any cause at all. In no other country, I think, but this, could a man have been subject to such a life-long persecution, when once his innocence had been clearly established.

Had I crawled forth a rescued victim from the rack in the horrible dungeons of the Inquisition,—had I heaved myself up from a half bastinado in China, or been torn from the just-entering, ghastly impaling stake in Barbary,—had I dropped alive from the knout in Russia, or come off with a gashed neck from the half-mortal, scarce-in-time-retracted scimitar of an executioneering slave in Turkey,—I might have borne about the remnant of this frame (the mangled trophy of reprieved innocence) with credit to myself in any one of those barbarous countries. No scorn, at least, would have mingled with the pity (small as it might be) with which what was left of me would have been surveyed.

The singularity of my case has often led me to inquire into the reasons of the general levity with which the subject of hanging is treated as a topic in this country. I say as a topic: for let the very persons who speak so lightly of the thing at a distance be brought to view the real scene,—let the platform be *bona fide* exhibited, and the trembling culprit brought forth,—the case is changed; but as a topic of conversation, I appeal to the vulgar jokes which pass current in every street. But why mention them, when the politest authors have agreed in making use of this subject as a source of the ridiculous? Swift, and Pope, and Prior, are fond of recurring to it. Gay has built an entire drama upon this single foundation. The whole interest of the *Beggar's Opera* may be said to hang upon it. To such writers as Fielding and Smollett it is a perfect *bon bouche*.—Hear the facetious Tom Brown, in his *Comical View of London and Westminster*, describe the *Order of the Show at one of the Tyburn Executions* in his time:—"Mr. Ordinary visits his melancholy flock in Newgate by eight. Doleful procession up Holborn Hill about eleven. Men handsome and proper that were never thought so before, which is some comfort, however. Arrive at the fatal place by twelve. Burnt brandy, women, and Sabbath-breaking, repented of. Some few penitential drops fall under the gallows. Sheriff's men, parson, pickpockets, criminals, all very busy. The last concluding peremptory psalm struck up. Show over by one."—In this sportive strain does this misguided wit think proper to play with a subject so serious, which yet he would hardly have done, if he had not known that there existed a predisposition in the habits of his unaccountable countrymen to consider the subject as a jest. But what shall we say to Shakspere, who (not to mention the solution which the Gravedigger in *Hamlet* gives of his fellow-workman's problem), in that scene in *Measure for Measure*, where the Clown calls upon Master Barnardine to get up and be hanged, which he declines on the score of being sleepy, has actually gone out of his way to gratify this amiable propensity in his countrymen; for it is plain, from the use that was to be made of his head, and from Abhorson's asking, "Is the axe upon the block, sirrah?" that beheading, and not hanging, was the punishment to which Barnardine was destined. But Shakspere knew that the axe and block were pregnant with no ludicrous images, and therefore falsified the historic truth of his own drama (if I may so speak) rather than he would leave out such excellent matter for a jest as the suspending of a fellow-creature in mid-air has been ever esteemed to be by Englishmen.

One reason why the ludicrous never fails to intrude itself into our contemplations upon this mode of death, I suppose to be, the absurd posture into which a man is thrown who is condemned to dance, as the vulgar delight to express it, upon nothing. To see him whisking and wavering in the air,

As the wind you know will wave a man;[1]

to behold the vacant carcase, from which the life is newly dislodged, shifting between earth and heaven, the sport of every gust; like a weathercock, serving to shew from which point the wind blows; like a maukin, fit only to scare away birds; like a nest left to swing upon a bough when the bird is flown; these are uses to which we cannot without a mixture of spleen and contempt behold the human carcase reduced. We string up dogs, foxes, bats, moles, weasels. Man surely deserves a steadier death.

Another reason why the ludicrous associates more forcibly with this than with any other mode of punishment, I cannot help thinking to be, the senseless costume with which old prescription has thought fit to clothe the exit of malefactors in this country. Let a man do what he will to abstract from his imagination all idea of the whimsical, something of it will come across him when he contemplates the figure of a fellow-creature in the day-time (in however distressing a situation) in a nightcap.

[1] Hieronimo in the *Spanish Tragedy*.

Whether it be that this nocturnal addition has something discordant with daylight, or that it is the dress which we are seen in at those times when we are "seen," as the Angel in Milton expresses it, "least wise;" this I am afraid will always be the case; unless indeed, as in my instance, some strong personal feeling overpower the ludicrous altogether. To me, when I reflect upon the train of misfortunes which have pursued me through life, owing to that accursed drapery, the cap presents as purely frightful an object as the sleeveless yellow coat and devil-painted mitre of the San Benitos. An ancestor of mine, who suffered for his loyalty in the time of the civil wars, was so sensible of the truth of what I am here advancing, that on the morning of execution, no entreaties could prevail upon him to submit to the odious dishabille, as he called it, but he insisted upon wearing, and actually suffered in, the identical flowing periwig which he is painted in, in the gallery belonging to my uncle's seat in ——shire.

Suffer me, Mr. Editor, before I quit the subject, to say a word or two respecting the minister of justice in this country; in plain words, I mean the hangman. It has always appeared to me that, in the mode of inflicting capital punishments with us, there is too much of the ministry of the human hand. The guillotine, as performing its functions more of itself and sparing human agency, though a cruel and disgusting exhibition, in my mind, has many ways the advantage over *our way*. In beheading, indeed, as it was formerly practised in England, and in whipping to death, as is sometimes practised now, the hand of man is no doubt sufficiently busy; but there is something less repugnant in these downright blows than in the officious barber-like ministerings of *the other*. To have a fellow with his hangman's hands fumbling about your collar, adjusting the thing as your valet would regulate your cravat, valuing himself on his menial dexterity——

I never shall forget meeting my rascal,—I mean the

fellow who officiated for me,—in London last winter. I think I see him now,—in a waistcoat that had been mine, —smirking along as if he knew me——

In some parts of Germany, that fellow's office is by law declared infamous, and his posterity incapable of being ennobled. They have hereditary hangmen, or had at least, in the same manner as they had hereditary other great officers of state; and the hangman's families of two adjoining parishes intermarried with each other to keep the breed entire. I wish something of the same kind were established in England.

But it is time to quit a subject which teems with disagreeable images——

Permit me to subscribe myself, Mr. Editor, Your unfortunate friend,

PENSILIS.

ON THE MELANCHOLY OF TAILORS.

<blockquote>
Sedet, æternumque sedebit,
Infelix Theseus.　　　　　VIRGIL.
</blockquote>

THAT there is a professional melancholy, if I may so express myself, incident to the occupation of a tailor, is a fact which I think very few will venture to dispute. I may safely appeal to my readers, whether they ever knew one of that faculty that was not of a temperament, to say the least, far removed from mercurial or jovial.

Observe the suspicious gravity of their gait. The peacock is not more tender, from a consciousness of his peculiar infirmity, than a gentleman of this profession is of being known by the same infallible testimonies of his occupation. "Walk, that I may know thee."

Do you ever see him go whistling along the footpath like a carman, or brush through a crowd like a baker, or go smiling to himself like a lover? Is he forward to thrust into mobs, or to make one at the ballad-singer's audiences? Does he not rather slink by assemblies and meetings of the people, as one that wisely declines popular observation?

How extremely rare is a noisy tailor! a mirthful and obstreperous tailor!

"At my nativity," says Sir Thomas Browne, "my ascendant was the earthly sign of Scorpius; I was born in the planetary hour of Saturn, and I think I have a piece of that leaden planet in me." One would think that he were anatomising a tailor! save that to the latter's occupation, methinks, a woollen planet would seem more consonant, and that he should be born when the sun was in Aries. He goes on. "I am no way facetious, nor disposed for the mirth and galliardise of company." How true a type of the whole trade! Eminently economical of his words, you shall seldom hear a jest come from one of them. He sometimes furnishes subject for a repartee, but rarely (I think) contributes one *ore proprio*.

Drink itself does not seem to elevate him, or at least to call out of him any of the external indications of vanity. I cannot say that it never causes his pride to swell, but it never breaks out. I am even fearful that it may swell and rankle to an alarming degree inwardly. For pride is near of kin to melancholy;—a hurtful obstruction from the ordinary outlets of vanity being shut. It is this stoppage which engenders proud humours. Therefore a tailor may be proud. I think he is never vain. The display of his gaudy patterns in that book of his which emulates the rainbow, never raises any inflations of that emotion in him, corresponding to what the wig-maker (for instance) evinces, when he expatiates on a curl or a bit of hair. He spreads them forth with a sullen incapacity for pleasure, a real or affected indifference to grandeur. Cloth of gold neither seems to elate, nor cloth of frize to depress him—according to the beautiful motto which formed the modest impresse of the shield worn by Charles Brandon at his marriage with the king's sister. Nay, I doubt whether he would discover any vain-glorious complacence in his colours, though "Iris" herself "dipt the woof."

In further corroboration of this argument—who ever saw the wedding of a tailor announced in the newspapers, or the birth of his eldest son?

When was a tailor known to give a dance, or to be himself a good dancer, or to perform exquisitely on the tight rope, or to shine in any such light and airy pastimes? to sing, or play on the violin?

Do they much care for public rejoicings, lightings up, ringing of bells, firing of cannons, etc.?

Valiant I know they can be; but I appeal to those who were witnesses to the exploits of Eliot's famous troop, whether in their fiercest charges they betrayed anything of that thoughtless oblivion of death with which a Frenchman jigs into battle, or whether they did not shew more of the melancholy valour of the Spaniard, upon whom they charged; that deliberate courage which contemplation and sedentary habits breathe?

Are they often great newsmongers?—I have known some few among them arrive at the dignity of speculative politicians; but that light and cheerful every-day interest in the affairs and goings-on of the world, which makes the barber [1] such delightful company, I think is rarely observable in them.

This characteristic pensiveness in them being so notorious, I wonder none of those writers, who have expressly treated of melancholy, should have mentioned it. Burton, whose book is an excellent abstract of all the authors in that kind who preceded him, and who treats of every species of this malady, from the *hypochondriacal* or *windy* to the *heroical* or *love melancholy*, has strangely omitted it. Shakspere himself has overlooked it. "I have neither the scholar's melancholy (saith Jaques) which is emulation; nor the courtier's, which is proud; nor the soldier's, which is politic; nor the lover's, which is all these:"—

---

[1] Having incidentally mentioned the barber, in a comparison of professional temperaments, I hope no other trade will take offence, or look upon it as an incivility done to them, if I say, that in courtesy, humanity, and all the conversational and social graces which "gladden life," I esteem no profession comparable to his. Indeed so great is the goodwill which I bear to this useful and agreeable body of men, that, residing in one of the Inns of Court (where the best specimens of them are to be found, except perhaps at the universities) there are seven of them to whom I am personally known, and who never pass me without the compliment of the hat on either side. My truly polite and urbane friend, Mr. A———m, of Flower-de-luce-court, in Fleet Street, will forgive my mention of him in particular. I can truly say, that I never spent a quarter of an hour under his hands without deriving some profit from the agreeable discussions, which are always going on there.

and then, when you might expect him to have brought in, "nor the tailor's, which is so and so"—he comes to an end of his enumeration, and falls to a defining of his own melancholy.

Milton likewise has omitted it, where he had so fair an opportunity of bringing it in, in his *Penseroso*.

But the partial omissions of historians proving nothing against the existence of any well-attested fact, I shall proceed and endeavour to ascertain the causes why this pensive turn should be so predominant in people of this profession above all others.

And first, may it not be, that the custom of wearing apparel being derived to us from the fall, and one of the most mortifying products of that unhappy event, a certain *seriousness* (to say no more of it) may in the order of things have been intended to be impressed upon the minds of that race of men to whom in all ages the care of contriving the human apparel has been entrusted,— to keep up the memory of the first institution of clothes, and serve as a standing remonstrance against those vanities, which the absurd conversion of a memorial of our shame into an ornament of our persons was destined to produce? Correspondent in some sort to this, it may be remarked, that the tailor sitting over a cave or hollow place, in the cabalistic language of his order, is said to have *certain melancholy regions* always open under his feet. But waiving further inquiry into final causes, where the best of us can only wander in the dark, let us try to discover the efficient causes of this melancholy.

I think, then, that they may be reduced to two, omitting some subordinate ones, viz. the sedentary habits of the tailor; something peculiar in his diet.

First, his *sedentary habits*.—In Doctor Norris' famous narrative of the frenzy of Mr. John Dennis, the patient, being questioned as to the occasion of the swelling in his legs, replies that it came "by criticism;" to which the learned doctor seeming to demur, as to a distemper which he had never read of, Dennis (who appears not to have been mad upon all subjects) rejoins with some warmth, that it was no distemper, but a noble art! that he had sat fourteen hours a day at it: and that the other was a pretty doctor not to know that there was a communication between the brain and the legs.

When we consider that this sitting for fourteen hours continuously, which the critic probably practised only while he was writing his "remarks," is no more than what the tailor, in the ordinary pursuance of his art, submits to daily (Sundays excepted) throughout the year, shall we wonder to find the brain affected, and in a manner overclouded, from that indissoluble sympathy between the noble and less noble parts of the body, which Dennis hints at? The unnatural and painful manner of his sitting must also greatly aggravate the evil, insomuch that I have sometimes ventured to liken tailors at their boards to so many envious Junos, *sitting cross-legged to hinder the birth of their own felicity.* The legs transversed thus ✕ crosswise, or decussated, was among the ancients the posture of malediction. The Turks, who practise it at this day, are noted to be a melancholy people.

Secondly, his *diet.*—To which purpose I find a most remarkable passage in Burton, in his chapter entitled "Bad diet a cause of melancholy." "Amongst herbs to be eaten (he says) I find gourds, cucumbers, melons, disallowed; but especially CABBAGE. It causeth troublesome dreams, and sends up black vapours to the brain. Galen, *loc. affect.* lib. 3, cap. 6, of all herbs condemns CABBAGE. And Isaack, lib. 2, cap. 1, *animæ gravitatem facit,* it brings heaviness to the soul." I could not omit so flattering a testimony from an author, who, having no theory of his own to serve, has so unconsciously contributed to the confirmation of mine. It is well known that this last named vegetable has, from the earliest periods which we can discover, constituted almost the sole food of this extraordinary race of people.

BURTON, *Junior.*

HOSPITA ON THE IMMODERATE INDULGENCE OF THE PLEASURES OF THE PALATE.

To the Editor of the Reflector.

Mr. Reflector—My husband and I are fond of company, and being in easy circumstances, we are seldom without a party to dinner two or three days in a week. The utmost cordiality has hitherto prevailed at our meetings; but there is a young gentleman, a near relation of my husband's, that has lately come among us, whose preposterous behaviour bids fair, if not timely checked, to disturb our tranquillity. He is too great a favourite with my husband in other respects, for me to remonstrate with him in any other than this distant way. A letter printed in your publication may catch his eye; for he is a great reader, and makes a point of seeing all the new things that come out. Indeed, he is by no means deficient in understanding. My husband says that he has a good deal of wit; but for my part I cannot say I am any judge of that, having seldom observed him open his mouth, except for purposes very foreign to conversation. In short, Sir, this young gentleman's failing is, an immoderate indulgence of his palate. The first time he dined with us, he thought it necessary to extenuate the length of time he kept the dinner on the table, by declaring that he had taken a very long walk in the morning, and came in fasting; but as that excuse could not serve above once or twice at most, he has latterly dropped the mask altogether, and chosen to appear in his own proper colours without reserve or apology.

You cannot imagine how unpleasant his conduct has become. His way of staring at the dishes as they are brought in, has absolutely something immodest in it: it is like the stare of an impudent man of fashion at a fine woman, when she first comes into a room. I am positively in pain for the dishes, and cannot help thinking they have consciousness, and will be put out of countenance, he treats them so like what they are not.

Then again he makes no scruple of keeping a joint of meat on the table, after the cheese and fruit are brought in, till he has what he calls *done with it*. Now how awkward this looks, where there are ladies, you may judge, Mr. Reflector,—how it disturbs the order and comfort of a meal. And yet I always make a point of helping him first, contrary to all good manners,—before any of my female friends are helped,—that he may avoid this very error. I wish he would eat before he comes out.

What makes his proceedings more particularly offensive at our house is, that my husband, though out of common politeness he is obliged to set dishes of animal food before his visitors, yet himself and his whole family (myself included) feed entirely on vegetables. We have a theory, that animal food is neither wholesome nor natural to man; and even vegetables we refuse to eat until they have undergone the operation of fire, in consideration of those numberless little living creatures which the glass helps us to detect in every fibre of the plant or root before it be dressed. On the same theory we boil our water, which is our only drink, before we suffer it to come to table. Our children are perfect little Pythagoreans: it would do you good to see them in their nursery, stuffing their dried fruits, figs, raisins, and *milk*, which is the only approach to animal food which is allowed. They have no notion how the substance of a creature that ever had life can become food for another creature. A beefsteak is an absurdity to them; a mutton-chop, a solecism in terms; a cutlet, a word absolutely without any meaning; a butcher is nonsense, except so far as it is taken for a man who delights in blood, or a hero. In this happy state of innocence we have kept their minds, not allowing them to go into the kitchen, or to hear of any preparations for the dressing of animal food, or even to know that such things are practised. But as a state of ignorance is incompatible with a certain age; and as my eldest girl, who is ten years old next Midsummer, must shortly be introduced into the world and sit at table with us, where she will see some things which will shock all her received notions, I have been endeavouring by little and little to break her mind, and prepare it for the disagreeable impressions which must be forced upon it. The first hint I gave her upon the subject, I could see her recoil from it with the same horror with which we listen to a tale of Anthropophagism; but she has gradually grown more reconciled to it in some measure, from my telling her that it was the custom of the world,—to which, however senseless, we must submit so far as we could do it with innocence, not to give offence; and she has shewn so much strength of mind on other occasions, which I have no doubt is owing to the calmness and serenity superinduced by her diet, that I am in good hopes, when the proper season for her *début* arrives, she may be brought to endure the sight of a roasted chicken or a dish of sweetbreads, for the first time, without fainting. Such being the nature of our little household, you may guess what inroads into the economy of it,— what revolutions and turnings of things upside down, the example of such a feeder as Mr. —— is calculated to produce.

I wonder at a time like the present, when the scarcity of every kind of food is so painfully acknowledged, that *shame* has no effect upon him. Can he have read Mr. Malthus's *Thoughts on the Ratio of Food to Population?*

Can he think it reasonable that one man should consume the sustenance of many?

The young gentleman has an agreeable air and person, such as are not unlikely to recommend him on the score of matrimony. But his fortune is not over large; and what prudent young woman would think of embarking hers with a man who would bring three or four mouths (or what is equivalent to them) into a family? She might as reasonably choose a widower in the same circumstances with three or four children.

I cannot think who he takes after. His father and mother, by all accounts, were very moderate eaters; only I have heard that the latter swallowed her victuals very fast, and the former had a tedious custom of sitting long at his meals. Perhaps he takes after both.

I wish you would turn this in your thoughts, Mr. Reflector, and give us your ideas on the subject of excessive eating; and, particularly, of animal food.

HOSPITA.

EDAX ON APPETITE.

To the Editor of the Reflector.

MR. REFLECTOR—I am going to lay before you a case of the most iniquitous persecution that ever poor devil suffered.

You must know, then, that I have been visited with a calamity ever since my birth. How shall I mention it without offending delicacy? Yet, out it must. My sufferings, then, have all arisen from a most inordinate appetite——

Not for wealth, not for vast possessions,—then might I have hoped to find a cure in some of those precepts of philosophers or poets,—those *verba et voces* which Horace speaks of:

"quibus hunc lenire dolorem
Possis, et magnam morbi deponere partem;"

not for glory, not for fame, not for applause,—for against this disease, too, he tells us there are certain piacula, or, as Pope has chosen to render it,

"rhymes, which fresh and fresh applied,
Will cure the arrant'st puppy of his pride;"

nor yet for pleasure, properly so called: the strict and virtuous lessons which I received in early life from the best of parents—a pious clergyman of the Church of England, now no more,—I trust have rendered me sufficiently secure on that side:—

No, sir, for none of these things: but an appetite, in

its coarsest and least metaphorical sense,—an appetite for *food*.

The exorbitances of my arrow-root and pap-dish days I cannot go back far enough to remember, only I have been told, that my mother's constitution not admitting of my being nursed at home, the woman who had the care of me for that purpose used to make most extravagant demands for my pretended excesses in that kind; which my parents, rather than believe anything unpleasant of me, chose to impute to the known covetousness and mercenary disposition of that sort of people. This blindness continued on their part after I was sent for home, up to the period when it was thought proper, on account of my advanced age, that I should mix with other boys more unreservedly than I had hitherto done. I was accordingly sent to boarding-school.

Here the melancholy truth became too apparent to be disguised. The prying republic of which a great school consists, soon found me out: there was no shifting the blame any longer upon other people's shoulders,—no good-natured maid to take upon herself the enormities of which I stood accused in the article of bread and butter, besides the crying sin of stolen ends of puddings, and cold pies strangely missing. The truth was but too manifest in my looks,—in the evident signs of inanition which I exhibited after the fullest meals, in spite of the double allowance which my master was privately instructed by my kind parents to give me. The sense of the ridiculous, which is but too much alive in grown persons, is tenfold more active and alert in boys. Once detected, I was the constant butt of their arrows,—the mark against which every puny leveller directed his little shaft of scorn. The very Graduses and Thesauruses were raked for phrases to pelt me with by the tiny pedants. *Ventri natus,—Ventri deditus,—Vesana gula,—Escarum gurges,—Dapibus indulgens,—Non dans frœna gulæ,—Sectans lautæ fercula mensæ*, resounded wheresoever I passed. I led a weary life, suffering the penalties of guilt for that which was no crime, but only following the blameless dictates of nature. The remembrance of those childish reproaches haunts me yet oftentimes in my dreams. My school-days come again, and the horror I used to feel, when in some silent corner retired from the notice of my unfeeling play-fellows, I have sat to mumble the solitary slice of gingerbread allotted me by the bounty of considerate friends, and have ached at heart because I could not spare a portion of it, as I saw other boys do, to some favourite boy;—for if I know my own heart, I was never selfish,—never possessed a luxury which I did not hasten to communicate to others; but my food, alas! was none; it was an indispensable necessary; I could as soon have spared the blood in my veins, as have parted that with my companions.

'Well, no one stage of suffering lasts for ever: we should grow reconciled to it at length, I suppose, if it did. The miseries of my school-days had their end; I was once more restored to the paternal dwelling. The affectionate solicitude of my parents was directed to the good-natured purpose of concealing even from myself the infirmity which haunted me. I was continually told that I was growing, and the appetite I displayed was humanely represented as being nothing more than a symptom and an effect of that. I used even to be complimented upon it. But this temporary fiction could not endure above a year or two. I ceased to grow, but alas! I did not cease my demands for alimentary sustenance.

Those times are long since passed, and with them have ceased to exist the fond concealment,—the indulgent blindness,—the delicate overlooking,—the compassionate fiction. I and my infirmity are left exposed and bare to the broad, unwinking eye of the world, which nothing can elude. My meals are scanned, my mouthfuls weighed in a balance: that which appetite demands, is set down to the account of gluttony,—a sin which my whole soul abhors, nay, which Nature herself has put it out of my power to commit. I am constitutionally disenabled from that vice; for how can he be guilty of excess, who never can get enough? Let them cease, then, to watch my plate; and leave off their ungracious comparisons of it to the seven baskets of fragments, and the supernaturally replenished cup of old Baucis; and be thankful that their more phlegmatic stomachs, not their virtue, have saved them from the like reproaches. I do not see that any of them desist from eating till the holy rage of hunger, as some one calls it, is supplied. Alas! I am doomed to stop short of that continence.

What am I to do? I am, by disposition, inclined to conviviality, and the social meal. I am no gourmand: I require no dainties: I should despise the board of Heliogabalus, except for its long sitting. Those vivacious, long-continued meals of the latter Romans, indeed, I justly envy; but the kind of fare which the Curii and Dentati put up with, I could be content with. Dentatus I have been called, among other unsavoury jests. Double-meal is another name which my acquaintance have palmed upon me, for an innocent piece of policy which I put in practice for some time without being found out; which was,—going the round of my friends, beginning with the most primitive feeders among them, who take their dinner about one o'clock, and so successively dropping in upon the next and the next, till by the time I got among my more fashionable intimates, whose hour was six or seven, I have nearly made up the body of a just and complete meal (as I reckon it), without taking more than one dinner (as they account of dinners) at one person's house. Since I have been found out, I endeavour to make up by a damper, as I call it, at home, before I go out. But alas! with me, increase of appetite truly grows by what it feeds on. What is peculiarly offensive to me at those dinner-parties is, the senseless custom of cheese, and the dessert afterwards. I have a rational antipathy to the former; and for fruit, and those other vain vegetable substitutes for meat (meat, the only legitimate aliment for human creatures since the flood, as I take it to be deduced from that permission, or ordinance rather, given to Noah and his descendants), I hold them in perfect contempt. Hay for horses. I remember a pretty apologue, which Mandeville tells very much to this purpose in his Fable of the Bees:—He brings in a Lion arguing with a Merchant, who had ventured to expostulate with this king of beasts upon his violent methods of feeding. The Lion thus retorts:—"Savage I am; but no creature can be called cruel but what either by malice or insensibility extinguishes his natural pity. The Lion was born without compassion; we follow the instinct of our nature; the gods have appointed us to live upon the waste and spoil of other animals, and as long as we can meet with dead ones, we never hunt after the living; 'tis only man, mischievous man, that can make death a sport. Nature taught your stomach to crave nothing but vegetables.—(Under favour of the Lion, if he meant to assert this universally of mankind, it is not true. However, what he says presently is very sensible.)—Your violent fondness to change, and greater eagerness after novelties, have prompted you to the destruction of animals without justice or necessity. The Lion has a ferment within him, that consumes the toughest skin and hardest bones, as well as the flesh of all animals without exception. Your squeamish stomach, in which the digestive heat is weak and inconsiderable, won't so much as admit of the most tender parts of them, unless above half the concoction has been performed by artificial fire beforehand; and yet what animal have you spared, to satisfy the caprices of a languid appetite? Languid I say; for what is man's hunger if compared with the Lion's? Yours, when it is at the worst, makes you faint; mine makes me mad: oft have I tried with roots and herbs to allay the violence of it, but in vain; nothing but large quantities of flesh can any ways appease it."—Allowing for the Lion not having a prophetic instinct to take in every *lusus naturæ* that was possible of the human appetite, he was, generally speaking, in the right; and the Merchant was so impressed with his argument that, we are told, he replied not, but fainted away. O, Mr. Reflector, that I were not obliged to add, that the creature who thus argues was but a type of me! Miserable man! *I am that Lion.* " Oft have I tried with roots and herbs to allay that violence, but in vain; nothing but——"

Those tales which are renewed as often as the editors of papers want to fill up a space in their unfeeling columns, of great eaters,—people that devour whole geese and legs of mutton *for wagers*, are sometimes attempted to be drawn to a parallel with my case. This wilful confounding of motives and circumstances, which make all the difference of moral or immoral in actions, just suits the sort of talent which some of my acquaintance pride themselves upon. *Wagers!*—I thank heaven I was never mercenary, nor could consent to prostitute a gift (though but a left-handed one) of nature, to the enlarging of my worldly substance; prudent as the necessities, which that fatal gift have involved me in, might have made such a prostitution to appear in the eyes of an indelicate world.

Rather let me say, that to the satisfaction of that talent which was given me, I have been content to sacrifice no common expectations; for such I had from an old lady, a near relation of our family, in whose good graces I had the fortune to stand, till one fatal evening——. You have seen, Mr. Reflector, if you have ever passed your time much in country towns, the kind of suppers which elderly ladies in those places have lying in petto in an adjoining parlour, next to that where they are entertaining their periodically-invited coevals with cards and muffins. The cloth is usually spread some half-hour before the final rubber is decided, whence they adjourn to sup upon what may emphatically be called *nothing*. A sliver of ham, purposely contrived to be transparent to shew the china-dish through it, neighbouring a slip of invisible brawn, which abuts upon something they call a tartlet, as that is bravely supported by an atom of marmalade, flanked in its turn by a grain of potted beef, with a power of such dishlings, *minims of hospitality*, spread in defiance of human nature, or rather with an utter ignorance of what it demands. Being engaged at one of these card parties, I was obliged to go a little before *supper-time* (as they facetiously call the point of time in which they are taking these shadowy refections), and the old lady, with a sort of fear shining through the smile of courteous hospitality that beamed in her countenance, begged me to step into the next room and take something before I went out in the cold,—a proposal which lay not in my nature to deny. Indignant at the airy prospect I saw before me, I set to, and in a trice despatched the whole meal intended for eleven persons,— fish, flesh, fowl, pastry,—to the sprigs of garnishing parsley, and the last fearful custard that quaked upon the board. I need not describe the consternation, when in due time the dowagers adjourned from their cards. Where was the supper?—and the servants' answer, Mr. —— had eat it all. That freak, however, jested me out of a good three hundred pounds a year, which I afterwards was informed for a certainty the old lady meant to leave me. I mention it not in illustration of the unhappy faculty which I am possessed of; for any unlucky wag of a school-boy, with a tolerable appetite, could have done as much without feeling any hurt after it,—only that you may judge whether I am a man likely to set my talent to sale, or to require the pitiful stimulus of a wager.

I have read in Pliny, or in some author of that stamp, of a reptile in Africa, whose venom is of that hot, destructive quality, that wheresoever it fastens its tooth, the whole substance of the animal that has been bitten in a few seconds is reduced to dust, crumbles away, and absolutely disappears; it is called from this quality, the Annihilator. Why am I forced to seek, in all the most prodigious and portentous facts of Natural History, for creatures typical of myself. *I am that Snake, that Annihilator:* "wherever I fasten, in a few seconds——"

O happy sick men, that are groaning under the want of that very thing, the excess of which is my torment! O fortunate, too fortunate, if you knew your happiness, invalids! What would I not give to exchange this fierce concoctive and digestive heat,—this rabid fury which vexes me, which tears and torments me,—for your quiet, mortified, hermit-like, subdued, and sanctified stomachs, —your cool, chastened inclinations, and coy desires for food!

To what unhappy figuration of the parts intestine I owe this unnatural craving I must leave to the anatomists and the physicians to determine: they, like the rest of the world, have doubtless their eye upon me; and as I have been cut up alive by the sarcasms of my friends, so I shudder when I contemplate the probability that this animal frame, when its restless appetites shall have ceased their importunity, may be cut up also (horrible suggestion!) to determine in what system of solids or fluids this original sin of my constitution lay lurking. What work will they make with their acids and alkalines, their serums and coagulums, effervescences, viscous matter, bile, chyle, and acrimonious juices, to explain that cause which nature, who willed the effect to punish me for my sins, may no less have determined to keep in the dark from them, to punish them for their presumption.

You may ask, Mr. Reflector, to what purpose is my appeal to you: what can you do for me? Alas! I know too well that my case is out of the reach of advice,—out of the reach of consolation. But it is some relief to the wounded heart to impart its tale of misery; and some of my acquaintance, who may read my case in your pages, under a borrowed name, may be induced to give it a more humane consideration than I could ever yet obtain from them under my own. Make them, if possible, to *reflect*, that an original peculiarity of constitution is no crime; that not that which goes into the mouth desecrates a man, but that which comes out of it,—such as sarcasm, bitter jests, mocks and taunts, and ill-natured observations;

and let them consider, if there be such things (which we have all heard of) as Pious Treachery, Innocent Adultery, etc., whether there may not be also such a thing as Innocent Gluttony. — I shall only subscribe myself, your afflicted Servant,

EDAX.

MR. H———:

A FARCE,—IN TWO ACTS.

As it was performed at Drury Lane Theatre, December 1806.

"*Mr. H———*, thou wert DAMNED. Bright shone the morning on the play-bills that announced thy appearance, and the streets were filled with the buzz of persons asking one another if they would go to see *Mr. H———*, and answering that they would certainly; but before night the gaiety, not of the author, but of his friends and the town, was eclipsed, for thou wert DAMNED! Hadst thou been anonymous, thou haply mightst have lived. But thou didst come to an untimely end for thy tricks, and for want of a better name to pass them off."—*Theatrical Examiner.*

CHARACTERS.

Mr. H———	*Mr. Elliston.*
BELVIL	*Mr. Bartley.*
LANDLORD PRY	*Mr. Wewitzer.*
MELESINDA	*Miss Mellon.*
MAID TO MELESINDA	*Mrs. Harlowe.*

GENTLEMEN, LADIES, WAITERS, SERVANTS, ETC.

SCENE.—*Bath.*

PROLOGUE.

SPOKEN BY MR. ELLISTON.

IF we have sinn'd in paring down a name,
All civil well-bred authors do the same,
Survey the columns of our daily writers—
You'll find that some Initials are great fighters.

How fierce the shock, how fatal is the jar,
When Ensign W. meets Lieutenant R.
With two stout seconds, just of their own gizzard,
Cross Captain X. and rough old General Izzard!
Letter to letter spreads the dire alarms,
Till half the Alphabet is up in arms.
Nor with less lustre have Initials shone,
To grace the gentler annals of crim. con.
Where the dispensers of the public lash
Soft penance give—a letter and a dash——
Where vice reduced in size shrinks to a failing,
And loses half her grossness by curtailing.
Faux pas are told in such a modest way,—
The affair of Colonel B—— with Mrs. A——
You must forgive them—for what is there, say,
Which such a pliant Vowel must not grant
To such a very pressing Consonant?
Or who poetic justice dares dispute,
When, mildly melting at a lover's suit,
The wife's a Liquid, her good man a Mute?
Even in the homelier scenes of honest life,
The coarse-spun intercourse of man and wife,
Initials I am told have taken place
Of Deary, Spouse, and that old-fashion'd race;
And Cabbage, ask'd by Brother Snip to tea,
Replies, "I'll come—but it don't rest with me—
I always leaves them things to Mrs. C."
O should this mincing fashion ever spread
From names of living heroes to the dead,
How would Ambition sigh, and hang the head,
As each loved syllable should melt away—
Her Alexander turn'd into great A.—
A single C. her Cæsar to express—
Her Scipio shrunk into a Roman S.;—
And, nick'd and dock'd to these new modes of speech,
Great Hannibal himself a Mr. H.

ACT I.

SCENE.—*A Public Room in an Inn—Landlord, Waiters, Gentlemen, etc.   Enter* MR. H.

Mr. H. Landlord, has the man brought home my boots?

Land. Yes, sir.

Mr. H. You have paid him?

Land. There is the receipt, sir, only not quite filled up; no name, only blank—"Blank, Dr. to Zekiel Spanish for one pair of best hessians." Now, sir, he wishes to know what name he shall put in—who he shall say "Dr."

Mr. H. Why, Mr. H., to be sure.

Land. So I told him, sir; but Zekiel has some qualms about it. He says, he thinks that Mr. H. only would not stand good in law.

Mr. H. Rot his impertinence! bid him put in Nebuchadnezzar, and not trouble me with his scruples.

Land. I shall, sir. [*Exit.*

Enter a Waiter.

Wait. Sir, Squire Level's man is below, with a hare and a brace of pheasants for Mr. H.

Mr. H. Give the man half-a-crown, and bid him return my best respects to his master. Presents, it seems, will find me out, with any name, or no name.

Enter 2d Waiter.

2d Wait. Sir, the man that makes up the Directory is at the door.

Mr. H. Give him a shilling; that is what these fellows come for.

2d Wait. He has sent up to know by what name your Honour will please to be inserted.

Mr. H. Zounds, fellow! I give him a shilling for leaving out my name, not for putting it in. This is one of the plaguy comforts of going anonymous.

[*Exit 2d Waiter.*

Enter 3d Waiter.

3d Wait. Two letters for Mr. H. [*Exit.*

Mr. H. From ladies (*opens them*). This from Melesinda, to remind me of the morning call I promised; the pretty creature positively languishes to be made Mrs. H. I believe I must indulge her (*affectedly*). This from her cousin, to bespeak me to some party, I suppose (*opening it*)—Oh, "this evening"—"Tea and cards"—(*surveying himself with complacency*). Dear H., thou art certainly a pretty fellow. I wonder what makes thee such a favourite among the ladies; I wish it may not be owing to the concealment of thy unfortunate——pshaw!

Enter 4th Waiter.

4th Wait. Sir, one Mr. Printagain is inquiring for you.

Mr. H. Oh, I remember, the poet: he is publishing by subscription. Give him a guinea, and tell him he may put me down.

4th Wait. What name shall I tell him, sir?

Mr. H. Zounds! he is a poet; let him fancy a name.

[*Exit 4th Waiter.*

Enter 5th Waiter.

5th Wait. Sir, Bartlemy the lame beggar, that you sent a private donation to last Monday, has by some accident discovered his benefactor, and is at the door waiting to return thanks.

Mr. H. Oh, poor fellow, who could put it into his head? Now I shall be teased by all his tribe, when once this is known. Well, tell him I am glad I could be of any service to him, and send him away.

5th Wait. I would have done so, sir; but the object of his call now, he says, is only to know who he is obliged to.

Mr. H. Why, me.

5th Wait. Yes, sir.

Mr. H. Me, me, me—who else, to be sure?

5th Wait. Yes, sir; but he is anxious to know the name of his benefactor.

Mr. H. Here is a pampered rogue of a beggar, that cannot be obliged to a gentleman in the way of his profession, but he must know the name, birth, parentage, and education of his benefactor. I warrant you, next he will require a certificate of one's good behaviour, and a magistrate's license in one's pocket, lawfully empowering So-and-so to———give an alms. Anything more?

5th Wait. Yes, sir: here has been Mr. Patriot, with the county petition to sign; and Mr. Failtime, that owes so much money, has sent to remind you of your promise to bail him.

Mr. H. Neither of which I can do while I have no name. Here is more of the plaguy comforts of going anonymous, that one can neither serve one's friend nor one's country. Damn it, a man had better be without a nose than without a name! I will not live long in this mutilated, dismembered state; I will to Melesinda this instant, and try to forget these vexations. Melesinda! there is music in the name; but then, hang it! there is none in mine to answer to it. [*Exit.*

(*While* Mr. H. *has been speaking, two gentlemen have been observing him curiously.*)

1st Gent. Who the devil is this extraordinary personage?

2d Gent. Who? why, 'tis Mr. H.

1st Gent. Has he no more name?

2d Gent. None that has yet transpired. No more! why, that single letter has been enough to inflame the imaginations of all the ladies in Bath. He has been here but a fortnight, and is already received into all the first families.

1st Gent. Wonderful! yet nobody knows who he is, or where he comes from!

2d Gent. He is vastly rich, gives away money as if he had infinity; dresses well, as you see; and for address, the mothers are all dying for fear the daughters should get him; and for the daughters, he may command them as absolutely as———. Melesinda, the rich heiress, 'tis thought, will carry him.

1st Gent. And is it possible that a mere anonymous———

2d Gent. Phoo! that is the charm, Who is he? and What is he? and What is his name?———The man with the great nose on his face never excited more of the gaping passion of wonderment in the dames of Strasburg than this new-comer with the single letter to his name has lighted up among the wives and maids of Bath; his simply having lodgings here draws more visitors to the house than an election. Come with me to the parade, and I will show you more of him. [*Exeunt.*

SCENE.—*In the Street.*

MR. H. *walking*, BELVIL *meeting him*.

Bel. My old Jamaica schoolfellow, that I have not seen for so many years? it must, it can be no other than Jack (*going up to him*). My dear Ho———

Mr. H. (*stopping his mouth*). Ho———! the devil—hush!

Bel. Why, sure it is———

Mr. H. It is; it is your old friend Jack, that shall be nameless.

Bel. My dear Ho———

Mr. H. (*stopping him*). Don't name it.

Bel. Name what?

Mr. H. My cursed unfortunate name. I have reasons to conceal it for a time.

Bel. I understand you—Creditors, Jack?

Mr. H. No, I assure you.

Bel. Snapped up a ward, peradventure, and the whole Chancery at your heels?

Mr. H. I don't use to travel with such cumbersome luggage.

Bel. You ha'n't taken a purse?

Mr. H. To relieve you at once from all disgraceful conjectures, you must know 'tis nothing but the sound of my name.

Bel. Ridiculous! 'Tis true yours is none of the most romantic, but what can that signify in a man?

Mr. H. You must understand that I am in some credit with the ladies.

Bel. With the ladies!

Mr. H. And truly I think not without some pretensions. My fortune——

Bel. Sufficiently splendid, if I may judge from your appearance.

Mr. H. My figure——

Bel. Airy, gay, and imposing.

Mr. H. My parts——

Bel. Bright.

Mr. H. My conversation——

Bel. Equally remote from flippancy and taciturnity.

Mr. H. But then my name—damn my name!

Bel. Childish!

Mr. H. Not so. Oh! Belvil, you are blest with one which sighing virgins may repeat without a blush, and for it change the paternal. But what virgin of any delicacy (and I require some in a wife) would endure to be called Mrs.————?

Bel. Ha! ha! ha! most absurd! Did not Clementina Falconbridge—the romantic Clementina Falconbridge—fancy Tommy Potts? and Rosabella Sweetlips sacrifice her mellifluous appellative to Jack Deady? Matilda, her cousin, married a Gubbins, and her sister Amelia a Clutterbuck.

Mr. H. Potts is tolerable, Deady is sufferable, Gubbins is bearable, and Clutterbuck is endurable, but Ho——

Bel. Hush! Jack, don't betray yourself. But you are really ashamed of thé family name?

Mr. H. Ay, and of my father that begot me, and my father's father, and all their forefathers that have borne it since the Conquest.

Bel. But how do you know the women are so squeamish?

Mr. H. I have tried them. I tell you there is neither maiden of sixteen nor widow of sixty but would turn up their noses at it. I have been refused by nineteen virgins, twenty-nine relicts, and two old maids.

Bel. That was hard indeed, Jack!

Mr. H. Parsons have stuck at publishing the banns, because they averred it was a heathenish name; parents have lingered their consent, because they suspected it was a fictitious name; and rivals have declined my challenges, because they pretended it was an ungentlemanly name.

Bel. Ha! ha! ha! but what course do you mean to pursue?

Mr. H. To engage the affections of some generous girl, who will be content to take me as Mr. H.

Bel. Mr. H.?

Mr. H. Yes, that is the name I go by here; you know one likes to be as near the truth as possible.

Bel. Certainly. But what then?—to get her to consent——

Mr. H. To accompany me to the altar without a name——: in short, to suspend her curiosity (that is all) till the moment the priest shall pronounce the irrevocable charm which makes two names one.

Bel. And that name——and then she must be pleased, ha! Jack?

Mr. H. Exactly such a girl it has been my fortune to meet with. Heark'ee (*whispers*)——(*musing*) yet, hang it! 'tis cruel to betray her confidence.

Bel. But the family name, Jack?

Mr. H. As you say, the family name must be perpetuated.

Bel. Though it be but a homely one.

Mr. H. True; but, come, I will show you the house where dwells this credulous melting fair.

Bel. Ha, ha! my old friend dwindled down to one letter. [*Exeunt.*

Scene.—*An apartment in* Melesinda's *House.*

Melesinda *sola, as if musing.*

Mel. H., H., H.? Sure it must be something precious by its being concealed. It can't be Homer, that is a heathen's name; nor Horatio, that is no surname; what if it be Hamlet? the Lord Hamlet—pretty, and I his poor distracted Ophelia! No, 'tis none of these; 'tis Harcourt or Hargrave, or some such sounding name, or Howard—high-born Howard—that would do. Maybe it is Harley; methinks my H. resembles Harley—the feeling Harley. But I hear him, and from his own lips I will once for ever be resolved.

Enter Mr. H.

Mr. H. My dear Melesinda!

Mel. My dear H., that is all you give me power to swear allegiance to,—to be enamoured of inarticulate sounds, and call with sighs upon an empty letter. But I will know.

Mr. H. My dear Melesinda, press me no more for the disclosure of that which in the face of day so soon must be revealed. Call it whim, humour, caprice in me. Suppose I have sworn an oath never, till the ceremony of our marriage is over, to disclose my true name.

Mel. Oh! H., H., H., I cherish here a fire of restless curiosity which consumes me. 'Tis appetite, passion; call it whim, caprice in me. Suppose I have sworn I must and will know it this very night.

Mr. H. Ungenerous Melesinda! I implore you to give me this one proof of your confidence. The holy vow once past, your H. shall not have a secret to withhold.

Mel. My H. has overcome : his Melesinda shall pine away and die before she dares express a saucy inclination; but what shall I call you till we are married ?

Mr. H. Call me ? call me anything. Call me Love, Love! Ay, Love, Love will do very well.

Mel. How many syllables is it, Love ?

Mr. H. How many ? ud, that is coming to the question with a vengeance. One, two, three, four,—what does it signify how many syllables ?

Mel. How many syllables, Love ?

Mr. H. My Melesinda's mind, I had hoped, was superior to this childish curiosity.

Mel. How many letters are there in it ?

[*Exit* MR. H., *followed by* MELESINDA *repeating the question.*]

SCENE.—*A Room in the Inn. Two Waiters disputing.*

1st Wait. Sir Harbottle Hammond, you may depend upon it!

2d Wait. Sir Harry Hardcastle, I tell you!

1st Wait. The Hammonds of Huntingdonshire.

2d Wait. The Hardcastles of Hertfordshire.

1st Wait. The Hammonds.

2d Wait. Don't tell me! does not Hardcastle begin with an H ?

1st Wait. So does Hammond, for that matter.

2d Wait. Faith, so it does, if you go to spell it. I did not think of that. I begin to be of your opinion; he is certainly a Hammond.

1st Wait. Here comes Susan Chambermaid, may be she can tell.

Enter SUSAN.

Both. Well, Susan, have you heard anything who this strange gentleman is?

Sus. Haven't you heard? it's all come out; Mrs. Guesswell, the parson's widow, has been here about it. I overheard her talking in confidence to Mrs. Setter and Mrs. Pointer, and she says they were holding a sort of a *cummitty* about it.

Both. What? What?

Sus. There can't be a doubt of it, she says, what from his *figger* and the appearance he cuts, and his *sumpshous* way of living, and above all from the remarkable circumstance that his surname should begin with an H., that he must be——

Both. Well? Well?

Sus. Neither more nor less than the Prince——

Both. Prince!

Sus. The Prince of Hessy-Cassel in disguise.

Both. Very likely. Very likely.

Sus. Oh, there can't be a doubt on it. Mrs. Guesswell says she knows it.

1st Wait. Now, if we could be sure that the Prince of Hessy What-do-you-call-him was in England on his travels.

2d Wait. Get a newspaper. Look in the newspapers.

Sus. Fiddle of the newspapers! who else can it be?

Both. That is very true (*gravely*).

Enter LANDLORD.

Land. Here—Susan! James! Philip! where are you all? The London coach is come in, and there is Mr. Fillaside, the fat passenger, has been bawling for somebody to help him off with his boots. (*The Chambermaid and Waiters slip out.*)

(*Solus.*) The house is turned upside down since the

strange gentleman came into it. Nothing but guessing and speculating, and speculating and guessing; waiters and chambermaids getting into corners and speculating, ostlers and stable-boys speculating in the yard. I believe the very horses in the stable are speculating too, for there they stand in a musing posture, nothing for them to eat, and not seeming to care whether they have anything or no; and, after all, what does it signify? I hate such curious ——odso, I must take this box up into his bedroom—he charged me to see to it myself—I hate such inquisitive —— I wonder what is in it?—it feels heavy. (*Reads*) "Leases, title-deeds, wills." Here, now, a man might satisfy his curiosity at once. Deeds must have names to them, so must leases and wills. But I wouldn't—no I wouldn't—— it is a pretty box too—prettily dovetailed. I admire the fashion of it much. But I'd cut my fingers off before I'd do such a dirty—what have I to do—— curse the keys, how they rattle!—rattle in one's pockets —the keys and the halfpence (*takes out a bunch and plays with them*). I wonder if any of these would fit? One might just try them; but I wouldn't lift up the lid if they did. Oh no, what should I be the richer for knowing? (*All this time he tries the keys one by one.*) What's his name to me?—a thousand names begin with an H. I hate people that are always prying, poking and prying into things,—thrusting their finger into one place —a mighty little hole this—and their keys into another. O Lord! little rusty fits it! but what is that to me? I wouldn't go to—no, no—but it is odd little rusty should just happen—— (*While he is turning up the lid of the box,* MR. H. *enters behind him unperceived.*)

Mr. H. What are you about, you dog?

Land. O Lord, sir! pardon; no thief, as I hope to be saved. Little Pry was always honest.

Mr. H. What else could move you to open that box?

Land. Sir, don't kill me, and I will confess the whole truth. This box happened to be lying—that is, I happened to be carrying this box, and I happened to have my keys out, and so—little rusty happened to fit——

Mr. H. So little rusty happened to fit!—and would not a rope fit that rogue's neck? I see the papers have not been moved—all is safe; but it was as well to frighten him a little (*aside*). Come, Landlord, as I think you honest, and suspected you only intended to gratify a little foolish curiosity——

Land. That was all, sir, upon my veracity.

Mr. H. For this time I will pass it over. Your name is Pry, I think?

Land. Yes, sir, Jeremiah Pry, at your service.

Mr. H. An apt name; you have a prying temper;—I mean, some little curiosity—a sort of inquisitiveness about you.

Land. A natural thirst after knowledge you may call it, sir. When a boy, I was never easy but when I was thrusting up the lids of some of my schoolfellows' boxes,—not to steal anything, upon my honour, sir—only to see what was in them; have had pens stuck in my eyes for peeping through key-holes after knowledge; could never see a cold pie with the legs dangling out at top but my fingers were for lifting up the crust,—just to try if it were pigeon or partridge,—for no other reason in the world. Surely, I think, my passion for nuts was owing to the pleasure of cracking the shell to get at something concealed, more than to any delight I took in eating the kernel. In short, sir, this appetite has grown with my growth.

Mr. H. You will certainly be hanged some day for peeping into some bureau or other, just to see what is in it.

Land. That is my fear, sir. The thumps and kicks I have had for peering into parcels, and turning of letters inside out,—just for curiosity! The blankets I have been made to dance in for searching parish registers for old ladies' ages,—just for curiosity! Once I was dragged through a horse-pond, only for peeping into a closet that had glass doors to it, while my Lady Bluegarters was undressing,—just for curiosity!

Mr. H. A very harmless piece of curiosity, truly! And now, Mr. Pry, first have the goodness to leave that box with me, and then do me the favour to carry your curiosity so far as to inquire if my servants are within.

Land. I shall, sir. Here! David! Jonathan!—I think I hear them coming,—shall make bold to leave you, sir. [*Exit.*

Mr. H. Another tolerable specimen of the comforts of going anonymous!

Enter two Footmen.

1*st Foot.* You speak first.

2*d Foot.* No, you had better speak.

1*st Foot.* You promised to begin.

Mr. H. They have something to say to me. The rascals want their wages raised, I suppose; there is always a favour to be asked when they come smiling. Well, poor rogues, service is but a hard bargain at the best. I think I must not be close with them. Well, David—well, Jonathan.

1*st Foot.* We have served your Honour faithfully——

2*d Foot.* Hope your Honour won't take offence——

Mr. H. The old story, I suppose—wages?

1*st Foot.* That's not it, your Honour.

2*d Foot.* You speak.

1*st Foot.* But if your Honour would just be pleased to——

2*d Foot.* Only be pleased to—

Mr. H. Be quick with what you have to say, for I am in haste.

1*st Foot.* Just to——

2*d Foot.* Let us know who it is——

1*st Foot.* Who it is we have the honour to serve.

Mr. H. Why, me, me, me! you serve me!

2*d Foot.* Yes, sir; but we do not know who you are.

Mr. H. Childish curiosity! do not you serve a rich master, a gay master, an indulgent master?

1st Foot. Ah, sir! the figure you make is to us, your poor servants, the principal mortification.

2d Foot. When we get over a pot at the public-house, or in a gentleman's kitchen, or elsewhere—as poor servants must have their pleasures—when the question goes round, who is your master? and who do you serve? and one says, I serve Lord So-and-so, and another, I am Squire Such-a-one's footman——

1st Foot. We have nothing to say for it, but that we serve Mr. H.

2d Foot. Or Squire H.

Mr. H. Really you are a couple of pretty modest, reasonable personages; but I hope you will take it as no offence, gentlemen, if, upon a dispassionate review of all that you have said, I think fit not to tell you any more of my name than I have chosen, for especial purposes, to communicate to the rest of the world.

1st Foot. Why then, sir, you may suit yourself.

2d Foot. We tell you plainly, we cannot stay.

1st Foot. We don't choose to serve Mr. H.

2d Foot. Nor any Mr. or Squire in the alphabet——

1st Foot. That lives in Chris-cross Row.

Mr. H. Go, for a couple of ungrateful, inquisitive, senseless rascals! Go hang, starve, or drown! Rogues, to speak thus irreverently of the alphabet! I shall live to see you glad to serve old Q—to curl the wig of great S—adjust the dot of little i—stand behind the chair of X, Y, Z—wear the livery of Et-cætera—and ride behind the sulky of And-by-it-self-and! [*Exit in a rage.*

ACT II.

Scene.—*A handsome Apartment well lighted, Tea, Cards, etc.—A Large Party of Ladies and Gentlemen, among them* Melesinda.

1st Lady. I wonder when the charming man will be here!

2d Lady. He is a delightful creature! Such a polish——

3d Lady. Such an air in all that he does or says——

4th Lady. Yet gifted with a strong understanding——

5th Lady. But has your ladyship the remotest idea of what his true name is?

1st Lady. They say his very servants do not know it. His French valet, that has lived with him these two years——

2d Lady. There, madam, I must beg leave to set you right: my coachman——

1st Lady. I have it from the very best authority, my footman——

2d Lady. Then, madam, you have set your servants on——

1st Lady. No, madam, I would scorn any such little mean ways of coming at a secret. For my part, I don't think any secret of that consequence.

2d Lady. That's just like me; I make a rule of troubling my head about nobody's business but my own.

Mel. But then she takes care to make everybody's business her own, and so to justify herself that way—— (*aside*).

1st Lady. My dear Melesinda, you look thoughtful.

Mel. Nothing.

2d Lady. Give it a name.

Mel. Perhaps it is nameless.

1st Lady. As the object—— Come, never blush nor

deny it, child. Bless me! what great ugly thing is that, that dangles at your bosom?

Mel. This? it is a cross: how do you like it?

2d Lady. A cross! Well, to me it looks for all the world like a great staring H? (*Here a general laugh.*)

Mel. Malicious creatures! Believe me, it is a cross, and nothing but a cross.

1st Lady. A cross, I believe, you would willingly hang at!

Mel. Intolerable spite!

[Mr. H. *is announced.*

Enter Mr. H.

1st Lady. Oh, Mr. H., we are so glad——

2d Lady. We have been so dull——

3d Lady. So perfectly lifeless! You owe it to us to be more than commonly entertaining.

Mr. H. Ladies, this is so obliging——

4th Lady. Oh, Mr. H., those ranunculas you said were dying, pretty things! they have got up——

5th Lady. I have worked that sprig you commended. I want you to come——

Mr. H. Ladies——

6th Lady. I have sent for that piece of music from London.

Mr. H. The Mozart—(*seeing* Melesinda)—Melesinda!

Several Ladies at once. Nay, positively, Melesinda, you shan't engross him all to yourself.

[*While the Ladies are pressing about* Mr. H. *the Gentlemen show signs of displeasure.*

1st Gent. We shan't be able to edge in a word, now this coxcomb is come.

2d Gent. Damn him! I will affront him.

1st Gent. Sir, with your leave, I have a word to say to one of these ladies.

2d Gent. If we could be heard——

(*The Ladies pay no attention but to* MR. H.)

Mr. H. You see, gentlemen, how the matter stands. (*Hums an air.*) I am not my own master: positively, I exist and breathe but to be agreeable to these—— Did you speak?

1st Gent. And affects absence of mind, puppy!

Mr. H. Who spoke of absence of mind?—did you, madam? How do you do, Lady Wearwell—how do? I did not see your ladyship before. What was I about to say?—oh!—absence of mind. I am the most unhappy dog in that way—sometimes spurt out the strangest things—the most *mal-à-propos*—without meaning to give the least offence, upon my honour—sheer absence of mind —things I would have given the world not to have said.

1st Gent. Do you hear the coxcomb?

1st Lady. Great wits, they say——

2d Lady. Your fine geniuses are most given——

3d Lady. Men of bright parts are commonly too vivacious——

Mr. H. But you shall hear. I was to dine the other day at a great Nabob's, that must be nameless, who, between ourselves, is strongly suspected of—being very rich, that's all. John, my valet, who knows my foible, cautioned me, while he was dressing me—as he usually does where he thinks there's a danger of my committing a *lapsus*—to take care in my conversation how I made any allusion, direct or indirect, to presents—you understand me? I set out double-charged with my fellow's consideration and my own, and, to do myself justice, behaved with tolerable circumspection for the first half hour or so—till at last a gentleman in company, who was indulging a free vein of raillery at the expense of the ladies, stumbled upon that expression of the poet which calls them "fair defects."

1st Lady. It is Pope, I believe, who says it.

Mr. H. No, madam, Milton. Where was I? Oh, "fair defects." This gave occasion to a critic in company to deliver his opinion on the phrase—that led to an enumeration of all the various words which might have been used instead of "defect," as want, absence, poverty, deficiency, lack. This moment I, who had not been attending to the progress of the argument (as the *dénoûment* will show), starting suddenly up out of one of my reveries, by some unfortunate connection of ideas, which the last fatal word had excited, the devil put it into my head to turn round to the Nabob, who was sitting next me, and in a very marked manner (as it seemed to the company) to put the question to him, "Pray, sir, what may be the exact value of a lac of rupees?" You may guess the confusion which followed.

1st Lady. What a distressing circumstance!

2d Lady. To a delicate mind——

3d Lady. How embarrassing——

4th Lady. I declare I quite pity you.

1st Gent. Puppy!

Mr. H. A Baronet at the table, seeing my dilemma, jogged my elbow; and a good-natured Duchess, who does everything with a grace peculiar to herself, trod on my toes at that instant: this brought me to myself, and—covered with blushes, and pitied by all the ladies—I withdrew.

1st Lady. How charmingly he tells a story!

2d Lady. But how distressing!

Mr. H. Lord Squandercounsel, who is my particular friend, was pleased to rally me in his inimitable way upon it next day. I shall never forget a sensible thing he said on the occasion—speaking of absence of mind, my foible—says he, my dear Hogs——

Several Ladies. Hogs——what?—ha!

Mr. H. My dear Hogsflesh—my name—*here a universal scream*)—Oh, my cursed unfortunate tongue!—H., I mean—Where was I?

1st Lady. Filthy!—abominable!

2d Lady. Unutterable!

3d Lady. Hogs——foh!

4th Lady. Disgusting!
5th Lady. Vile!
6th Lady. Shocking!
1st Lady. Odious!
2d Lady. Hogs——pah!
3d Lady. A smelling bottle—look to Miss Melesinda. Poor thing! it is no wonder. You had better keep off from her, Mr. Hogsflesh, and not be pressing about her in her circumstances.
1st Gent. Good time of day to you, Mr. Hogsflesh!
2d Gent. The compliments of the season to you, Mr. Hogsflesh!
Mr. H. This is too much—flesh and blood cannot endure it.
1st Gent. What flesh? hog's-flesh?
2d Gent. How he sets up his bristles!
Mr. H. Bristles!
1st Gent. He looks as fierce as a hog in armour.
Mr. H. A hog!——Madam!——(*here he severally accosts the Ladies, who by turns repel him*).
1st Lady. Extremely obliged to you for your attentions; but don't want a partner.
2d Lady. Greatly flattered by your preference; but believe I shall remain single.
3d Lady. Shall always acknowledge your politeness; but have no thoughts of altering my condition.
4th Lady. Always be happy to respect you as a friend; but you must not look for anything further.
5th Lady. No doubt of your ability to make any woman happy; but have no thoughts of changing my name.
6th Lady. Must tell you, sir, that if, by your insinuations, you think to prevail with me, you have got the wrong sow by the ear. Does he think any lady would go to pig with him?
Old Lady. Must beg you to be less particular in your addresses to me. Does he take me for a Jew, to long after forbidden meats?

Mr. H. I shall go mad!—to be refused by old Mother Damnable—she that's so old, nobody knows whether she was ever married or no, but passes for a maid by courtesy; her juvenile exploits being beyond the farthest stretch of tradition!—old Mother Damnable!

[*Exeunt all, either pitying or seeming to avoid him.*

SCENE.—*The Street.* BELVIL *and another Gentleman.*

Bel. Poor Jack! I am really sorry for him. The account which you give me of his mortifying change of reception at the assembly would be highly diverting if it gave me less pain to hear it. With all his amusing absurdities, and amongst them—not the least—a predominant desire to be thought well of by the fair sex, he has an abundant share of good-nature, and is a man of honour. Notwithstanding all that has happened, Melesinda may do worse than take him yet. But did the women resent it so deeply as you say?

Gent. Oh, intolerably! They fled him as fearfully, when 'twas once blown, as a man would be avoided who was suddenly discovered to have marks of the plague, and as fast,—when before they had been ready to devour the foolishest thing he could say.

Bel. Ha! ha! so frail is the tenure by which these women's favourites commonly hold their envied pre-eminence! Well, I must go find him out and comfort him. I suppose I shall find him at the inn.

Gent. Either there or at Melesinda's. Adieu!

[*Exeunt.*

SCENE.—MR. H——'s *Apartment.*

Mr. H. (*solus*). Was ever anything so mortifying? to be refused by old Mother Damnable!—with such parts and address, and the little squeamish devils to dislike me for a name—a sound!—Oh, my cursed name! that it was something I could be revenged on! if it were alive, that I might tread upon it, or crush it, or pummel it, or kick it, or spit it out—for it sticks in my throat and will choke me.

My plaguy ancestors! if they had left me but a Van or a Mac, or an Irish O', it had been something to qualify it.—Mynheer Van Hogsflesh,—or Sawney MacHogsflesh, —or Sir Phelim O'Hogsflesh,—but downright blunt——. If it had been any other name in the world, I could have borne it. If it had been the name of a beast, as Bull, Fox, Kid, Lamb, Wolf, Lion; or of a bird, as Sparrow, Hawk, Buzzard, Daw, Finch, Nightingale; or of a fish, as Sprat, Herring, Salmon; or the name of a thing, as Ginger, Hay, Wood; or of a colour, as Black, Gray, White, Green; or of a sound, as Bray; or the name of a month, as March, May; or of a place, as Barnet, Baldock, Hitchin; or the name of a coin, as Farthing, Penny, Twopenny; or of a profession, as Butcher, Baker, Carpenter, Piper, Fisher, Fletcher, Fowler, Glover; or a Jew's name, as Solomons, Isaacs, Jacobs; or a personal name, as Foot, Leg, Crookshanks, Heaviside, Sidebottom, Longbottom, Ramsbottom, Winterbottom; or a long name, as Blanchenhagen, or Blanchenhausen; or a short name, as Crib, Crisp, Crips, Tag, Trot, Tub, Phips, Padge, Papps, or Prig, or Wig, or Pip, or Trip; Trip had been something, but Ho——.

(Walks about in great agitation,—recovering his calmness a little, sits down.)

Farewell the most distant thoughts of marriage—the finger-circling ring, the purity-figuring glove, the envy-pining bridesmaids, the wishing parson, and the simpering clerk! Farewell the ambiguous blush-raising joke, the titter-provoking pun, the morning-stirring drum!—No son of mine shall exist to bear my ill-fated name! No nurse come chuckling to tell me it is a boy! No midwife, leering at me from under the lids of professional gravity! I dreamed of caudle (*sings in a melancholy tone*)—Lullaby, Lullaby,—hush-a-by-baby!—how like its papa it is!—(*makes motions as if he was nursing*). And then, when grown up, "Is this your son, sir?" "Yes, sir, a poor copy of me,—a sad young dog!—just what his father was at his age. I have four more at home." Oh! oh! oh!

Enter LANDLORD.

Mr. H. Landlord, I must pack up to-night; you will see all my things got ready.

Land. Hope your Honour does not intend to quit the "Blue Boar,"—sorry anything has happened.

Mr. H. He has heard it all.

Land. Your Honour has had some mortification, to be sure, as a man may say; you have brought your pigs to a fine market.

Mr. H. Pigs!

Land. What then? take old Pry's advice, and never mind it. Don't scorch your crackling for 'em, sir.

Mr. H. Scorch my crackling!—a queer phrase; but I suppose he don't mean to affront me.

Land. What is done can't be undone; you can't make a silken purse out of a sow's ear.

Mr. H. As you say, landlord, thinking of a thing does. but augment it.

Land. Does but *hogment* it, indeed, sir.

Mr. H. Hogment it!—damn it! I said augment it.

Land. Lord, sir, 'tis not everybody has such gift of fine phrases as your Honour, that can lard his discourse.

Mr. H. Lard!

Land. Suppose they do smoke you——

Mr. H. Smoke me?

Land. One of my phrases; never mind my words, sir, my meaning is good. We all mean the same thing, only you express yourself one way, and I another, that's all. The meaning's the same; it is all pork.

Mr. H. That's another of your phrases, I presume. (*Bell rings, and the landlord called for.*)

Land. Anon, anon.
Mr. H. Oh, I wish I were anonymous!
[*Exeunt several ways.*

Scene.—Melesinda's *Apartment.*

Melesinda *and* Maid.

Maid. Lord, madam! before I'd take on as you do about a foolish—what signifies a name? Hogs—Hogs—what is it?—is just as good as any other, for what I see.

Mel. Ignorant creature! yet she is perhaps blest in the absence of those ideas which, while they add a zest to the few pleasures which fall to the lot of superior natures to enjoy, doubly edge the——

Maid. Superior natures!—a fig! If he's hog by name, he's not hog by nature—that don't follow; his name don't make him anything, does it? He don't grunt the more for it, nor squeak, that ever I hear; he likes his victuals out of a plate, as other Christians do; you never see him go to the trough——

Mel. Unfeeling wretch! yet possibly her intentions——

Maid. For instance, madam, my name is Finch—Betty Finch. I don't whistle the more for that, nor long after canary-seed while I can get good wholesome mutton—no, nor you can't catch me by throwing salt on my tail. If you come to that, hadn't I a young man used to come after me—they said courted me—his name was Lion—Francis Lion, a tailor; but though he was fond enough of me, for all that he never offered to eat me.

Mel. How fortunate that the discovery has been made before it was too late! Had I listened to his deceits, and, as the perfidious man had almost persuaded me, precipitated myself into an inextricable engagement before——

Maid. No great harm if you had. You'd only have

bought a pig in a poke—and what then? Oh, here he comes creeping——

Enter MR. H., *abject.*

Go to her, Mr. Hogs — Hogs — Hogsbristles — what's your name? Don't be afraid, man—don't give it up—she's not crying—only *summat* has made her eyes red—she has got a sty in her eye, I believe—(*going*).

Mel. You are not going, Betty?

Maid. Oh, madam, never mind me—I shall be back in the twinkling of a pig's whisker, as they say. [*Exit.*

Mr. H. Melesinda, you behold before you a wretch who would have betrayed your confidence, but it was love that prompted him; who would have tricked you by an unworthy concealment into a participation of that disgrace which a superficial world has agreed to attach to a name—but with it you would have shared a fortune not contemptible, and a heart—but 'tis over now. That name he is content to bear alone—to go where the persecuted syllables shall be no more heard, or excite no meaning—some spot where his native tongue has never penetrated, nor any of his countrymen have landed, to plant their unfeeling satire, their brutal wit, and national ill manners—where no Englishman—— (*Here* MELESINDA, *who has been pouting during this speech, fetches a deep sigh.*) Some yet undiscovered Otaheite, where witless, unapprehensive savages shall innocently pronounce the ill-fated sounds, and think them not inharmonious.

Mel. Oh!

Mr. H. Who knows but among the female natives might be found——

Mel. Sir! (*raising her head*).

Mr. H. One who would be more kind than—some Oberea—Queen Oberea.

Mel. Oh!

Mr. H. Or what if I were to seek for proofs of reciprocal esteem among unprejudiced African maids in Monomotopa?

Enter SERVANT.

Serv. Mr. Belvil. [*Exit.*

Enter BELVIL.

Mr. H. In Monomotopa (*musing*).

Bel. Heyday, Jack! what means this mortified face? nothing has happened, I hope, between this lady and you? I beg pardon, madam, but understanding my friend was with you, I took the liberty of seeking him here. Some little difference possibly which a third person can adjust—not a word—will you, madam, as this gentleman's friend, suffer me to be the arbitrator—strange!—hark'ee, Jack, nothing has come out, has there?—you understand me. Oh, I guess how it is—somebody has got at your secret. You haven't blabbed it yourself, have you?—ha! ha! ha! I could find in my heart—Jack, what would you give me if I should relieve you——

Mr. H. No power of man can relieve me (*sighs*), but it must lie at the root—gnawing at the root—here it will lie.

Bel. No power of man?—not a common man, I grant you; for instance, a subject—it's out of the power of any subject.

Mr. H. Gnawing at the root—there it will lie.

Bel. Such a thing has been known as a name to be changed; but not by a subject (*shows a Gazette*).

Mr. H. Gnawing at the root (*suddenly snatches the paper out of* BELVIL'S *hand*); ha! pish! nonsense! give it me—what! (*reads*) promotions, bankrupts—a great many bankrupts this week—there it will lie (*lays it down, takes it up again, and reads*)—"The King has been graciously pleased"—gnawing at the root—"graciously pleased to grant unto John Hogsflesh"—the devil—

"Hogsflesh, Esq., of Sty Hall, in the county of Hants, his royal license and authority"—O Lord! O Lord!—"that he and his issue"—me and my issue—"may take and use the surname and arms of Bacon"—Bacon, the surname and arms of Bacon!—"in pursuance of an injunction contained in the last will and testament of Nicholas Bacon, Esq., his late uncle, as well as out of grateful respect to his memory:"—grateful respect, poor old soul!——here's more—"and that such arms may be first duly exemplified"—they shall, I will take care of that—"according to the laws of arms, and recorded in the Heralds' Office."

Bel. Come, madam, give me leave to put my own interpretation upon your silence, and to plead for my friend, that now that only obstacle which seemed to stand in the way of your union is removed, you will suffer me to complete the happiness which my news seems to have brought him, by introducing him with a new claim to your favour, by the name of Mr. Bacon. (*Takes their hands and joins them, which* MELESINDA *seems to give consent to with a smile.*)

Mr. H. Generous Melesinda!—my dear friend—"he and his issue,"—me and my issue—O Lord!

Bel. I wish you joy, Jack, with all my heart!

Mr. H. Bacon, Bacon, Bacon—how odd it sounds! I could never be tired of hearing it. There was Lord Chancellor Bacon. Methinks I have some of the Verulam blood in me already—methinks I could look through Nature—there was Friar Bacon, a conjurer—I feel as if I could conjure too——

Enter a SERVANT.

Serv. Two young ladies and an old lady are at the door, inquiring if you see company, madam.

Mr. H. "Surname and arms"——

Mel. Show them up.—My dear Mr. Bacon, moderate your joy!

Enter three Ladies, being part of those who were at the assembly.

1st *Lady.* My dear Melesinda, how do you do?

2d *Lady.* How do you do? We have been so concerned for you——

Old Lady. We have been so concerned—(*seeing him*) Mr. Hogsflesh——

Mr. H. There's no such person—nor there never was—nor 'tis not fit there should be—" surname and arms——"

Bel. It is true what my friend would express; we have been all in a mistake, ladies. Very true, the name of this gentleman was what you call it, but it is so no longer. The succession to the long-contested Bacon estate is at length decided, and with it my friend succeeds to the name of his deceased relative.

Mr. H. "His Majesty has been graciously pleased——"

1st *Lady.* I am sure we all join in hearty congratulation—(*sighs*).

2d *Lady.* And wish you joy with all our hearts—(*heighho!*).

Old Lady. And hope you will enjoy the name and estate many years—(*cries*).

Bel. Ha! ha! ha! mortify them a little, Jack.

1st *Lady.* Hope you intend to stay——

2d *Lady.* With us some time——

Old Lady. In these parts.

Mr. H. Ladies, for your congratulations I thank you; for the favours you have lavished on me, and in particular for this lady's (*turning to the old Lady*) good opinion, I rest your debtor. As to any future favours—(*accosts them severally in the order in which he was refused by them at the assembly*)—Madam, shall always acknowledge your politeness; but at present, you see, I am engaged with a partner. Always be happy to respect you as a friend, but you must not look for anything further. Must

beg of you to be less particular in your addresses to me.
Ladies all, with this piece of advice, of Bath and you—

   Your ever grateful servant takes his leave.
   Lay your plans surer when you plot to grieve;
   See, while you kindly mean to mortify
   Another, the wild arrow do not fly,
   And gall yourself. For once you've been mistaken;
   Your shafts have miss'd their aim—Hogsflesh has saved
      his Bacon!

NOTES.

Sonnets (p. 1).—These sonnets are the earliest of Lamb's experiments in verse. They were written at the age of twenty, and tell of his attachment to Ann Simmons—the *Anna* of the sonnets, the Alice Winterton of his later writings, the girl whose acquaintance he made during his visits to his grandmother at Blakesware in Hertfordshire. See Talfourd's *Final Memorials*, Letter to Coleridge 1796 :—" The following sonnet was composed during a walk down to Hertfordshire early in the last summer :—

'The Lord of Light shakes off his drowsyhed,' etc.

The last line is a copy of Bowles' 'To the green hamlet in the peaceful plain.' Your ears are not so very fastidious: many people would not like words so prosaic and familiar in a sonnet as Islington and Hertfordshire. The next was written within a day or two of the last, on revisiting a spot where the scene was laid of my first sonnet, 'that mock'd my steps with many a lonely glade' :—

'When last I roved these winding wood-walks green,' etc.

The next retains a few lines from a sonnet of mine which you once remarked had no 'body of thought' in it. I agree with you, but have preserved a part of it, and it runs thus. I flatter myself you will like it :—

'A timid grace sits trembling in her eye,' etc.

The next and last I value most of all. 'Twas composed close upon the heels of the last, in that very wood I had in mind when I wrote 'Methinks how dainty sweet' :—

'We were two pretty babes, the youngest she,' etc."

Of these early sonnets there are several versions—as first written by Lamb; then as altered by Coleridge; and lastly as revised by Lamb, when reissued in the volumes of 1818. They are given here according to this latest revision. All readers of

Lamb's Letters will remember his soreness about Coleridge's alterations of his sonnets, and his pathetic "Coleridge! spare my ewe-lambs."

Sonnet 7 (p. 4).—Written by Lamb in the winter of 1795-96, when in temporary confinement at the asylum at Hoxton. See letter to Coleridge of 1796. The sonnet that follows, though belonging to a later date, is inserted here in accordance with a wish of Lamb expressed in a letter to Coleridge:—"If the fraternal sentiment conveyed in the following lines will atone for the total want of anything like merit or genius in it, I desire you will print it next after my other sonnet to my sister." For whatever reason, these lines were afterwards withdrawn from publication, and were not printed in Lamb's lifetime.

Sonnet 9 (p. 5).—A voyage to Margate with his sister in the *Old Margate Hoy*, afterwards celebrated in *Elia*, seems to have been the occasion of this sonnet.

Sonnet 10 (p. 5).—There is some doubt as to the authorship of this sonnet. It is signed C. L. in the first edition of Coleridge's Poems (Bristol, 1796), and is included among Lamb's contributions to the second edition of these poems in the following year. But it had appeared with the signature S. T. C. in a series of sonnets published by Coleridge in the *Morning Chronicle* in 1794; and is once again claimed for Coleridge in the third edition of his poems in 1803. On the whole it seems likely that it was a joint composition of the two friends, and was finally surrendered by Lamb to his companion. Lamb did not include it in the first collected edition of his works in 1818.

To Sara and her Samuel (p. 6).—Written on occasion of a disappointment. Lamb had unsuccessfully asked leave of absence from his office to visit Coleridge and his wife at Bristol. The lines were sent in a letter to Coleridge of July 5, 1796, and were printed in the January following in the *Monthly Magazine*. Talfourd points out how strangely Lamb confounds the Avon of Bristol with that of Stratford-on-Avon.

To the Poet Cowper (p. 7).—"I fear you will not accord entirely with my sentiments of Cowper as expressed above (perhaps scarcely just); but the poor gentleman has just recovered from his lunacies, and that begets pity; and pity, love; and love, admiration; and then it goes hard with people but they lie!" (Letter to Coleridge, July 1796.)

Blank Verse (p. 7).—The seven poems that follow are from the second edition of Coleridge's Poems, 1797. These, and the sonnets already given, were prefaced by the following dedication :—" The few following poems, creatures of the Fancy and the Feeling, in life's more *vacant* hours, produced, for the most part, by Love in Idleness, are, with all a brother's fondness, inscribed to Mary Ann Lamb, the author's best friend and sister."

To Charles Lloyd (p. 11).—See letter to Coleridge of 1797 :— "You have learned by this time, with surprise no doubt, that Lloyd is with me in town. The emotions I felt on his coming so unlooked for are not ill expressed in what follows, and what, if you do not object to them as too personal, and to the world obscure or otherwise wanting in worth, I should wish to make part of our little volume."

A Vision of Repentance (p. 13).—From the supplement to the volume of 1797, not dated, but sent by Lamb to Coleridge in a letter of April 15, 1797.

To Charles Lloyd (p. 15).—The blank verse that follows is from the joint volume *Blank Verse by Charles Lloyd and Charles Lamb*, 1798. "The following I wrote when I had returned from C. Lloyd, leaving him behind me at Burton with Southey. To understand some of it you must remember that at that time he was very much perplexed in mind." (*Letter to Coleridge*, 1797.)

Written on the day of my Aunt's Funeral (p. 16).—See letter to Coleridge, January 5, 1797. "My poor old aunt whom you have seen, the kindest, goodest creature to me when I was at school; who used to toddle there to bring me good things, when I, schoolboy like, only despised her for it, and used to be ashamed to see her come and sit herself down on the old coal-hole steps as you went into the old Grammar School, and open her apron, and bring out her bason, with some nice thing she had caused to be saved for me; the good old creature is now lying on her death-bed. . . . She says, poor thing, she is glad she is come home to die with me."

Written a year after the Events (p. 17).—Sent to Coleridge in a letter of September 1797, with the following heading—(" Friday next, Coleridge, is the day on which my mother died ").

Written soon after the preceding Poem (p. 19).—Sent by Lamb to Southey, and mentioned by the latter in a note to his friend Wynn, November 20, 1797—"I know that our tastes differ much in poetry, and yet I think you must like these lines by Charles Lamb. I believe you know his history, and the dreadful death of his mother."

The old familar Faces (p. 21).—Dated by Lamb, January 1798. The first stanza was omitted by him when the poem was reprinted in 1818, in common with other poems that bore reference to his mother's death. The allusion in the fifth stanza—

"I had a friend, a kinder friend has no man"—

was to Coleridge, between whom and Lamb the relations had been for some time the reverse of cordial. There had been little jealousies and wounded vanities in connection with the joint volume of poems. As a poet, Coleridge was already showing himself possessed of powers far greater than Lamb's, and moreover he had been of late disposed to ridicule that affectation of simplicity which had marked the early poems of himself and his friend. In November 1797 Coleridge printed in the *Monthly Magazine* three sonnets, signed *Nehemiah Higginbottom*, ostensibly intended to parody certain characteristics of his own earlier manner. Unfortunately, if a parody on himself, it was doubly so on his fellow-poet; and it seems impossible to doubt that the second of these effusions was somewhat ungenerously aimed at Lamb, and intended to give pain. It runs thus—

To Simplicity.

O! I do love thee, meek Simplicity!
For of thy lays the lulling simpleness
Goes to my heart, and soothes each small distress,
Distress though small, yet haply great to me!
'Tis true on Lady Fortune's gentlest pad
I amble on; yet, though I know not why,
So sad I am—but should a friend and I
Grow cool and miff, O! I am very sad!
And then with sonnets and with sympathy
My dreamy bosom's mystic woes I pall;
Now of my false friend plaining plaintively,
Now raving at mankind in general;
But whether sad or fierce, 'tis simple all,
All very simple, meek Simplicity!

The "friend of my bosom" was Lamb's new friend Charles Lloyd, who had taken Coleridge's place as his nearest friend and confidant. I have preserved in the last stanza the italics originally used by Lamb in alluding to the lady whose doors were now closed upon him—"*Some are taken from me.*" See my Memoir of Lamb in the *Men of Letters* Series.

Living without God in the World (p. 23).—Contributed by Lamb to the first volume of Cottle's *Annual Anthology*. See Letter of Lamb to Southey of November 28, 1798.

John Woodvil (p. 25).—Published in a thin duodecimo volume in 1802. It was written three years earlier, and shown to Coleridge and Southey, who strongly dissuaded Lamb from printing it. At Christmas 1799 Lamb offered it to John Kemble, then manager of Drury Lane, but it was not unnaturally declined. The influences under which the play was written are pointed out in Lamb's dedicatory letter to Coleridge, prefixed to the collected edition of his works in 1818. The title originally chosen for the play was *Pride's Cure.* Lamb defends this title in a letter to Manning of December 1799. "I meant his (*i.e.* John Woodvil's) punishment, not alone to be a cure for his daily and habitual pride, but the direct consequence and appropriate punishment of a particular act of pride." Southey writes to Charles Danvers in December 1801:—"Lamb and his sister see us often; he is printing his play, which will please you by the exquisite beauty of its poetry, and provoke you by the exquisite silliness of its story." It was reviewed in the *Edinburgh* of April 1803.

The Witch (p. 66).—Originally written as an episode in *John Woodvil,* the characters being, instead of the "old servant and stranger," Sandford, Sir Walter Woodvil's steward, and Margaret. See letter of Lamb to Southey, April 20, 1799. "The following is a second extract from my tragedy, *that is to be.* 'Tis narrated by an old steward to Margaret, orphan ward of Sir Walter Woodvil. . . . I expect you to like the old woman's curse." See also a letter to Manning of November 3, 1800:—"At last I have written to Kemble to know the event of my play, which was presented last Christmas. As I suspected, came an answer back that the copy was lost, and could not be found; no hint that anybody had to this day ever looked into it, with a courteous (reasonable !) request of another copy (if I had one by me), and a promise of a definitive answer in a week. I could not resist so facile and moderate a demand, so scribbled out another, omitting sundry things, *such as the witch* story, about half of the forest scene (which is too leisurely for story), and transposing that soliloquy about England getting drunk."

A Ballad: noting the difference of Rich and Poor (p. 68).— See letter to Coleridge, August 6, 1800 :—"I have hit off the following in imitation of old English poetry which, I imagine, I am a dab at. The measure is unmeasurable; but it most resembles that beautiful ballad, The Old and Young Courtier; and in its feature of taking the extremes of two situations for just parallel, it resembles the old poetry certainly."

Ballad from the German (p. 69).—During Lamb's connection with the press (1800-1803), one of his joint schemes with Coleridge was to versify prose translations of German poems supplied by the latter. We may suppose that this paraphrase of Thekla's song in *Wallenstein* was one of these experiments. Coleridge, in a note to his translation of *Wallenstein* in 1800, introduced a slightly different version, with the following preface:—"I cannot but add here an imitation of this song, with which the author of 'The Tale of Rosamund Gray and Blind Margaret' has favoured me, and which appears to me to have caught the happiest manner of our old ballads—

> ' The clouds are black'ning, the storms threat'ning,
> The cavern doth mutter, the greenwood moan ;
> Billows are breaking, the damsel's heart aching,
> Thus in the dark night she singeth alone,
>   Her eye upward roving :
>
> ' The world is empty, the heart is dead surely,
> In this world plainly all seemeth amiss ;
> To thy heaven, Holy One, take home thy little one,
> I have partaken of all earth's bliss
>   Both living and loving.'"

Whether this was Lamb's first draft, or whether it is Lamb's version revised by Coleridge, cannot now be determined.

Hester (p. 69).—Lamb writes to Manning in 1803 :—" I send you some verses I have made on the death of a young Quaker you may have heard me speak of as being in love with for some years while I lived at Pentonville, though I had never spoken to her in my life. She died about a month since." Her name was Hester Savory, but no other fact about her seems recoverable. It was in 1800 that Lamb was living in Chapel Street, Pentonville.

A Farewell to Tobacco (p. 70).—Published in Leigh Hunt's *Reflector* (iv. 1811). Sent in a letter to Wordsworth and his sister, in September 1805 :—" I wish you may think this a handsome farewell to my 'Friendly Traitress.' Tobacco has been my evening comfort and my morning curse for these five years ; and you know how difficult it is from refraining to pick one's lips even, when it has become a habit. This poem is the only one which I have finished since so long as when I wrote 'Hester Savory.' I have had it in my head to do it these two years, but tobacco stood in its own light when it gave me headaches that prevented my singing its praises. Now you have got it, you have got all my store, for I have absolutely not another line . . . The 'Tobacco' being a little in the way of Wither (whom Southey so much likes), perhaps you will somehow convey it to him with my kind remembrances." The Ode bears, in fact, traces and reminiscences of many old authors. The metre is Wither's, and the alternate praise and abuse of his theme is borrowed from the *Author's Abstract of Melancholy*, prefixed to Burton's *Anatomy*. The couplet—

" Stinking'st of the stinking kind,
Filth of the mouth and fog of the mind,"

is a parody of one in Flecknoe's *Invocation to Silence* (1674),

" Offspring of a heavenly kind,
Frost of the mouth and thaw of the mind."

Lines on the Celebrated Picture by Leonardo da Vinci (p. 75).— In the 1818 volumes Lamb printed four copies of verses on subjects connected with this painter—the other three being by his sister Mary. It is evident, from his letters of this period, that he was increasingly interested in the works of Leonardo. See the Elia Essay—*Old China*.

To T. L. H.—a Child (p. 83).—Thornton Leigh Hunt, the eldest child of Leigh Hunt. The occasion of these lines was the imprisonment of Leigh Hunt in the Surrey gaol, from 1813 to 1815, for the *Examiner* libel on the Prince Regent. Hunt writes in his autobiography :—" My eldest little boy, to whom Lamb addressed some charming verses on the occasion, was my constant companion, and we used to play all sorts of juvenile games together. It was, probably, in dreaming of these games (but the words had a more touching effect on my ear) that he exclaimed one night in his sleep, ' No ! I'm not lost, I'm found.' " Charles and Mary Lamb were constant visitors at the prison. Hunt adds :—" The Lambs came to comfort me in all weathers, hail or sunshine, in daylight and in darkness, even in the dreadful frost and snow of the beginning of 1814."

To Miss Kelly (p. 84).—The four following sonnets appear for the first time in the volumes of 1818, and the date and occasion of their composition cannot be ascertained. It is interesting to know that the sonnet on the Family Name attracted the attention of Goethe. When Crabb Robinson visited Weimar in 1829, in conversation with Goethe he asked " whether he knew the name of Lamb." " Oh yes ! Did he not write a pretty sonnet on his own name ? " " Charles Lamb," adds Robinson, " though he always affected contempt for Goethe, yet was manifestly pleased that his name was known to him." The mingled sarcasm and pathos of the sonnet to John Lamb will not escape the reader's attention.

Written at Cambridge (p. 87).—The majority of the poems that follow are from the " *Album Verses, with a few others,*" published by Edward Moxon in 1830. The following was the dedication to this volume :—

"DEAR MOXON—I do not know to whom a Dedication of these Trifles is more properly due than to yourself. You suggested the printing of them. You were desirous of exhibiting a specimen of the *manner* in which publications, entrusted to your future care, would appear. With more propriety, perhaps, the 'Christmas,' or some other of your own simple, unpretending, compositions might have served this purpose. But I forgot— you have bid a long adieu to the Muses. I had on my hands sundry copies of Verses, written for *Albums*—

'These books, kept by modern young ladies for show,
Of which their plain grandmothers nothing did know,'

or otherwise floating about in Periodicals, which you have chosen in this manner to embody. I feel little interest in this publication. They are simply *Advertisement Verses*.

"It is not for me, nor you, to allude in public to the kindness of our honoured Friend, under whose auspices you are become a Bookseller. May that fine-minded Veteran in Verse enjoy life long enough to see his patronage justified! I venture to predict that your habits of industry, and your cheerful spirit, will carry you through the world.—I am, dear Moxon, your friend and sincere Well-wisher, CHARLES LAMB.
"ENFIELD, 1*st June* 1830."

The "Veteran in Verse" was Samuel Rogers, who enjoyed life for a quarter of a century longer. The little volume was roughly handled by the reviewers, whose unfriendly comments were repelled by Southey in a sonnet contributed to the *Times* newspaper. Lamb writes to Bernard Barton in August 1830 :— "Thank you for your warm interest about my little volume, for the critics on which I care the five hundred thousandth part of a half farthing. I am too old a militant for that. How noble though in R. S. to come forward for an old friend who had treated him so unworthily. . . . What a clamour against a poor collection of Album Verses, as if we had put forth an Epic."

Work (p. 88).—Published in the *Examiner* in 1822.

Leisure (p. 88).—*London Magazine*, April 1821.

In the Album of Lucy Barton (p. 89).—Written at Bernard Barton's request, and sent in a letter to him of September 30, 1824 :—"I am ill at these numbers, but if the above be not too mean to have a place in thy daughter's sanctum, take them with pleasure."

The Young Catechist (p. 91).—"Apropos of Van Balen, an artist who painted me lately had painted a blackamoor praying, and not filling his canvas, stuffed in his little girl aside of blacky, gaping at him unmeaningly, and then did not know what to call it. Now, for a picture to be promoted to the exhibition (Suffolk Street) as *historical*, a subject is requisite. What does Mr. T. but christen it the 'Young Catechist,' and published it with dialogue following, which dubbed it an historical painting. Nothing to a friend at need." (Letter to B. Barton, 1827.)

On an infant dying as soon as born (p. 93).—Written on occasion of the death of the first child of Thomas Hood. In the Memorials of Hood by his daughter we find this reference to the event:—"The first few years of his married life were the most unclouded my father ever knew. The young couple resided for some years in Robert Street, Adelphi. Here was born their first child, which to their great grief scarcely survived its birth. In looking over some old papers I found a few tiny curls of golden hair, as soft as the finest silk, wrapped in a yellow and timeworn paper inscribed in my father's handwriting:—

'Little eyes that scarce did see,
Little lips that never smiled;
Alas! my little dear dead child,
Death is thy father, and not me,
I but embraced thee, soon as he!'

On this occasion those exquisite lines of Charles Lamb's—'On an infant dying as soon as born,' were written and sent to my father and mother." It is interesting to put side by side these two copies of verses. They are curiously characteristic of the different genius of these two great humorists.

The Christening (p. 95).—From *Blackwood's Magazine*, May 1829. Written on the baptism of a child of Charles and Mary Gisburne May, at Enfield, in May 1829.

The Gipsy's Malison (p. 96).—The origin of these lines is told in an amusing letter of Lamb's to Mr. Procter (Barry Cornwall) of January 29, 1829:—"When Miss Ouldcroft (who is now Mrs. Reddam) was at Enfield, which she was in summer time, and owed her health to its sun and genial influences, she visited (with young-lady-like impertinence) a poor man's cottage that had a pretty baby (O the yearning!), gave it fine caps and sweetmeats. On a day, broke into the parlour our two maids uproarious. 'O maam! who do you think Miss Ouldcroft (they pronounce it Holcroft) has been working a cap for?' 'A child,' answered Mary, in true Shandean female simplicity. ''Tis the man's child as was taken up for sheep-stealing.' Miss Ouldcroft was staggered and would have cut the connection, but by main force I made her go and take her leave of her protégée. I thought, if she went no more, the Abactor, or Abactor's wife (*vide* Ainsworth), would suppose she had heard something; and I have delicacy for a sheep-stealer. The overseer's actually overhauled a mutton pie at the baker's (his first, last, and only hope of mutton pie), which he never came to eat, and thence inferred his guilt. *Per occasionem cujus* I framed the sonnet; observe its elaborate construction. I was four days about it." The sonnet appeared in *Blackwood* for January 1829. Lamb had already written to Procter—"Did you see a sonnet of mine in *Blackwood's* last? Curious construction. Elaborata facilitas! and now I'll tell. 'Twas written for 'The Gem,' but the Editors declined it, on the plea that it would *shock all mothers*, so they published *The Widow* instead. I am born out of time."

To a young Friend on her twenty-first Birthday (p. 103).—To Emma Isola, the adopted daughter of Charles and Mary Lamb, and afterwards the wife of Edward Moxon. The "respected grandsire" was an Italian refugee who had settled in Cambridge and supported himself as a teacher of languages. Two eminent poets, Gray and Wordsworth, learned Italian from him.

Harmony in Unlikeness (p. 105). The "fair Maria" is, of course, Mary Lamb, and "Emma Brown," the Miss Isola of the two preceding poems. As Mary Lamb had at this time well passed her sixtieth year, the tender playfulness of these lines will not pass unnoticed.

To a celebrated Female Performer in "The Blind Boy" (p. 105).—Lamb's old favourite, Miss Kelly.

Translations from the Latin of Vincent Bourne (p. 109).—Lamb had made the acquaintance of Vincent Bourne's Latin Poems in 1815. He writes to Wordsworth in that year: "Since I saw you I have had a treat in the reading way, which comes not every day, the Latin Poems of V. Bourne, which were quite new to me. What a heart that man had! all laid out upon town scenes, a proper counterpoise to *some people's* rural extravaganzas. Why I mention him is, that your *Power of Music* reminded me of his poem of the *Ballad Singer in the Seven Dials* . . . . What a sweet, unpretending, pretty-mannered, *matterful* creature, sucking from every flower, making a flower of everything, his diction all Latin, and his thoughts all English. Bless him! Latin wasn't good enough for him. Why wasn't he content with the language which Gay and Prior wrote in?" It will be remembered that Cowper entertained the same high admiration for Bourne, whose pupil he had been at Westminster, and translated some of the best of his Latin poems.

Epicedium. Going or Gone (p. 119).—Contributed to Hone's *Table Book* in 1827. After the sixth stanza there were originally the two following, carrying on the description of "Old Dorrell":—

> "Had he mended in right time,
> He need not in night-time
> (That black hour and fright-time)
>   Till sexton interred him,
> Have groaned in his coffin,
> While demons stood scoffing—
> You'd ha' thought him a coughing—
>   My own father [1] heard him.
>
> Could gain so importune
> With occasion opportune,
> That for a poor Fortune,
>   That should have been ours, [2]
> In soul he should venture
> To pierce the dim centre
> Where will-forgers enter,
>   Amid the dark Powers."

Old Dorrell is mentioned elsewhere by Lamb, as one from whom his family had had "expectations." See the Elia Essay *New Year's Eve:*—"It was better that our family should have missed that legacy which old Dorrell cheated us of, than that I should have at this moment two thousand pounds *in banco*, and be without the idea of that specious old rogue." The other persons named in these verses are mostly old inhabitants of the village of Widford, which he knew so well in the happy Blakesware days. Mrs. Tween of Widford has kindly furnished me with particulars of some of these. Ben Carter the gardener, and Lilly the postillion, were servants of the Plumer family—the latter "a diminutive man with a remarkable red face." His gravestone is in Widford churchyard. He died at the advanced age of 89, in October 1812. Clemitson was the tenant of what is called Blakesware Farm. Clapton was another Widford farmer (buried May 8, 1802). Mrs. Tween tells me that the "elder Mr. and Mrs. Plumer of Blakesware always went out in a carriage and four, with Lilly as Postillion, two outriders, and a couple of carriage-dogs."

Kitty "Wheatley" is probably a mistake (for Lamb had a "royal disdain" for accuracy in spelling) for Whately. The

---

[1] Who sat up with him.
[2] I have this fact from parental tradition only.

Rev. Joseph Whately, vicar of Widford, married Jane Plumer, sister of the Mr. Plumer who sat in the House of Commons for Hertfordshire; and the "Kitty" here referred to was probably one of his daughters. Joseph Whately's youngest child became Archbishop of Dublin.

The Wife's Trial (p. 122).—Written in the summer of 1827. Lamb writes to Barton, August 10 :—"I am trying my hand at a drama, in two acts, founded on Crabbe's 'Confidant,' *mutatis mutandis.*" The change to which Lamb thus directs attention concerns the precise nature of the secret which the malicious friend holds *in terrorem* over the wife's head. Again, on August 28, Lamb writes to the same friend :—"Yesterday I sent off my tragi-comedy to Mr. Kemble. Wish it luck. I made it all ('tis blank verse, and I think of the true old dramatic cut), or most of it, in the green lanes about Enfield." The little drama was not found suitable for the stage, and was ultimately published in *Blackwood* for December 1828.

To a Friend, on his Marriage (p. 152).—Evidently to Edward Moxon, who married Emma Isola in July of this year, 1833.

Free thoughts on several eminent Composers (p. 154).—Sent in a letter to William Ayrton in May 1830. The little note, exquisitely humorous, has been kindly placed at my disposal by Mr. W. S. Ayrton of Saltburn. It is as follows :—

"ENFIELD, Thursday.
(No other date.)

"DEAR AYRTON—Novello paid us a visit yesterday, and I very much wished you with us. Our conversation was principally, as you may suppose, upon *Music;* and he, desiring me to give him my real opinion respecting the distinct grades of excellence in all the eminent Composers of the Italian, German, and English Schools, I have done it, rather to oblige him than from any overweening opinion I have of my own judgment in that science. Such as it is, I submit it to better critics, and am, dear Ayrton, yours sincerely, CH. LAMB."

To Margaret W—— (p. 155).—Lamb's last verses, written only a few weeks before his death in December of the same year. It is pleasant to find what sweet and graceful fancies were still at his command in the gloomy loneliness of his last days. The lines were first printed in the *Athenæum* of March 14, 1835.

Rosamund Gray (p. 157).—Written and published in 1798, when Lamb was in his twenty-fourth year, under the title of "A Tale of Rosamund Gray and Old Blind Margaret." The earliest reference by Lamb to the story is in a letter to Southey, undated, but apparently of October 1798. Southey was at this time living at Westbury, near Bristol, writing many of his shorter poems and ballads, and sending them to Lamb for his criticism and revision. One of these poems, a short tale in verse, called "The Ruined Cottage," had been thus submitted to Lamb, and he writes back as follows:—"I thank you heartily for the Eclogue which pleases me mightily, being so full of picture-work and circumstances. I find no fault in it, unless perhaps that Joanna's ruin is a catastrophe too trite; and this is not the first or second time you have clothed your indignation in verse, in a tale of ruined innocence. The old lady, spinning in the sun, I hope would not disdain to claim some kindred with old Margaret."

"Old Margaret" is the grandmother in the story of *Rosamund Gray*, and here begin the many curious coincidences afforded by the tale. Southey's Eclogue, with some slight variations of detail, is in fact Lamb's story told over again in a hundred and twenty lines of blank verse—a pious old grandmother, a lovely grandchild, a seduction, and the consequent death of the old lady. That Southey should have sent the poem to Lamb, without apologising for using his material, seems as strange as that Lamb should have received it with no further expression of surprise than that just quoted. Lamb goes on to criticise some points in his friend's treatment of the subject, and adds— "I am thinking, I believe, of the song—

' An old woman clothed in gray,
   Whose daughter was charming and young,
 And she was deluded away
   By Roger's false flattering tongue.'

A Roger-Lothario would be a novel character; I think you might paint him very well. You may think this a very silly suggestion, and so indeed it is; but in good truth, nothing else but the first words of that foolish ballad put me upon scribbling my *Rosamund*."

It might be assumed that this was one of Lamb's ordinary hoaxes, were it not that in the last lines of his story he makes the villain of the tale, Matravis, in the course of his delirious wanderings, to sing "a song about *an old woman clothed in gray*." But it is quite as likely that his story recalled to him the ribald old ballad as that it was suggested by it.

The story is indeed, as I have said elsewhere, made up of strange and fantastic ingredients. The scene is laid in Widford, the Hertfordshire village close to Blakesware, where the happiest days of Lamb's childhood had been passed, and where he had formed the first and only love attachment of his life. In a cottage, about half a mile from Blakesware Hall (bearing the incongruous name of Blenheims), lived the girl who is believed by the people of Widford to be the original of Rosamund Gray, but whose actual name was Ann (or Nancy) Simmons, the *Anna* of Lamb's early sonnets, the Alice W—n of the Essays of Elia. But though real persons seem to be indicated in the story, the events in which they take part are without foundation in fact, for the girl who won the heart of Charles Lamb married prosperously, and lived to an advanced age. Lamb found a name for his heroine in a song "Rosamund Gray," by his early friend Lloyd, published in "Poems on various Subjects" (Carlisle, 1795). Nothing but the name could certainly have been found by Lamb in the prosaic commonplace of this effusion, of which a single stanza will suffice as specimen—

> " If actions are great, no one cares if they're good,
>   A tyrant's a reverenced name,
> The grant of renown is imprinted in blood,
>   And a sword is a passport to fame.
> And I've marked honest virtue with misery bowed,
>   Tho' she urge inoffensive her way;
> Yes, feelings I've marked that would honour the proud,
>   In the bosom of Rosamund Gray."

But it was quite in Lamb's manner to appropriate any name that was associated with a personal friend, or had lately struck him in his reading; and though it is a "far cry" from Charles Lloyd to Christopher Marlowe, we are not surprised to find that the villain of the story should be named Matravis (a slip of spelling, we may be sure, for Matrevis), one of the assassins who murder the king in Marlowe's *Edward the Second*. The remaining characters in the tale are sentimentalised abstractions of himself and his sister Mary (Allan and Elinor Clare), his old grandmother, Mrs. Field, Coleridge (the schoolfellow who precedes Allan Clare to college), and a few of the servants and villagers of Blakesware and Widford. Of the original of Matravis (if such ever existed) we know nothing. As a creation he is absolutely characterless and shadowy, but there are sentences in the story containing allusions so bitterly incisive, and yet so irrelevant to the story he takes part in, that it is impossible to doubt that Lamb had in view some old enemy from whom he or his family had suffered injury. How otherwise are we to account for the detail that Matravis had once "paid his court to Elinor Clare," or for the outbursts in Elinor's letter to Maria, "O ye Matravises of the age," or for the mention of the dream that Allan was dead, and that Matravis "put on mourning for him"?—allusions with no bearing on Lamb's story, and which can only be attributed to an overmastering desire of the moment to unburden himself of a personal grievance.

The "unique" character of the romance, which Talfourd lays stress upon, lies in a curious combination of the utterly artificial method of the sentimental fiction of Lamb's day, with a vein of real genius and poetry, which no conventionalities could obliterate. The theatrical platitudes of Elinor Clare's letters to her cousin are not at all more false to nature than those of the two friends in *Julia de Roubigné*, from which they are closely copied ; but they offend the taste the more, because in Mackenzie all is alike hollow, and in Lamb they stand out against a background of truth and genuine sensibility. But there is—the truth must be said—a tinge of *insanity* in the story. Two years before, its author had been for a time under restraint, and since then, though he never again needed this protection against himself, he had undergone an agony such as few men are called upon to endure. But through whatever "dim and perilous ways" the intellect is sounding on, we never lose touch of the sweet and human heart that beats underneath. Shelley was not overstating the truth when he wrote to Leigh Hunt, "What a lovely thing is his *Rosamund Gray!* How much knowledge of the sweetest and deepest part of our nature in it!" The mellow autumn light on garden and cottage was never more perfectly felt by poet or painter than in the opening pages of this story. If the clouds gather afterwards, we wonder and are sorry—even as when they gather at the close round one of the matchless lyrics of William Blake.

Curious Fragments (p. 197).—Published in 1801, in the small volume containing *John Woodvil*.

In March 1800 Lamb, writing to Manning about his plans and projects, tells how Coleridge had introduced him to Daniel Stuart of the *Morning Post*:—"He has lugged me to the brink of engaging to a newspaper, and has suggested to me for a first plan the forgery of a supposed manuscript of Burton, the anatomist of melancholy." Six months later he has to write that his idea of furnishing political squibs to the *Post* had come to nothing; but adds, "I had struck off two imitations of Burton, quite abstracted from any modern allusions, which it was my intent only to lug in from time to time to make 'em popular. Stuart has got these with an introductory letter ; but not hearing from him, I have ceased from my labours, but I write to him to-day to get a final answer. I am afraid they won't do for a paper. Burton is a scarce gentleman, not much known, else I had done 'em pretty well. I have also hit off a few lines in the name of Burton, being a *Conceit of Diabolic Possession*. Burton was a man often assailed by deepest melancholy, and at other times much given to laughing and jesting, as is the way with melancholy men. I will send them you; they were almost extempore, and no great things; but you will indulge them." They were not found suitable for the *Morning Post*. "Fate and 'Wisest Stuart' say, No," and Lamb accordingly printed them in the following year with his *John Woodvil*, having in the meantime changed the name of the lines from *Conceit of Diabolic Possession* to *Hypochondriacus*.

Recollections of Christ's Hospital (p. 206).—A paper contributed by Lamb to the *Gentleman's Magazine* in 1813. It appeared in two instalments—in the June of that year, and in the supplement to the annual volume. When Lamb reprinted the essay in his volume of 1818 he omitted the opening paragraphs, which were as follows:—

"A great deal has been said about the governors of this Hospital abusing their right of presentation by presenting the children of opulent parents to the Institution. This may have been the case in an instance or two; and what wonder, in an establishment consisting, in town and country, of upwards of a thousand boys! But I believe there is no great danger of an abuse of this sort ever becoming very general. There is an old quality in human nature which will perpetually present an adequate preventive to this evil. While the coarse blue coat and the yellow hose shall continue to be the costume of the school (and never may modern refinement innovate upon the venerable fashion!) the sons of the aristocracy of this country, cleric or laic, will not often be obtruded upon this seminary.

"I own I wish there were more room for such complaints. I cannot but think that a sprinkling of the sons of respectable parents among them has an admirable tendency to liberalise the whole mass, and that to the great proportion of clergymen's children in particular which are to be found among them it is owing that the foundation has not long since degenerated into a mere charity-school, as it must do upon the plan so hotly recommended by some reformists, of recruiting its ranks from the offspring of none but the very lowest of the people.

"I am not learned enough in the history of the Hospital to say by what steps it may have departed from the letter of its original charter; but, believing it, as it is at present constituted, to be a great practical benefit, I am not anxious to revert to first principles, to overturn a positive good, under pretence of restoring something which existed in the days of Edward the Sixth, when the face of everything around us was as different as can be from the present. Since that time the opportunities of instruction to the very lowest classes (of as much instruction as may be beneficial and not pernicious to them) have multiplied beyond what the prophetic spirit of the first suggester of this charity[1] could have predicted, or the wishes of that holy man have even aspired to. There are parochial schools, and Bell's and Lancaster's, with their arms open to receive every son of ignorance, and disperse the last fog of uninstructed darkness which dwells upon the land. What harm, then, if in the heart of this noble city, there should be left one receptacle where parents of rather more liberal views, but whose time-straitened circumstances do not admit of affording their children that better sort of education which they themselves, not without cost to their parents, have received, may without cost send their sons? For such Christ's Hospital unfolds her bounty."

What was the immediate occasion of Lamb's paper it is impossible to say, but about four years previously the question of the right of governors to present certain candidates, sons of gentlemen, to the foundation, had arisen and been discussed with some bitterness in the newspapers of the day. The son of the Vicar of Edmonton, a Mr. Dawson Warren, had been presented to the school, and a member of the Common Council had drawn attention to the case as contrary to the spirit of the regulations in force as to candidates for admission. The question was carefully inquired into, and after much debate the case of Mr. Warren's son was decided in his favour, and a committee drew up a new form of presentation which has remained substantially in force to the present day. It is obviously to this incident, and the public interest aroused by it, that the opening sentences of the original essay refer.

Lamb reprinted the bulk of his essay under its present title (it had been originally headed *On Christ's Hospital, and the character of the Christ's Hospital Boys*) in his collected works in 1818. Two years later he followed it up with the Elia Essay, *Christ's Hospital five and thirty years ago*, in which (assuming the character of a second writer criticising his predecessor) he deals in lighter fashion with some other aspects of the school. The character of James Boyer, the headmaster, is drawn in both essays with the utmost frankness. Coleridge, in his *Table Talk*, relates some experiences which leave no doubt that Lamb's picture was not overdrawn. "The discipline at Christ's Hospital in my time was ultra-Spartan; all domestic ties were to be put aside. 'Boy!' I remember Boyer saying to me once when I was crying the first day of my return after the holidays, 'Boy! the school is your father! Boy! the school is your mother! Boy! the school is your brother! Boy! the school is your sister! the school is your first cousin, and your second cousin, and all the rest of your relations! Let's have no more crying!'"

---

[1] Bishop Ridley, in a sermon preached before King Edward the Sixth.

On the Tragedies of Shakspere (p. 220).—From Leigh Hunt's *Reflector*, where it appeared in 1811, under the title of *Theatralia, No.* 1, *on Garrick and Acting*. It was signed with the letter "X."

In my Memoir of Charles Lamb, in the *Men of Letters* Series, I have dwelt upon the curious mixture of truth and paradox supplied by this essay. The most obvious criticism upon the paper is that it proves too much, and makes all theatrical representations not only superfluous, but actually injurious to the effect of a drama. Lamb seems to have awakened to a consciousness of this before the close of his argument, for he admits that the method employed would extend with equal force to Shakspere's comedies, and that it would be "no very difficult task" to show "why Falstaff, Shallow, Sir Hugh Evans and the rest, are equally incompatible with stage representation." Happily, we possess such criticism of Lamb's upon the best acting of his day as shows that he could on occasion feel very strongly what the drama may owe to its interpreters on the stage. We have only to recall his description of Mrs. Jordan's Viola or Bensley's Malvolio. In fact, while we read the present paper we are reminded of a story of the late Charles Austin and the prize essay, and feel that Lamb could have written, if not "a much better one," certainly one at least as good "on the other side." It is hardly needful to point out that the essay contains some of the noblest criticism ever written, and that in protesting against the eighteenth century adapters of Shakspere Lamb was doing an unexampled service to the cause of true art. Cibber's version of *Richard III.* kept the stage up to yesterday; Tate's *Lear* was finally set aside by Macready in 1838.

The following letter of Lamb's, bearing on the subject of these alterations of Shakspere, may appropriately be given here. It is practically new, for it was contributed to the *Spectator* in November 1828, and has never (to my knowledge) been reprinted:—

"SHAKSPERE'S IMPROVERS.

"To the Editor of the *Spectator*.

"SIR—Partaking in your indignation at the sickly stuff interpolated by Tate in the genuine play of *King Lear*, I beg to lay before you certain kindred enormities that you may be less aware of, which that co-dilutor of Sternhold and Hopkins, with his compeers, were suffered—nay, encouraged—by an English public of a century and a half ago to perpetrate upon the dramas of Shakspere.

"I speak from imperfect recollection of one of these new versions which I have seen, namely, of *Coriolanus*—by the same hand which touched up *King Lear*—in which he, the said Nahum, not deeming his author's catastrophe enough striking, makes Aufidius (if my memory fail me not) violate the person of the wife, and mangle the body of the little son of his Roman rival. Shadwell, another improver, in his version of *Timon of Athens*, a copy of which (167⅞) is lying before me, omits the character of Flavius, the kind-hearted steward, that fine exception to the air of general perfidy in the play, which would else be too oppressive to reader or spectator; and substitutes for it a kind female who is supposed to be attached to Timon to the last, thus making the moral of the piece to consist in showing, not the hollowness of friendships conciliated by a mere undistinguishing prodigality, but the superiority of woman's love to the friendships of men. Evandra too has a rival in the affections of the noble Athenian. So impossible did these blockheads imagine it to be to interest the feelings of an audience without an intrigue, that the misanthrope Timon must whine and the daughterly Cordelia must whimper their love affections before they could hope to touch the gentle hearts in the boxes! Had one of these gentry taken in hand to improve the fine Scriptural story of Joseph and his brethren, we should have had a love-passion introduced to make the mere fraternal interest of the piece go down—an episode of the amours of Reuben or Issachar with the fair Mizraim of Egypt.

"Thus Evandra closes the eyes of Shadwell's dying Timon, who it seems has poisoned himself:—

'*Evan.* Oh my dear Lord! why do you stoop and bend
Like flowers o'ercharged with dew, whose yielding stalks
Cannot support them?
'*Timon.* So now my weary pilgrimage on earth
Is almost finished! now my best Evandra,
I charge thee by our loves, our mutual loves,
Live, and live happy after me, and if
A thought of Timon comes into thy mind,
And brings a tear from thee—
   (*What then? why, then*)
       let some diversion
Banish it.'

And so, after some more drivel of the same stamp, the noble Timon dies. And was not this a dainty dish to set before an audience of the Duke's Theatre in the year 167⅞? Yet Betterton then acted Timon, and his wife Evandra.

"I now come to the London Acting Edition of *Macbeth* of the same date, 1678 (played, if I remember, by the same players at the same house), from which I made a few rough extracts when I visited the British Museum for the sake of selecting from the

'Garrick Plays.' As I can scarcely expect to be believed upon my own word, as to what our ancestors at that time were willing to accept, for Shakspere, I refer the reader to that collection to verify my report. Who the improver[1] was in this instance we are left to guess, for the title page leaves us to conjecture. Possibly the players each one separately contributed his new reading, which was silently adopted. Flesh and blood could not at this time of day submit to a thorough perusal of the thing; but, from a glance or two of casual inspection, I am enabled to lay before the reader a few flowers. In one of the lyric parts Hecate is made to say—

—'On a corner of the moon,
A drop my spectacles have found,
I'll catch it.'

"Hecate, the solemn president of classic enchantments, thence adopted into the romantic—the triform Hecate—wearing spectacles to assist old sight!—(No. 4 or No. 5, as the opticians class them, is not said)—one may as well fancy Cerberus in a bran-new collar, or the "dreaded name of Demogorgon" in jack-boots. Among the ingredients of the cauldron is enumerated, not a *tiger's*, but—what? Reader—

'A Dutchman's chawdron.'

"We were about that time engaged in a war with Holland. Again, Macduff being about to journey across the heath,—the 'blasted heath,'—answers his lady who cautiously demands of him, 'Are you afoot?'—

' Knowing the way to be both short and easy,
And that the chariot did attend me here,
I have adventured '—

From which we may infer that the Thane of Fife lived as a nobleman ought to do, and kept his carriage. Again, the same nobleman, on the morning after Duncan's murder, says, 'Rising this morning early, I went to look out of my window, I could scarce see further than my heath.' And indeed the original author informs us that it had been a 'rough night,' so that the improver does not wander far from his text. The exquisite familiarity of this prose-patch was doubtlessly intended by the improver to break the tiresome monotony of Shakspere's blank verse. In conclusion, Lady Macbeth is brought in repentant and counselling her husband to give up the crown for conscience sake. *Item*, she sees a ghost, which

---

[1] Mr. Swinburne points out to me that it was Sir William Davenant.

is all the time invisible to *him*. Such was the *Macbeth* which Betterton acted, and a contemporary audience took on trust for Shakspere's.   C. L."

Characters of Dramatic Writers Contemporary with Shakspere (p. 241).—Chosen by Lamb in 1818, for publication in his collected works, from the "Specimens of English Dramatic Poets, who lived about the time of Shakspere," published in 1808. His prefatory words explain that he here selects such criticisms as would be intelligible and interesting apart from the passages to which they refer.

Specimens from the Writings of Fuller, the Church Historian (p. 262).—First printed in Leigh Hunt's *Reflector*, No. iv. 1811.

On the Genius and Character of Hogarth (p. 272).—The *Reflector*, No. iii. 1811. The "old-fashioned house in ——shire" was Blakesware in Hertfordshire. See letter of Lamb to Southey in October 1799 :—"I have but just got your letter, being returned from Herts, where I have passed a few red-letter days with much pleasure. I would describe the country to you, as you have done by Devonshire, but alas! I am a poor pen at that same. I could tell you of an old house with a tapestry bedroom, the 'judgment of Solomon' composing one panel, and 'Actaeon spying Diana naked' the other. I could tell of an old marble hall, with Hogarth's prints, and the Roman Caesars in marble hung round."

On the Poetical Works of George Wither (p. 295).—First printed in Lamb's works, 1818. These critical remarks were, in the first instance, marginal notes made by Lamb in an interleaved copy of Wither's *Philarete* and other poems, edited and printed by Lamb's friend and old schoolfellow, John Matthew Gutch, at his private press at Bristol. Mr. Gutch, in the appendix to his *Lyttel Geste of Robin Hode* (1847), thus tells the story of their origin :—

"It was in the year 1809 that the editor's attention was first directed to Wither's publications, and his admiration of his poems gradually increased as many of his rare pieces fell into his hands, particularly those which Mr. Park had collected, with many of that gentleman's valuable annotations interspersed in their pages. He was encouraged to proceed in his selection by his warm-hearted friend and schoolfellow, Charles Lamb, who, it will be seen by the following letter, first became acquainted with Wither's poems through the editor :—

'DEAR GUTCH—I did not see your brother who brought me Wither, but I understood he said you were daily expecting to come to town; this has prevented my writing. The books have pleased me excessively; I should think you could not have made a better selection. I never saw *Philarete* before—judge of my pleasure. I could not forbear scribbling certain critiques in pencil on the blank leaves. Shall I send them, or may I expect to see you in town? Some of them are remarks on the character of Wither and of his writings. Do you mean to have anything of that kind? What I have said on *Philarete* is poor, but I think some of the rest not so bad; perhaps I have exceeded my commission in scrawling over the copies, but my delight therein must excuse me, and pencil marks will rub out. Where is the life? Write, for I am quite in the dark. Yours, with many thanks, C. LAMB.

'Perhaps I could digest the few critiques prefixed to the "Satires," "Shepherds' Hunting," etc., into a short abstract of Wither's character and works, at the end of his life. But, may be, you don't want anything, and have said all you wish in the life.

'*April* 9, 1810, London.'

"These pencil-marks Charles Lamb afterwards requested the editor to return to him, and they formed the matter of one of his papers in the collection of his works first published in 1818."

Mr. Gutch was quite wrong in supposing that Lamb first became acquainted with Wither through this privately printed edition. What Lamb says is that he there met with *Philarete* for the first time. Four years earlier we find Lamb referring to Wither as one of his favourite writers. (See note to the *Farewell to Tobacco*.) And from Wither he had borrowed the rhymed couplet which remained to the end of his life the metre he most affected.

The interleaved copy referred to by Mr. Gutch is now in the possession of Mr. A. C. Swinburne, and through his kindness I have been enabled to make a careful examination of it. An early copy of Gutch's edition was, in the first instance, interleaved, and sent to Lamb for his corrections of the press and suggestions as to emendations of the text, where corrupt or doubtful. These he furnished, together with criticisms and other remarks, written on the blank pages. Mr. Gutch seems then to have sent on the volumes to Dr. G. F. Nott, the editor of Surrey's and Wyatt's Poems. Dr. Nott added his quota of corrections and suggestions, and the volumes once more found their way into the hands of Lamb, who proceeds (*more suo*) to criticise the last interloper with the utmost freedom of language and (as may well be believed) with a critical acumen that leaves Dr. Nott far behind. The necessity for continually differing from this rival critic finds abundant scope for grim jest in connection with his opponent's surname, "It should *not*, Nott!" occurring over and over again, with slight variations of form. Many of Lamb's interjectional remarks and desperate plays upon words would hardly bear the dignity of type; but now and again occurs some such fine outburst as the following. On Wither's Satire ix. *On Ambition*, Dr. Nott remarks, "A very dull essay indeed," whereupon Lamb turns upon him with fury, "Why double-dull it with thy dull commentary? Have you nothing to cry out but 'very dull,' 'a little better,' 'this has some spirit,' 'this is prosaic'? Foh! If the sun of Wither withdraw awhile, clamour not for joy, Owl, it will out again, and blear thy envious eyes."

And the shortest of Lamb's marginal comments often contain some felicity of expression which could have fallen from none but himself, as when Wither, in the Satire *On Presumption*, asks—

> "How, then, will those presumptuous fellows speed?
> Who think (forsooth) because that once a yeere
> They can afford the poor some slender cheere;
> Observe their country feasts, or common doles,
> And entertain their Christmas wassail bowls,
> Or else because that for the churches good,
> They in defence of *Hock-tide* custome stood,
> A Whitsun-ale, or some such godly motion,"

Lamb quietly notes, "The Puritan pokes out his tender horns here."

Which Drayton seems to have felt (p. 300).—The quotation from Drayton is from the Ode "To Himself, and the Harp," in which occur the noble lines:—

> Apollo and the nine
> Forbid no man their shrine,
> That cometh with hands pure;
> Else they be so divine,
> They will not him endure.

It is a notable instance of the lack of care with which Lamb's text has been dealt with by editors, that from the first appearance of this paper in 1818 to the present time, an error has been allowed to remain that makes nonsense of Drayton's lines. "Slake" has been from the first misprinted "Stake."

The Londoner (p. 301).—This short essay is in the form of a letter to Leigh Hunt's *Reflector*, but as a matter of fact it never appeared in any of the four numbers to which that periodical extended. It had probably been sent to Hunt for publication, and been prevented from appearing by the early collapse of the venture.

The paper was written many years before—as far back indeed as 1802. In a letter to Manning of February in that year, after defending his new play, *John Woodvil*, against certain criticisms of his friend, he adds somewhat abruptly, "I will now transcribe 'The Londoner' (No. 1), and wind up all with affection and humble servant at the end." Then followed, according to Talfourd, a transcription of this very paper. The subject of it was fresh in Lamb's thoughts or memory, and the essay is indeed an expansion of a passage in a letter to Wordsworth of about a year before—"I have passed all my days in London until I have found as many and intense local attachments as any of you mountaineers can have done with dead nature. The lighted shops of the Strand and Fleet Street; the innumerable trades, tradesmen, and customers, coaches, wagons, playhouses; all the bustle and wickedness round about Covent Garden; the very women of the town; the watchmen, drunken scenes, rattles, life awake, if you awake, at all hours of the night; the impossibility of being dull in Fleet Street; the crowds, the very dirt and mud, the sun shining upon houses and pavements, the print-shops, the old book-stalls, parsons cheapening books, coffee-houses, steams of soup from kitchens, the pantomimes—London itself a pantomime and a masquerade—all these things work themselves into my mind and feed me without a power of satiating me. The wonder of these sights impels me into night walks about her crowded streets, and I often shed tears in the motley Strand from fulness of joy at so much life—all these things must be strange to you, so are your rural emotions to me. But, consider, what must I have been doing all my life not to have lent great portions of my heart with usury to such scenes?"

The last sentence of this passage is repeated, it will be noticed, almost word for word, in the present essay. Lamb's affection for the great city was one of the most real and permanent of his life. When he was living, in later years, in Covent Garden, he heads a letter to Payne Collier, "The Garden of England," and such indeed it was to him. Like Dr. Johnson returning from the Hebrides, he "resumed existence" only when he came back to the familiar surroundings of Fleet Street. There lies before me an unpublished letter of Lamb's to his old fellow-clerk in the India House, Mr. Dodwell, written only a few weeks after he had settled at Enfield and ceased for ever to be a "Londoner." The letter is full of varied interest, of wild fun interspersed with truly "Elian" subtleties, and I make no apology for printing a portion of it. The original is in the possession of the family of the late Mr. Arthur Loveday of Wardington, Banbury, through whose kindness I am able to give it:—

" ENFIELD CHASE,
nearly opposite to the 1st Chapel, or, better to define it, east side, opposite a white house in which a Mrs. Vaughan (in ill health) still resides.
October 7, 1827.

"MY DEAR DODWELL—Your little pig found his way to Enfield this morning, without his feet, or rather his little feet came first, and, as I guessed, the rest of him soon followed. He is quite a beauty. It was a pity to kill him, or *rather*, as Rice would say, it would have been a pity *not* to kill him in his state of innocence. He might have lived to be corrupted by the ways of the world, and for all his delicate promise have turned out, like an old tea-broker you and I remember, a lump of fat rusty *Bacon*. . . . Your kind letter has left a relish upon my taste, it read warm and short as to-morrow's crackling. I am not quite so comfortable at home yet as I should be else in the neatest compactest house I ever got, a perfect God-send, but for some weeks I must enjoy it alone. *She* always comes round again. It is a house of a few years' standing, built (for its size with every convenience) by an old humorist for himself, which he tired of as soon as he got warm in it. Grates, locks, a pump, convenience indescribable, and cheap as if it had been old and craved repairs. For me, who always take the first thing that offers, how lucky that the best should first offer itself! My books, my prints, are up, and I seem (so like this room I write in is to a room there) to have come here transported in the night, like Gulliver in his flying house; and to add to the deception, the new river has come down from Islington with me. 'Twas what I wished—to move my *house*, and I have realised it. Only instead of company seven nights in the week, I see my friends on the first day of it, and enjoy six real Sabbaths. The museum is a loss, but I am not so far but I can visit it occasionally, and I have exhausted the plays there.

'Indisputably I shall allow no sage and onion to be crammed into the throat of so tender a suckling.

'Bread and milk, with some odoriferous mint, and the liveret minced.

'Come and tell me when he cries, that I may catch his little eyes.

'And do it nice and *crips*' (that's the cook's word).

2 D

"You'll excuse me, I have been only speaking to Becky about the dinner to-morrow. After it, a glass of seldom-drunk wine to my friend Dodwell, and, if she will give a stranger leave, to Mrs. Dodwell; then to the memory of the last, and of the last but one, learned Dodwell, of whom, but not whom, I have read so much. . . ."

On Burial Societies, and the Character of an Undertaker (p. 304).—Leigh Hunt's *Reflector*. (No. iii. Art. xiii. 1811.)

On the danger of confounding Moral with Personal Deformity (p. 311).—Leigh Hunt's *Reflector*. (No. ii. Art. xv. 1811.)

On the Inconveniences resulting from being Hanged (p. 319).— (Leigh Hunt's *Reflector*, No. ii. Art. xii. 1811.) The leading idea of this essay was afterwards made by Lamb the subject of a farce called "The Pawnbroker's Daughter," which, after various ineffectual attempts to produce it upon the stage, he finally published in *Blackwood* for January 1830. There is now lying before me a note of Lamb's to the elder Charles Mathews, accompanying a copy of the farce, which he submitted to Mathews' approval for production at the Adelphi. The note is dated October 27, 1828. Lamb's desire for success as a dramatist remained with him to the end of his life.

The idea of *hanging*, with all its grim accessories, was a favourite one with this strange humorist. Readers of his correspondence will recall a Latin epigram on the subject, written for a school-boy, and sent to Southey in a letter of May 1830. My friend Archdeacon Hessey has quite lately published in the pages of a school magazine (conducted by the boys of Merchant Taylors School) the true history of this epigram, and kindly allows me to transfer it to my notes. The composition of epigrams in Latin and in English was part of the regular *curriculum* of Merchant Taylors. "We boys," writes Dr. Hessey, "were allowed to obtain assistance from our friends (if we could) in this sort of composition, though in other matters we were bound to draw upon our own resources.

"The subjects for 1830 were *Suum Cuique* and *Brevis esse laboro*. After some three or four exercise nights I confess that I was literally 'at my wits' end.' But a brilliant idea struck me. I had frequently, boy as I was, seen Charles Lamb at my father's house, and once, in 1825 or 1826, I had been taken to have tea with him and his sister, Mary Lamb, at their little house, Colebrook Cottage, a whitish-brown tenement, standing by itself close to the New River at Islington. He was very kind, as he always was to young people, and very quaint. I told him that I had devoured his 'Roast Pig,' and he congratulated me on possessing a thorough school-boy's appetite. And he was pleased when I mentioned my having seen the boys at Christ's Hospital at their public suppers, which then took place on the Sunday evenings in Lent. 'Could this good-natured and humorous old gentleman be prevailed upon to give me an Epigram?' 'I don't know,' said my father, to whom I put the question, 'but I will ask him, at any rate, and send him the mottos.' In a day or two there arrived from Enfield, to which Lamb had removed some time in 1827, not one, but two epigrams, one on each subject. That on *Suum Cuique* was in Latin, and was suggested by the grim satisfaction which had recently been expressed by the public at the capture and execution of some notorious highwayman. . . . I have now before me the copies of them as they were shown up to the head-master, with the names of J. A. Hessey and F. Hessey attached to them respectively." Dr. Hessey proceeds to give the authentic text of the Latin epigram, which I may be allowed to repeat, especially as a misprint in Talfourd's version has never been corrected by later editors :—

"SUUM CUIQUE.

" Adsciscit sibi divitias et opes alienas
  Fur, rapiens, spolians, quod mihi quodque tibi
Proprium erat—temnens haec verba Meumque Tuumque.
  Omne Suum est. Tandem cuique suum tribuit.
Dat laqueo collum : vestes vah ! carnifici dat :
  Sese Diabolo : sic bene, Cuique Suum."

On the Melancholy of Tailors (p. 330).—This paper first appeared in the *Champion* of December 4, 1814, then edited by John Scott, afterwards editor of the *London Magazine*. The paper seems to be referred to by Lamb in a letter to Wordsworth, written just after or just before its appearance in print, in the end of November 1814. The "Burton" mentioned refers to his having signed the essay "Burton *junior*":—

"DEAR W.—Your experience about tailors seems to be in point blank opposition to Burton, as much as the author of 'The Excursion' does, *toto cœlo*, differ in his notion of a country life from the picture which W. H. (William Hazlitt) has exhibited of the same. But with a little explanation you and B. may be reconciled. It is evident that he confined his observations to the genuine native London tailor. What freaks tailor-nature may take in the country is not for him to give account of. And certainly some of the freaks recorded do give an idea of the persons in question being beside themselves, rather than in harmony with the common, moderate, self-enjoyment of the rest of mankind. A flying-tailor, I venture to say, is no more *in rerum naturâ* than a flying-horse or a gryphon. His wheeling his airy flight from the precipice you mention had a parallel in the melancholy Jew who toppled from the monument. Were his limbs ever found? Then, the man who cures diseases by words is evidently an inspired tailor. Burton never affirmed that the art of sewing disqualified the practiser of it from being a fit organ for supernatural revelation. He never enters into such subjects. 'Tis the common, uninspired tailor which he speaks of. Again, the person who makes his smiles to be *heard*, is evidently a man under possession; a demoniac tailor. A greater hell than his own must have a hand in this. I am not certain that the cause which you advocate has much reason for triumph. You seem to me to substitute light-headedness for light-heartedness by a trick, or not to know the difference. I confess a grinning tailor would shock me. Enough of tailors!"

The title and the signature of this essay declare the source of its inspiration. It is likely enough that the mention by the original Burton of *cabbage* as a "melancholy diet" suggested the whole paper. *Cabbage*—in its double sense of the vegetable so called and of stealing—has been long a calumnious jest at the expense of tailors, from a supposed inclination in them to appropriate odd scraps and remnants of the cloth entrusted to them. This expression, and the grim title (referred to in this letter) given to the dark cavity beneath a tailor's working-board into which the fragments of "cabbage" were dropped, were favourite jests with Lamb. See the stanza in his "Satan in search of a wife," the Devil having fallen in love with a tailor's daughter:—

"Who is she that by night from her balcony looks
On a garden where *cabbage* is springing?
'Tis the tailor's fair lass———."

Hospita on the Immoderate Indulgence of the Pleasures of the Palate (p. 335).—The *Reflector*, No. iv. 1811.

Edax on Appetite (p. 339).—The *Reflector*, No. iv. 1811.

Mr. H., a Farce, in two Acts (p. 348).—Lamb's letters to Wordsworth and Manning in the summer of 1806 are full of almost childish delight in the prospect of the first performance of his farce. Thus he writes to Manning in China:—"Now, you'd like to know the subject. The title is 'Mr. H.,' no more; how simple, how taking! A great H sprawling over the playbill, and attracting eyes at every corner. The story is a coxcomb appearing at Bath, vastly rich—all the ladies dying for him—all bursting to know who he is—but he goes by no other name than Mr. H., a curiosity like that of the dames of Strasburg about the man with the great nose. But I won't tell you any more about it. Yes, I will: but I can't give you any idea how I've done it. I'll just tell you that after much vehement admiration, when his true name comes out, 'Hogsflesh,' all the women shun him, avoid him, and not one can be found to change her name for him—that's the idea—how flat it is here—but how whimsical in the farce; and only think how hard upon one it is that the ship is despatched to-morrow, and my triumph cannot be ascertained till the Wednesday after —but all China will ring of it by and by."

The looked-for triumph was, as every one knows, to be exchanged for summary failure. "Great curiosity," says Talfourd, who was evidently among the audience, "was excited by the announcement; the house was crowded to the ceiling; and the audience impatiently awaited the conclusion of the long, dull, intolerable opera of 'The Travellers,' by which it was preceded. At length Mr. Elliston, the hero of the farce, entered, gaily dressed and in happiest spirits—enough, but not too much elated—and delivered the prologue with great vivacity and success. The farce began; at first it was much applauded, but the wit seemed wire-drawn, and when the curtain fell on the first act the friends of the author began to fear. The second act dragged heavily on, as second acts of farces will do; a rout at Bath, peopled with ill-dressed and over-dressed actors and actresses, increased the disposition to yawn; and when the moment of disclosure came, and nothing worse than the name *Hogsflesh* was heard, the audience resented the long play on their curiosity, and would hear no more. Lamb, with his sister, sat, as he anticipated, in the front of the pit, and having joined in encoring the prologue, the brilliancy of which injured the farce, he gave way with equal pliancy to the common feeling, and hissed and hooted as loudly as any of his neighbours. The next morning's play-bill contained a veracious announcement that 'the new farce of Mr. H., performed for the first time last night, was received by an overflowing audience with universal applause, and will be repeated for the second time to-morrow;' but the stage lamps never that morrow saw! Elliston would have tried it again, but Lamb saw at once that the case was hopeless, and consoled his friends with a century of puns for the wreck of his dramatic hopes."

Crabb Robinson was also present at the first performance, and confirms Talfourd's account in every respect. He adds: "The prologue was very well received. Indeed it could not fail, being one of the very best in the language. But on the disclosure of the name the squeamishness of the vulgar taste in the pit shewed itself by hisses, and I recollect that Lamb joined, and was probably the loudest hisser in the house." Hazlitt in his "Table Talk" Essay "On great and little things" adds yet a few more details to the history of the event: "I remember when Lamb's farce was damned (for damned it was, that's certain) I used to dream every night for a month after (and then I vowed I would plague myself no more about it) that it was revived at one of the minor or provincial theatres with great success, that such and such retrenchments had been made in it, and that it was thought it might do at the other House. I had heard, indeed (this was told in confidence to Lamb), that Gentleman Lewis was present on the night of its performance, and said that if he had had it he would have made it, by a few judicious curtailments, 'the most popular little thing that had been brought out for some time.' How often did I conjure up in recollection the full diapason of applause at the end of the prologue, and hear my ingenious friend in the first row of the pit roar with laughter at his own wit!" And Hazlitt's Recollections end with the passage beginning "Mr. H., thou wert damned," which Lamb prefixed to his farce when he published it for the first time in 1818, and which has been preserved in that place as a fit and appropriate preface ever since.

Neither the inadequacy of the secret in the case of the hero's name nor its vulgarity seems to have been the real secret of the public resentment. An able American critic, Mr. J. Brander Matthews, gives the true cause. "The fault of the piece," he writes, "the fatal fault, was the keeping of the secret from the spectators. To keep a secret is a misconception of true theatrical effect, an improper method of sustaining dramatic suspense. An audience is interested not in what the end may be, but in the means whereby that end is to be reached. . . . If the audience that night had been slily let into the secret in an early scene they would have had double enjoyment in watching the futile endeavours of the *dramatis personæ* to divine it, and they would not have been disappointed when Mr. Hogsflesh let slip his full patronymic. Kept in ignorance, the spectators joined the actors in speculation, and when the word was revealed they were not amused by the disgust of the actors, so annoyed were they that they had been puzzled by a vulgar name. Perhaps, too, there was a certain reaction after the undue expectancy raised by the prologue. Lamb wrote to Wordsworth that 'the number of friends they had in the House was astonishing.' Now nothing is so dangerous on the first night of a new play as a large number of friends in the audience. One is greatly inclined to regret that Lamb did not yield to Elliston, and let the play be acted again. If it had had a second chance the injudicious friends would have been absent, and the name of the hero would have been noised abroad, and, once in the possession of this secret, the audience might well have laughed long and heartily at the hero's misadventures."

I do not know whether it has been noticed that Lamb's

prologue is suggested by Garrick's to the *School for Scandal.* It was but thirty years since Sheridan's plays were written, and the fascination of his mannerisms still controlled all writers of comedy. Lamb's wit, however, was not of the Congreve type, and he had to rely mainly on vivacity of manner, and a too liberal sprinkling of puns and such verbal humour. It is hardly unfair to him to suggest that the last words of the farce, "Hogsflesh has saved his Bacon," were the first thought of, and that the farce was written to lead up to them.

The surname Hogsflesh, it may be added, is by no means confined to Lamb's farce. Mr. Leslie, the artist, in his delightful book on the Thames, mentions a school-fellow of that name, and the editor has heard, not remotely, of a family bearing the name, who, with a coyness that would have delighted Lamb, softened the obnoxious syllables into *Ho'flesh.* Lamb had probably met with the name in real life, and his prompt fancy had at once seized upon its farcical capabilities. The farce seems never to have been acted in public in England since its summary rejection in December 1806. But it was played at an amateur performance by the late C. J. Mathews in 1822, as recorded in the actor's memoirs. In America the fate of the little play has been different. Three months after its performance at Drury Lane it was produced in New York. It was produced later, in 1812, in Philadelphia, at the Chestnut Street Th— and had a considerable run.

I append a list of the works of Lamb published during his lifetime, in which the writings included in this volume originally appeared:—

(1.) *Poems on various Subjects,* by S. T. Coleridge, late of Jesus College, Cambridge. London: printed for C. G. and J. Robinsons and J. Cottle, bookseller, Bristol. 1796. (Contains four sonnets, signed C. L.)

(2.) *Poems,* by S. T. Coleridge. Second edition—to which are now added Poems by Charles Lamb and Charles Lloyd. Printed by N. Biggs for J. Cottle, Bristol, and Messrs. Robinsons, London. 1797.

(3.) *Blank Verse,* by Charles Lloyd and Charles Lamb. London: printed by T. Bensley for John and Arthur Arch, No. 23 Grace Church Street. 1798.

(4.) *A Tale of Rosamund Gray and Old Blind Margaret,* by Charles Lamb. London: printed for Lee and Hurst, No. 32 Paternoster Row. 1798.

(5.) *John Woodvil, a Tragedy,* by C. Lamb, to which are added Fragments of Burton, the author of the *Anatomy of Melancholy.* London. 1802.

(6.) *Specimens of English Dramatic Poets, who lived about the time of Shakspere, with Notes,* by Charles Lamb. London. 1808.

(7.) *The Works of Charles Lamb.* In two volumes. London. 1818.

(8.) *Album Verses, with a few others,* by Charles Lamb. London. 1830.

THE END.

www.ingramcontent.com/pod-product-compliance
Lightning Source LLC
Chambersburg PA
CBHW051737300426
44115CB00007B/600